Jonathan
much success
with more!
Donna Bailey

Power Moms

The New Rules for Engaging
MOM INFLUENCERS
Who Drive Brand Choice

MARIA T. BAILEY

Power Moms

The New Rules for Engaging Mom Influencers Who Drive Brand Choice

Maria T. Bailey

F I R S T E D I T I O N

ISBN: 978-1-936214-42-6

Library of Congress Control Number: 2011925474

Edited by Lisa Pliscou

Proofread by Karen Kibler

Index by Jean Jesensky, Endswell Indexing

PLEASE NOTE: The number of social media followers reflect the information available at the time this book was compiled in October 2010.

www.WyattMacKenzie.com

(541) 964-3314

Requests for permission or further information should be addressed to:
Wyatt-MacKenzie Publishing, 15115 Highway 36, Deadwood, Oregon 97430

Dedication

To my children, Madison, Owen, Keenan and Morgan, who make me so proud every single day. Thank you for allowing me to be your mom.

TABLE OF CONTENTS

Introduction ... 1

SECTION 1
The Mom Market ... 11

SECTION 2
Power Moms ... 47

SECTION 3
The Big Black Book of Power Moms
Directory ... 79

SECTION 4
Moms Worth Mentioning ... 277

SECTION 5
Celebrity Moms ... 299

SECTION 6
Global Moms ... 317

SECTION 7
Influential Dads ... 329

Acknowledgements ... 341

Footnotes ... 343

Index ... 345

Introduction

A publisher once told me that I'd written everything that could be written about the subject of Marketing and Moms. The number of people interested in my topic, she said, was relatively small and an exclusive niche. She went on to tell me that there weren't enough changes in the subject to warrant another book.

Well, that was three books and many readers ago. While my books haven't earned a spot on the *New York Times* bestseller list—at least, not yet—they *are* published in 12 languages and the insights I've provided in them have helped companies earn millions in additional revenue. For this reason, I utilize her words as the inspiration for my writing. Not only does the competitor in me feel challenged to prove her wrong, but also the overachiever in me utilizes them to stay true to delivering value to you, my reader. I'm not going to write a new book just to prove one can be written. Rather, I write one when I think there is enough valuable information, insights and shifts in the market to warrant a new book.

If you're not familiar with the series of Mom Marketing books I've written, I hope you'll allow me to retrace the evolution that's led to *Power Moms*. It began 11 years ago with *The Women's Home-Based Business Book of Answers* (Prima). Few people know that this was my first book because my second, *Marketing to Moms: Getting Your Share of the Trillion Dollar Market* (Random House), made a big impression in the marketing world. But it was that first book that opened the door to so many of the Power Moms you'll meet later in this book. Life really does come full circle!

Marketing to Moms was the first book to examine the spending power of mothers and focus on the lucrative subset of female consumers in the U.S.: those with offspring. It was really *Trillion-Dollar Moms: Marketing to a New Generation of Mothers* (Random House) that impacted my career the most and finally caught the attention of companies who were willing to invest in connecting with the Mom Market. Both the passage of time and the changing generational makeup of the mom segment gave me another reason to write about the spending habits of mothers. I think it was the $1.7 trillion dollars that mothers were contributing to the economy that got the attention of brands like Coca-Cola and HP, but I don't mind taking some of the credit as well.

After all, it was through many hours of number-crunching that I calculated the impressive number that's now used by everyone from the United States government to my own competitors, often without being attributed. They say when your information becomes mainstream that you've made it. This probably means I could have stopped writing at that point. I wanted to try my hand at a non-business book next, so I authored *Ultimate Mom* (HCI), a collection of inspirational and personal stories by mothers across America. While it was fun, it didn't require me to do the research that I love so much in writing business books.

I have a passion for studying consumer behavior and then linking together social influences to predict trends and identify tactics that will drive a desired outcome to these trends and behaviors. For instance, if my research shows that 60% of moms don't know what they are cooking at 4 pm, and many of them are in their cars racing from one practice field to another, I enjoy creating the tactic that will provide Mom with a dinner solution while selling more roasted chickens for Walmart. When I saw moms beginning to use technology in surprising new ways—like synchronizing soccer schedules or socializing at Twitter parties—I decided it was time to write *Mom 3.0: Marketing with Mothers by Leveraging New Media and Technology* (Wyatt-MacKenzie).

But I can't take all the credit for my book ideas. They often come from my clients or prospective clients. The idea for *Trillion-Dollar Moms* evolved out of a conversation with Dave Williams at Best Buy. I was working on a project to convert many of their stores to mom-friendly floor plans when Dave asked me if Best Buy should be marketing to the age of the child or the age of the mother. He had observed that moms with toddlers were 25 to 45 years old and belonged to three distinct generations. His question seemed like a great research project for me, as well as a great book for others, so I turned it into *Trillion-Dollar Moms.* This book came about the same way. It got its chapters from questions I receive from clients and others wanting to tap the Mom Market.

My passion for writing about Power Moms stems from two questions presented to me by marketers. The first one emerged with the rise of Mom Bloggers. At least once a day, every day, someone will ask me, "How do I get to the Mom Bloggers who influence other mothers?" It's a good question but one that makes me cringe. Here's why.

Mom Bloggers are indeed influencers and I myself am a Mom Blogger. However, these women are only a small component of the Power Moms among the 83 million mothers in the U.S. In fact, according to my research, only about one-third of all moms read blogs. This means that if a marketer solely looks to Blogging Moms to reach the market, they are leaving 70% untouched. That's a lot of consumers not hearing your message. The truth is that Power Moms can be found online and offline.

This is the single most important theme of this book. Power Moms are online *and* offline. And they're not only moms who blog. They are moms who lead parent-teacher organizations; moms who orchestrate bake sales; and moms who run businesses. They are the go-to moms in the bleachers at the Little League field down the street from your office.

The second question that provided inspiration for this book comes from our clients who are sometimes puzzled when we tell them, "We'll leverage our relationships with Power Moms to create buzz for your brand." They look at us with a blank stare and ask, "How do you find the PTO mom in Des Moines, Iowa?" The answer is simple: we network with other Power Moms. Granted, we've had a decade to develop the relationships we have with Mom Influencers throughout the world, but it all began by starting a dialogue with one Power Mom.

I've realized over the years that as easy as it seems for me, it can seem like a daunting task to a marketer looking for national exposure or a time-consuming challenge for a startup on the fast track to success. And this is why I've written *Power Moms*. I wanted to create a resource that will help you identify the Mom Influencers who align with your brand, your goals and your marketing needs. It was my intent to create a *big* "little black book" of Power Moms.

You might be asking yourself why I would want to give away all this information to people who might never become paying clients. It doesn't seem to make much sense, does it? The fact is, my firm, BSM Media, can offer marketers much more than just an email introduction to their marketing strategy. Another reason I'm willing to share my relationships with you and the ability to connect with these influencers is that these women deserve your attention. I want to shine a spotlight on the long list of impressive Power Moms included in this "black book" and help brand marketers realize that Word of Mom Marketing goes beyond sending Mom Bloggers free product samples. There are many ways to utilize the power of moms and many types of Power Moms who can help you reach your goals. I hope you will agree after becoming familiar with them that they are an amazing group of women.

There have been many benefits to the incredible journey I call my career. I've traveled to exotic places, worked with some of the biggest brands in the world, seen my name in the *Wall Street Journal*, received calls from Celebrity Moms and CEOs and, importantly, shown my children that it's possible to be passionate about your job. The most valuable gift, however, has been the opportunity to meet thousands of incredible mothers around the globe. It would be difficult to describe each amazing mark these women are making on the world beyond raising their own children. I've met mom inventors, authors, activists, politicians and community organizers. I've crossed paths with mothers who have made millions and moms who are saving millions of other women time and money while earning very little themselves. They are passionate about their ideas, products and way of parenting.

I first met Molly Gold of Go Mom! (www.gomominc.com) 10 years ago when she was producing "The Go Mom Planner" to distribute online and later in Target, Walgreens and office supply stores. We traded business stories on the phone for more than four years until we eventually had the opportunity to meet face to face. The night she picked me up at Reagan International Airport, we sat up talking in a hotel room for hours like schoolgirls. Today, she is impacting the lives of thousands of mothers online and offline with her innovative digital planner and other products and services. There she is, in a quiet suburban neighborhood in Carey, North Carolina, influencing, impacting and engaging moms all over the world while being Molly Gold, mom of three, influencing, impacting and engaging with moms at swim team and baseball practices.

Another great example is Daisy Sutherland, well known on Twitter as @drmommy. She's the mother of five with a private practice in Tampa, homeschooling her children, authoring two books and impacting, influencing and engaging with mothers online at drmommyonline.com and via Facebook and MomTV.com. On the weekends, she's actively involved in her church and service projects.

Both of these women are examples of the extraordinary impact moms are making in the physical world as well as online. These women are doing remarkable things in their physical and virtual communities and along the way they're sharing product information, recommending brands and partnering with marketing teams to create buzz among their peers. Their reach goes well beyond a Technorati or Klout score; Google Analytics cannot measure their sphere of influence. They are authentic, real and trusted by their peers. These Power Moms can be your best marketing partners—or your worst nightmare when disappointed by bad service. It's my intent for you to find the right mom for your product and establish a relevant dialogue with her in order to reach your marketing goals. This isn't a book you'll read through once. It's a resource, a go-to guide you can use over and over again.

How to Use Your Big Black Book of Power Moms

Your Black Book of Power Moms is divided into several sections and contains over 335 Mom Influencers in total. The first section includes moms interviewed by the BSM Media team during the fall of 2010. You can imagine what a monumental task it was gathering information from over 300 busy women during the holiday season! The women we selected to interview are moms who we have identified over the years to be true influencers. We utilize a proprietary system called the Mom Matrix to identify Power Moms; I'll describe this more fully in section 3. My team asked these women to tell us about their involvement online and offline and to tell us how companies can engage with them as a marketing partner. We also asked for their unfiltered thoughts on marketing to mothers and the role influence plays in building buzz in the world of moms online and off. Many of these women were brutal in their honesty and their responses are published verbatim.

You will see that common themes begin to emerge. Mothers tend to build their sphere of influence around a personal passion. Common interests and business goals separate these women into distinct categories of influence. For instance, you'll discover a passionate group of Coupon Moms who like Method, home care and personal care products; they're a viable group of Power Moms with whom to engage in conversation. Coupon-oriented and frugal moms make good partners for retailers like Old Navy or economy-minded consumer product brands.

Ultimately there were a number of influential mothers who, for a variety of reasons, we were unable to interview. Nonetheless these are Power Moms who also deserve your attention; you'll find them in the "Worth Mentioning" section of the directory. We gathered information about them from their websites, bios, prior personal conversations and other sources. We hope it will serve as a starting point in learning more about these mothers.

We felt it was important to include international moms as well. Thanks to the rapid growth of social media, moms are interacting with each other across oceans and continents. So we wanted to introduce to you some of these moms we know and others outside the U.S. who have caught our attention. You'll find them in the "Global Power Moms" section of the directory.

Finally, there are two groups of influencers who might be somewhat unexpected but cannot be ignored when exploring the topic of moms and influence. The first is Celebrity Moms: the mothers who grace the pages of *People* and *Us Weekly* and whose children lay the foundation for the latest fashion trends. Many marketers inquire about the impact these women make as spokespersons for their products. Therefore, I decided it was relevant to give my thoughts on who's hot and who's not while identifying the real Power Moms among celebrities with children.

And last but not least, the second group is Dad Influencers. Yes, I said it—the D word. With more and more couples making the decision about who will be the alpha earner after the first child is born, along with increasing media attention toward stay-at-home dads, fathers are getting more attention from marketers and Power Moms alike. Just as with moms, our dad section includes fathers who are influencing and engaging offline as well as online. It's a new group and one we see growing in size in the future.

While I did my best to include a variety and cross section of Power Moms, I know there are many we were unable to include in this book. That's the risk you take when you embark on naming individuals and making lists. A deserving person always gets left off. In advance, I apologize for the omission of any worthy moms who didn't make this directory. If, after becoming acquainted with the moms and dads listed here, you still don't find the moms who meet your objectives, let me know. This is an open invitation to email me (Maria@bsmmedia.com) or tweet me (@MomTalkRadio) and I'll be happy to point you in the right direction.

I know there's a group of moms out there for every brand, every product and every marketing goal. I hope this book will serve as an invaluable resource with pages tagged and names underlined in yellow for many years to come. May you find great success in engaging, influencing and impacting with moms.

Section 1
The Mom Market

It seems like an obvious choice for marketers to target mothers, as they represent the largest and most lucrative consumer segment. However, even after countless articles have appeared and my own four books have been published, there remains a group of marketing professionals who need to be persuaded that targeting mothers will increase their sales. On the flip side, if you are one of those marketing professionals who believes in the power of mom spending, you might be surprised that anyone has missed the marketing frenzy fueled by Mom Bloggers. And if you are a Mom Blogger, you may not be aware that the attention now given to mothers did not always exist.

Over a decade ago, when I published my first book on the Mom Market, *Marketing to Moms,* it was 1999 and no one, not even the U.S. government, had quantified the impact of mothers on the American economy. I recall sitting in our offices with Rachael Bender, my business partner at the time, and shifting through pages and pages of data to calculate the annual spending of U.S. mothers. It was countless hours of interpreting numbers to get to the $1.7 trillion figure that is often quoted in the media and even on the websites of marketers who have hung

"Marketing to Moms" agency shingles. Every now and then a savvy research analyst or tough editor will ask me how it was calculated.

The short answer is that the annual spending of mothers is determined through data from the U.S. Census Report and the Department of Agriculture which is the agency that tracks spending. Overlaid on this calculation is the amount of household spending a mother controls. Here's where it starts getting more complicated. In order to come to the most accurate conclusion, you must consider the structure of the household. Single mothers control almost 98% of the household income while married women control 85%.

The greatest change in variables since we began calculating mom spending is the increased number of single moms. In fact, according to the U.S. Census 2000 Report, single moms are the fastest-growing segment of the population and currently number over 10 million. You can see as this number increases so does the annual spending of mothers. This is not the only fact contributing to the increase. Mothers are increasingly starting businesses, being involved in eldercare and influencing the larger purchases in their household. Women are also becoming mothers at younger *and* older ages, widening the pool of population that falls into the category of "female with at least one child living in the home." (Just a side note: we do not calculate women under 18 with a child because we feel that their spending habits may be affected by other supporting factors.)

Every year, my team recalculates the data to determine the current spending of the 83 million U.S. women with children. As you can imagine, the number climbs year after year. Today, mothers in the U.S. control over $2.4 trillion a year. Single mothers alone account for $174 billion in annual spending.[1] As I often say, $2.4 trillion is more than the gross national product of Portugal, Australia and Spain combined. It's a lot of money!

What this represents is a utopia for companies that have a product, service or information source for moms, which in my mind is just about everyone. I'll assume you are reading this because you understand the marketing value of moms and want to connect with the most influential of mothers—the Power Mom. For this reason, I'll devote only a small portion of this section to the actual numbers behind their spending power and will concentrate instead on helping you understand the personality, behaviors and characteristics of today's mother.

As a scientist by education, I think understanding the equation of {Behavior + Environmental Elements = Desired Reaction} is helpful in creating a loyal connection with moms and increasing the ROI (return on investment) of your marketing programs. I won't bore you with a ton of numbers but will give you the ones that matter in the equation of success.

The Mom Spend

Moms have emerged as a powerful and influential consumer group. Companies once saw them only as purchasers of diapers and groceries. Today, mothers are not only controlling household spending, they're spending money in business as well. Women, many of whom are mothers, are starting an estimated 4 million businesses a year.[2] They are buying office supplies, copiers, fax machines, computers and accounting and legal services. Looking for a way to balance a career and family, mothers are starting home-based businesses at four times the rate of their male counterparts.[3] These companies range from small one-person service providers to multimillion-dollar businesses. Women employed outside the home control $1.5 trillion in spending for business.[4] This spending is coming not just from mothers in business for themselves but also from mothers employed by others.

A Census Bureau report cites that even among mothers with very young children, more than 60% are in the labor force.[5] A typical middle manager will decide many things: for example, how to budget advertising expenses, where her department goes for a celebration luncheon or whether to send a colleague to an out-of-town meeting. There's a good chance that the middle manager is a mother.

Moms represent not only power in the U.S. economy but in politics as well. Mothers represent an important bloc of voters for candidates, particularly those running for president. The so-called "Soccer Mom" contingent helped put Bill Clinton in the White House in 1996. In the last four presidential elections, suburban mothers have represented one-fifth of all the votes cast.[6] I had the fortunate opportunity, before her untimely death, to spend time with Elizabeth Edwards, ex-wife of former presidential candidate John Edwards, and she agreed that U.S. mothers represent one of the most untapped pools of voters today.

We sat for nearly four hours discussing the power of mothers to drive political change. She knew about the political blogs written by Power Moms such as Erin Kotecki Vest, known online as Queen of Spain (www.queenofspainblog.com and on Twitter as @queenofspain), and Joanne Bamberger (www.PunditMom.com and @punditmom).

Moms' Money

According to the U.S. Department of Agriculture, the agency that tracks family expenditures, an average-income family will spend $165,630 on a child by the time he or she reaches 18 years of age.[7]

Parents with incomes of $38,000 to $64,000 spent $18,510 on miscellaneous items for the average child from birth through age 18. This includes spending on entertainment, reading material, VCRs and wireless devices, summer camps and lessons.[8]

Females outnumber males in the United States by over 6 million (roughly 6%) and a significant percentage have at least one child. There are 141,606,000 women with children in the U.S.[9]

Woman-owned businesses generate $1.15 trillion in sales.[10]

Women-owned businesses employ 9.2 million people.[11]

U.S. women spend more than $3.7 trillion annually on consumer goods and services, plus another $1.5 trillion as purchasing agents for businesses. As a group, U.S. women constitute the number-three market in the world, with their collective buying power exceeding that of the economy of Japan.[12]

Women sign 80% of all checks written in the United States. According to BabyCenter (www.babycenter.com), the average child will cost $338,000 by the time she or he finishes a public college. Before a child is 18 years old, his or her parent(s) will have spent $105,000 on housing, $41,400 on food and $17,400 on healthcare.[13]

It's a fair conclusion that the amount of money mothers control in the U.S. will continue to grow at least for the next decade; marketers will want to tap this lucrative market. We'll start broad by covering the "Mom Marketing 101" section I include in almost every talk I give and in some of my other books as well. It's the basics; it's the foundation. Understanding the market in general and then drilling down to the Power Mom concept will give you all the knowledge you need to launch the right marketing programs for your brand.

It's All in a Mom's Day

There's a lot going on in the busy day of a mother. Moms are doing more than just spending money. They are engaged in everything from washing clothes to budgeting business plans. They are online, offline and off-road. Moms are chatting, tweeting and blogging with friends, family and strangers. One thing they all have in common is that they are time-starved. According to BSM Media research, 64% of moms say they have given up sleep in order to get work/chores done so that they could spend time with their child. The role of mother in today's society can be isolating and is one of the key motivations for moms to adopt social media friendships via blogs, Twitter and Facebook. Seventy-four percent of moms surveyed admitted feeling isolated from family and friends after giving birth. Perhaps this is why over 60% of them chat and socialize with other moms online.

While online, they are sharing information and empowering themselves and others to do more with less time. Over 30% have blogged, with 66% having posted a message on a board or chatted online. Moms share a lot. The moms who share the most, with the important factor of credibility among their peers, are Power Moms. (We'll look at this more closely in the next section.)

Additionally, 65% of mothers ask another mom for advice before a large purchase. They also share memories. Moms are the chief family archivist, taking 80% of the photos. In fact, you'll meet a lot of Power Moms in the directory who focus their passion (and influence) on photography. They like to customize products and have fueled the growth of customizable brands such as Build-A-Bear Workshop, M&M.com (customizable candy) and American Girl dolls.

Moms are efficient. In fact, 55% indicate they have their Halloween planned prior to Labor Day and 65% have thought about their fall calendar by the time the first day of school rolls around.

I've sliced and diced mom behavior in many ways over the years. In *Marketing to Moms,* I focused on moms in general and in 2005 my focus turned to examining the three generations of mothers in *Trillion-Dollar Moms.* In *Mom 3.0,* I discussed how brands can connect with consumers using social media. Today many of the core values and motivators remain the same for moms while their consumer behaviors and media engagement have changed. I use the word "engagement" here rather than "consumption" because today's mothers are using media and technology to actively engage in marketing, shopping and interacting with companies.

In fact, the popularity of mothers as *active* consumers and marketing partners has become such a hot commodity that a dark side has evolved in some mothers. It can be seen in the sense of entitlement that some of the most influential moms exhibit toward marketers. Many of these moms don't realize that a decade ago most companies never paid attention to mothers. They were content stirring their marketing dollars toward the female market in general. Just as some of today's most popular Mom Bloggers/ Influencers were becoming mothers for the first time, the marketing frenzy started. At first they were enamored by the attention and free product. Now that a value on their influence has been established, some seem to have forgotten that the attention paid to mothers is a recent phenomenon. Since this is all they know, however, these moms feel entitled to new standards when in actuality the entire Marketing to Moms industry is still in the very early stages of evolution.

Don't get me wrong, a mom's time is valuable and you will see how strongly that reality is emphasized as you get to know the moms in this book. However, we all—moms and companies alike—need to find the middle ground between authenticity and entitlement. It's not necessary for me to write more on the pay for influence debate because you will hear firsthand from the moms in the directory who'll shed a diverse light on the subject.

When I wrote *Trillion-Dollar Moms,* I did so because I felt it was important to illustrate that from a marketing point of view, all moms are not alike. I also wanted to dispel the myth that all Mom Influencers were "Soccer Moms." Additionally, at the time a societal shift was occurring in the Mom Market. Women from three distinct generations were, for the first time in history, becoming mothers. Older Boomer moms were giving birth in hospital rooms right next door to 20-year-old Millennials. It's safe to say that today's Baby Boomers are leaving the age of childbearing; however, many are still mothers of younger children. A 46-year-old Boomer can be parenting children as young as two or three years old in some cases. For this reason, I believe a condensed overview is beneficial for marketers trying to tap the Mom Market.

Defining the Generations

The U.S. Census describes Baby Boomers as people born between 1946 and 1964. Of them, approximately 40 million are mothers. Generation Xers were born between 1965 and 1980 and account for 15.6 million mothers. Generation Y or Millennials, as some call them, were born between 1981 and 1995. Although they currently represent the smallest pool of mothers, they are expected to increase the current number of 4 million births a year as they begin to become mothers.

Generation Y:	1981–1995	57 million
Generation X:	1965–1980	50 million
Baby Boomers:	1946–1965	70 million

Boomer Moms

Mothers of this generation no longer function within the boundaries of generational characteristics as their predecessors did. Instead, Boomer moms are likely to take on the behaviors of the cohort whose children are the same age as their own. For instance, a 45-year-old Boomer mother who has a toddler will likely behave like Gen X moms who have toddlers. This is a critical piece of information for marketers who have been segmenting mothers by their age rather than by the age of their children. Our research proves that the age of the child is a far more critical segmenting tool than the age of the mother. This was the big takeaway in *Trillion-Dollar Moms* and this paradigm still exists today.

Boomer moms are the group dubbed "Soccer Moms." They have an elevated sense of style and are willing to pay more for the items they value. They will purchase their children's clothing at Target and their shoes at Nordstrom. Their disposable income is slightly higher than that of the two generations of mothers that follow, as they are further along in their life stage. Nostalgic marketing works well with Boomers because they seek opportunities to recreate their own childhood memories for their children. Many of these women have blazed the trail juggling work and family and because of this it takes a village to raise their children.

They feel extremely time-starved as they struggle for balance in their lives. This is why recreating memories is important to them. If they can rely on certain brands to leave the same pleasant memories in the minds of their children then it's one less challenge for them to maneuver.

For instance, if a Boomer is shopping for crayons and she's standing in front of the Crayola and Rose Art brands, she will likely select Crayola because she remembers the scent of fresh Crayolas on the first day of school. It helps her feel confident that the first day of school will be as special for her own child thanks to Crayola. Buying crayons is now off the overcrowded task list for this Boomer mom.

Family enrichment is very important because she is always trying to squeeze in quality time with the family. Marketers can leverage her values by not only creating memories but also by helping her create experiences for her to enjoy with her family. For instance, Disney created the Social Media Mom Celebration which allows top social media mom influencers to bring their children with them to the Happiest Place on Earth.

Boomers with older children are now becoming empty-nesters. With their newfound freedom, they're starting businesses and discovering new hobbies without relinquishing their role as a mother. Boomer influencers tend to belong to more offline organizations because this was a common behavior as they were growing up, in contrast to the Millennials and Generation Xers who belong to online groups such as BabyCenter circles and Facebook fan pages. A Boomer mom serves as an influencer to both of her younger cohorts as someone who has "been there, done that." Keep in mind that a Boomer mom can be an effective Power Mom even if her children are out of the home. Younger mothers look to her for wisdom and insights.

Generation X Mothers

These women have grown up with technology in all forms and with multimedia advertising, with more options for receiving and seeking information than all previous generations combined. As mothers, they expect marketers to appeal to their multisensory communication behaviors. They will challenge marketers to think well beyond the typical marketing toolbox to deliver messages in new ways that smoothly integrate into their lifestyle.

Generation X moms are currently 31 to 46 years old and comprise the group born between 1965 and the early 80s. They number approximately 51 million and, as a whole, this segment represents approximately 25% of the population.[14] Generation X is particularly difficult to generalize because it a highly diverse generation, composed of more ethnic backgrounds than any of its predecessors. It includes the largest population of naturalized citizens in U.S history.[15] Thanks to negative and often unfounded media coverage that depicted them as a generation that was lazy, whiny, cynical and disloyal, one common theme exists within this group of men and women. They hate to be called "Xers."

Generation Xers are also known as the generation of "latchkey kids," which was a description for children who (symbolically) carried keys around their necks so they could let themselves in after school while their mothers were at work.. These children were required to become self-reliant and fend for themselves while their Boomer mothers worked away from home. The outcome of long hours alone produced a generation that grew up confident in their problem-solving abilities.

One of the greatest influencing factors of this generation is divorce. This was the first generation since the June Cleaver household of the 50s to have to learn to manage a lifestyle with divorced parents, splitting their time between two households and developing relationships with blended families. Some experts estimate that nearly half of Gen Xers grew up in divorced households, based on the U.S. Census Bureau number that 50% of marriages in the late 60s and 70s ended in divorce.

One effect of the instability they witnessed among their parents was a lack of desire to get married. According to the 2000 Census, single mothers comprise the fastest-growing demographic in the U.S.[16] Surprisingly, this group is not growing as the outcome of increased divorce but rather out of new moms' decisions to postpone marriage, regardless of unplanned pregnancies. In addition, the freedom to stay single is made easier by the Generation X mom's ability to financially support her family on her own.

Although most moms will solicit the advice of their own mothers after giving birth for the first time, the traditional relationship can sometimes shift from simply mother-daughter interaction to a friendship based on the common experience of motherhood, and the mother's advice suddenly carries double weight. However, it should be noted that because of the nature of a Gen Xer to be self-reliant and create his or her own solutions, they might often make their own decision based on what's right for them personally.

When a Gen X mother is seeking advice on baby food, she'll typically turn to her friends or members of a peer group and ask them to share their personal stories and experiences with various brands. Gen X moms like stories because they illustrate the individuality of different situations. They allow her to see that there is more than one way to do things. Once she gets insights from peers, she'll likely share this information with her mother who, as a new Baby Boomer grandmother, will tell her how things were when she was a child and what brands she used to feed her babies as a young mother. The Gen X mom will discount stories of the "old days" in an attempt to forget her own unstable childhood and avoid recreating it for her child. What changes the scenario is that the Gen X mom has now repositioned her mother as a friend rather than just her mom and will extrapolate the valuable facts from her mother's advice.

Generation Xers are on a quest for individuality. This goal can be seen as a motivator for many of these moms to build their own brands online via personal blogs, YouTube channels or MomTV shows. They feel that being their own person allows them to better control the uncertainties of the world they experienced as a child. The quest for individuality is seen on retail shelves with the popularity of personalized jewelry, sweaters, stationery and household items. It's also seen in the number of customized names for mom products. From "yoga moms" to "slacker moms," Generation X mothers are maintaining more of their own personal identity and adapting motherhood to fit with who they are as women.

A stable home life is the dream of many Generation Xers—particularly those who grew up as a latchkey child and/or as the product of divorce. It's been said that everything eventually comes back into style and this may be true also for the traditional nuclear family. The Cleaver family may come to mind, but once again I ask you to leave your preconceived visions of Mom aside. Today's Generation X mom desires to create a stable home life for herself and her children with or without a man. While Baby Boomer moms believed it took a village to raise a child, Generation X moms believe they independently control the experiences and parenting of their child.

Generation Xers desire to be a part of groups and have high expectations for them. They like to form and belong to groups where they can share ideas and find opportunities for growth, creating surrogate families of like-minded peers who share their vision of community and chosen family. With an unlimited number of groups that exist for just about every interest, personal value or belief, whether in person or virtually, Gen Xers can express their individuality and find common ground with others across the city or across the country. Groupings by Xers have spawned a myriad of new social interactions among all generations. They include Mommy and Me playgroups, Bible study groups, volunteering events and home parties. In fact, the home party plan business has grown to a $29.95 billion industry.[17] The tendency to belong to groups makes the Gen Xer a great Power Mom and is one of the reasons I suggest asking moms about their offline and group involvement rather than simply looking at their Technorati numbers to determine their sphere of influence.

The importance of education is perhaps one of the most notable parenting priorities among Generation X mothers. Gen X moms prefer to spend money on enriching experiences that will create lasting family memories such as unique vacations and adventure travel. It's not enough to simply buy airline tickets and stay in a run-of-the-mill resort.

Gen Xers are active consumers. They weigh their buying decisions against the personal and financial costs they set for themselves. In other words, before purchasing a product or service, they will decide if it's worth it for them in the investment of time and/or dollars. They are very realistic and define value against their sense of realism. They can't be sold, and see marketing at face value, looking past flash and sizzle to make purchases based on their own needs. They want results and benefits, plain and simple. Their pragmatic attitude about life is reflected in what they expect from marketers. They want real answers to real-life challenges. And this grounding in reality and the desire to speak the truth has birthed the new genre of television entertainment, reality TV, as well as the increased interest in live broadcasts, eliminating the ability of someone behind the scenes to manipulate the story or outcome.

Gen Xers are visual in their learning, a trait acquired while watching TV and exploring the early years of computer games and activities. They enjoy imagery but recognize that it is just an outcome of technology. Their ability to juggle tasks, a skill they learned as latchkey kids, enables them to absorb various multimedia messages at one time. They have the mental capacity to take in and process images that are being delivered to them through multiple channels. Gen X moms tend to be traditionalists, perhaps as a way to create stability for their children that they never had. The resurrection of nostalgic toys, games and retro designs has in large part been fueled by the Gen Xer's desire to hold on to a conservative, traditional family life.

Due to their independent thinking, Gen Xers have very strong opinions that contribute to their maven tendencies. This can work in favor of brands that win their praise but can be a curse for those who disappoint. Their ability to navigate technology makes their sphere of influence even more powerful. A typical Power Mom can easily take her praises and share them across multiple media channels or she can take her disgust and amplify it to thousands of peers within seconds. In fact, you will see that many of the moms in the later pages point to the lack of customer service as a motivator in projecting their opinions to their peers. It's a dangerous thing for a marketer to disappoint a Gen X Power Mom and even worse to communicate messages that seem unauthentic or transparently manipulative.

Generation Y

Born between 1983 and 1994, this group is most often defined by the fact that they graduated from high school in the new millennium. Today, the oldest "millennial moms" are 28. They number 70 million and make up 21% of the U.S. population.[18] For marketers, Generation Y presents the largest consumer group to emerge since the Baby Boomer generation. It is estimated that the U.S. population will grow by twice the current rate as Generation Y women become moms. As a consumer group, they control approximately $172 billion a year and influence $3,000 in family spending annually.[19]

Gen Y has enjoyed a prosperous childhood. Over two-thirds of the women have a television in their room and when they aren't absorbing traditional media visually, 70% of them are online. They are the most socioeconomically and ethnically diverse population in the history of the U.S. Minorities make up 34% of Generation Y, up from 24% of their Baby Boomer cohorts.[20] It is interesting to note that as of 2010, Hispanics make up the largest minority group in this generation. They comprise a diverse generation that is, in general, supportive of change that furthers inclusiveness and equality, such as acceptance of gay marriage.

Gen Ys have a passion for creating a better place to live and an understanding of the state of the world beyond their front yards. Although three out of four Gen Ys have a working mother, their mothers are quite different from those that raised the latchkey children of the prior generation.[21] These mothers turned their attention to nurturing their young rather than chasing material possessions and career titles as they feel their own mothers did. Gen Y mothers enjoy movies depicting nurturing parents who make childrearing the focus of their lives, and then end up enriched by the experience, such as *Three Men and a Baby* and *Parenthood.* They have a sincere interest in parenting in a style we describe as "get on the floor and play."

Self-confidence is one of the most defining traits of this generation, producing a spirit of ambition and passion that is illustrated in numerous areas. They are also aware of the damage done by previous generations to their world, and have grown up in a more environmentally sensitive milieu than any previous generations. Self-assured Gen Ys believe they can change the world and correct the problems caused by the less capable generations that came before them.

Technology has played a major role in shaping all aspects of the lives of Generation Ys. Perhaps one of the most formative uses of technology is in socializing with friends. Communicating with peers has long been a popular activity with teens, but while Boomers spent hours telephoning girlfriends and Gen Xers later used email, instant messaging is today's technology of choice. In fact, two-thirds of teenagers use instant messaging.[22] Platforms such as Facebook have helped Gen Y moms to avoid the traditional isolation that their Boomer mothers suffered from after childbirth. They can now Skype with girlfriends, join

Twitter parties with fellow moms or meet new friends during a MomTV online Mom Mixer. They belong to many online groups and have an attitude of "the more the merrier."

Gen Ys move and operate in groups, whether physically or virtually. The constant engagement these young mothers have experienced means they place a high premium on relationships and value a sense of strong loyalty among their cohorts. They are mothers who demonstrate a great deal of confidence in this role. The practice they've had absorbing all forms of media at once has equipped them with multitasking skills like no other generation before them. Since they view education as a lifelong process, they seek ways to engage their children in newly emerging technologies such as iPhone and iPad applications.

When Generation Ys make buying decisions, they draw on their mother's message to them as a child: they can be whatever they want to be. Today they have plenty of celebrity images to try on for themselves, from Christina Aguilera to Jennifer Garner. They process what they hear and see in advertising messages, decide what they want to be and what fits their lifestyle and select products that meet their needs. The Generation Y Power Mom uses her connectivity to share her discoveries with her friends and the many groups she belongs to in both the online and offline world.

If I were going to make a prediction about the Generation Y moms and those coming behind her, I would bet that fewer of these women will invest their time in blogging. Why? Because today's technology allows them the same benefits of sharing and socializing without the investment of time in creating content, building traffic and figuring out how to monetize it. The new moms who give birth today already have an established online network of friends on Facebook and may also be socializing on Twitter. If she wants to share baby photos, she can do it via her Snapfish account or Facebook page. If she wants to praise a brand, she can "like" it on Facebook, rather than write a 300-word product review to let her friends know her opinion. Generation Y Power Moms offer marketers the benefit of online audiences as well as offline groups.

Three Generations Coming Together

When it comes to Mom Marketing, one point I continually emphasize is that moms are always changing, as does their use of technology and buying styles.

Today's moms have evolved to a new place; however, what *hasn't* changed over the decade that I've been studying them is their core values. In fact, the core values I'm about to discuss can even be called global in scope. A mother in Japan places the same value on the health and safety of her child as the mama in South Africa or South Georgia. What changes is how they exhibit the value and the definition it carries within their culture. It's important to understand her core values for two reasons.

First, it provides a shared goal in establishing a meaningful dialogue with moms. Think about your closest friends. They've earned their spot in your circle of peers probably because you share a belief system, special interests and/or common priorities. It's the same criteria that mothers apply in developing relationships with brands, companies and service providers. If you can speak to one of her core goals, you will go a long way in developing a meaningful relationship with her.

The second reason it's important to understand her core values is that these values provide the foundation of motivations. You'll see later in this chapter how her desire to simplify her life leads to her motivation to keep lists and find simpler solutions to everyday tasks. A mother's core values should be the starting point for every campaign, product design or engagement you create with or for a mother. The five core values of mothers are health and safety, value, time, child enrichment and simplicity.

Core Value #1: Health and Safety

This ranks at the top of a mother's core value list. Nothing means more to her than keeping her family safe and raising healthy children. I recently sat in a restaurant in Peru. I watched moms from around the world feed their children breakfast. Now to the normal person, this would not be an interesting activity; for me, however, it was an exciting melting pot of insights. I was determined to find a common behavior within this group of mothers if one existed. Much to my family's dismay, I observed families for hours leaving the buffet line and sitting down to dine.

It didn't take long to find my common denominator. Approximately 90% of the moms I watched made sure their children had food and were eating before they began to eat themselves. Call it a primeval behavior, but just about every mom took the time to assure herself that the health of her child would be maintained by eating breakfast. It's a very strong value. Many moms will put their own needs and desires on a back burner to stay true to it.

In their desire to keep their children safe and healthy, moms look for the right goods and services. They want to feel that companies sincerely care about *their* health and well-being as well. There are many ways a company can leverage this core value with moms. Companies who design products that tell moms they understand and care about their healthcare needs demonstrate shared value through actions. It's not enough to just proclaim, "It's healthy." That approach doesn't work when a mom says it to her broccoli-hating child and it won't work in marketing.

Moms want a partner. They want someone to educate them and create a platform for discussion in the form of a blog or a fun tweet that they can share with other moms. They want to feel empowered by using your product. Many of the Power Moms in this directory will tell you that they're motivated to share information because they want to share good solutions with other moms.

Core Value #2: Saving Time

Saving time might also be termed convenience. However you choose to phrase it, moms value time. Sometimes they even value it more than money. Whether a woman has one child or ten, she's likely to feel she's starved for time.

Time for her family, time for herself, time to work, time for her spouse, and time for the house are just a few demands on a mother's time. The one type of time we don't want to talk to moms about anymore is "quality time," a loosely defined term that carries almost no meaning to mothers today. The term was overused in the mid-to-late 90s, and many mothers resent the term because it represents something not easily obtained and even less manageable.

Time is so precious that some mothers are willing to pay to gain a few extra minutes in their day. This is good for advertisers. Mothers' desire to find time can present a marketer with many communication channels. You can talk to mothers about how your product is going to give them more time, but another approach is to focus on what the mothers will do with the free time they gain by using your product.

One of the most effective campaign slogans I've seen in a while was for a bank touting its convenience. They promised that by banking with them, the customer would regain two hours in their week. However, it wasn't the two hours that was the motivator in the ad, it was this line: "We will give you two hours; what you do with them is your choice." It was brilliant in illustrating that what one mother would do with two hours is quite different from what another mom would do with the same time. The campaign allowed the potential customer to place her own perceived value on the hours saved, rather than the bank doing it for them in a cookie-cutter way.

Core Value #3: Value

Value is a word that moms understand well, particularly as they try to manage their family's finances. One of the greatest mistakes marketers and retailers make in relation to leveraging this value is confusing it with price. Value doesn't always mean price in the minds of moms. It is more closely aligned with quality. To determine the value of a product or service, mothers measure its quality, convenience and relevance against the price. If she knows that paying a little more for higher quality will ultimately save her in time that she won't have to spend replacing the original product when it fails her, it's worth the price. The *value* of the product is greater than the *price*.

Mothers don't necessarily want the cheapest product but they want to know that they're paying a competitive price and that the value comes in good quality, customer service and added benefits to her family. Here's where it all comes full circle. The benefits to her family will be measured against her core values. The more the benefits touch one of her core values, the greater the value it is assigned in her mind.

Core Value #1: Child Enrichment

Child enrichment speaks to the natural desire for mothers to breed superior offspring. It's the desire to do the job of mothering better than her own mother did or to provide her children with more than she herself had as a child. The trend is best illustrated within the Boomer segment of mothers. In the late 1980s and early 1990s many of these women accumulated material possessions like BMWs and Rolex watches as an outward sign of their success. Today, the children of this same generation have become the visual symbols of success. It has produced a generation of overscheduled children who are chauffeured from tennis to piano lessons and private schools that have newborns on waiting lists for admission. Messages that speak to mothers about bettering the lives of their children, enriching their experiences and creating more intelligent students can be seen in print and electronic ads. The success of Baby Einstein videos was based on mothers seeking a way to better stimulate young, developing brains with music and exposure to the arts. Today's moms want their children to be smart and successful, but they also want them to be happy.

It's one thing to want more for your child; however, too much of a good thing is never beneficial. Today many mothers have turned the value of child enrichment into an engagement in entitlement. These moms believe their children should be *entitled* to the better things in life and their offspring have come to expect it. This is one trend marketers have seized with great zest. Spa parties for six-year-olds, expensive boutiques for toddlers and preteen pedicures are among only a few of the initiatives created to capture the large population of entitlement-minded mothers.

Although sales in these categories are growing, I am beginning to see a turn in the tide. In a recent BSM Media survey of 300 mothers, 80% of them said they would like to keep their little girls "little" for a longer period of time and saw a direct link to these pint-sized luxuries as a contributing factor to accelerating their maturity. As moms go green, the economy weakens and the desire to simplify expands, I feel there will be a turn toward more educational, philanthropic and spiritual means of enrichment rather than materialistic ones.

The outcome to a mom's focus on child enrichment has a great deal to do with her desire to raise a happy, healthy adult. In fact, when we ask moms what it is that she wants most from her journey in motherhood, that desire tops the list. Surprisingly, it's not the smartest, wealthiest or most attractive adult when she gets right down to the answer. It's giving her child the tools, knowledge and experiences to become a happy adult. It's a "job well done" moment for her when she's achieved this goal.

Fortunately for marketers it's a long journey, with many opportunities to be her partner on the path of parenthood with products and services to help along the way. It's important for marketers to also realize that the memories created along the way hold a significant value to her as well. She knows that when the kids are grown, memories will be all the more important for both herself and the kids.

Marketers can leverage a mother's desire for family enrichment by speaking to the memories their product can create for the family. This is where nostalgic marketing emerges. Brands take mothers down memory lane in an attempt to help them relive childhood experiences that can be recreated for their own children. The message plays well to a mother's desire to create cherished memories for her own children.

A number of brands have recently joined in the bandwagon of nostalgic marketing in order to appeal to mothers. For example, in the recent "More Ovaltine, please" ads, the message is the same as the one today's mothers saw when they were children. This reuse is effective because it allows mothers to relive a pleasant childhood experience while providing a solution for getting their children to drink something they feel is nutritious.

Core Value #5: Simplicity

The search for balance includes simplifying one's life, growing spiritually and just feeling good. Marketers have done a good job in leveraging this value. It can be seen in magazine content, merchandising and of course advertising. Most obviously you can see it in the popularity of the magazine *Real Simple*. Take a stroll down the aisles of your neighborhood Target store and you'll find hundreds of products devoted to the idea of simplifying. You'll see shelf, closet and home office organizers, color-coded toy bins and seasonal celebration kits complete with holiday plates, cups and napkins. Everything in one store with one mission: to make life easier. According to a study by the Radcliffe Public Policy Center, 61% of Americans would be willing to trade money for family time: they'd give up some of their pay for more time with their children or other family members.

The value of simplification is that it produces time, the most important currency a mother possesses. You'll see in the directory how many Power Moms cite "solutions" as a key way to influence peers. You'll see that if you save Mom time or simplify her life, she's happy to share the good news with other mothers.

Values = Motivations

It may seem logical that a close look at Mom's values is important in shaping the dialogue you establish with her. Yet the impact of her values can be felt way beyond establishing a common ground. Understanding her values allows us to understand the "why" behind many of her actions. Her values form the foundation for the five key motivators that ultimately govern and direct her actions. These motivators are nurturing relationships; sharing; do it more simply; healthy, happy adults; and accomplishment.

In her quest to raise healthy, happy adults, moms need to nurture relationships. These are relationships not only between her and her child but between her children and extended family members, peers, teachers and the community at large. She values time so she seeks ways to do tasks more efficiently and in a simpler manner. This motivator will drive her to buy a new cleaning product or bundle product to create her own solutions. Mothers want to feel that they are enriching their family life through their actions so they seek this sense of accomplishment.

This quest for success motivates her to find the best vacation destination for each of her family members or to build a home-based business that allows her to stay in the home. As a marketer you want to touch her heart with one of her core values while leveraging one of her key motivators to produce an outcome that delivers the emotional fulfillment of reaching her goal. Let me give you one example. If I were a cell phone company attempting to sell a mom a wireless device for her child, I would speak to her value of safety while demonstrating to her how the wireless device can facilitate her ability to stay connected—more easily and simply—with her child. Safety is what she values, and nurturing relationships by staying connected is what motivates her to purchase the phone. These motivators run true for most mothers in today's Mom Market.

Now that you've got a basic knowledge of moms, their core values and their key motivators, it's time to introduce you to the emerging subsegments of mothers today.

Subsegments of Today's Moms

As has been discussed, there are all kinds of moms out there and today's technology has made it easier than ever for like-minded moms to band together. Have you ever wondered why and how people branch out into smaller groups, segmenting any particular market demographic? I can't speak to the male population or any ethnic groups, but I *can* help you understand moms.

We've talked about two crucial concepts in this chapter that will allow you to understand the creation of subsegments in today's Mom Market: first, the customization of motherhood being fueled by Generation X and Y mothers and secondly, the creation of peer groups based on common values. Customization will explain the "why" behind all the new distinctions among moms and common values will explain how they come to life.

It's important to understand these two contributing factors because it makes the task of Marketing to Moms far less intimidating. Without this knowledge a marketer could easily argue that too much segmentation exists to cost-effectively tap the market. The reality, however, is that while many segments of moms are popularized in the media with sexy names like "Eco Moms" and "Alpha Moms," they are all parts of the general population of mothers who have customized their role as a mom and joined together with others who share their values. By focusing on the five core values, marketers can establish a relevant dialogue no matter which segment of the Mom Market they're targeting.

Every day there seems to be a new segment of moms in the media or online. Personally, I think it's exciting to see motherhood evolve from the homogeneous days of June Cleaver. Today, mothers take pride in being a "slacker mom" or "no-drama mama" and social networks have given them a platform to join with other like-minded women. Additionally, you can always count on a public relations specialist to give media-savvy names to those moms who don't have the creativity to do so themselves. Step aside, Soccer Moms, let me introduce you to today's moms.

Mom Subsegments

I'm going to describe only a few of the many subsegments of moms as a way to illustrate how passion, value sets and priorities can form peer groups. Even more importantly, I want to highlight their differences and help you recognize that Power Moms exist in every single peer group. This is a significant realization because it will allow you to find the Power Moms influencers who are most closely aligned with your brand and products. I'll describe later how to use the Power Mom directory to your best advantage. Keep in mind that the more you know about a particular Power Mom's values and the segment she resides in, the better choice she will make for your brand.

Mojo Moms

These moms don't believe you have to lose your pre-mom identity just because you have a toddler in tow. According to Amy Tiemann, founder of Mojo Moms (MojoMoms.com), life is a lot more complex and interesting than any oversimplified idea of "opting out" or engaging in the "Mommy Wars" that you so often read about these days. She encourages women to continue developing their own interests and goals throughout life, shaping a career path over the long run that takes the family's needs and personal "seasons of leadership" into account.

You'll meet Power Mom Debi Silber, known as the Mojo Coach (themojocoach.com), in the directory section of this book. You'll be amazed at the reach of her online audience as well as her offline seminar following.

One thing is certain about Mojo Moms: the world needs the full range of talents that these moms have to offer! Mojo

Moms seek to discover who they are and how they can continue to share their talents with others while juggling the demands of a family.

Alpha Moms

A lot has been written in the media about Alpha Moms, albeit sometimes incorrectly defined. The term "Alpha Mom" is often used to define Mom Influencers. However, we know that Mom Influencers exist within all segments of mothers. Alpha Moms are just one of these subsegments. "Alpha Mom" is the new term for the "Super Mom" of the 90s. Think Martha Stewart on steroids. An Alpha Mom is a well-educated overachiever who takes multitasking to a new level. She is motivated by the satisfaction she earns by being "in the know" and the sense of accomplishment she achieves by doing it better and faster than her peers. She often holds a leadership position in her community such as PTO president or team mom.

Beta Moms

Consider these moms the opposite of the Alpha Mom. They aren't worried about the socks on the floor and pick their battles with their children. Experiences are more important than material items and giving Junior a little downtime is just fine in their home. Don't misunderstand them, though. They are moms and don't abuse their authoritative role, but their sense of what's important is self-defined. They are the moms who might forget to sign a permission slip or return a library book but they don't fret over it. René Sylver, author of *Good-Enough Mother: The Perfectly Imperfect Book of Parenting*, described it best in an interview with *USA Today*.

"Our children are people—not projects," she said. "Motherhood is not a contest. We get to the finish line. It's OK to chill out a little bit and let your kids be independent, and individuals, and revel in who they are."

Hybrid Moms

I've said it for years: segmenting the Mom Market into the "working" and "stay at home" categories is outdated and wrong. The growing number of hybrid moms proves it. These women, who choose to integrate a career or professional work into their in-home parenting life, are proud of their dual role. In fact, they even have their own community at HybridMom.com. Hybrid Moms put their role as mother first, yet take pride in melding a professional life into the extra hours of the day. With the growth of social media and moms who are running in-home businesses, the community of Hybrid Moms has grown quickly.

Moxie and Fitness Moms

Fitness and fun are what brings these moms together. Their mission is to support moms in their pursuit of a community of friends, fun and fitness. The term "Moxie Mom" was coined by Susan Lavelle in 2003 and it has quickly grown to include moms with the moxie to stay fit even after pregnancy. The Wii Fit and www.fromcouchto5K.com also did a great deal to generate growth in this segment of mothers as well.

The craze to get off the couch and introduce fitness into the life of a mom has spawned a new generation of marathoners who compare running schedules on Twitter and trade injury reports on Facebook. Power Moms in this segment include Carla Birnberg (www.mizfitonline.com),

Lisa Gully (www.workoutmommy.com) and Debi Silber (www.themojocoach.com), mentioned earlier in this chapter.

Eco Moms

Eco Moms are green with a capital "G." Interested in organic produce and low-impact living, concerned about toxins in her kitchen, this mom is about teaching her children to value the Earth's resources and making wise environmental choices. These Eco Moms are often highly educated women who are influenced by Celebrity Moms such as Sheryl Crow and Robin Wright Penn. These moms are not only washing in cold water and using low-energy light bulbs but they are organizing themselves in the name of their children's future.

One such mom maintains anonymity but writes a popular blog for moms called "GreenAndCleanMom" in which she regularly points out healthy and safe alternatives to the bad habits many less eco-minded moms possess. Another mom runs Green Mom Reviews (greenmomreviews.com), which highlights green, sustainable products. Marketers can witness the power of word of mouth marketing among mothers by visiting this site. You can find heavy-hitting influencers in this group like Annie, also known as @phdinparenting on Twitter. She is outspoken and passionate about educating moms and is not afraid to call out moms on Twitter.

Eco Moms are organizing into groups such as Parents for Climate Protection and EcoMom Alliance, redefining the definition and reality of "mommy groups." In research by BSM Media, we found that most mothers would like to do better in the area of going green; however, they feel that the media has failed to provide them solid information on how to achieve this goal. Many moms cited a lack of true definition to marketing terms such as "organic" and "natural" as their downfall in becoming truly green. One mom told me, "The whole 'green' theme has become like 'fat-free' was in the nineties. Everything has 'organic' or 'natural' on the label, making me wonder what these words really mean to me and my family."

Coupon Super Savers

Blame it on the economy or the fact that many Blogging Moms give up disposable income when they choose to stay at home, but there is a cult-like following of frugal moms in the online and offline spheres. I admit that before the recession-like economy affected my family, I closely watched this group of moms as an interested observer and could appreciate their energy and excitement, even if I didn't have the urge to clip coupons. But it was only a matter of time until the economy made our family rethink our budget, too.

When that moment of truth arrived, I knew exactly where to turn for help. I went to Andrea Deckard, founder of www.savingslifestyle.com . She not only taught me how to clip coupons but by visiting her blog, I could find out when and where to use them to get the most for my dollar. I may sound like a born-again shopper, but literally in one month my grocery bill went from $350 a week to $150–$175 a week. Of course, I had to give up a closet to my stockpiled groceries, but with a family of six plus a few animals to feed, it was worth it. What's that? You don't know what a stockpile is? Well, just ask one of the many frugal moms you'll meet in the directory.

Yummy Mummies

Think Victoria Beckham, Kelly Ripa and Nicole Richie. These are the new moms, driven by pop culture, who aren't ready to give up their taste for fashion and style just because they're toting diapers in their Kate Spade bag. According to London-based Polly Williams, author of *Yummy Mummy*, "what happens when hipster 30-somethings breed" is a Yummy Mummy. The growth of this segment has been fueled by the media focus on celebrity mothers like Angelina Jolie, Halle Barry and Jennifer Garner who, with their little bundles of joys on their hips, retain their prepregnancy figure and flare. Like many other Generation X moms who are customizing their definition of motherhood, these women don't believe that childbirth or adoption has to mean losing their personal identity.

Companies trying to reach this segment of mothers need to consider the style of their product as to how it fits into their self-image of parenthood. The best example of this is the diaper bag. Long gone are the Winnie the Pooh quilted bags in baby blue. Instead these Yummy Mummies tote Kate Spade bags, which from the outside appear to be a typical oversized black bag—with the functionality of a diaper bag hidden inside. We included a section of Celebrity Moms in our directory to give you a sense of who are true influencers among everyday moms and who are just actresses with kids. Believe it or not, not every Mom Celebrity makes a good influencer in the minds of Main Street moms. I'll leave it at Octomom.

Mompreneurs

They don't consider themselves working mothers yet they own businesses. Mompreneurs are business owners who put their role as mother before their identity as entrepreneur. Their motivation to launch a business is largely fueled out of their desire to become an in-home mother, enabling them to spend more time with their children. Some are accidental business owners. The companies they run range from eBay auctions to franchise businesses. Two of the most famous moms among this group are Lisa Druxman, founder of Stroller Strides, and Julie Aigner Clark, founder of Baby Einstein. Both of these moms created well-known, revenue-generating brands on a global scale from the confines of their own home with kids beneath their feet. You'll meet several moms in our Power Mom directory who are part of the Huggies MomInspired™ program (www.HuggiesMomInspired.com). These are mom inventors who have received a grant from Huggies to take their idea or product to the next business level. Thousands of moms vie for the grants during each round of registration.

Whether it's an eBay business or a product company with inventory in Walmart, these business owners make great Power Moms because they interact with women from a variety of backgrounds and professional industries.

These are just a few of the mom groups you'll find in today's market. Remember that regardless of the name they hook their identity to, these moms all possess a link to the five core values described earlier. They also have leaders and followers in the mix, Power Moms and peers who can be influenced.

Now that you're familiar with moms in general, let's turn our attention to the Power Moms: the moms you need to carry your message, create the buzz and endorse your product.

Section 2
Power Moms

I call them Power Moms. Others call them Mom Influencers. Whatever term you use to identify them, they are the go-to moms: the moms who share information with peers, direct fellow stroller pushers to retailers and to pilot their minivans to recommended destinations. Their product knowledge and brand opinions are so sought after in certain circles that they control the destiny of some marketing efforts. A product can live and die by the powerful word of mouth of these mothers. Their opinions can also make the headlines of the New York Times or Huffington Post in a less than favorable manner.

As we've discussed, Power Moms possess immense power to change events, launch brands and use technology in ways that programmers never intended it to be used. Many of these women are propelling the growth of technology in the Mom Market well beyond the latest trends. They're pushing the envelope in blogging, podcasting and videocasting and because of their influence, others are following. Twitter parties and online "Mom Mixers" would not exist had it not been for the creativity and innovation of these mothers.

Marketers have always known about the importance of word of mouth marketing. Now, with today's technology, word of mouth in the Mom Market is on steroids. Understanding the behaviors of such a powerfully influential consumer group is imperative to the success of brands trying to connect with mothers. I believe that most marketers are aware of this importance; however, in the excitement of being able to track the power of moms passing along information online, many have forgotten the power of moms offline. Remember, offline word of mouth hasn't gone away and in many ways remains as valuable as a few good tweets during a Twitter party or a "like" on Facebook. I suggest that savvy Power Mom marketers reacquaint themselves with the offline power of Mom Influencers while better leveraging the influence of social media moms.

Winning the heart of a Power Mom is a marketer's dream come true. Her loyalty can earn you thousands of dollars in sales, numerous mentions throughout her day and perhaps millions of impressions online in blogs, podcasts or videos. Nothing beats a third-party Power Mom endorsement of your product. According to research conducted by BSM Media, 70% of moms purchase products based on another mother's recommendation.

Consider the results of 2008 research released from BabyCenter, the largest online resource for pregnant women and new moms. According to their survey, an audience of mothers engages in 109 word-of-mouth conversations a week. Sixty percent of conversations among these mothers-to-be and new moms include product recommendations. Research also illustrates that they are gathering those recommendations in both the physical and virtual word. In a survey of 300 social media moms, defined as moms who actively participate in more than one social media activity, 85% of them responded that they recommend products and services to other moms offline as well as through their social media outlets. Additionally, we asked these same mothers how often they purchased a product another mother recommended to them. It was not surprising that 99% said they had. What *was* surprising was that 90% revealed they'd bought a product they'd heard about on Twitter.

For years, I've been writing about the importance of walking in Mom's shoes to deliver your message in all the places a mother travels throughout her day. This confirms that you must position yourself offline as well as online. A marketer needs to make certain that moms are creating a buzz in the carpool lane, in the grocery store and at the office as well as in a Facebook thread. That's a lot of places for one marketer to be but the task is not impossible to accomplish with the help of Power Mom. Becoming familiar with these women and engaging them in talking about your brand or product goes a long way in creating Word of Mom Marketing online and offline.

A great deal is written and spoken about word of mouth marketing. Its evolution as a formalized marketing tactic has been fueled by social media. Prior to 1995, there was no formalized association for marketing professionals interested in understanding the mechanism of how one consumer passes on information to another. The launch of the Word of Mouth Marketing Association (WOMMA) created an organization dedicated to discussion and understanding and with it came a new wave of interest. Shortly afterwards, Tremor, a division of Proctor and

Gamble, launched Vocal Point as its delivery vehicle for word of mouth marketing in the Mom Market. Marketers took notice, as did Mom Bloggers and online advertisers.

In the early 2000s, everyone from Mom Bloggers to media companies created aggregate lists of influencers to sell to marketers desperate to create buzz among moms. What used to happen as a natural, rather mysterious phenomenon has become a calculated marketing tactic. Some marketing purists still believe that true viral buzz only happens without the strong intervention of a brand manager but even with this philosophy they've got to agree that a Mom Influencer *can* fuel the viral engine.

To fully appreciate the impact of a Power Mom, let's examine her most powerful tool: Word of Mom. Remember she carries it with her offline and online, in her minivan, on her wireless device, in her grocery basket and on her Facebook page. It's passed between moms in local communities by marketing programs that engage moms with products and messages to share with their peers. Online Word of Mom provokes mothers to forward emails and give recommendations to other moms within their virtual communities.

There are two very important parts to generating Word of Mom. First, finding the right moms, which should be made easier by reading this book, and secondly, arming the Power Mom with the tools to share your message. At BSM Media, we measure the results of these two steps to determine the success of any marketing program. We ask two very important questions of every single marketing program: Did we reach the right moms? And if we did, what was the total sphere of influence of the Power Moms who delivered our client's message?

This is very different from the typical manner in which marketers have been measuring success, particularly online. For years, it's been about the number of impressions. However, we believe that the message is far more powerful, even with fewer impressions, if the right "mom messenger" is delivering the message to the moms who are a fit for your product.

In a recent Word of Mom program with Power Moms, 82% of moms reported telling 30–50 other moms about our client's product. During another program, BSM Media was able to garner 1.5 million mom-generated impressions for a client's brand. These are great results, but the most important element is the delivery channel: another mom. As mentioned earlier, the majority of moms (70%) purchase a product based on another mom's recommendation. The numbers may seem less impressive if compared with, say, a blizzard of banners appearing on large mom portals on the Web. But their true significance quickly emerges when you consider the full scope of influence via those Power Moms.

Using conservative numbers, if 60% of the 1 million mom-generated impressions caused a chain reaction of those mothers telling even 20 other moms, your brand message has reached over 5 million moms. That's the power of what we call the "mom sphere of influence." Your marketing message transcends the first tier of mothers to reach a secondary and tertiary group of consumers who all heard about your product from another mother. This is powerful marketing at its best.

The optimum engagement for marketers is to gain the seal of approval by Power Mom, but have you ever wondered what motivates a mom to be your brand evangelist (a term coined by a fellow author Jackie Huba)? Or why other moms respect a Power Mom so much? Well, you're about to find out, as we shift our focus and take you inside the minds of Power Moms and learn how marketers can identify, engage and empower them to sell their brand.

A Power Mom's Motivation

Power Moms are the "go-to" moms within their peer group. You can find her sitting in the bleachers at almost any Little League game. She is the mom who others turn to, not only for the score but also for recommendations on retailers and dinner ideas. She confidently shares her thoughts, opinions and most of all, little-known knowledge and facts. In many instances, you can find her on Twitter while serving hot dogs during her volunteer hours or texting friends while listening to piano lessons. Other moms gather around her and listen avidly as she dishes out her insights. Within the pyramid of her peers she sits on the top, pointing the way to more information and recommendations.

It takes time to know all the things she knows. She surfs the Internet, reads product labels, combs through magazines and watches for a great deal via a blog. As a result, this mom can tell you about the hottest lipstick color, back-to-school trends and what shoes Tori Spelling's children are wearing for the holidays. What motivates her to always be in the know? Recall the five core values of a mom we discussed in section one. This mom is highly motivated by her need to share, nurture relationships and demonstrate that she can do it better and more simply. She enjoys her position at the top of her peer pyramid because it gives her that sense of accomplishment that she strives to obtain. This is the self-made Power Mom. Her reign at the top is quite intentional.

There's a second type of Power Mom who earns her position more by accident than by design. We will discuss her as we look at the qualities that make up a Power Mom. You'll learn that some moms become Power Moms by virtue of their social situations.

Making of a Power Mom

Power Moms earn their spot at the top of the pyramid of peers by their extensive breadth of knowledge. In the late 1990s, my team at BSM Media and I began to see some commonalities among Power Moms. More and more companies were asking us to engage influencers in marketing programs for them, which meant we had to seek out the most influential moms in the nation.

Today we seek out the most influential moms, mums and mamas because the interest in these women has rapidly grown on a global scale. Initially, we leveraged many existing relationships but also considered referrals from other Power Moms. We found that these media mavens not only recommend the best stroller to purchase for a newborn, they also recommend other moms like themselves.

Soon we had relationships with thousands of Power Moms across the U.S. Today we also have thousands of relationships around the globe. You can ask me for a name of a Mom Influencer in San Diego and I can give you 10 without blinking an eye. My first call would be to Cindy Robinson, mother of four, on the board of directors for Parents

Connect and a business owner. If you wanted to know a Power Mom in Chicago, I'd give you the name of Julie Marchese, mother of four boys including twins, church group leader, part-time teacher and team mom. In Washington, DC, I would definitely recommend Amy Lupold Bair of Resourcefulmommy.com. In the online world, if you asked me for a "turbo tweeter," I'd point you to Shellie Ross, @Military_mom, or Daisy Sutherland, @DrMommy.

The more we networked with Power Moms, the more we noticed common traits or qualities among them. In fact, we identified roughly 20 shared behaviors and traits that make them an influencer. We analyzed and plotted these qualities and eventually developed the Mom Matrix, a system of 18 common behaviors that position a mom to be a distributor of marketing, product and brand information. These are the behaviors that make her most likely to be a true Power Mom rather than a mom who simply speaks to a few other moms over the course of her day. While not every Power Mom exhibits every trait, our experience and observations illustrate that some combination of these qualities ultimately propel her to the status of Power Mom among her peers. I'll explain why after we look at some of the traits.

Among the characteristics of a Power Mom are the following:

- Mothers of multiples
- Mothers of physically-challenged children
- Mothers who have suffered a tragedy
- Mothers who hold a leadership position in their community
- Moms who are published, whether traditionally or self-published
- Moms who control a media outlet such as website, newsletter or blog
- Moms with more than three children
- Moms who run a business
- Mothers who have exhibited a strong nonprofit commitment
- Moms of preschoolers
- Moms who are engaged in *multiple* platforms of social media

A combination of two or three of these behaviors allows you to identify moms who have strong established social networks. In word of mouth marketing, these networks are leveraged as outlets for her to share marketing messages. At BSM Media, we use our Power Mom Matrix to screen potential moms and rate them against the behaviors we seek as influencers. We feel that it is not sufficient to merely ask moms if they're willing to talk to other moms about a product or to set a number of interactions she conducts with other moms as criteria. You need Power Moms who are truly influencers and respected among their peers.

Be aware that there are moms who make it a habit, or even a business, to enter online sweepstakes, participate in focus groups or register to test products. Along with the media hype of Mom Blogging and free products, a new generation of Mom Bloggers has emerged whose primary motivation is free product. Marketers should avoid these women because their motivations are transparent to other moms who tune out their product reviews. It's well known among their peers. As a marketer, you want to engage the most respected authority in the peer group.

Let's take a minute and examine why some of these traits produce a Power Mom. A mom of multiples, for example, is viewed as a go-to mom because, in the eyes of her peers who parent singletons, there is a perception that it takes more know-how to parent twins or triplets; *this* mom has a greater need for convenience and ease, and likely uses additional products. Thus, if the mom of multiples has greater needs as a mother, the deduction by her peers is that she must know more about parenting.

I remember, as the mother of three babies under two years of age, mothers of singletons gawking in amazement that I really could handle my three. It's this feeling of amazement that puts the mom of multiples on the road to becoming an influencer. This same kind of mom logic applies to moms of physically-challenged children and moms who have survived a tragedy, whether it's a divorce or family illness. The feeling of her peers is that somehow it takes more knowledge to weather their storm; they must possess some kind of insight perhaps not so readily available to other moms with less complicated lives. These are the moms who accidentally become Power Moms because of often uncontrollable circumstances.

The emergence of technologies such as self-publishing, blogging, podcasting and videocasting have produced a whole new breed of Power Moms. These self-declared, self-made experts have utilized technology to build up audiences of moms who respect and admire their opinions. Liz Gumbiner of Cool Mom Picks, Gabrielle Blair of Design Mom and Jo-Lynne Shane of Parenting Squad are just a few of these influential mothers who frequently suggest products to solution-seeking mothers. They control publications, websites, e-newsletters and blog posts, and through those, they influence audiences who read, listen and engage with them. These are the kinds of moms who've taken on the role of PTA president and gone even further—way further. Many of these women have created influence by becoming authors and reaching moms around the globe. Elizabeth Pantley, author of several parenting books, travels around the world speaking to mothers about baby's sleep habits and potty training; Melanie Nelson, author and blogger at Blogging101.com talks to women worldwide on Twitter as @melanienelson.

All of these women are Mom Influencers and their impact on other mothers is immeasurable. But let's not forget the old-fashioned mom mavens who use minimal technology in their community interactions but still influence many mothers throughout their daily activities. As an example, I'd like to tell you about my good friend Jennifer Calhoun, mother of two and executive at a major technology manufacturer. (The danger of interacting with me as a mother is that one day you might end up in a book or PowerPoint presentation!) She doesn't blog or tweet but recommends product every time she shows up at a volleyball game in a new outfit or posts new photos on Facebook or serves the latest bottle of wine at a moms' night out event. There are plenty of great Power Moms who are not Mommy Bloggers and you find them right there in your local marketplaces. They are the Girl Scout leaders, PTO presidents, daycare providers, teachers, bake sale chairwomen and others who hold leadership positions and influence their peer groups. These mothers, although possessing a smaller reach, can nonetheless impact sales and brand awareness in local markets.

Mining the Power of Power Moms

When it comes to Power Moms, the most commonly asked question by marketers is "Where do we find them?" Now that you have your "little black book" of big influencers in hand, a key part of the challenge is met. You could also pay someone to find them for you, but I caution you to learn what process they use to determine that a mom is a Power Mom.

There are companies out there who are *paying* people to sign up and that's how they build their databases. You can imagine how startled I was when a young gentleman called me recently to solicit my services in building his company's influencer database. His proposal was to pay me $2 for each mom I convinced to register. My skin was crawling as I turned down the offer. Today, I watch from the sidelines as I see this same company sell its database of supposed influencers to unsuspecting, yet eager marketers. My high standards of professionalism will not allow me to spread the word about the source of their "influencers," although I cringe at the thought of it all. Companies who sell Mom Influencer lists typically charge between $100–$150 per influencer. You may be inclined to pay the price but do be aware of *how* they are finding their Power Moms.

If the directory I've assembled for you here doesn't meet all your Power Mom needs and you need more, you may decide to mine them on your own. There are a few important tactics you can deploy to find Mom Influencers. First, identify the right Power Mom for your company's needs and goals. Not all Power Moms are influencers in all circles. For instance, if you have a prenatal product, your best influencer is a mom of a toddler or a mom who is pregnant for the second or third time. Moms look up to moms who have already experienced the parenting stage they're currently in. They seek information from experienced mothers who are elevated peers.

As we've discussed already, not all Power Moms are created equal. Influencers can be found in each and every subsegment of moms, from Alpha to Beta mothers. Once you've decided the right life-stage and demographic criteria for your influencer, determine if there is a common interest you would like to share with your Power Mom. For instance, if you're a brand manager promoting a healthy cereal, you want to seek Power Mom who shares the passion of eating right. Not only will this shared interest deepen your relationship with her, but it makes her recommendation of your product more credible among her peer group. For example, Lisa Druxman, founder of Stroller Strides, would be the perfect Power Mom for a healthy food product because she lives a healthy lifestyle and leads a company with 750 health-conscious mom groups across the United States.

Social media has made this easier for you. You can follow moms on Twitter and see who talks most about the focus of your company. For instance, Jennifer Cherry, a mom who produces a morning sickness remedy called B-Natal, can easily search Twitter via www.summize.com and find moms who are giving out morning sickness advice via Twitter. Summize.com is the Google of Twitter and will give you a real-time read on who is tweeting about what topics. Social media is your crystal ball into which moms are talking about what problems or which mothers are seeking the advice of other moms. The moms dishing out the advice are the moms you want to target. Go get your Power Mom.

When it comes to offline Mom Influencers, local publications can be a great mining tool. Toward the back of these publications you can find listings of mom organizations and playgroups. These listings often post the leader's name and phone number. You can often find calendar events for mom groups, such as Mothers of Twins or moms' meetups. A friendly phone call to the organizer can end in not only enlisting her help, but also gaining referrals to other local Power Moms.

You can also find these physical-world mom organizations by searching online. Often a simple search by location, interest and any combination of the words "mom" or "mothers" can normally turn up local mom organizations. Again, an email or phone call to the leader of these groups can uncover a Mom Influencer. Sites such as www.iplay-groups.com can also serve as a way to identify moms who organize other moms. Their database will allow you to search geographically.

Engaging with Your Power Mom

Once you have located the right Power Mom for your brand, it's time to start the conversation. Much like dating, or at least the way it was in the 80s, you don't jump into the relationship. It's important to introduce yourself, then clearly define the purpose of your contact and the expectations for the relationship. Remember, a relationship means that it is a mutually beneficial partnership and "here's a free product" doesn't count. I've tried to give you enough information in this directory to allow you to get to know the goals of the individual moms and how they prefer to work with brands. This information will go a long way to opening the door. Most likely once you say, "I saw you in Maria Bailey's book..." you'll probably have your entrée. (Think of me as your wing-mom instead of your wingman.) Be honest. Be open. Power Moms don't bite unless you deceive them or do something really stupid like send Jewish Mom Bloggers Easter egg decorating tips. Yes, it's happened. Sadly enough it happened twice in 12 months when the same Jewish moms received tuna recipes for Lent the following year. I just tell my clients to be themselves and to remember many of these women are business owners as well as moms, so treat them professionally.

Marketing with Power Moms

Now that you've identified the right Power Mom for your brand, how do you engage with them to help you market your product? My team at BSM Media has conducted over 5,000 Mom Influencer programs, enlisting over 1 million Power Moms over the past decade. Based on a client's budget, we design customized programs to fit their goals. The good news is that, unlike other marketing initiatives, money doesn't necessarily govern the results of these programs. Our experience working with budgets ranging from $10,000 to $100,000 has allowed us to hone in on the key elements necessary in leveraging Power Mom. And for the cost of this book, I'm going to share them with you now.

In order to engage these influencers with your message, the first component to offer is some type of exclusive nugget of information that elevates them among their peers. As we discussed earlier, this nugget provides the knowledge that motivates her to share with her friends. Access to unknown facts, product previews and special offers are all things that keep her on top of the peer pyramid.

Keep in mind that as the influence of some moms has grown, so has their price tag for leveraging their influence. It will take much more than a free product preview, for example, to have Trisha Haas of MomDot.com talk about your product on her site. She will, however, talk about mom-friendly products that never happen her way via a marketer.

Let's take a moment and talk about the nasty ongoing discussion among Mom Bloggers: to be paid or not to be paid, that is the question. A decade ago when I wrote my first book on Marketing to Moms I could only dream that marketers would someday appreciate the influence of mothers. Today, not only have brands recognized the value of moms, but moms have come to realize their value among companies.

There is a constant debate, sometimes very heated among moms, about the true definition of that value. Every time a Mom Blogger posts about the topic of payment for reviews or product mentions, a long trail of comments blankets the posts, followed by a firestorm on Twitter. Many a mom has been verbally chastised for taking product instead of cash and selling her sphere of influence for free stuff.

It's important to truly understand where a mom, particularly a blogger, stands on this issue before reaching out to her. Most women have a very clear explanation on their site regarding reviews as well as a Federal Trade Commission disclosure statement. The latter promotes transparency to audiences; it protects you as a brand and the Mom Blogger against false claims or any appearance of a conflict of interest. (Read more at http://news.cnet.com/8301-13578_3-10269962-38.html#ixzz1AMY1C7Mu).

While you're analyzing a mom's position on pay-for-post influence, it's important to define your own. Do you *want* influence that is motivated by money? Or do you want to garner true praise for your product? If it's simply online impressions and reach you're striving to obtain, then the first option is absolutely viable. However, if you're seeking deeper relationships and emotion-based praise of your product, you're more likely to obtain this by winning over a mom who really loves the features and benefits of your product.

Let's assume you've moved beyond the question of pay-for-play influence. Next, it's important to also give her something to share with others. It's great to empower her with information to spread for you, but to give her something she can actually share will double your results. One of the major complaints of Mom Bloggers in particular is the endless flow of meaningless and generic press releases flooding their in-boxes. They normally start off, "We love your blog and thought you would want to share this information with your readers." This approach is often met with a quick click of the "delete" key.

Another complaint is the mystery deliveries to their doorstep. Many marketers simply send samples to influencers and hope these Mom Influencers will begin telling others about the product. This approach not only lacks the personal touch so important to moms, it's missing the key element of sharing: having something significant to share with other moms. A better approach might be to include some valuable coupons along with the product; this allows her to share a discount with her peers, once she has fallen in love with your product.

Think about the last time someone shared an online promo code or a retailer's 25% coupon with you. You likely felt grateful and/or loyal to that person in some way. This is the same emotion that fuels word of mouth. There are moms who have built entire Facebook pages, YouTube channels and blogs around sharing coupon codes because they love helping other moms save money.

The third element of your Power Mom program, budget permitting, is something special for her child. Moms love for others to show attention to their children. Of course, if your product is focused more on Mom herself, this is not as important to your program. Here's an example. To launch ZhuZhu Pets into the market, we not only gave moms the toy hamster to review but we gave her child the very first Zhuniverse play sets. Many of them could not wait to brag, in a friendly way of course, that their family had the toy that others could only find on eBay with a high price tag.

This partnership with Power Mom has been credited with what some industry experts call the most successful launch of a toy product in the world. These efforts helped ZhuZhu Pets receive "Toy of the Year" distinctions in 2009 *and* 2010. During the holiday season, marketers once again leveraged Power Mom influencers by giving them each 100 toys to donate to a charity of their choice. This campaign—called "Random Acts of Zhu"—created a great deal of goodwill as well as numerous positive blog posts and tweets. More importantly, it utilized online influencers to deliver product and messaging to offline audiences.

One final thought. Be sure to give moms ideas on how they might help you spread the word. In a Cartoon Network program with 10,000 of our Power Moms, we sent branded tattoos and stickers, among other items. In the package, we included a letter to the mom with ideas as to where they could distribute these items. We took into consideration the kinds of solutions that moms are always seeking for activities such as Scout troop meetings, birthday parties, classroom reward boxes and bag stuffers for event favors. Our suggestion was for the mom to send them into their child's classroom as a fun reward or use them to fill birthday piñatas. Ideas such as these help moms position themselves as heroes, not only among peers, but to their children as well. Can you imagine how cool it would be to have a mom who has access to early movie previews or Cartoon Network tattoos that no one else has? Very cool!

You can also create exciting experiences for the mom to share with her child. Gift cards for a mother and child to visit a Build-A-Bear Workshop or a shopping spree at

Macy's also work well to win Mom's loyalty. We've even coordinated programs where we create events that give moms the night off while dads take care of the kids for a moms' night out. Moms really like these types of programs because it achieves two of their goals. First, Dad gets to spend some fun time with the kids and second, it results in a well-deserved night off.

Another example of a cohesive Power Mom program is in-home parties. We call them MommyParties (www.mommyparties.com). Nestlé Nesquik was very successful in using them to launch a new product in several Western states. With the help of BSM Media, they engaged Power Moms in trying samples of their shelf-safe chocolate milk. Rather than just sending samples, Nestle sent each mom suggestions for holding a "chocolate milk and cookies" mixer. The Nesquik party package also included a plush toy for their children.

This Word of Mom program was a huge success. Eighty percent of all mothers invited other moms into their home to sample the milk at their preview party. The best news for Nestlé was that on average these moms told 20–30 other moms about the shelf-stable milk. Nestlé successfully became a part of the mom dialogue going on between Power Moms and their peers. Sales in the test market were so strong that a national rollout occurred six months earlier than the expected target date.

Disney found similar success with home-based parties called In-Home Celebrations. Unlike Nestlé, Disney used its own database of Mom Influencers. These were moms who had proclaimed their interest in the brand by registering to participate in the program. Over 1,000 moms hosted parties with the Disney party kits they received. Some mothers even supplemented the kits and threw parties for 50–100 people. The power of Power Mom produced millions of online impressions and reached thousands of moms offline. Best of all, the cost of the program was 50% less than other similar word-of-mouth programs.

Before we conclude this discussion on how to successfully market with Power Mom, it's important to mention a key aspect of your programs: measurement. Some argue that it's nearly impossible to measure word of mouth; however, if you set this expectation with your moms as a part of the program's description, there *are* ways to calculate results. At BSM Media, we utilize several tools, from online surveys to post-event interviews that include intent to purchase, mentions to other moms and general feedback. Be sure to build your Power Mom program against established goals. Establish your benchmarks *before* you launch the program so that you can clearly define the call to action that will support your goals.

Power Mom Activities

There are a number of program types marketers can launch to partner with Power Mom. Among them are Power Mom Mixers®, in-home parties, influencer campaigns and advisory boards. All of these programs should include the marketing tactics described above. Only the execution of these tactics changes from program to program.

Power Mom Mixers

These grassroots marketing programs are the perfect combination of viral marketing and Mom Influencers and can be conducted in from 1 to 100 markets. Basically, a Power Mom Mixer is an exclusive, invitation-only special event hosted for Power Moms. We've done everything from pedicure parties to fashion shows for these influencers. During the event, a company or brand representative, hopefully a mom, adds a special touch and personalized interaction with the guest moms. It's a great way to put a face to your brand by letting the moms know there are like-minded mothers behind your products. Samples, previews and displays enhance the event as well.

Power Mom Mixers should be fun and provide a platform for moms to socialize with other moms. They can also be educational. HP hosted Power Mom Mixers inside of Longs Drugstores in California last year. The events had a social feel to them, but also educated moms on how to enhance their digital photos. Even during leisure time, moms are still multitaskers so this dual approach works well. Moms should leave the event with coupons or items to share with their peers.

Power Mom Mixers can also be held online. You might wonder, "Who can moms mix with via their laptops?" With moms, if there's a will, there's a way. Online Power Mom Mixers take place using live video on MomTV.com. Moms gather in front of the computer and watch a Live Social host who leads the conversation via video and gives away prizes while playing trivia games. Moms join via a live chat room or take part via Twitter. For information about online social media Mom Mixers, you can contact ElizaBeth@momtv.com.

More about In-Home Parties and MommyParties

Everyone loves a party and the best part of a Power Mom in-home party is that you create a platform for the mom to showcase her Mavenism. (Yes, it's a word.) The party lets the Maven share with her peers, not only what she knows but also the products or brand messages you supply for the party. In-home parties and MommyParties are more effective in the summer months when moms are looking for boredom-busting activities.

We've conducted over 100,000 in-home parties with Power Moms. The easier you make it for the mom to hold a fun get-together, the greater the response you'll have from her and her guests. The program begins when you invite Power Moms to serve as party hosts. The simplest explanation of this initiative is that each Power Mom hostess invites her peers to enjoy an in-home, themed party designed around your product or brand messaging. The hostess receives a party box which contains everything she needs to conduct her party. Depending upon your budget and your goals, the supplies in the box can be increased or decreased according to the size of the party. Should you be fortunate enough to have a large budget, you opt for uber-party kits large enough for Scout leaders or other mom leaders to host large grassroots parties. Although we call them in-home parties, we always tell moms that the party can be conducted during a planned playgroup at the playground or a prearranged meeting of moms. The idea is to create an event that gets your brand in front of moms.

The box should include an instruction sheet as well as any combination of party favors, invitations, snack recipes, product samples, coupons, company literature, decorations, door prizes and a special hostess gift. In the best of budgetary times, a hostess would receive a box with all these elements inside. For more realistic budgets, there are a few cost-cutting possibilities. Are there pieces you can house online? Remember, every component in the box adds weight, which adds postage, which in turn adds expense to your program. An online printable invitation can be created and moms can be pointed to a microsite to download recipes, activities and games to play during the party. However, the hostess letter with instruction sheet is too important to put online. It's your communication with moms and needs to be personal and engaging. It should also include the post-event measurement instructions, whether it's a paper survey or a URL to an online polling tool.

In-home parties using Power Mom hostesses can be very effective. A consumer product company recently hosted in-home Power Mom Mixers to introduce a new line of products. Not only did over 12,000 moms volunteer to host parties on behalf of the company, but the mothers who qualified to become hostesses exceeded the anticipated sample distribution by 50%.

An entertainment client recently sponsored Dino-Mite Mom Parties with 500 preschool mothers. Each mom received a party kit filled with party activities, recipes for snacks, samples, coupons and other shareable promotional items. The turnkey program resulted in thousands of word-of-mouth mentions and hundreds of thousands of online blog impressions. In fact, 82% of moms told at least 15 other moms about the brand.

You might be surprised what moms are willing to do for your product. Last year, we held painting parties in seven cities across the U.S. The goal was to introduce a new

Benjamin Moore paint with special marbleizing qualities. Moms actually invited friends into their home to repaint their living room walls. The program was very successful.

Influencers Programs

Moms don't have to throw a party to spread the word for you. With a compelling program, moms will carry your message, product samples and coupons with them during their typically busy days, scattering them along the way. The best influencer programs take into consideration all the components of an in-home party, only without the party. We often send Power Moms a product kit with ideas on sharing it with others. This is a good initiative when your campaign is based on coupon distribution. Moms are happy to leave a handful at the school office or daycare reception desk.

The best part is that a mom with influence is more likely to get approval to leave your coupons at the pediatrician's office than your average big-name company. Companies can also leverage a solely online influencer program by recruiting Mom Bloggers or other online social media Mom Influencers, such as webmasters and podcasters. We call these programs Online Media Tours. Again, you want to work with moms you know. I've done most of the work that I would otherwise be instructing you to do by compiling this directory. I still suggest that you get familiar with the onlinePower Moms you select from this book. Read their blogs, listen to the podcasts and/or watch their videos on MomTV. You can also reach non–media controlling moms with online programs. Instead of sending snail mail packets to each Power Mom, marketers can establish a microsite with e-coupons, buttons, e-cards and prewritten emails that can be easily forwarded to other moms along with audio or video files. Whatever you load on the site, just make it easy to forward and make sure it includes a call to action.

Advisory Boards and Mom Panels

Another effective way to engage a Power Mom is to create advisory boards or Mom Panels. They are a great way to formally establish a group of influential moms and align them with your brand. Here again, some moms are now requiring payment for this type of role. Ironically, many of the moms now demanding payment are the same moms who served on the early Mom Panels and used them as a stepping stone into the limelight of Power Momism. This is another situation where you'll have to determine your values and budget for such an endeavor. The size of the panel is optional. We've created advisory boards of moms as large as 100 for some clients, and as small as 10 for others. Again, budget and goals will dictate this.

Keep in mind that size doesn't necessarily limit the effectiveness of your panel. If you select moms with the right personalities and an existing audience of followers, you can obtain as much or more success than by creating a board of 100 poorly selected mothers. Another limiting factor to your success is the level of engagement you provide these moms, not only in product development, access to company personnel and involvement in marketing campaigns, but also with other moms. Remember, this is the world of *interactive* engagement. It doesn't serve the audience well if you have an advisory board of moms with whom they cannot interact. It's about sharing ideas, but not in a one-way direction.

You should select your Power Mom in much the same way we've already described in this chapter. Common interests, shared passion and a clear outline of expectations are essential to your success. Companies can utilize mom advisory boards in many ways. They make great sounding boards and focus groups for new products, ad campaigns and marketing ideas. They can be used as spokespersons and online experts. We created a mom advisory panel for one client and the moms, many of whom were authors, supplied the company with content for both online and offline publications. Lifetime has done something similar with their group of Lifetime Moms. In fact, they've been able to create an entire site as well as ad packages for clients around their influencer panel.

Having moms produce content is a great way to give them the opportunity to gain visibility among their peers and exposure for their own brands—while the company receives free content. Best of all, content is written for moms, by moms. It creates a win-win situation for both sides, but only if the moms see a flow of traffic to their sites or it helps them get other Power Mom gigs. In justifying the expense for a program like this, you may want to spread the expense across research, content and word of mouth marketing. Properly set up, your Mom Panel can save you expense in all three areas.

It's worth mentioning that not all Mom Panels have to be created from moms outside of the company. Some of the best influencers can be the moms who work to develop and promote your products every day. Take advantage of their passion and experience and share it with other moms who are your target as consumers. Orbitz has done this. They recently created a panel of 20 employees with children of varied ages. Among the topics these parents discuss online, in an interactive forum, are cruise tips and babysitters while on vacation.

Like any other marketing program, there are right and wrong ways to execute this type of initiative and in today's viral world, moms can create as much buzz as you hope to generate through a successful program.

Let's start off by analyzing McDonald's Mom Panel. In May of 2006, McDonald's announced the creation of a group they called Quality Correspondents. They do have a global Mom Panel, but the goals of the programs differ and for our purposes we will focus on Quality Correspondents.

According to the McDonald's website, "the Quality Correspondents represent real moms across the country. They come with different backgrounds, questions and perspectives, but with one thing in common: They are moms who care what their families eat. The Moms' Quality Correspondents, like you, want to know that they're providing quality, nutritious food to their families. The Moms will have unprecedented access to the McDonald's system to see how McDonald's serves millions of customers quality food every day. They will ask the kinds of questions that you yourself want answered, and will share their experiences via online journals, videos, and photos. We invite you to join this journey by following along, and interacting with the Moms by submitting your own questions."

And what does the Quality Correspondent program offer the average mom? According to McDonald's microsite, www.mcdonaldsmom.com, "In addition, by joining the online community, you'll receive regular updates about the Correspondents' activities." The site has profiles of the six moms selected as well as their journals of special McDonald's field trips. Also included is a Q&A section. It seems like a great program on the surface, right?

Wrong.

The problems with McDonald's mom program started way back at the beginning with the call for entries. When the company solicited moms to apply for the six-member board, reports are that they received 10,000 to 30,000 entries—all moms eager to help market the brand. I must confess that as a mom who started her teen career under the golden arches, I even applied. A McDonald's loyalist who specializes in Marketing to Moms with a radio and television show, I thought I was a shoo-in for the job. And I was willing to lend my expertise and audience access without compensation. Apparently at least 10,000 other moms thought the same thing. I filled out the application and waited for a response but one never came. In fact, I learned about the winning women only because a McDonald's public relations firm sent a press release to Mom Talk Radio. It was the only correspondence I got from the company until the first newsletter. There was no automated thank-you email, no alternative way for me to become engaged—nothing at all.

As a marketer, I recognized a missed opportunity for McDonald's. If 10,000 moms raise their hand to volunteer to help me market my brand to other moms, I'm not going to turn them away. I'm going to find some way, any way, for them to feel at least minimally engaged in our company. As a mother, I felt like I had given my time to a company that didn't even do the one thing I ask of my children on a daily basis: say thank you.

Apparently, I was not the only mother who went away disappointed. In fact, many moms circulated emails, posted blogs about the program and one mom even set up a website calling herself the "7th Mom." McDonald's gained visibility, just not the kind they were seeking. Even marketing publications wrote about the flaws in the program. The missed opportunities continue even today, as does the less than positive mom buzz.

In McDonald's defense, it appears that the legal department is running the program. First, the selection of the ethnically diverse membership was seen as a deliberate attempt to be politically correct. Second, the panel does not allow for any interactivity between the McDonald's Correspondents and other moms. In a time when two-way dialogues and interactive communication are the expectations of most mothers online, McDonald's is providing merely "the chance to receive regular updates." To me, it's unclear what value this offers moms who are expecting an online community as McDonald's promises. The definition of an online community for Millennial and Generation X moms is a place where they can share with like-minded moms. Other than submitting questions, there is no way for outside moms to share or engage with the Correspondents. Again, I am sure that the legal team didn't want to deal with the unknown elements of consumer-generated content and this was the compromise.

My final comment on McDonald's program is about another missed opportunity, and one that they may not even realize yet. The electronic newsletter that moms receive with updates cannot be forwarded. I've tried it several times myself. If a mom views something interesting, there's no way for her to share it with a friend. It's an easy element to change but one that can make a big difference. McDonald's is, however, making some changes and expansions in the program that could salvage their initial effort. Recently, the Quality Correspondents made a special appearance on iVillage's "In the Loop" show to talk about their experiences in the volunteer program. During the show, McDonald's gave out $5 gift cards and free samples of its fruit and walnut salad to the audience. It was creative and fun and involved other moms. They also recently announced the formation of some local Correspondent programs which could go a long way toward engaging additional mothers.

Now let's focus on best-in-class programs and take a look at the Walt Disney World Moms Panel. In the spirit of full disclosure, let me first say that although I'm now engaged in working with Disney on offshoot programs of the Mom Panel, I *have* worked on elements of the initial program.

The Disney Moms Panel was created by the marketing team at Walt Disney World under the direction of Leanne Jakubowski. The goal was to create a forum for vacation-planning moms where they could get insights from moms just like themselves. The response to Disney's call for entries was overwhelming. In just a few short days, over 10,000 moms applied for a spot on the 12-member panel. Disney created the same excitement among moms that McDonald's had just a few months earlier. The difference is that Disney decided to find a way to engage the 10,000 moms who didn't make the final cut. They kept in contact with applicants and soon after announcing the names of the 12 Disney mom panelists, they extended an invitation to the other moms to join a newly created, yet exclusive group called the Mickey Moms Club.

Incidentally, this group didn't have a name initially because the first entry into the interactive community was to ask the members to name their group. The participating moms selected Mickey Moms Club. In the true fashion of Disney, they surprised and delighted the Mickey Moms Club members with an exclusive membership kit mailed to their homes. Today, members can submit questions, receive special emails and information, read profiles of other moms and interact with other members. Disney successfully turned what could have been 10,000 disgruntled moms into brand evangelists. Meanwhile, the Walt Disney World Moms Panel has generated hundreds of viewers' questions, tips and advice. It now includes dads as well as aunties from several countries and the Mickey Moms Club is over 50,000 strong.

Mom Influencers are an integral link among mediums, content and other moms—delivering to mothers the benefits that Web 2.0 promises to bring to the Internet. Who knows? Maybe they're the missing link that developers are now trying to replicate in order to take the Internet to the next level. It wouldn't be surprising. Moms know what other mothers are seeking in content, as well as the delivery channels that make it easy for moms to obtain what they need.

Power Moms are the partners you want to include in your marketing strategy. They talk, share and engage with you and your target market. Ensure the success of your efforts by finding the right Mom Influencers for your brand, engage them in a win-win relationship and give them the platform and tools to share with other mothers. Entertain, educate and empower them and you will enlist the services of your most effective brand evangelists in the Mom Market.

Section 3

Power Moms Directory

Name: Amanda Acuna

Children: Two, ages 8 and 5 (both girls)

Hometown: Lake Arrowhead, CA

Company Name(s): Mom Blogger; Mommy Mandy

Short description of business: I started MommyMandy in 2004 when my husband and I started to try and conceive our second daughter. MommyMandy became an outlet for me to talk about my struggles and eventually talk about my pregnancy; over the years MommyMandy has evolved to a valuable resource for parents.

Websites or Blogs you own: Mommy Mandy http://mommymandy.com

Approximate audience size: 50,000 a month

Facebook Id: Amanda Acuna

Twitter Id: @mommymandy

Approximate # of followers: 4,000

Online Involvements and associations: American Girl Parent Ambassadors, Frigidaire Test Drive, Bee Squad for BumbleBee Foods, Snapfish Selects, The Motherhood, VTech Voices

How many moms do you typically interact with during the week offline? Around 100

What's the best way for companies to reach you as an influencer or as a mom? Email: amanda@mommymandy.com

What do you think is the biggest mistake companies make in trying to work with moms? They expect us to do everything for free, but a lot of mom bloggers blog to help as a supplemental income for their family. While we don't always want something in return, a nice thank you would be great!

How do you define influence among moms? Someone who helps moms grow.

Name: Lorraine Akemann

Children: Two, ages 7 and 5

Hometown: Bay Area (Redwood City), California

Company Name(s): My Busy Kit; Moms With Apps

Short description of business: My Busy Kit makes portable activity kits to keep children creatively entertained while out and about. Moms With Apps is a collaborative community of independent mobile app developers (mostly parents who have made their own apps). Moms With Apps was spearheaded by four moms who connected over Twitter. They quickly recognized the family-friendly nature in each of their apps and suggested a brainstorming session on cross-marketing. What started as a small conference call soon grew into a diverse collaboration of developers. Founders include Alesha Bishop and Jill Seman from MomMaps, Lynette Mattke from PicPocket Books, and Lorraine Akemann from My Busy Kit.

Websites or Blogs you own: My Busy Kit www.mybusykit.com, Moms With Apps http://momswithapps.com, Keeps Me Smiling www.keepsmesmiling.com

Approximate audience size: 10,000 unique visitors/50,000 page views per month

Facebook Id: MomsWithApps

Twitter Id: @momswithapps

Approximate # of followers: 1,300

What's the best way for companies to reach you as an influencer or as a mom? Email: lorraineakemann@gmail.com

How is the best way to work with you and your company? Interacting with us over Facebook has been a very effective way to facilitate interaction from our audience. Our site is http://www.facebook.com/momswithapps.

What do you think is the biggest mistake companies make in trying to work with moms? Impersonal messages that look like they are distributed from a PR list. We like to work with real people, on a first name basis. Anything else is substandard.

Are there companies who you feel are doing a great job connecting with moms? Yes, an organization called: The Thinking Person's Guide to Autism. Also, BlogHer is a great organization for Moms.

How do you feel you influence moms online? By only projecting resourceful and timely information, not clutter. No one has time for advertisements. You need to give them what they want, when they need it, and have it summarized in a neat and compelling way.

How can companies best support your business or mission as a mom? Don't have a long drawn out message. Just get to the point. There might be a crying baby in the stroller. Tell us what you want to tell us, tell us why it's important, offer an incentive, and move on. If it's good, we'll remember and will tell a friend. That's your best marketing right there.

What motivates you to tell other moms (good or bad) about a company, brand or product? If it helped my family get through the day in a more harmonious, educational, or enriching way, it's a win.

Name: Jen Alamilla

Children: One, age 14

City and home state: Lilburn, GA

Company Name(s): Real Women Real Money Work From Home

Short description of business: I teach women how to work from home using their computer and their telephone. I feature only legitimate companies that I have tested first. Usually it is something unique such as advertising on their car for cash, being a mock juror, data entry from home for flower companies, making extra money participating in paid surveys and focus groups. It has to be legit, no scams or spam. I also feature unique ways to save money, such as depression era cooking recipes.

I started my blog because of the recession. I had a lot of tips for making and saving extra money and I was at my computer and telephone all day anyway when I owned the maid service, so I would blog my tips. I hate seeing pyramids and MLMs and all that stuff and people getting sucked into it so I wanted to feature real, legit ways to make extra money to help folks get through the recession. I started offering savings tips as well. Nothing is better than getting an email from a reader who was going to get their lights turned off and found out they could make a little money from home to help out.

Websites or Blogs you own: Real Women Real Money Work From Home http://www.realwomenrealmoneyworkfromhome.blogspot.com

Approximate audience size: Now up to 2,000 hits a month and growing. It has doubled in the last month.

Websites or blogs you contribute to: About 20 ezine type websites, Yahoo Shine

Facebook Id: Jen Alamillo

Twitter Id: @jh0816

Online Involvements and associations: BzzAgent, Mom Ambassador, Crowdtap, Houseparty, MomCentral, She Speaks, Vocalpoint

How many moms do you typically interact with during the week offline? 100

Offline Involvements: Women's Small Business Group Lilburn (I got into that when I owned a maid service; it was during this time that I started the blog), PTA, my daughter's multiple athletic activities, Humane Society, Georgia Poodle Rescue

How do you feel you influence moms online? I help them learn how to save and make extra money, so my readers are the budget-motivated moms. It is not that they do not spend any money; they just want to spend it in the smartest way possible. I try to help them look outside the box for ways to do that. That is what makes it fun for me and for them.

Is there one moment when you realized you were impacting the life/lives of others? I received an email in the WORST of the recession from a lady who had NO MONEY to feed her kids breakfast. Because of a suggestion of mine, she was able to pick up some extra cash. This happened very quickly for her. One day she is thinking, there is not going to be anything to eat on so-and-so day, then she finds my blog and reads my posts, takes my advice and is able to buy breakfast cereal a couple days later just in time. That made it very real to me. I never expected that. That is when I realized this was so much more special than running a maid service. That was just the first of many emails from readers telling me how I affected them. It was an incredible moment that is difficult to describe with words. I do not think I have ever done anything more important. I NEVER expected to do that by blogging. When I am off, my readers email me, Facebook me, leave comments wanting to know when I am coming back. They are waiting for the information. The economy is still rough for a lot of folks.

What motivates you to tell other moms (good or bad) about a company, brand or product? If it saved me time, money or a headache. If my family really likes it. If I really enjoyed it. If it is really new or different. Sometimes it depends on the mom. One of my friends is big on organics right now, so we tell each other about anything we find that is good and organic.

Final words: Again, moms wear so many hats, we have influence in a lot of places. I remember the first time I went to buy a car and all the good ol' boy salesmen did not take me seriously. I had to call my dad to come up there and then they took me seriously. (Then my dad and I walked out of there and went to another dealership and let the first one know WHY!) I don't get treated that way at dealerships anymore (that was 20 years ago). Women are the decision makers. I hear it all the time, men at the store saying to their wives, "whatever you want, Dear!" They know it is easier on them that way!

Name: Beth Alferink

Number of children and ages: Two, ages 2 and 4 (both boys)

City and home state: Mansfield, Texas

Company Name(s): Laughing Chicks and Beth Austin Designs

Short description of business: Laughing Chicks & Beth Austin Designs encompass my jewelry design and direct sales companies that are just getting started. I'm so excited to finally have an avenue for my creative spirit and can't wait to share my visions for style and design with everyone. I started my blog as my initial creative outlet from my full-time job in 2008 shortly after my second son was born. As my blog grew and I worked with more and more companies and met more and more amazing women, I realized that I really wanted to get back to my true love of jewelry design. Luckily in November 2010, I was able to start production of the initial product lines and expect to launch fully in 2011. I am also in direct sales for Gypsy & Co because their clothing and boot line really fits the image that I want to portray in my jewelry line. The two companies together were a perfect fit. Right now, I don't plan for an exit strategy. I plan to continue to grow all facets of my creative side in the hopes of leaving my current full-time position in the next three years.

Websites or Blogs you own: Two Monkeys & a Washtub http://www.twomonkeysawashtub.com, Gypsy & Co. by Beth http://beth.gypsyandco.com

Approximate audience size: 5,500 site visits monthly

Facebook Id: Two Monkeys and a Washtub

Twitter Id: @monkeyswashtub

Approximate # of followers: >1,000

Online Involvements and associations: I'm a member of MomSelect, Double Duty Divas, One2One Network, Family Review Network, and Mom Central, Purex Insider, Soft Scrub Club, and Juicy Bunch (Juicy Juice) Member.

How many moms do you typically interact with during the week offline? 20-30

Offline Involvements: Mansfield Early Childhood PTA and mommy playgroups; volunteer at the local animal shelters, provide goods and food to community food banks, and I run the annual office toy drive for donations for the local community.

How do you define influence among moms? Influence is not just following the crowd, but truly relying on one another's thoughts and passions in life to truly define who you are as a person. If you can make a difference through what you say and do in how one person feels about themselves, cares for their family, or steps back and reevaluates their daily activities through something you say or do then you have truly influenced another person.

How do you feel you influence moms online? Honesty in discussions and building online relationships help build influence online. It's also about sharing yourself, your strengths, weaknesses, likes and dislikes, so that your online friends truly become friends.

What motivates you to tell other moms (good or bad) about a company, brand or product? Customer service is really a motivating factor for me! Regardless of how I really feel about a product or company, if I'm treated really well then I'll pass that along. Just because something isn't my taste doesn't mean it isn't a perfect fit for someone else and if a company excels at customer service then really their products will carry that same level of pride in ownership, too!

Name: Betsy Arndt

Children: Two, ages 6 and 2 (both girls)

Hometown: Wilmington, NC

Facebook Id: Betsy Arndt

Approximate # of followers: 200+

Twitter Id: @ejsweets

Approximate # of followers: 100

Online Involvements and associations: Vocal Point, Novartis Shop Talk, Circle of Moms, Café Mom, Pampers Online Community, Huggies, Panel Polls, Bzzagent, PineCone research

How many moms do you typically interact with during the week offline? My company started in 2009 when my friends were begging me to teach them how to save money like I did, picking up FREEbies and only spending $50 per week on groceries for a family of 5.

Offline Involvements: MOMS Club, PTA, Room Parent for a 1st grade class. Our MOMS club does at least one community service project each year—food drives, yard sales (profits are donated to a local organization like the Domestic Violence Shelter), blood and bone marrow drives ... just to name a few. I do volunteer work for my daughter's school and have done everything from teacher prep work to helping with large fundraisers.

What's the best way for companies to reach you as an influencer or as a mom? Ask for my opinions and ideas. I love surveys and am a member of multiple sites that allow me to participate in surveys on a variety of topics. Some send products to review, others just show concepts and ask for thoughts in response. If you reach out to me and give me opportunities to share my thoughts and experiences, I'll most likely have more confidence in your company or product and want to share that with other moms.

How is the best way to work with you and your company? I believe the best way is a combination of social media, print, radio, and even in-person. Online opportunities are endless; you could have chat groups, surveys, product discussions, etc., and those allow moms to participate when it is most convenient for them. Even as I type this, I have a two-year-old pulling on me and constantly interrupting but you don't have to deal with that! Print, radio, and TV allow you to get information out to a mass population. In-person activities, such as focus groups or product testing, will give you the most honest and real reactions of those involved. It all depends on what your goal is and how you best want to accomplish it.

What do you think is the biggest mistake companies make in trying to work with moms? Many companies don't take moms' opinions seriously because we aren't earning an income for what we do. Moms are the ultimate multi-taskers and we fill so many different roles. Just because we don't have a degree in the field, doesn't mean we don't know what we are talking about.

How do you feel you influence moms online? I influence moms online by sharing my opinions, experiences, thoughts, and ideas about topics relating to motherhood. It may be on an online message board, through Facebook, or even just an email to another mom. Do I know everything? Absolutely NOT! Do I have information that could help other moms? Absolutely. I think it's extremely important to be a good listener and to be supportive of others regardless of whether or not you agree.

How can companies best support your business or mission as a mom? I want quality products for my children that don't cost me an arm and a leg. It infuriates me that there have been so many recalls on children's toys, baby care items like high-chairs, and over-the-counter medicines. If you are a company that makes children's products, you had better take all the steps necessary to ensure that it is safe for my child. If not, you lose my trust and my business. If you have a product and want to know how to improve it or whether or not a child likes it, send out some samples and get feedback from both the child and parent. Don't just test it in a laboratory. Reach out to moms in any way you can to help provide the best products possible. Providing opportunities to get feedback from parents and in turn, producing quality products, will support my mission as a mom by allowing me to feel confident that I am doing everything I can to provide a safe, nurturing, and educational environment for my child.

What motivates you to tell other moms (good or bad) about a company, brand or product? I'm motivated to tell other moms about a company, brand, or product simply because I want to help them in any way possible. Moms are too often short on time and money and we are always looking for ways to improve how we take care of our children. I've shared the good and bad about these things as they've related to me but it's important to remember that people are different, children are different, and what worked for me, might not work for you. If a product injured my child and I know a parent that is considering purchasing it, I'll share my experience in an attempt to spare them the same trauma. If a product worked wonders in helping my child potty train, I'll let other moms know so that hopefully it helps them, too. Our main goal is all the same—happy, healthy families—so why not work together to achieve that?

Name: Bridget Axtell

Children: Two, ages 10 and 7

Hometown: Rathdrum, ID

Short Description of Business: I started my blog to share my frugal deals and freebies with others. I'm a stay-at-home mom and I strive to make my money and resources stretch farther to benefit my family!

Websites or Blogs you own: Being Frugal and Making it Work
http://cheekymommaof2.blogspot.com

Approximate audience size: 825

Websites or blogs you contribute to: Gather.com

Facebook Id: Being Frugal and Making it Work

Twitter Id: @cheekymommaof2

Approximate # of followers: 340

Online Involvements and associations: TwitterMoms, The Product Review Place, MyBlogSpark, Mom Bloggers, Giveaway Blogs, Blog Frog, One2One Network, She Speaks

What's the best way for companies to reach you as an influencer or as a mom?
Cheekymommaof2@live.com

What do you think is the biggest mistake companies make in trying to work with moms? Not being patient and understanding. As a busy mom, oftentimes life gets in the way. We do our best to get things done on time, but sometimes we just can't make it!

How do you feel you influence moms online? Word of mouth is a very valuable resource. If enough moms post positive or negative reviews, there is going to be an impact!

Name: Amy Lupold Bair

Children: Two, ages 6 and 4

Hometown: Olney, MD

Company Name(s): Resourceful Mommy Media http://resourcefulmommymedia.com

Short description of business: Resourceful Mommy Media includes daily publishing of original content at ResourcefulMommy.com; social media marketing including blog tours, contests, and ambassador programs at GlobalInfluenceNetwork.com; and Twitter Party hosting with Sitewarmings by Resourceful Mommy, the number one Twitter marketing event. I began blogging in the summer of 2008 with the intention of launching a freelance writing career. In order to promote my own blog, I created a marketing concept called a Twitter Party complete with a topic of conversation, expert panelists, and prizes or "Goody Bags." During the first party to promote my site, three people reached out to me to have me hold a similar event for them. From there my business Sitewarmings by Resourceful Mommy was born, and as that business and my freelance writing grew, I launched Resourceful Mommy Media, LLC. In February of 2009, I launched a blog network now called the Global Influence Network, which has grown to include over 1200 bloggers. The purpose of the network is to provide income and opportunities for bloggers as well as to work with nonprofits on public service campaigns. We frequently work with the Ad Council to promote issues such as child passenger safety and drunk driving awareness. Exit strategy? Developing one is next on the long list of things to do in 2011.

Websites or Blogs you own: Global Influence http://www.globalinfluencenetwork.com/, Resourceful Mommy http://resourcefulmommy.com, Resourceful Mommy Media http://resourcefulmommymedia.com/

Approximate audience size: 1,000+ bloggers, 15,000 unique monthly visitors plus 1800 daily subscribers

Websites or blogs you contribute to: LifetimeMoms.com, Momformation.com, MOMeoMagazine.com

Facebook Id: Resourceful Mommy

Twitter Id: @ResourcefulMom

Approximate # of followers: 24,000

Online Involvements and associations: Disney Social Media Moms Celebration planner, Frito-Lay Fabulous 15 blogger

How many moms do you typically interact with during the week offline? Between school drop-off, pick-up, activities and MOMS Club events, in the typical week I interact with 30 to 40 moms.

What's the best way for companies to reach you as an influencer or as a mom? Through the contact form at http://resourcefulmommymedia.com

How is the best way to work with you and your company? While Resourceful Mommy

Media organizes local focus groups, online seminars, and other blogger outreach events, we are most known for our social media campaigns to create buzz around a topic or product.

What do you think is the biggest mistake companies make in trying to work with moms? The biggest mistake that companies make in trying to work with moms is that they often ignore an incredible skill set and focus simply on the buying power or online influence of moms. I find that there are many times I am brought into a project to provide the unique perspective of an online mom, and during my time as a consultant, other skills and insights I can offer are not utilized.

Are there companies who you feel are doing a great job connecting with moms? I've been impressed with some of the outreach from Proctor and Gamble including the ways they've partnered with online moms.

How do you feel you influence moms online? The platforms I mainly use are Twitter, Facebook, and my personal blog, but by far I am most influential on Twitter. Over the last two and a half years, moms on Twitter have come to know and trust me as a fellow mom, not just as a blogger or marketing professional. They ask me for advice on anything from the best toy for an 18-month-old to which Magic Your Way package to book at Walt Disney World. I've found Twitter to be the most effective tool in my influence arsenal because the real time interaction simply cannot be matched.

Is there one moment when you realized you were impacting the life/lives of others? I think that the first few times moms came to me and said, "I bought such and such after tweeting with you and my son loves it," I realized that my opinions weren't just being lumped together with those of others, but were being singled out as worthwhile and trusted. Since then I've received the most joy from hearing that a great tip or tool I've shared on ResourcefulMommy.com has made a mom's life easier or advice I've shared on travel to Walt Disney World has saved a family money. The biggest moment for me, however, was when I heard from a mom several months after hosting a Twitter Party in celebration of National Adoption Month. After attending the event, this particular mom felt called to foster to adopt and has since had an infant placed in her family, hopefully permanently. There is nothing more rewarding than that.

How can companies best support your business or mission as a mom? The best way for companies to support what I am doing is to continue to explore options to hire moms as consultants, writers, graphic designers, or as a location to place advertising. They should continue to seek our opinions and invest in our conferences and events.

What motivates you to tell other moms (good or bad) about a company, brand or product? The number one motivation for me is finding that a product or brand is unique in some way. One product that stands out in my mind is the Sippy Straw Cleaner. It is a low cost item that has incredible value for every parent because it solves an issue that all parents face: how to properly clean the flexible straws of sippy cups. Once a product impresses me, I'm a fan for life, and I love to share that with everyone.

Final words: My hope is that online moms who have passionately voiced their concerns or approval of products and brands will use that same influence and passion to champion a variety of causes that affect the future of our children. It is much easier for moms to put the power of their brand behind a benign product than it is to do the same for a controversial issue, but I hope that this is the future of online mom influence.

Power Moms Directory

Name: Mimi Baker

Children: Four, ages 19, 17, 11, and 7

Hometown: Annandale, MN

Websites or Blogs you own: Woven by Words http://wovenbywords.blogspot.com/ and Marvelous Mom Reviews http://marvelousmomreviews.blogspot.com/

Approximate audience size: 920

Twitter Id: @bigguysmama

Approximate # of followers: 1,940

What's the best way for companies to reach you as an influencer or as a mom? Email: mnjesusfreak@gmail.com

What do you think is the biggest mistake companies make in trying to work with moms? Expecting us to do something for nothing. Writing online reviews is becoming a business for many moms and to ask us to do something for a company without any compensation is unrealistic. I also think the companies don't give us enough credit for the amount of time it takes to create our reviews, put the information out there on a daily basis for everyone to see.

Are there companies who you feel are doing a great job connecting with moms? Growing Tree Toys, Hasbro

How do you feel you influence moms online? On my WbW site I share honestly about myself and my family life. On my MMR site I do family friendly product reviews. First of all, everyone who has visited my site at least once knows that there won't be anything inappropriate. I do my best to let moms know about the products I would use in my home and share my opinion as honestly as I know how.

Is there one moment when you realized you were impacting the life/lives of others? I was doing one of the Twitter parties I attend and I recognized that some of the others were having a hard time; we started chatting aside from the party. It worked out well and I enjoyed spending my time connecting with people as an encourager.

How can companies best support your business or mission as a mom? I sometimes miss the opportunity to work with certain companies because of the number of followers I have, which the companies consider to be too few...I understand that, but I need to work with quality companies to build those follower numbers. It would be great if they would look through some of my posts to get an idea of how well I do my reviews and base their partnership with me on that. I do realize they are in the business of making money and they want bloggers with a high number of followers and traffic.

How do you feel companies can best connect with moms, particularly those who are influencers? Having an email available on a Press page or a Marketing page at their site would be helpful. So often I search and search for someone to connect with to share about my site and what I can offer and I come up dry. Emailing directly to an influencer is a great way to connect and it makes me feel like I'm doing my job when a company reaches out to me.

Final words: I think we are making more of an impact in today's world than in the past. Moms who have stayed home and impacted their immediate area are now able to blog and affect thousands of people. In most areas we are becoming a force to be reckoned with.

Name: Suzanne Bastien

Children: Six, ages 19, 16, 15, 9, 3 and 2

Hometown: Centennial, Colorado

Websites or Blogs you own: Crunchy Green Mom Http://crunchygreenmom.blogspot.com

Approximate audience size: 1000

Facebook Id: Crunchy Green Mom

Twitter Id: @CrunchyGreenMom

Online Involvements and associations: I work with Yahoo Mom's Board, MomSelect

What do you think is the biggest mistake companies make in trying to work with moms? They seem to talk "down" to us, as if we have no idea what we are doing with blogs, social media, etc.

Are there companies who you feel are doing a great job connecting with moms? Yahoo is a GREAT company to work with; I also love CSN and Green Tree Toys.

How do you define influence among moms? We are a strong force; just like face-to-face, we learn online which moms to listen to when it comes to products. When I see a complaint about a company by one of those moms, I listen more.

How do you feel you influence moms offline? Is it more than chatting in the carpool line? Yes, we have moms' groups, we go to local businesses and learn about them. We leave the mom life behind and become our own person with goals, dreams and a lot of laughter.

How can companies best support your business or mission as a mom? Green Tree Toys and Yahoo offer us options for our kids. They can publish articles to help other moms during Breast Cancer month or to prepare for the first day of school, and help moms find eco friendly toys that are priced reasonably and are easy to find.

How do you feel companies can best connect with moms, particularly those who are influencers? Write to us, learn our names and actually read our blogs if you say you are going to. Don't assume that Eco-moms are all non-vaccinating moms. Learn about us and give us the option to learn about you.

Final words: I am finding more and more coupon sites, etc., that are updated daily, with moms informing each other which stores not to patronize because the staff is not knowledgeable about the coupon rules and it's a fight to use coupons there. Businesses, train your staff; we are listening to the bloggers.

Name: Amy Baxter

Children: Three, ages 13, 11, and 8

Hometown: Atlanta, GA

Company Name(s): Buzzy4shots.com, MMJ Labs

Short description of business: Creating, testing, and manufacturing personal pain prevention products. I came up with the idea on August 4, 2004 (I know the date because we videotaped after the Eureka moment); I filed for a business license in Georgia in August, 2006, and filed patents in October, 2006. I would have preferred to find a big pharma company to take the idea and run with it, but they all said Buzzy needed to be disposable or that needle pain wasn't a big deal. Since I knew the impact Buzzy had on my kids, and since I fundamentally disagree with disposable products just for the sake of making more money, I decided to go forward with the idea myself. One critical turning point was when my husband said, "How will you feel every time you see a child crying with a shot if you DON'T try it?" The cost of not knowing whether I could have made a difference helped tip the balance. Our mission is to provide personal pain relief which is tested and effective, and our goal is to change the culture of medical pain relief to one in which patients are empowered to take pain relief into their own hands. Our current goal is to grow the body of literature and sales to the point where a consumer company will take over the device and distribute the product widely. The most ideal scenario would allow me to continue researching the potential applications of the combination of vibration and cold for pain relief.

Websites or Blogs you own: Buzzy 4 Shots www.buzzy4shots.com

Approximate audience size: 1000 hits/day

Websites or blogs you contribute to: ziggetyzoom, people.com, medscape, special-needs

Facebook Id: buzzy4shot

Twitter Id: @buzzy4shots

How many moms do you typically interact with during the week offline? 100

Offline Involvements: International Women's Forum, Women's forum of Georgia, American Academy of Pediatrics, American College of Emergency Physicians, Child Life Council, Society for Procedural Sedation, Pediatric Emergency Medicine Associates, Research Mentor

How do you feel you influence moms online? By writing medical advice in simple, no nonsense and humorous ways, I can break down the barriers between the medical community and common sense.

Is there one moment when you realized you were impacting the life/lives of others? As a new faculty member, I got a letter with a sweet picture of a baby I'd taken care of in the emergency department saying "Thank you for saving my life." That card buoyed me in down times for years. Since that time, through Buzzy I get about one note a month from a person or family whose life has been changed. Sometimes Buzzy decreased needle drama for a child's home shots, or altered an adult's willingness to get the flu vaccine, or in one case changed a man's decision to quit dialysis. As an emergency doctor you have the privilege of helping at most one life at a time, but with a really great product the impact can be much more wide-spread.

How do you feel you influence moms offline? Is it more than chatting in the carpool line? Since my job gives me a unique perspective on children's health, I am often asked for medical advice and second opinions. One of my neighbors once said, "I don't think you realize how seriously everyone takes your opinion." The gravity of this is that I am pretty lax about physical play safety, and about germs, and to a certain extent about hygiene, and I don't necessarily want people being influenced by my slackness. If I haven't seen someone in the emergency department permanently damaged by an activity, I permit my kids to do it. They play on trampolines that have nets, but NEVER ride bikes without a helmet or run with food in their mouths.

How can companies best support your business or mission as a mom? If I'm going to be doing business with a company, being Skype-tolerant is huge. Don't make me travel to a meeting; facilitate online connections.

What motivates you to tell other moms (good or bad) about a company, brand or product? I'm attracted to uniqueness and quality. If I hear about a brilliant time-saver or see something I've never seen before, I'm much more likely to feel the urge to tell other moms; I definitely like the satisfaction of finding out about the next big thing first. I rarely get irritated enough about a product to run it down, though. Cute is also a biggie for me.

How do you feel companies can best connect with moms, particularly those who are influencers? In this world of mass-communication, personal letters on real paper with real ink signatures stand out. If someone found me via any of my activities (hospital, start-up groups, Women's Forum) and sent a letter TO ME, I'd consider it much more strongly.

Final words: I think my opinion of the competence of women I meet in the work force is enhanced when I find out they're moms. There seems to be an external as well as internal shift in the perception of moms in the work force today; even a decade ago, competence among working moms was not initially inferred. The improved influence of moms in the world today now connotes competitive job skills, which has diminished the unfair bias against hiring moms.

Name: Heather Belden

Children: Four, ages 16, 15, 7 and 19 months

Hometown: Gwinn,Michigan

Website or Blogs you own: Saving for 6 http://savingfor6.blogspot.com/

Facebook Id: Saving For 6

Approximate # of followers: 24

Twitter Id: @SavingFor6

Online Involvements and associations: MILLS ADVISORY PANEL, Nesquik Shakers, Fishfull ambassador

How many moms do you typically interact with during the week offline? 20+

Offline Involvements: Girl Scout Volunteer, Playgroup

Are there companies who you feel are doing a great job connecting with moms? General Mills

How do you define influence among moms? Moms trust other moms' opinions and experiences. This is what defines influence: whether you're trying or not, anytime you are interacting with another mom you are usually influencing them in some way.

How do you feel you influence moms offline? Is it more than chatting in the carpool line? I have four kids, ages 16 years to 19 months, so between groups , activities, and work I interact with a lot of moms. It is more than just chatting in line. Every mom I interact with I can find at least one thing we have in common.

What motivates you to tell other moms (good or bad) about a company, brand or product? I will tell others if using the product is memorable in some way, that it works or somehow makes life better, if the product is good; or even if it is bad as long as the company is quick and pleasant in rectifying the situation.

How do you feel companies can best connect with moms, particularly those who are influencers? Contact them directly, also Social Media and websites designed to connect moms and companies.

Final words: I think moms are a huge influence in every aspect of today's world, and that their influence will just keep getting stronger. They used to say "it's a man's world"; now it's a mom's world.

Name: Amy Bellgardt

Children: Two, ages 3 and 10 (both boys)

Hometown: Edmond, Oklahoma

Company Name (s): Mom Spark Media

Short description of business: Mom Spark Media is a social media company that not only connects mom bloggers with brands, but also offers a supportive community and blogging education to its members. The Mom Spark blog also offers articles on parenting, product reviews, crafts, recipes, blogging articles and more topics that moms love! After working on blogger outreach and community for over a year, I decided to give Mom Spark Media an official name in August 2010. Mom Spark Media's main mission is to help mom bloggers grow by offering special opportunities, education and community support.

Website or Blogs you own: MomSpark.net, MomSparkMedia.com, MomMadeThat.com, NerdGirlCentral.com

Approximate audience size: With all sites combined, 30,000+.

Facebook Id: Amy Bellgardt

Twitter Id: @MomSpark

Approximate # of followers: 19,000

Online Involvements and associations: Rayovac Brand Ambassador

How is the best way to work with you and your company? Brands can work with me as a blogger (reviews, paid posts, brand ambassador programs, etc.), or in a larger fashion as a social media company doing large blogger outreach.

What do you think is the biggest mistake companies make in trying to work with moms? The biggest mistake companies make in trying to work with moms is underestimating their talents, knowledge, and worth.

How do you define influence among moms? I see a high-influence mom as one who is extroverted, honest, and hard working. Yes, size of audiences helps.

Name: Kathy Benuck

Children: Three

Hometown: Bedford, NH

Company Name(s): JK Design www.jkdsgn.com, All About Being Organized www.allaboutbeingorganized.com, www.besteverchristmas.com

Short description of business: My companies are based on my passion for photography, web design, website hosting, and creative work for corporate clients (logo design, publication design, writing, etc.).

Offline Involvements: I serve in leadership positions for several civic, social, cultural, and charitable organizations, and am a very active member and former officer of a large women's organization; I am active in multiple political campaigns and organizations; have organized a major community event for children; serve as a substitute teacher at the middle school and high school level; serve on a School

Board subcommittee and on the Board of Governors for local public access television station.

What's the best way for companies to reach you as an influencer or as a mom? Email: kathybenuck@comcast.net

Name: Tisha Berg

Children: Two, ages 6 and 4 (both girls)

Hometown: Burbank, CA

Company Name(s): Biz Mommy

Short description of business: As a "Blogger-preneur" I show moms how to start their own home-based businesses and *then* market their products or services through blogging and other online marketing strategies. My company started in 2009 after I had worked on several work-from-home projects. I wanted to help other moms who needed to stay home with their kids but still had the desire to contribute to the household income. My goal is to help women and moms uncover their innate talents so that they can create a home-based business they feel passionate about and then teach them blogging and internet marketing skills so that they can market their business most effectively.

Websites or Blogs you own: Biz Mommy http://bizmommy.com, What Matters Right Now http://whatmattersrightnow.com

Approximate audience size: 450 blog subscribers

Websites or blogs you contribute to: Working Mother Magazine http://www.wowrkingmother.com, The Los Angeles Examiner http://www.examiner.com, About One http://www.aboutone.com, Project You http://www.projectyoumagazine.com/, ComLuv http://www.comluv.com, Virgin Blogger Notes http://www.virginbloggersnotes.com

Facebook Id: Tisha Berg, The Biz Mommy Work From Home Job Board

Twitter Id: @TishaBerg

Approximate # of followers: 2,700

Online Involvements and associations: Twitter Moms Elite, Project You Partner, Clever 1000 member

Offline Involvements: PTA, Toastmasters, The Momtrepreneur Exchange, local food shelters, Big Sunday, 4Good

What's the best way for companies to reach you as an influencer or as a mom? Directly! tisha@tishaberg.com or on Twitter: @TishaBerg

Are there companies who you feel are doing a great job connecting with moms? I've seen a lot of big brands out there who are doing a great job connecting with the mom community! In my personal experience, X-Box, Hewlet Packard, Yoplait and ProFlowers have run some generous campaigns that stressed getting input from the moms involved.

How do you define influence among moms? In a nutshell, influence would be the ability to get other moms to take action in support of a cause or promotion. But I think more importantly, it's about having a respected voice that you can use to inspire and educate the mom community on matters that are important to them and their particular lifestyles.

Is there one moment when you realized you were impacting the life/lives of others? The main reason Social Media is so great is that you get immediate response from your fans/followers. When I started my Facebook group to help moms find out about work-from-home job opportunities, the messages that so many women sent to me to thank me for what I was doing to help them were real eye-openers. They made me realize that I was definitely on the right path.

How can companies best support your business or mission as a mom? By keeping in mind the dual roles and many hats that work-from-home parents must constantly balance and then addressing those concerns when we are pitched or marketed to.

What motivates you to tell other moms (good or bad) about a company, brand or product? The BIG thing for me is customer service. Good service will always have me raving to others about how a certain company really "gets it."

Name: Emily Berry

Children: Two, ages 6 and 2

Hometown: Germantown, OH

Employer: Fulltime at Miami University

Short description of business: My cousin and co-blogger, Jenny Rapson, started Mommin' It Up in 2007 as a way to share the entertaining conversations we had with other people. We made each other laugh, and we thought we might make someone else laugh as well. We also wanted to create a way to chronicle our lives and the lives of our children.

Websites or Blogs you own: Mommin' It Up http://momminitup.com

Approximate audience size: 20,000 unique visitors per month

Facebook Id: Mommin It Up and Emily Burns Berry

Approximate # of followers: 2,300 combined

Twitter Id: @momminitup

Approximate # of followers: 4,700

Online Involvements and associations: I have been a Frigidaire Test Drive Mom, a Milano cookie Milano Maven, a Disney Magical Mom, and a Granite Transformations TrendSetter Blogger. I was sponsored by Lands' End for BlogHer '09 and by Intel for Blissdom '10, and I will be representing Lands' End once again at Blissdom '11. I also have strong relationships with Tide, TJ Maxx, Yummie Tummie, Weight Watchers and many more local and nationwide brands.

Offline Involvements: I work full time and I have been enrolled in graduate school for the past two years, and I'm part of a book club that has about 10 members, all of whom are moms. Additionally, my family and I are members of a local church. My family and I participate in the JDRF Walk for the Cure each year and we are involved in our church.

What's the best way for companies to reach you as an influencer or as a mom? I generally hear from companies first through email emily@momminitup.com.

What do you think is the biggest mistake companies make in trying to work with moms? While the tide is changing, I think companies still under-value the influence moms have and the time and effort they put into their promotions.

Are there companies who you feel are doing a great job connecting with moms? Walt Disney World has done absolutely amazing things with their social media presence. By creating the Moms Panel, hosting "Magical Moms" tours and having such a presence on Facebook and Twitter, they are, in my opinion, the gold standard for marketing to moms.

How do you define influence among moms? I define influence as trust. Moms look to other moms for advice on everything from breastfeeding and sleep training to cell phone rules and Internet safety. They're looking for advice regarding what they're most passionate about—their children—and they aren't going to take just anyone's word. They want advice and opinions from people they trust, whether it's their sisters, their neighbors, or their favorite mom blogger. Mom bloggers have an incredibly strong sphere of influence because their readers feel as though they know them and they trust their opinions. Bloggers put their lives out there in a way that fosters trust.

What motivates you to tell other moms (good or bad) about a company, brand or product? I genuinely enjoy spreading the word about products that have worked for me or brands I believe in. When a crayon went through my dryer and stained our clothes and Tide Stain Release took out the marks immediately, you can be sure I was tweeting and posting about it! Because of my online following, I am always cautious and thoughtful before making any remarks about companies and brands that could be perceived negatively.

How do you feel companies can best connect with moms, particularly those who are influencers? The absolute best way to connect with moms is to form relationships. Start on their turf—interact with them on Twitter, send personal emails, become their Facebook friends. Get to know them, but also let them get to know you. Blogger events are a fantastic way to show off your product or service but to also make personal connections that will create lasting relationships.

Name: Jill Berry

Children: Three, ages 14, 12, and 7

Hometown: Woodbine, MD

Company Name(s): Musings from Me

Short description of business: Musings from Me is my blog. I use it as a portal for my online presence, social media influence, and writing. I launched my blog in 2008 and got serious in the spring of 2009, then started attending conferences and joined networks such as MomSelect. I use my blog as a way to get product reviews, brand ambassador gigs, social media campaigns, and writing assignments.

Websites or Blogs you own: Musings from Me http://www.musingsfromme.com

Approximate audience size: 2,000/month

Websites or blogs you contribute to: Savvy Source DC, Oyster Locals Blo, Baltimore Parenting Tweens, Examiner DC City Mommy, Baltimore City Mommy, Type Parent

Facebook Id: Jill Richardson Berry

Approximate # of followers: 1,050

Twitter Id: @MusingsfromMe

Approximate # of followers: 2,000 total

Online Involvements and associations: The View Mom, Unilever Family Dish Ambassador, Soft Scrub Mom, General Hospital Mom, Yoursphere Mom, Orlando Mom

How many moms do you typically interact with during the week offline? 20

Offline Involvements: PTA in elementary, middle, and high schools, Church Book Club, volunteering at elementary school for Read-to-Me with primary grade students

What's the best way for companies to reach you as an influencer or as a mom? Twitter. Email: jillanneberry@msn.com. Facebook.

Are there companies who you feel are doing a great job connecting with moms? Zhu Zhu Pets. Nerf. Hasbro.

How can companies best support your business or mission as a mom? PAY ME! Stop asking me to write a post based on a press release! Also, I need to see, play with, or experience the product or event in order to write a review. A press release or a video clip will not make me blog about the product.

Final words: Moms are and have always been a force to be reckoned with. Moms and women need to be paid the same as men. Moms influence what their children buy. Companies should look to moms as the "shapers of spenders and citizens of the future."

Name: Suz Besecker

Children: Two, ages 4 and 1

Hometown: Longwood, Florida

Websites or Blogs you own: Not Your Typical Mommy (http://www.notyourtypicalmommy.com)

Approximate audience size: 2,500+ hits a month.

Websites or blogs you contribute(d) to: NYTM, Morris Bunch Blog, RookieMoms

Twitter Id: @NYTMBlog

Approximate # of followers: 1,268

Online Involvements and associations: Infantino Test Drive Mom, Happy and Healthy Mom Reviews, Kolcraft Mom.

What's the best way for companies to reach you as an influencer or as a mom? Shoot me an email nytmblog@gmail.com, send me a tweet. Engage me anyway you can, I'm game for almost anything.

What do you think is the biggest mistake companies make in trying to work with moms? They assume that moms aren't as smart as we are. Most of us are highly educated, college graduates that chose to leave our professions to raise our children. We make 90% of the household decisions and we deserve to be treated rightly so. The biggest mistake most companies make is believing that our time isn't worth anything. Moms that blog or work social media need to be compensated; throwing us a measly gift card (while the card is appreciated) doesn't cover all the time and energy we put into our work. We are passionate about our work so companies should be passionate about us.

Are there companies who you feel are doing a great job connecting with moms? Kolcraft has great people working with them and Bravado! Designs has a great rep that answers any Twitter questions you ask. Some brands never respond to any Twitter questions.

How do you define influence among moms? A mom's word is solid gold. If a Mom I know warns me about a product, or tells me her horror story, I learn from it. I take it in and use it when making decisions. I trust the Moms I know online and offline for their valued opinions. There's no reason for them to be dishonest in their reviews or thoughts about products, baby issues and mommy issues. A mom, online, doesn't have to have a bazillion followers just to be trusted. Even the smallest of bloggers has a strong voice.

How do you feel you influence moms online? I influence moms online by engaging them in discussions, asking for opinions, begging for help with questions I can't answer on my own or that I can't trust Dr. Google to answer. I influence by giving all I've got to my blog, my online friends and any panels, groups or Twitter parties I attend. I am honest, open and clear about everything I put out in social media.

How can companies best support your business or mission as a mom? Companies can support me by trusting in me and my work, by giving me free range to be open and honest about anything I write. Plus, compensation is a great support.

How do you feel companies can best connect with moms, particularly those who are influencers? Send an email. Send a gift basket. Send a tweet. Get out there and say, "Hello."

Final words: Moms are great, we are raising the next generation, and we can help you rule the world.

Name: Clair Boone

Children: Two, ages 2 and newborn

Hometown: Highland, Indiana

Short description of business: In late 2008, I bought diapers for 20 cents a pack and amazed some friends. They wanted help with saving money; then it caught on all across the USA and especially in my community.

Websites or Blogs you own: Mummy Deals www.mummydeals.org

Approximate audience size: Over 50,000 hits/month on the blog; I also write for others online, for three newspapers, and appear on local radio biweekly.

Websites or blogs you contribute to: www.Wisebread.com, three newspapers, WJOB FM, www.MomStyleNews.com

Facebook Id: Mummydeals

Approximate # of followers: 2,100

Twitter Id: MummyDeals

Approximate # of followers: 4,000

Online Involvements and associations: Mom Bloggers Club, My Blog Spark, Mom Select, Mom Central, Operation Christmas Child Blogger 2010, Feld Entertainment Activator

How many moms do you typically interact with during the week offline? 50+

Offline Involvements: (Groups, memberships): MOPS Member, Living Word CHUR41 Member, Local Coffee Break, Bible study, teaching two classes/month on saving money, heavy involvement at church, and advocate for operation Christmas child

What's the best way for companies to reach you as an influencer or as a mom? Email: mummydeals@yahoo.com

What do you think is the biggest mistake companies make in trying to work with moms? Addressing letters, "Dear Mom Blogger," not researching me well in order to pitch things I may be interested in.

How can companies best support your business or mission as a mom? Understand me, I'm passionate about helping others save money on everyday expenses so that they will have extra money to help others.

What motivates you to tell other moms (good or bad) about a company, brand or product? A really good or bad experience, something I believe in.

Name: Nicole Brady

Children: Two, ages 7 and 6

Hometown: Bettendorf, IA

Websites or Blogs you own: SAHM Ramblings http://www.SahmRamblings.com, SAHM Reviews http://www.SahmReviews.com

Twitter Id: @SahmReviews

Approximate # of followers: 1120

Online Involvements and associations: Tropicana Juicy Rewards Ambassador, Guest at Build-A-Bear World Connect (2010)

How many moms do you typically interact with during the week offline? Between school activities, swim team, friendships, gym membership and just out and about, I would say my personal involvement is with 30-40 moms ... conservatively.

What's the best way for companies to reach you as an influencer or as a mom? If you know me personally, you'll have a better chance of connecting with me. As a blogger, there's nothing I frown upon more than an email beginning "Hello Blogger" or even "Hello SahmReviews." Take a few minutes to read some of my blog posts to get a feel for who I am, what my kids are like or something important that has happened to me. But more importantly, don't ask me to support your product or service if it isn't something I've tried or had a chance to test out.

What do you think is the biggest mistake companies make in trying to work with mom bloggers?
(1) Giving moms a title of Ambassador when they just recently tried the product or haven't tried it at all. To be an ambassador, you need to know the ins and outs of a product and be able to provide input to the brand about mistakes they need to correct! An ambassador that provides nothing but feel-good rhetoric will be transparent to skeptics whereas an honest and sincere ambassador is easier to relate to ... and believe.

(2) Moms are busy. Add blogging into the mix and they are busier. If I love a product, I'll gladly talk about it but that has nothing to do with someone contacting me. Too many companies send moms (or bloggers in general) emails in the form of press releases expecting us to regurgitate it to our readers. I'll speak for only myself and say "No, thank you." My mailbox is bogged down with a lot of stuff: press releases make it worse. Some companies ask me to talk about their products without providing samples or compensation of any kind. If you plan to contact a blogger, the MINIMUM you should be offering is to send a sample. Along the same line, if they want to up the ante, they can ALSO say "I have an additional sample of my products to give away to your readers."

Are there companies who you feel are doing a great job connecting with moms? I could provide the names of various companies that "get" social media and that have provided the opportunity for me to work with brands in different aspects. But one company stands out by far: Build-A-Bear Workshop is one of the best companies that I have connected. They don't simply ask, "What do you think?" They go a step further and ask, "How does that make you feel?" and "What suggestions do you have for improving?" Even something as simple as a problem with the website is corrected swiftly when brought to light.

How do you feel you influence moms online? I don't hard-sell things to my readers on my blogs or followers and friends on social media platforms and message boards. I believe my influence online is subtle ... I try to provide open, honest feedback about how products and services integrate into my life and that of my family. If those around me (online or offline) are able to relate my story to their own life, they are going to be more likely to try something out than if I simply said, "This product does this and this and this. You should try it."

How do you feel you influence moms offline? Is it more than chatting in the carpool line? Yes, it's more than chatting in the carpool line. It's about building friendships and respect. As an example, extra-curricular activities don't last only 5 or 10 minutes. They last long enough for moms to have real, in-depth conversations about what we're up to, where we eat, what is on our children's Christmas lists (and our own) while listening as someone tries to resolve whatever conflict the day has presented. Even more, moms find time to bond and become friends. Friends look to friends for advice on problems but also on "what works and what doesn't." Offline, I'm that person at the gym who welcomes you to the class the first time you are there, asks your name, finds YOU if the instructor says "find a partner" then says to you, "See you next time." I influence people offline by being myself, by being sincere and caring. People ask my opinion about things because they know I'll be honest.

What motivates you to tell other moms (good or bad) about a company, brand or product? What motivates me is excitement, necessity or opportunity. I'm not one to randomly say, "Have you tried the new Dunkin Donuts Holiday-Flavored Coffees?" Instead, I'm the one who chimes in when someone complains about the coffee they're drinking and I offer, "Have you tried the new Dunkin Donuts Coffee?" However, if I just tried something new that people don't know about, I go into brag mode about it: "Did you know that Snickers has a new candy bar coming out?"

How do you feel companies can best connect with moms, particularly those who are influencers? Understand me: my excitement, my pains, my promises, my exhaustion, my pitfalls. Realize what my troubles are when I'm juggling healthy meals, hectic schedules, homework and more. Relate to it and provide comfort and assistance regardless of whether it benefits your brand directly. Trust me, it will come back to you in trickle-down rewards.

Name: Angela Breidenbach

Children: Six, ages 26, 24, 24, 21, 21, and 19

Hometown: Missoula, MT

Company Name(s): Gems of Wisdom (MyGemofWisdom.com)

Short description of business: Speaker (keynote, women's events, and conferences) author, life/relationship coach, jewelry that matches the *Gems of Wisdom: For a Treasure-filled Life* book due out May 2011 from Journey Press (a Sheaf House imprint). The jewelry also helps support the Sanctuary of Hope Homes in Kenya. In addition to non-fiction lifestyle and relationship books, I write cookbooks (three so far), articles, e-zine articles, and blog. I started Gems of Wisdom to coach, mentor, and live a missional lifestyle while hoping to inspire others to do the same in April 2009. My mission is to empower other women to reach out and change the world around them, to enlighten, educate, and encourage more intentional living through empowerment.

Websites or Blogs you own: Angela Breidenbach www.AngelaBreidenbach.com personal website linked to all the other websites & blogs, Gems of Wisdom www.MyGemOfWisdom.com for jewelry, missions, books, coaching, God Uses Broken Vessels www.GodUsesBrokenVessels.com personal blog.

Approximate audience size: About 3,000+ publicly, but my reading audience includes 10K from the Christian Fiction Online Magazine for the last 2 years and the Afictionado's several thousand readers as well.

Websites or blogs you contribute to: www.thefaithgirls.com

Facebook Id: Angela Breidenbach (Angie)

Twitter Id: @AngBreidenbach

Approximate # of followers: 720

Online Involvements and associations: American Christian Fiction Writers, RWA (Romance Writers of America), I'm on the Faith, Hope, and Love loop, Finish the Book as well as the Montana Romance Writers state chapter of RWA, AWSA (Advanced Writers and Speakers Association) and TwitterMoms.

Offline Involvements: All of my associations have both online and offline presence. ACFW, AWSA, RWA/FHL & MT Romance Writers, Weight Watchers (I'm a leader and ambassador) and my church. I speak to a few hundred people most weekends through Weight Watchers meetings and church duties.

Offline Community Service: Assisting Minister for my congregation, Mrs. Montana International 2009, Jadyn Fred Foundation spokesperson and supporter via a portion of every cookbook sold goes to the JFF, Hope's Promise Orphan Ministries spokesperson and supporter through jewelry sales that directly support two Sanctuary of Hope Orphan Homes in Kenya. I also work with the Montana Meth Project throughout the year on short projects.

What's the best way for companies to reach you as an influencer or as a mom? As an influencer, to ask me to participate or to speak, contact via my website or Facebook contact info. My Facebook account is set up so that it messages me automatically for direct messages that would include business communication. As a mom or to market to me, use Facebook. I don't feel spammed there. I can choose to ignore if it doesn't meet my needs. Otherwise I feel spammed because they've entered my private domain in my email if it isn't something I've solicited. If they're doing some sort of mass promo, the best way is to invite me via one of the Facebook events. I can choose to participate if it meets my needs and I usually read at least a little of the event invitation.

What do you think is the biggest mistake companies make in trying to work with moms? Not having an easily accessible website (too complicated to use in short increments) and sending junk mail with tons of small print. Moms don't have time to decipher. They read in short bursts. I also think a common mistake is in being too corporate. Make a woman feel helpless and she avoids you. Build friendship and trust and she'll be loyal and bring her friends. So translate this to policies and procedures. Red tape and corporate immobile policy is a sure fire way to losing trust.

How do you define influence among moms? Influence is when someone uses your idea or advice personally. Influence is empowering, educating, and motivating their choices so that those choices change the way the mom interacts in the world around her.

Is there one moment when you realized you were impacting the life/lives of others? I think the moment I realized was more a compilation of happenings. The moment was putting them all together for the "ah hah." Women would come talk to me; ask advice, share burdens or worries. Then they'd come back again to tell me how it worked out. As this happened more and more, I began to realize I had a calling, a purpose. I love to share ideas and wisdom to improve the lives of others.

How do you feel you influence moms offline? Is it more than chatting in the carpool line? Much more than chatting in the carpool line. Most carpool moms never leave the car. I meet one-on-one over coffee, email, phone calls. Influence is in the relationship. There is no influence without relationship. By listening, I can discern the need. Once I know the need, I can either help to fill it or refer them to someone else who can. But often, without relationship, you can't get to the need or even know one exists.

How can companies best support your business or mission as a mom? Look for common needs, wants, and desires in their customers that my work can solve. Use Gems of Wisdom as a tool to better serve their customers. The companies will build relationship with their customers by providing solutions to the needs of moms. It's about helping. When you help someone else to have better relationships, lifestyle, or experiences then they want to hear more about what you have to offer. It's a win/win. Ask me to speak for events where my topics encourage and educate women to inspire happier, healthier lives.

What motivates you to tell other moms (good or bad) about a company, brand or product? I want to help other women succeed or have a great experience. Women are wired to help others. Good or bad experiences with companies, brands, products are a natural for the nurturing way of a woman. We either want someone to have the great experience we did or we want to warn them away from a bad one. It's much less common to say nothing because our emotions are connected to how we provide for our families, friends, and the causes we believe in.

Name: Janis Brett Elspas

Children: Four, ages 13 (triplets) and 15

Hometown: Los Angeles, CA

Company Name(s): MommyBlogExpert.com

Short description of business: Mommy Blog focuses on enhancing family living for moms, dads, kids and extended family members. I also provide support for other moms who blog and the brands targeting us, including publishing a free list of all the mom and women blogger conferences with links to them on my site. I also do PR consulting under the business name Janis Elspas Communications.

Prior to transitioning to a full-time mommy blogger about 2 years ago, I worked in public relations and corporate communications for 25+ years and as a traditional journalist as a nationally-syndicated columnist for Copley News Service.

Websites or Blogs you own: MommyBlogExpert.com and JanisElspas.com

Approximate audience size: I have about 1,800 unique visitors to my blog each month.

Websites or blogs you contribute to: I am a regular contributing paid columnist to Zulily's and DealPop's blogs. In addition, as a volunteer, I handle media relations for The Triplet Connection and write The Triplet Connection National Convention's blog.

Facebook Id: Mommy Blog Expert

Approximate # of followers: 120 Facebook followers

Twitter Id: @MommyBlogExpert

Approximate # of followers: 5,800

Online Involvements and associations: I was a The View Ambassador and I am currently a HerInteractive Ambassador as well as on the Advisory Board of SheBlogs. I am also on the HIPsters Panel and am a Nielsen Consumer Panelist. I am also a long-time member of Public Relations Society of America and also The Triplet Connection.

How many moms do you typically interact with during the week offline? 25-30

Offline Community Service: The Triplet Connection, Strides Riding Center, Big Sunday (city-wide community service year round in L.A).

What's the best way for companies to reach you as an influencer or as a mom? I prefer email, but also make myself available by phone and I always love interacting on the various women's and moms' social media networks I'm active in, some of which I've listed above.

How can companies best support your business or mission as a mom? Be open to working with us side by side. Many of us are mommy bloggers now, but we are formerly highly-regarded professionals in the workforce in fields such as law, journalism, medicine, the sciences and arts and more. We are intelligent and appreciate being treated with mutual respect.

What motivates you to tell other moms (good or bad) about a company, brand or product? The quality of the product, company, brand, etc., the way that customer service plays into it, and how the company treats consumers is very important in my overall feelings on how I view and talk about companies and their products.

Final words: As stated above, I think brands would be wise to appreciate and acknowledge the influence we have collectively as females with kids, not only over our own families, but on all fronts: economically, politically, socially, educationally and otherwise.

Name: Candice Broom

Number of children and ages: 2, ages 3 and 6

Websites or Blogs you own: Mom Most Traveled http://www.mommosttraveled.com

Approximate audience size: 14,000 unique visitors each month

Facebook Id: CanCan Mom Most Traveled

Approximate # of followers: 650

Twitter Id: @MomMostTraveled

Approximate # of followers: 4,400

Online Involvements and associations: Mom Select, Mom Central, Team Mom

How many moms do you typically interact with during the week offline? Dozens! I am a 3K preschool teacher and interact with moms daily!

What do you think is the biggest mistake companies make in trying to work with moms? I get a little weary of the "ooo, girlfriend! We are so in this together!" tone. I might be a mom but I don't necessarily identify with every mom everywhere. Being a mom is a part of my identity, and motherhood is paved with millions of tiny choices which every mother navigates differently. We might be on the same journey but we don't see or experience or feel all the same things.

How do you define influence among moms? I think the influential moms are confident and caring, validating and outgoing: the person who you would go to for mom advice ... you could have a different influencer for "gear," one for "fashion," one for "bargains," one for "education," one for "entertaining"; chances are that these words instantly bring to mind a friend or writer who is your trusted guru in these specialty areas.

How do you feel companies can best connect with moms, particularly those who are influencers? I would like to see more companies formally hire moms for advisory positions instead of paying in gift cards and samples. I think this will be the next step.

Last words: In a phase of life (raising children) that used to mean isolation from society, the internet allows us to connect and have a voice. I was the only mom in my social circle to use cloth diapers, but I found a wealth of support, information, and even community online. The same goes for my vegetarian lifestyle and my love for travel. But moms can also connect online and be a part of the world at large, supporting political candidates or charities with their time and words. All without leaving the house! Or ... from the comfort of a coffee shop with free WiFi.

Name: Cindy Buccieri

Children: Two, ages 10 and 7

Hometown: Melbourne, Florida

Company Name(s): I have three blogs: Busy Mom's Tips, Blogging Hints and the Work at Home Helper. However, the company name is simply my name Cindy Buccieri.

Short description of business: I am the creator and author of three blogs. Busy Mom's Tips was my first blog and is dedicated to helping busy moms make their lives a little easier so that they have more time to spend with their families. Blogging Hints provides tips and advice for new bloggers just starting out and The Work at Home Helper offers advice and work-at-home job suggestions for those who want to work from home.

I launched my first blog, Busy Mom's Tips, in September 2009. The motivation for this blog was to provide busy mothers like myself with helpful tips on making their lives a little easier. My goal was to provide cost and time saving tips for planning family vacations, home decorating ideas, meal planning suggestions, saving money, house cleaning tips and offer helpful product reviews. A year later, in August 2010 and September 2010, Blogging Hints and The Work at Home Helper were launched respectively.

Websites or Blogs you own: Busy Mom's Tips http://www.busy-moms-tips-blog.com, Blogging Hints http://blogging-hints.blogspot.com and The Work at Home Helper http://www.workathomehelper.com

Approximate audience size: 10,000 per month

Websites or blogs you contribute to: I contribute to eHow.com and Associated Content. I was recently a guest blogger on Bobbypinsboardwalk.com.

Facebook Id: Busy Mom's Tips and Blogging Hints

Twitter Id: @busymomstips, @blogginghints and @workathomehelpr

Approximate # of followers: 520

Online Involvements and associations: Pssst.... with General Mills, Buzz Agent, She Blogs, Miles of Marketing and Moms Central.

How many moms do you typically interact with during the week offline? Approximately 25 moms.

What's the best way for companies to reach you as an influencer or as a mom? My email address is contact@busy-moms-tips.com.

How is the best way to work with you and your company? I'm open for all types of media. I enjoy posting product reviews and hosting giveaways on my blogs and I actively communicate with the Twitter and Facebook followers. I haven't ventured into the video or radio arena but I'm interested in those outlets as well.

What do you think is the biggest mistake companies make in trying to work with moms? In my experience, the biggest mistake companies have made in trying to work with me is that they don't follow up. I receive initial contact emails soliciting my interest and when I respond to the email, I don't receive a response. I believe those companies are losing a great source for marketing with my blogs and me.

How do you define influence among moms? Mothers tend to listen to and take the advice of other mothers, especially those who have experienced something first hand. Influence among moms is defined as sharing your thoughts, experiences and suggestions with other mothers in hopes of helping them make a decision or make their life a little easier.

How do you feel you influence moms online? From the comments I receive either through email or from my blog, I know that I'm making a difference in other mothers' lives. Whenever I come across a way to save money or a way to make a task more efficient, I share it with my readers so that they, too, can benefit from what I've learned. The same is true for bloggers and job seekers that I've helped. I want to let them know what I've learned so that they don't have to spend their precious time searching the Internet looking for the answers. I give them those answers.

How can companies best support your business or mission as a mom? Provide me with opportunities to market their products and services through reviews or giveaways. Let me help them get the word out to other mothers.

What motivates you to tell other moms (good or bad) about a company, brand or product? I enjoy helping others. I want to let other moms know if I come across a product that is really great. However, I also want to let them know if I know of something that is a waste of money or could be potentially unsafe for their children. In a post about a family vacation to Williamsburg, Virginia, I wanted to let other mothers know that it is well worth it to buy a refillable cup. I also let them know that it is advisable for them to ride the bus around the town as it is a lot of walking for small children.

Final words: As mothers, we tend to put our families before ourselves. Due to our constantly busy lives, mothers at times may miss out on important information about the economy and politics. In most cases, mothers are tuned into what is happening with the educational system as this directly relates to their children's education and future. Women like me are necessary to help get information out there to other mothers.

Name: Jennifer Bullock

Children: Two, ages 3.5 and 7 months

Hometown: Charlotte, NC

Websites or Blogs you own: Mommy B Knows Best www.MommyBKnowsBest.com and Aw Shucks It's the Bullocks www.awshucksitsthebullocks.com

Approximate audience size: 2,500

Websites or blogs you contribute to: Blogcritics.org, MommyBKnowsBest.com and awshucksitsthebullocks.com

Facebook Id: MommyBKnowsBest

Twitter Id: @MommyBKnowsBest

Approximate # of followers: 2,690

Online Involvements and associations: Member of Mom Bloggers Club, Member of Playground Divas and Charlotte Bloggers Meetup Groups, Mom Maven, Medela Moms

How many moms do you typically interact with during the week offline? 100

Offline Involvements: Playground Divas Meetup Group, and Charlotte Mommies, Service days at Florence Crittenton Women's Shelter, regular donations to trailer home out reach

Are there companies who you feel are doing a great job connecting with moms? Yes, definitely. I love Agoo and Bebe Au Lait; they're two great companies and are great about working with moms.

How do you define influence among moms? I think influence is not only causing a mom to purchase a specific product but it's to get her thinking about her purchases in general, the way she's doing things with her children and helping her make the best choices for her family; real influence is getting someone to think about topics beyond the subject of the writing.

What motivates you to tell other moms (good or bad) about a company, brand or product? I have been giving my friends/other moms my opinions since I became a mom. I feel as if there's much to be learned from other moms, experienced moms, and we have an obligation to tell other moms so that they don't make the same mistakes as we did or so that they can enjoy great products, too. Plus I always love to support a great company or tout their customer service; you frequently hear negative comments coming from people but great comments aren't as easy to come by. Having worked in the customer service industry, I know how important positive feedback can be, too, so I'm sure to give it when credit is due.

Final words: I think in general moms talk with each other. I'll chat up a random mom in the grocery line and we'll be best friends by the time she hands the cashier her last coupon; we'll talk about life, husbands, schools, politics, anything. I think that's one of the best things about being a mom is that you can automatically relate to another mom no matter what your background.

Name: Amy Byrd

Children: Two, ages 14 and 6

Hometown: Iron City, TN

Websites or Blogs you own: Wayland Cook http://waylandcook.blogspot.com/; Cooks Worldwide http://cooksworldwide.forumotion.net/index.htm

Facebook Id: Amy Jennifer Stone Byrd

Twitter Id: @waylandcook

Approximate # of followers: 850+

Online Involvements and associations: Allens Vegetable company

What do you think is the biggest mistake companies make in trying to work with moms? Talking in tech speak which some people don't understand.

How can companies best support your business or mission as a mom? They can support us by educating us better on their products.

Name: Kris Cain

Children: Four, ages 7 and 4 (two sets of twins)

Hometown: South Suburbs of Chicago, IL

Company Name(s): LTG Media, http://ltgmedia.com, Kris Cain Photography, http://kriscainphotography.com

Short description of business: Kris Cain Photography: photography of events around the Chicago area; I do portraits, and parties, etc. LTG Media: Social Media Services, Web Design, and Events. I have been doing the photography part of my business for about 7 years. It started as a hobby and quickly expanded to a business. What I love is that I work when I want. I do not have to take any job if I am not able, and I can quit at any time without a major loss. LTG Media is a new venture that has been floating around in my head for some time. Though I have been doing web design for several years, I am finally putting a name with that part of my presence and creating a site, etc., to go along with it as well as expanding my services.

Websites or Blogs you own: A Techy Mom's Nerd Paradise, http://littletechgirl.com

Approximate audience size: about 11,000 pageviews per month

Websites or blogs you contribute to: Type-A Mom, http://typeamom.com, Family Technology Editor Examiner, http://examiner.com, Chicago Tech Gear Examiner, National Apple Gear Examiner, Mom Blog Magazine (http://momblogmagazine.com), Tech Editor BlogHer (http://blogher.com), Contributing Writer, The Chicago Moms (http://thechicagomoms.com), Contributing Writer, Technocratic (http://technorati.com), Contributing Writer, BitMoms (http://bitmoms.com), Blog Network Member

Facebook Id: littletechgirl.com

Twitter Id: @littletechgirl

Approximate # of followers: 5110

Online Involvements and associations: eBay Classifieds Ambassador, BitMoms Blog Network, AMD Mom

How is the best way to work with you and your company? I love establishing relationships with companies. Not just a one hit wonder so to speak. I like companies that come back again, say thank you, and remember you for future opportunities if you have proven yourself.

What do you think is the biggest mistake companies make in trying to work with moms? Asking the mom to perform many duties for free, such as planning events, or rounding up other moms, etc., or asking for more than one blog post without some sort of mutual agreement on compensation.

How do you define influence among moms? What amazes me with moms, specifically the mom blogging community, is how close-knit we are when needed. Information can spread quickly and moms will band together to help one another. The same applies when getting out the word on a new product. Influence is determined by how well the peer moms are willing to listen and heed advice from one another.

How can companies best support your business or mission as a mom? I love getting companies involved in promoting events, and providing products to help moms. I have many ideas in my head that I hope to act on that can benefit many. On my main blog, companies provide products for me to review which helps keep my blog fresh with new content and helps consumers in making purchase decisions.

How do you feel companies can best connect with moms, particularly those who are influencers? I think Ambassador Programs, or social media jobs are great starts in getting moms involved with helping to share information and getting other moms involved. If a mom feels taken care of by a company, she is more likely to tell all her friends.

Final words: I think this is a great time for moms in social media. Companies have taken notice of the fact that moms influence a LOT of the household buying decisions. We also have the ability to either help or hurt right away by word of mouth. Companies can find some great moms out here that can manage campaigns, or write for them in a professional manner. Moms are used to multitasking and handle it well and get it all done.

Name: Sheri Carpenter

Children: Three, ages 12, 8, and 6

Hometown: Old Hickory Tennessee

Company Name(s): Scentsy Wickless –Candles—Independent Consultant

Short description of business: Flameless, Sootless, leadless, Scentsy Wickless Candles are powered by a 25-watt light bulb so they never get hot to the touch. Our wax is non toxic so it is safe for kids and pets. We also offer room sprays, travel tins, scent circles, fragrance foam, and Scentsy Buddies. Also, I am an Independent Consultant. I started my business in January of 2010 because I love the products. I am also hoping to grow my business to the point where I can work it full time and provide a better life for my family. I have a team of 4 people so far and they are great people to work with. I love what I do and my motivation is my family and children. I want to provide a good life for them and a stable life. My goals are to be able to work this business full time and live comfortably without struggling anymore.

Websites or Blogs you own: Sensible Aromas http://sensiblearomas.com, Miracle Momas http://miraclemomas.net, One Busy Moma http://onebusymoma.com and Coffee Shop Deals http://www.coffeeshopdeals.com

Approximate audience size: Miracle Momas, 22,000 views per month, One Busy Moma, 11,000 views per month, Coffee Shop Deals (open just a month so far) 8,000 views

Facebook Id: Sheri Carpenter

Twitter Id: @SheriCarpenter

Approximate # of followers: 3350

Online Involvements and associations: SITS, SheSpeaks,SheBlogs, Crowd Tap, Tomoson

What's the best way for companies to reach you as an influencer or as a mom? Email at onebusymoma@comcast.net.

Are there companies who you feel are doing a great job connecting with moms? There are quite a few companies I think are doing a great job. I can't name all of them, of course, but the ones I have worked with that are completely awesome that I can name right off the top of my head are: Oneida, Fantasy Jewelry Box, Jewelry Stylist, McNeil Designs.

How do you feel you influence moms online? I influence moms online by blogging and connecting. I am always meeting new people and talking with people. I feel that I influence them mainly through the blogs that I write. I write about a wide variety of things from business to parenting and I get great responses from my readers. So I feel that I influence them or help them in their decision-making on the topics that I write about.

Is there one moment when you realized you were impacting the life/lives of others? The moment when I realized I was impacting others' lives came after an article that I did for a Work At Home Mom; she emailed me about 2 weeks later letting me know that her sales had gone up and she added 2 new team members just from the article that I wrote and posted for her.

How do you feel companies can best connect with moms, particularly those who are influencers? I think companies can best connect with moms by going straight to the source. I have learned that working through programs or influencer sites you don't always get the whole story or the real statistics so I recommend checking us out for yourself. Ask the questions you want to know and let us answer them instead of having someone else answer them for us.

Name: Felicia Carter

Children: Two, ages 3 and 2 months (both boys)

Hometown: Asheville, NC

Websites or Blogs you own: Go Graham Go http://www.gograhamgo.com

Facebook Id: Go Graham Go

Twitter Id: @gograhamgo

Approximate # of followers: 5,162

Online Involvements and associations: Kellogg's, Chuggington, ShooShoos, Wisk, OfficeMax, Infantino, Scrubbing Bubbles, Mom Central, Mom Bloggers Club, The Motherhood

How many moms do you typically interact with during the week offline? 50 or more

Offline Involvements: Youth leader at church, Mother Goose Library Time

What's the best way for companies to reach you as an influencer or as a mom? By email Felicia@gograhamgo.com

Are there companies who you feel are doing a great job connecting with moms? Brands like Kellogg's and Pampers are taking the time to be personal and really get to know the audience.

How do you feel you influence moms offline? Is it more than chatting in the carpool line? I feel like I am the go-to person when there is a problem. I try to be the voice of reason and prompt action if action is required.

What motivates you to tell other moms (good or bad) about a company, brand or product? I always have to ask myself, "Would other moms want to know about this?"

Name: Geri Chase

Children: Two, ages 11 and 9 (both boys)

Hometown: Surprise, Arizona

Short description of business: I Am Boymom, once it is up and running, will be dedicated to products and information aimed at moms who seek advice and help in raising their male children. Helping Our Warriors is a nonprofit corporation dedicated to strengthening military families.

Websites or Blogs you own: I Am Boymom http://iamboymom.blogspot.com/ and Helping Our Warriors

Approximate audience size: 200 a month

Facebook Id: Geri Tanner Chase

Twitter Id: @iamboymom

Approximate # of followers: 320

Online Involvements and associations: Soft Scrub Captain, Feld Family Entertainment Family Activator, Member of MomSelect, MomCentral and One2One Mom Review Networks, SheKnows Food Club Member, House Party Hostess

How many moms do you typically interact with during the week offline? 30-100

Offline Involvements: Teacher for Women's group at church, Cub Scout assistant, Founding Director of Helping Our Warriors Nonprofit, Helping Our Warriors, Church projects, school volunteer

What do you think is the biggest mistake companies make in trying to work with moms? Assuming that we are all the same. Yes, we all have some of the same issues when it comes to rearing children, but our families and our family dynamics are so incredibly unique! Work at getting to know us as individual families a little bit! Another mistake companies make is sending out requests to review products that don't pertain to me or my family. Don't send me an offer to review a toy for a 3-month-old when my kids are almost pre-teens. That tells me you have put no effort into getting to know me or my family. Also, many PR folks assume that we will write about anything on our blogs just to fill space. Many moms have turned their blogs into businesses and do not work for free, nor should they. I don't mind writing a post about an event that contributes to a good cause and not being compensated for it, *i.e.*, breast cancer, but I'm not going to spend my time writing about your 60% off sale on toilet seats so that you can make a ton of money off free publicity. If you want my endorsement, you need to offer something in return (maybe I need a new toilet seat! I do have boys with aiming issues!).

Are there companies who you feel are doing a great job connecting with moms? I loved working with Cepia LLC (Zhu Zhu Pets). They offered a fantastic product, they offered a really fun way to try out the product and most importantly, they listened to the feedback they got from the moms they worked with. I mentioned a specific issue I had with one of their items in my blog review and within a day or so I was contacted by a toy engineer from Cepia asking me to try the new and improved version of their product that had been changed to address some of our comments. That shows me that a) they stand behind their products, b) they listen to and respect their customers, and c) they do not want to waste consumers' hard-earned cash on toys that don't work. I love supporting companies with integrity!

I would say that RideMakerz did a great job at connecting with moms as well. I thought they really researched their target audience and reached out to those of us who are always looking for unique and fun activities geared toward boys. They gave my boys personal attention and treated them so well that my boys love going back there because of the memories of their first visit.

Disney gets the whole Mom thing. Of course, they've been at it a long time and they've had plenty of opportunities to watch moms struggling with toddler melt-downs, teenage boredom, etc. I think Disney does a great job communicating with moms regarding new events and attractions that cater to different age groups. They really go out of their way to create family friendly experiences.

How do you feel you influence moms online? I feel I can be a voice of experience and reason when it comes to sharing my experiences with companies and products with other moms, especially those who are concerned about making sure the money they spend is not being wasted on inferior products. I am honest when I share my experiences and include the good, the bad and the ugly so that my readers and followers get a full picture of what my experience with a product or company was really like. It's the only way they can really make an informed decision about where and how to spend their hard earned dollars! On a personal level, I tend to be pretty open and honest about how I experience life ... it's kind of like Geri in real time. If I feel it or think it, I have a need to express it. I think lots of moms have thoughts and feelings that aren't always pretty or perfect regarding motherhood, but are sometimes reticent to say "Hey this is hard and it sucks some days." I have no problem talking (writing) realistically about the demands that motherhood places on us as individuals and I have no problem talking about my struggle with that role, as well as my struggle to overcome my past and become who I want to be as I raise my kids. I think other moms appreciate the candor and that what I feel and share resonates with many women who can't always pull it together to be the idyllic "June Cleaver" type of mom we all thought we were supposed to be.

How do you feel you influence moms offline? Is it more than chatting in the carpool line? Sure it's more than chatting in the carpool line. A big reason my opinions or ideas carry any weight with any of my friends and acquaintances is that they know I really do care about them and what is going on in their lives. They know that I listen to them and that when I can help them, I will. Whether it's offering information or watching your kid ... whatever. Nobody's going to listen to some jerk that really doesn't give a hoot about what kinds of things affect you and your family. People can tell when you are sincere and when you aren't. But honestly? Carpool lines and football practices are some of the best times to bond and share with other moms. Sometimes it's the only time we have during the day to engage in adult conversation! And simple questions like "What have you been doing today?" open the door for me to actually talk about what I've been doing, so I share. Or they share and we all end up trying to support and uplift one another!

I think the key to being an influencer is establishing yourself as a person who is actively involved with issues that affect most of us at some level or another, whether it's saving money or working for a charity. And then you have to not be afraid to talk about those issues when you have the chance. When people talk to you about what you've been doing and you can tell them in great detail with lots of enthusiasm about the product you just reviewed or the charity event you just attended, you engage them and get them thinking about how they can do the same.

How can companies best support your business or mission as a mom? Offer us opportunities that help us grow, not only as moms, but as businesswomen, too. Some of us do not have marketing or business degrees, so be patient with us while we develop some of the skills we need to be more productive, or better yet ... mentor us. Know that our families will always come first and allow enough time with projects for us to plan around family events and schedules. Last minute is sometimes hard for busy moms to pull off. Also, don't be offended if we turn down offers to promote products that either don't work for our family demographic or may not align with our core values. There's nothing worse than making an apology for not wanting to take on a project and being treated poorly by a company because of my choice. Sometimes it's just not a good match and companies need to be okay with that.

Final words: There are so many things our children face today that we did not have to face as children. At the same time, there is so much more knowledge and information available to parents to help them raise their kids that wasn't available for our parents. I think just the wealth and availability of all that information already gives us more power to influence than previous generations of mothers. And not just in the area of parenting! The advent of websites like Blogher and She Speaks and MomCentral has put more moms than ever before in the unique position to exert influence in political, economic and educational arenas. Home schooling is a perfect example of how social media has been used to dispel myths and stigmas surrounding home education, and amazing curriculums have been developed and shared as a result of moms being able to share their experiences. The development of blogging and social media has allowed moms, who would not normally have a voice, an opportunity to effect change from anywhere in the world where they can access a computer! How amazing is that? And how many wonderful things have been done because of this new technology!?

But I think we have to be careful to use that influence properly. For me, I have to do a gut check once in awhile to make sure that I am using my influence for good and not evil. There have been a couple of offers I've had to turn down because I didn't think my core values aligned with the product or company. There have been blog posts that I have deleted because I realized that spilling my guts for the world to see might not be in the best interest of me or my family, no matter how much I wanted to share the anguish or anger with my readers. In the end, I have to answer to myself, my family and my followers, on and offline. I don't want to lose the trust of my readers and friends because I got too caught up in the hype and my message got lost, you know? Like Peter Parker's Uncle said: "With great power comes great responsibility." The power and instantaneous nature of the internet can uplift and support or it can permanently damage lives and reputations. As Moms with Influence, we have a responsibility to make sure that what we put out there doesn't cause harm or purposely mislead the people who trust us to give them good and honest information.

Name: Tricia Chinn Campbell

Children: Two, ages 3 and newborn

Hometown: Silverthorne, CO

Company Name(s): I have a couple small businesses: Happenstance Jewelry—glass, tile, scrabble, and domino fashion jewelry, Green T Marketing—marketing, consulting, Swanky Tails—ponytail holders/accessories

Short description of business: The idea was to be a stay-at-home mom but to bring in some income—while keeping my creativity moving. I didn't want to fall out from the market (of advertising and marketing) but where I live, people don't want to or seem to understand the need to pay you what you're worth or for your experience—so I decided to start a jewelry company. I'm hoping to get a few projects from time to time with my marketing consulting business, and would love to get into mom-to-mom marketing some way; since I a baby in December 2010, it may be a little difficult. In the meantime, my jewelry company has allowed me to get into some fun boutiques as well as have jewelry parties around town, thus keeping me in touch with lots of moms and other women.

Websites or Blogs you own: Happenstance Jewelry sweethappenstance.com, Green T Marketing greentmarketing.com, Swanky Tails myswankytails.com

Online Involvements and associations: I created a group page called "The Cool Gals Network" which is basically a place for everybody to not only network work-wise, but to also include information on any nonprofit organizations and events they or their businesses are holding.

What do you think is the biggest mistake companies make in trying to work with moms? It's a mistake to assume that being a mom is our only passion or that it's all we know or all we are. We're regular women—although it is nice to be recognized or to be "touched" with certain sentiments as a mom.

Are there companies who you feel are doing a great job connecting with moms? There was a great ad for Toyota Sienna with the mom who first talked about how the thought of getting a minivan made her cry ... but with her Sienna, she thinks it's super stylish ... she's in there watching TV and doing her nails, in her robe, etc.: funny and so relevant.

How do you define influence among moms? These days we have moms who are more educated, moms who have experienced a full life before children. They've taken these life experiences, work skills, etc., and have been able to apply them in how they raise their kids, in how they make decisions for the children; they are more proactive women who get active in their children's lives, school work, etc. They're not going to let others raise their kids ... they're going to be very involved.

How can companies best support your business or mission as a mom? Create more recognized mom groups, forums, websites ... any place where we can identify with each other on different but similar levels.

How do you feel companies can best connect with moms, particularly those who are influencers? Get their product or service in front of those influencers, and pay them to create focus groups.

Name: Charlene

Children: One, age 12 months

Hometown: Boston, MA

Company Name(s): Charlene Chronicles

Short description of business: A discovery portal for Moms and their families, primarily in Metro-west Massachusetts, which I started in October 2009. I heard from moms who were frustrated with having to search through many sites to find family-friendly businesses and events that are located west of Boston. CharleneChronicles was created to provide that information for them and my mission is to be a resource for those events and services, as well as to highlight trendy and classy products for moms and their children. I do not have an exit strategy as I plan on doing this for quite some time.

Websites or Blogs you own: CharleneChronicles.com

Approximate audience size: 2,000

Websites or blogs you contribute to: I have contributed to Sittercity.com, IsisParenting.com and Boston Parent Bloggers.

Facebook Id: Charlene Chronicles

Twitter Id: @CharChronicles

Approximate # of followers: 720

Online Involvements and associations: Twitter Moms, MomSelect, Boston Parent Bloggers, MommyBlogs, Mom Blog Network, BloggyMoms.

Offline Involvements: Member of Bar Associations and Industry Groups

What's the best way for companies to reach you as an influencer or as a mom? Email at Charlene@CharleneChronicles.com

What do you think is the biggest mistake companies make in trying to work with moms? Presuming we always work for free.

How do you feel you influence moms online? By providing them with information they might not have received otherwise.

How do you feel you influence moms offline? Is it more than chatting in the carpool line? If someone is looking for a suggestion on a baby or child product, or a fitness routine, they often ask me for my advice. So I often influence their buying patterns and motivate them to make healthier habits.

How do you feel companies can best connect with moms, particularly those who are influencers? I think the companies that are doing a good job have Mom Panels, where the company actively and consistently seeks the input of moms. It starts there and the rest follows as a result.

Do you have any additional thoughts on the influence of moms in any area of today's world? I believe that the moms of today are more educated than ever before. They can see through companies' flashy ads and want a quality product or service. Companies used to pat moms on the head. Now companies are kissing Mom's $%& because moms have started to dictate what should be in the market, not the other way around. Companies used to say, "This is what we have so you better like it." Now moms are saying, "I don't like what you have and you better fix it."

Name: Danielle Clawson Fletcher

Children: Three, ages 17, 13 and 3

Hometown: Charlotte, NC

Company Name(s): oh, how posh!

Short description of business: oh, how posh! offers inspiring ideas and stylish trends for creating fabulous holiday parties, cocktail parties, and everyday get-togethers. We love all things pretty and pristine and we love sharing our ideas, we aspire to help you create beautiful celebrations with style. We feel that every day should be celebrated, no matter how big or small the celebration. I started oh, how posh! in September 2008. I have been doing corporate event planning for over ten years and always talked to my parents and everyone else about starting my own business for event planning and sharing ideas on how to plan the perfect party. My father passed away in August 2008, and that motivated me to do what I love to do before it's too late. My father never had the chance to see my company and what I have been able to achieve, but my mother has.

Websites or Blogs you own: oh, how posh! http://www.ohhowposh.com/

Approximate audience size: 1,500 daily hits

Facebook Id: oh, how posh!

Offline Involvements: Charlotte Business Women Leaders, Event Professionals of Charlotte, Catherine's House, Ronald McDonald House, Charlotte Rescue Mission

How do you feel you influence moms offline? Is it more than chatting in the carpool line? Listening and taking into account others' experiences and advice.

What motivates you to tell other moms (good or bad) about a company, brand or product? My overall experience and how our family is affected.

Name: Amy Colton

Children: Three, ages 13, 11 and 7

Hometown: Evanston, IL

Company Name(s): Current Lifestyle Marketing

Short description of business: Public relations and social media marketing

Online Involvements and associations: Founding Board Member, Marketing to Moms Coalition

How many moms do you typically interact with during the week offline? 25

Offline Involvements: PTA, Church, Marketing to Mom Coalition

What do you think is the biggest mistake companies make in trying to work with moms? They fall into traps of clichés—girly color palettes, too many "busy mom" references. We know we are busy. Often it's easy to see that men have written the material, and it is based onwhat they assume we have going on.

Are there companies who you feel are doing a great job connecting with moms? I think Walmart is doing a good job, actually. The marketing takes a tongue-in-cheek approach—the TV spots often have humor. The spot for the Super Bowl in 2010 was funny, and showed that it's really moms buying everything to pull off the "guy" fest.

How do you define influence among moms? In my universe, it's one-on-one influence that makes the biggest impact. I don't have time to participate in online communities or organized mommy groups, but I do pay attention to what my friends on Facebook post, and most importantly what moms on the playground talk about. Influence among moms is sparking the opportunity for a mother to stop and listen—to a new piece of news, a new idea or trend, or something funny to share.

How do you feel you influence moms offline? Is it more than chatting in the carpool line? It is many things: chatting on the playground, talking to other parents as you drop your kids off for activities, but also just sharing your experiences. I have found that I have influenced other mothers just by sharing what my family's days are like—how we deal with our kids' schedules, what it's like for me to be working full time, how things get messed up a lot. An open dialogue has the most influence, whether it's mom-to-mom or brand-to-mom.

What motivates you to tell other moms (good or bad) about a company, brand or product? It has to be something truly great to pass along—support for a cause I care about, a terrific product, or a special deal. But the threshold isn't as high for passing bad news along—moms are likely to share even small experiences that are bad as well as the big flops from brands.

Name: Randa Cote

Children: Two, ages 4 and 9 months

Hometown: San Diego, CA

Company Name(s): Moms in Business Unite

Short description of business: The Moms in Business Unite Conference is the vision of five women entrepreneurs who united to empower and educate the growing number of women in business. With nearly 40 years of combined entrepreneurial experience as well as eight children, we recognized a need for a forum that provides both business education and solutions for establishing a balanced work and family life. We created the Moms in Business Unite Conference to bring together accomplished instructors, relevant life and business topics, and a truly unique learning environment. This conference helps women and mom business owners pursue their entrepreneurial endeavors by providing tools, resources, and guidance for their journey through the various stages of business ownership.

Date started: September 2008

Motivation in launching it: Our committee unites under one primary passion "to help educate women to propel their businesses forward."

Mission: The Moms in Business Unite Conference is the leading professional resource that offers women inspiration and education to ignite their entrepreneurial dreams and propel them forward.

Exit strategy: have yet to determine this.

Websites or Blogs you own: www.momsinbusinessunite.com, www.spesolutions.com,

Approximate audience size: 500

Facebook Id: Moms in Business Unite Conference

Approximate # of followers: 200

Twitter Id: @MIBU_Conference

Approximate # of followers: 300

How many moms do you typically interact with during the week offline? 40-50

Offline Involvements: NAWBO, USD Alumni, 2006 Playgroup, 2010 Playgroup x2, Preschool Classroom Mom, San Diego Parent Connection, Women in SharePoint, SD SharePoint Users Group, Susan G. Komen Breast Cancer Awareness, American Cancer Society, Take Shape for Life, The Unity Center, Military Adopt a Family, Childcare for the Unity Center

What's the best way for companies to reach you as an influencer or as a mom? Email info@momsinbusinessunite.com

Is there one moment when you realized you were impacting the life/lives of others? Yes—at the end of our first conference when someone approached me and said "Randa, take in this moment, and realize that you changed lives today."

How do you feel you influence moms offline? Is it more than chatting in the carpool line? Yes, I constantly provide assistance, organization, and valuable information to everyone I meet or those who will listen—I love sharing knowledge! I try to get people involved in group activities. I have been the driving force to unite all the moms of preschoolers in my community and as a result they feel so much more connected and supported.

What motivates you to tell other moms (good or bad) about a company, brand or product? Unfortunately, very bad experiences always motivate me to communicate—but lately I have been trying to communicate the very good experiences, too. I personally love when I get prompted (with email or other means) to provide feedback about a product or service. In our busy lives, it really helps to be prompted. I have also been using the Facebook "Like" button on products or services that I support.

Name: Sarah Coulsey

Children: Two, ages 5 and 2

City and home state: Greenfield, MA

Company Name(s): Sarah's Blog Of Fun

Short description of business: A website for reviews, giveaways, games and just plain fun! I started my Blog in December of 2009. I started it to enter giveaways. In the last 10 months, I have turned it into a huge site that does just about everything! I host games, giveaways, reviews of lots of products, and just have fun.

Websites or Blogs you own: Sarah's Blog Of Fun www.sarahsblogoffun.com

Approximate audience size: 1,270 Followers, 7,000 page views per month

Twitter Id: @SarahsBlogOfFun

Approximate # of followers: 1,000

What's the best way for companies to reach you as an influencer or as a mom? Through my email: sarahcoulsey03@gmail.com

What do you think is the biggest mistake companies make in trying to work with moms? They try to get us to work for free. For me, blog posts take a lot of time. I work very hard on my reviews. It is not an easy job.

Are there companies who you feel are doing a great job connecting with moms? I have worked with a lot of different great companies. The two I am working with right now that are awesome are Spa Naturals, and Honeywell.

Is there one moment when you realized you were impacting the life/lives of others? When my followers started telling me they valued my opinion and trusted me!

How can companies best support your business or mission as a mom? If they keep sending me their products to review, I can keep doing my job.

Name: Laura K. Cowan

Children: One, age 17 months

Hometown: Ann Arbor, MI

Company Name(s): 29Diapers.com

Short description of business: Along with being a writer (the author of *Ecofrugal Baby: How To Save 70% Off Baby's First Year*, which is available in paperback and as an e-book) and editor, I am the founder of 29Diapers.com, a blog that teaches readers all about modern cloth diapers and how to be a frugal green parent. I was laid off from my job as a magazine copy chief just one month before becoming pregnant with my daughter. This was in 2008, just as the recession was beginning, and since I couldn't earn as much money just doing my freelance editing and writing work, I made it my job to *save* money. I became obsessive about finding out just how much money I could save on baby expenses, and soon my friends were coming to me for advice on how to save money on baby gear and how to use cloth diapers, which are super cute (really!) and save me $1000 per year and keep one ton of trash out of the landfills per year. I realized the knowledge I had acquired needed to go out to other new parents who were stressed out by the costs associated with having a baby and didn't know how easy and cute modern cloth diapers are. I started 29Diapers.com in April of 2010 and started hosting cloth diaper giveaways, packing the site with information about cloth diapers, and writing a blog series called Ecofrugal Fridays, which detailed all my best tips for saving money on each type of baby gear. That turned into my book, which I held my first book signing for on November 7, at the Barnes & Noble on Washtenaw Avenue in Ann Arbor, Michigan. To include my online fans in the event, I made a way for them to order the book directly from 29Diapers.com with a field to specify a recipient and custom message in their book, so I can sign the online copies along with the books sold in stores. Bookstores are starting to pick up the new title, and things are taking off. I'm very excited to be able to do what I love—write!—and help other new parents who are going through the same financial stress I felt two years ago. What a blessing to be able to do what I love while being a blessing to others!

Websites or Blogs you own: 29 Diapers, http://www.29diapers.com/

Approximate audience size: 1500 visitors/month

Facebook Id: 29 Diapers

Twitter Id: @29diapers

Approximate # of followers: 510

Online Involvements and associations: I am a member of the Ning Cloth Diapering Bloggers network, where I have made some great friends and professional connections. I am also a member of various mom blogger PR organizations but haven't found them to be very helpful in setting up giveaways or posts that would be of interest to my audience, so instead I pitch companies myself.

What's the best way for companies to reach you as an influencer or as a mom? Email: laurakcowan@gmail.com.

What do you think is the biggest mistake companies make in trying to work with moms? Treating them as "just" housewives. I don't know any moms who sit around eating bon bons after vacuuming! Being a mom and wife is the hardest job I've ever had, but on top of that, most moms are enormously influential, intelligent, and savvy people. This stay-at-home mom is writing a novel, promoting a nonfiction book, and running a blog that is hosting a HUGE month-long Christmas baby giveaway event. I think companies are starting to realize that they are lucky to get in with influential moms like me, who are building our own brands as well as theirs.

Are there companies who you feel are doing a great job connecting with moms? My favorite green parenting brands do a good job connecting with moms through blog giveaways and special promotions. Some of these include Boon, See Kai Run, Nifty Nappy, Thirsties, and Rockin' Green.

Is there one moment when you realized you were impacting the life/lives of others? I realized I was having an impact on the lives of others and the planet when my pregnant friends started asking me for information on cloth diapers. Every kid that is cloth diapered saves one ton of trash per year from going in the landfill, not to mention the manufacturing waste and oil saved from producing fewer disposable diapers.

How can companies best support your business or mission as a mom? My blog is only six months old but growing fast. I would love it if companies came to me to pitch giveaway or product review ideas. Linking to my blog, giveaway events, and telling people about the free classes and book signings I'm doing would also help me get the word out about great products and how to be a green parent on a tiny budget.

How do you feel companies can best connect with moms, particularly those who are influencers? Social media is the best way to connect with influential moms, because moms who have a large influence online are already on Facebook, Twitter, and the like.

Name: Anne Crane

Children: Six, ages 2, 10, 21, 23, and 17 (deceased)

Hometown: Wellington, FL

Websites or Blogs you own: Mommy Has to Work http://www.mommyhastowork.com/

Approximate audience size: 2,000

Websites or blogs you contribute to: Mama Buzz, Mom Select, Double Duty Divas, The Product Review Place, Mom Bloggers Club

Facebook Id: Anne Crane, Mommy Has to Work

Twitter Id: @mommyhastowork

Approximate # of followers: 1,500

Is there one moment when you realized you were impacting the life/lives of others? I preach going green to many. My neighbor has known about my blog and my "green" activities. Recently though, he commented that he did not realize that there are many small ways to recycle and be green that make a huge difference. He learned that from me.

How do you feel you influence moms offline? Is it more than chatting in the carpool line? I chat to the moms during drop off at my daughter's day care and on my son's field trips. I organize meetings at school to share products and help moms learn.

Name: Lucinda Cross

Children: Three, ages 9, 6, and 5months

Hometown: Yonkers, NY

Company Name(s): Corporate Mom Drop Outs

Short description of business: I started my company, called LC Associates, in 2006, and we provided outsourcing teams for small business owners. I then created Corporate Mom Drop Outs which provides online and offline marketing support for moms in transition from job to CEO for start-up businesses who need support in building a sustainable business model and lifestyle balance. I launched my business based on my own frustrations of working in Corporate America; I always had a side hustle, but I wanted to find a way to make more money and work from home and spend more time with my children. I then decided to write my letter of resignation after a situation where I was being questioned on my son's illness with the flu. I decided on that day that I refuse to have anyone control my life or how I operate with my children and when. My motivation came from my kids, from the low paycheck I was receiving and the income I was getting from doing my business part time. I left that job and now run a profitable and sustainable business model that provides mothers with the motivation and instruction to be all that they can be. I plan to create an online academy that will be a combination of all of the entrepreneurial programs I have done and joint ventures I have made with other industry leaders, which will allow moms a chance to receive the information they need in an instructional learning environment.

Websites or Blogs you own: Corporate Mom Dropouts www.corporatemom-dropouts.com, Lucinda Cross www.lucindacross.com, Super Mom Entrepreneur www.supermompreneur.com

Approximate audience size: 12,000

Websites or blogs you contribute to: NBC Momtourage www.momtourage.com, www.brandnewmommy.com, www.supermompreneur.com

Facebook Id: Lucinda Cross

Twitter Id: @corpmomdropout

How many moms do you typically interact with during the week offline? 50-100

Offline Involvements: Project Enterprise, Manhattan Chamber of Commerce, Women Chamber of Commerce, EWomens Network, The National Association of Black Female Entrepreneurs, Board of Education speaker, speak to numerous nonprofit organizations for women and young girls in High School

What's the best way for companies to reach you as an influencer or as a mom? Email: www.corporatemomdropouts.com

What do you think is the biggest mistake companies make in trying to work with moms? I think that companies miss out on building a relationship with the moms: placing moms in the marketing seat will make a huge difference in sales, by including real life images of moms at home, working moms, and images of moms with their families in their media campaigns.

Are there companies who you feel are doing a great job connecting with moms? Huggies, Toyota Sienna (Swagger Van), Johnson and Johnson

How do you feel you influence moms online? I influence moms in a positive and motivating way to take action. I walk my walk and talk my talk. I show moms that they can still be who they want to be, do what they want to do and take care of their family at the same time. As a mom with three kids under 10 years old, a husband and a full-time business. They see that I am pushing towards my goals and I am not using the kids as an excuse or the lack of time as an excuse. I go out of my comfort zone, out of my so-called target market, to influence other moms, such as those in prison, women in domestic violence situations, and women in social services. I influence moms by coaching them to believe in themselves, I assist them in creating products, starting businesses, and providing balancing tips for their family.

Is there one moment when you realized you were impacting the life/lives of others? When people are willing to pay me during a recession is when I knew I was impacting lives. I had over 30 women from Corporate America contact me from one organization who said that their supervisor directed them to my site for more information on how they can work from home, and maximize on their unemployment benefits. I connect with moms in faith-based organizations, nonprofit organizations, domestic violence groups, moms who were released from prison.

How can companies best support your business or mission as a mom? Companies can support Corporate Mom Drop Outs by, of course, monetary sponsorships that will allow me to train more moms, and equip more moms with the necessary tools to build their business. Corporate Mom Drop Outs needs to partner with many of these companies that provide home office organization equipment and office supplies as well as work/life balance tools.

How do you feel companies can best connect with moms, particularly those who are influencers? I feel companies should look at which influencers are communicating with other moms, and then presenting opportunities for the influencer to gain more exposure, becoming a brand ambassador of the company. Moms love to tell other moms, influencers love to be seen as the "go to person" or the person with the "connections." As an influencer I look for ways that I can support my economy of moms and how I can dominate the industry according to my niche, so if companies want to connect with the influencer they have to understand the mindset of an influencer which is different from the mindset of a mom consumer or product reviewer. Influencers like to have unique opportunities that will help showcase their relationship with the company and the exclusive connection they have to help others.

Final words: The influence of moms going back to school, getting a higher education, and learning in today's time has increased; moms are owning more businesses, not just women but moms are coming out of their shells. They are doing more than becoming a multi-level marketing representative, they are now using their creativity and their skills and techniques to create their own opportunities and are hiring other moms to help with building their business. So the influence of education and being socially connected is at an all-time high. We are connecting on social media, we are becoming tech savvy, we are not compromising our families any longer and more and more moms are becoming change makers, industry leaders and influencers.

Name: Lori Cunningham

Children: Two, ages 7 and 4

Hometown: Chino Hills, CA

Short description of business: It is my plan to start up a consulting business within the next year. I started my blog, the wellconnectedmom.com, as a way to jump in head first back into the working world after being absent for 8 years. Before my children were born, I worked for Nestle for 12 years in brand management, promotions, sales, IT, Internet technologies, and eBusiness consulting. After my eight-year hiatus, I began evaluating, "what is my passion?" I thought back to when I was in grade school where I would often go to the library to check out Popular Science. I LOVED looking at all of the futuristic projects and technologies which would change the way we live. Wow. I knew that I needed to work in the technology field again. Writing a blog is a visible way to add to my resume, create a large rolodex of contacts, and connect with other moms while affording me the flexibility to be home with my children.

I started my blog a little over a year ago. While being in my moms groups, I noticed that other moms only use 20% of the features/apps on their phones. Being a techy at heart, I created my blog to help moms better utilize gadgets to make their lives more efficient, fun, and better connected.

Websites or Blogs you own: The Well Connected Mom http://wellconnectedmom.com, The Well Connected Home http://thewellconnectedhome.com

Approximate audience size: 1,100 unique visitors

Websites or blogs you contribute to: Momtechnology.com, Chinohills.com, DivaToolbox.com, And WE Magazine for Women

Facebook Id: Well Connected Mom

Twitter Id: @wellconnectdmom

Approximate # of followers: 1,940

Online Involvements and associations: CrowdTap, MediaSpace Comunispace, AT&T Power Moms, LosetheLaptop.com, LG Innovation Lab, Microsoft Office 2010 case study

How many moms do you typically interact with during the week offline? 100-120

Offline Involvements: MOPS (Mothers of Preschoolers), BSF (Bible Study Fellowship), my daughter's and son's soccer teams, Awana's—Bible study group for my kids, PTA, involvement with my kids' schools/classrooms. Fender School of Music—provides low cost or no cost music lessons for kids. I help wherever needed. Also, I served on the board for the past six years (last three as Chair) for Alternate Avenues (http://alternateavenues.net), where we help women and men in unplanned pregnancies decipher their "true" choices. We provide free pregnancy testing, ultrasounds, consulting, and support through their pregnancies and afterwards. We also have support groups for women who have been through abortions (1 in 3 women) to help them forgive themselves and live life more fully. With over 43 million babies aborted since Roe versus Wade, we as a nation have lost countless generations of families. At Alternate Avenues, we help to build families through love and support.

What's the best way for companies to reach you as an influencer or as a mom? Ask me to become a Brand Ambassador which could include: using their products to write about, attending shows with the company and speaking about their products from a mom's point of view. They could actively promote my website/persona as a part of their marketing campaign. Companies can elevate mom bloggers to receive more publicity for their blog. The more publicity a blog has, the more impressions a brand receives.

What do you think is the biggest mistake companies make in trying to work with moms? Two things. First, when a mom is heavily involved with a project or contest with a large company, she puts a lot of heart and soul into it. When the contest is over, the company (or PR Company) moves on and sometimes doesn't even promote the results. This can be disheartening for the mom blogger. Second, many companies chase after the bigger bloggers, but with so many companies pursuing them, the big bloggers often can't invest the time in the companies that a smaller, hungrier blogger would.

Are there companies who you feel are doing a great job connecting with moms? Disney, V-Tech, Zhu-Zhu Pets, Kodak

How do you feel you influence moms online? Technology is changing at such a rapid pace, it's literally impossible to keep up on all fronts about the latest tech product and how it relates (if at all) to a mom. Moms look to me for relevance and solutions which make their lives easier. I have influence with moms online (and offline) because 1) I am a mom, 2) I am emotionally involved (technology is my passion!), and 3) I enjoy both reviewing innovative products that solve a mom's problems and then spreading the word about that product enthusiastically.

How can companies best support your business or mission as a mom? Exposure and creating a true partnership are the best ways a company can support me. Partnerships are important and I work hard to provide value to both the company I'm working for and the audience I'm writing to. Companies can support me as a mom by continuing to find ways their products are solutions to my problems.

What motivates you to tell other moms (good or bad) about a company, brand or product? The experience: if a product/company promises something and my expectations are exceeded in my experience of using it, I will tell (and show) a lot of people about it. For example, I love the Zeo personal sleep coach I reviewed as a follow-up from CES. It is an incredible find and most people have never heard of it. It monitors your sleep patterns and tells you how much time you spend in REM, light, and heavy sleep—as well as how many times you awaken—you get a graph charting this by every 15 minutes during your sleep time. It delivered on all its promises and more. I talk about my experience with the Zeo often.

How do you feel companies can best connect with moms, particularly those who are influencers? Create a genuine two-way relationship that carries on beyond just one event. As many moms aren't getting paid much to blog, companies could "invest" in the mom blogger to show that they care about her growing her blog or business. Investing could include advertising, sponsorships to big blogging events (where the company approaches the blogger first about it!), publicity for her blog, an offer to take care of expenses for classes, bringing her on as a consultant to help "train" their marketing department in communicating to moms, etc.

Final words: Moms hold a lot together—families, jobs, blogs, business, kids' schedules, job development, and concern for friends, acquaintances, and even families she doesn't know but her heart breaks for them. Many mom bloggers have been stay-at-home moms for a long time and didn't realize their self-worth. Blogs give them a chance to realize their importance in a personal and professional way. And mom bloggers are making an impact. This is evidenced by the number of corporate seminars and conferences focused on "connecting with moms." The Internet provides moms a chance to bond together in a way that wasn't possible years ago. They're taking up sisterhood in a new way and together they make a powerful stand.

Name: Onica Cupido

Children: One, age 2 ½

Hometown: New York, NY

Short description of business: Ten years ago, I started my online community to provide information and support for a group that wasn't being spoken to. As a woman and mother I had questions that no one was answering or thought were important to address. So I became a source for myself and the women in my group.

Websites or Blogs you own: Euphoria Luv Blog http://euphorialuv.wordpress.com/, Blasian Baby Notes http://blasianbabynotes.blogspot.com/, http://mommyfactor.blogspot.com/

Facebook Id: Euphoria Luv and Mommy Factor

Twitter Id: @EuphoriaLuv, @MommyFactor

Approximate # of followers: 4,300

How many moms do you typically interact with during the week offline? Over 100

What do you think is the biggest mistake companies make in trying to work with moms? They group all moms together. Each mom and her community is different with unique needs.

Is there one moment when you realized you were impacting the life/lives of others? There are many moments. When a complete stranger comes to me and says I know you and have been following you because what you talk about is also my life, my struggles, my thoughts. When they thank me for being a face for them as women, mothers and families, that's when I know I'm making an impact on lives.

How can companies best support your business or mission as a mom? By understanding that the mommy and family community is composed of many different forms and mixtures. Companies need to broaden their images and messages to reflect a broader range. If need be, devote a team to researching and targeting the multi-ethnic community.

What motivates you to tell other moms (good or bad) about a company, brand or product? Adding or taking away value to the mom's life. If a company, brand or product will not add something to value then I feel responsible to mention my thoughts and observations. The same if there's something I feel would add great value to another mom's life.

Name: Jeannine D'Addario

Children: One, age 10

Hometown: La Canada, CA

Employer: The Walt Disney Company

Short description of business: Entertainment and Licensing

Facebook Id: Jeannine D'Addario

Twitter Id: @JDaddario

Online Involvements and associations: Café Mom, Circle of Moms, Razorfish, Fast Company, Great Schools

How many moms do you typically interact with during the week offline? 10-20

Offline Involvements: PTA, Business School Alumni, YMCA, Girl Scouts, Girl Scouts, ASPCA/Humane Society

What's the best way for companies to reach you as an influencer or as a mom? Email Jeannine.DAddario@disney.com, online sites

How do you feel you influence moms online? I believe the best influence comes from one-on-one communication and storytelling. Having shared experiences is the key to influence.

Is there one moment when you realized you were impacting the life/lives of others? When I gave school advice to a friend and then saw her pass it on to all of her friends and so on.

How do you feel you influence moms offline? Is it more than chatting in the carpool line? Yes, it's lots of conversations and examples, and I get called for advice when moms see something my child has or has done or that I have done in the community.

How can companies best support your business or mission as a mom? MAKE LIFE EASIER. Stop overwhelming me with information that I don't want or need. I get too many emails, etc., and once I decide I don't want to participate, go away.

What motivates you to tell other moms (good or bad) about a company, brand or product? My personal experience. If it's great I will share, if it's horrible I will share, if it's neither I do not share, so amaze me, but don't disappoint me.

Name: Dori DeCarlo

Children: Three, ages 22, 21, and 18

Hometown: Bristol, CT

Company Name(s): S1 ~ The CLEAR Advantage!

Short description of business: S1 has a full line of clear bags and backpacks that assist with the safety issues in our schools, offices, airports, sports arenas and other public venues. S1—for Safety First—began after Columbine. As a mom I couldn't imagine what it would be like to kiss my children good-bye in the morning and not have them return from school because someone who was angry with the world smuggled in a gun. I wanted to design bags that would work for all as parents want safety, kids want cool. My children were instrumental in the design of our clear bags and backpacks. We began in 2005, and it took years in field testing, finding the right manufacturer and saving the money to start as I was unable to get funding. The first 4 bags were our Backpack, Mini Backpack (because I dislike seeing small children carry a backpack that hits them in the knees when they walk), Messenger Bag and Wheelchair Bag. The Wheelchair Bag was among the first products because I have worked with people with mobility issues, and didn't want to say to a kid in a wheelchair that *someday* our company will make a bag for you. Because of the rise of neck and back strain in our children, I worked with chiropractors on the ergonomic design of our bags so they would be healthy for the body. I'm a mom so I know where the bags break and added reinforced fabric-lined seams and heavy zippers and use the thickest materials available because I know how tough kids are on their bags. As we expanded into the workplace, so did our product line and then the Transportation Security Administration approached different bag manufacturers to ask us to develop checkpoint friendly laptop bags and backpacks, so we added them to our line; since it is not the "clear" that makes them checkpoint friendly, we developed a Made in the USA line that is 100% green! All in all we now have 19 different bags and backpacks in our line.

Websites or Blogs you own: Sl The Clear Advantage http://www.slbags.com, Sl The Clear Advantage http://www.slcheckpointfriendlybags.com, Word of Mom http://www.wordofmom.ning.com, Sl The Clear Advantage http://promoteclientsandsafetytogether.blogspot.com

Websites or blogs you contribute to: Online Security Authority, Entrepreneurial Success Stories

Facebook Id: Dori DeCarlo

Twitter Id: @Dori_Sl_Bags

Approximate # of followers: 2100

Online Involvements and associations: BlogTalkRadio Show Word of Mom, DSWA, NAFE, NAWBO, NFIB–Leadership Council BOD. I have been asked to participate in a number of panels for Mompreneurs and Entrepreneurs and do so whenever my schedule permits.

Offline Involvements: National Federation of Independent Business—I am on the Leadership Council Board of Directors and part of the Small Business Boot camp that was held in December 2010 for the new legislators: the camp helps legislators understand the needs of small business owners before they enact laws that will affect those owners! DSWA—Direct Selling Women's Association is a group in which I have just become involved. We meet monthly and I will be doing some speaking at their events. I also speak at different groups and showcases and schools on business building, marketing without a budget and the importance of an Elevator Pitch! I do business coaching and mentoring—sometimes for a fee—other times to give back.

What's the best way for companies to reach you as an influencer or as a mom? Sincerity! Whether it is a TV, radio, print or online ad or communication keep it real and it will resonate with me and I will, in turn, share it with others.

How do you feel you influence moms online? I try to share other Mompreneurs and their products and services through the social media sites I am active on and especially with Word of Mom on BlogTalkRadio.

Is there one moment when you realized you were impacting the life/lives of others? Through our product line I know that I have stopped someone from bringing something into schools that could harm others—and if I only stopped one—then I have done my job. My happiest moment within social media has been through my BTR show Word of Mom. One of my listeners and friends that I "met" on Twitter was one of the recipients of the Huggies® MomInspired™ Grants—how amazing is that!

How do you feel companies can best connect with moms, particularly those who are influencers? Supporting our missions by finding out who we are and what we do is a great way. They have advertising and marketing dollars that they should earmark for Mom-owned—not just women-owned—companies. Huggies is a great example of looking to moms to assist them with products and services that are making other moms' lives easier! More companies should follow suit and reach out to those Mompreneurs making a difference, and they should support our companies and missions. We are active online and they have the IT personnel to find us!

Final words: Moms support moms—which is what can set Mompreneurs apart from Entrepreneurs and Businesswomen. As new moms we turn to seasoned moms for advice and support. As our children grow, moms are there to help get them off the bus, carpool to school or games and share our children's triumphs and tough moments. When we begin home-based businesses other Mompreneurs become our mentors, guides and support systems. Politically we need to become active in supporting candidates who understand that family and small business go hand-in-hand. Social Media has taken us to new heights as we can reach other moms across the street or across continents. We support, educate and empower each other and I am proud that I am a Mompreneur that is making a difference in the lives of others!

Name: Jessica Denay

Chidlren: One, age 10

Hometown: Los Angeles, CA

Company Name(s): Hot Moms Club and Hollywood Hot Moms

Short description of business: Hot Moms Club is a multimedia brand on the pulse of celebrity mom trends but we help make them accessible to every mom. We speak to the moms as women, not just as parents, we believe you are not the best mom unless you are the best YOU! We see every mom as a Hot Mom; it is an attitude, a way of being, and it doesn't matter what age, shape or size, we help break loose the "Hot Mom" inside of you!

Hot Moms Club was started in Feb 2005 by my friend Joy Bergin and me, and it started out as a joke in my living room. We didn't have any business experience, we didn't even know what a domain name was! But we had a great idea and the timing was perfect. The web was different then, no one had heard of Youtube or Facebook.

We were one of the first sites to speak to moms in a cool empowering way, letting them know that motherhood broadened and expanded them, that they were not merely "just a mom." It was a fun concept, permission to still be fabulous after childbirth! Our motto resonated with mothers everywhere as well as with celebrity moms and we quickly had a devoted following.

Websites or Blogs you own: Hot Moms Club www.HotMomsClub.com, Hollywood Hot Moms www.HollywoodHotMoms.com

Approximate audience size: 68K

Websites or blogs you contribute to: www.people.com/ babies, OKmagazine.com, USmagazine.com/moms and babies

Facebook Id: Hot Moms Club

Approximate # of followers: 6K

Twitter Id: @HotMomsClubBuzz

Approximate # of followers: 3.5K

Online Involvements and associations: Brand Ambassador for Reebok Easy Tone shoes and the Ambassador for Youth for the National PTA

How many moms do you typically interact with during the week offline? 25-30

Offline Involvements: I spend my free time with my son or friends and family hiking, traveling or going to the beach. The Hot Moms Club hosts many celebrity events, most of which have a charity component; we have helped raise over 100K dollars and products for various charities. I also attend and support many charity events and functions.

How is the best way to work with you and your company? We have a 360 marketing approach, combining online, print, TV, high profile events, sampling and celebrity gifting.

Are there companies who you feel are doing a great job connecting with moms? Suave ran a great campaign a few years back, one of their tag lines was, " Don't let your kid's school bus be the only thing that turns heads!" It was brilliant. They also had a hilarious webisode series called In The Motherhood with Leah Remini and Jenny McCarthy.

Is there one moment when you realized you were impacting the life/lives of others? We received emails from moms all the time thanking us for our message and the content in our site and books, and it always makes you feel good to read that. I have also had friends who have seen me work hard to build the brand and business tell me how it inspires them and gives them hope that they can succeed in their dreams and pursuits.

Final words: Moms will always be powerful influencers of spending. As women we love to talk and socialize. The Internet and tools today make connecting so much easier and faster for us to spread advice and tips and ideas. As this medium grows so will our influence and voices.

Name: Melissa Denton

Children: I have fostered 5 in the past year and a half

Hometown: Loveland, CO

Company Name(s): MomTV's Adoption Angles

Short description of business: A weekly show on MomTV all about adoption. In January of 2009 I debuted MomTV's Adoption Angles. My mission for the show is for it to be informative, inspirational AND *FUN*. Although my heart is in foster care, the hope is to get the word out about all avenues of adoption (Fost/Adopt, Domestic & International) and also, to celebrate the people involved. My guests have ranged from birth moms, adoptees, authors, professionals (therapists), an Emmy award winner and families that have adopted. They share the good, the bad and the ugly. One thing they have in common is their passion for adoption and sharing the positives. So far, each and every guest has moved me to tears. No joke. I have no exit strategy and plan on doing the show as long as the Good Lord allows.

Websites or Blogs you own: Full Circle www.ourfullcircle.com and Host: MomTV's Adoption Angles http://www.momtv.com/adoption-angles

Approximate audience size: 200+ blog followers and the show varies by week

Websites or blogs you contribute to: Past contributions include: Mile High Mamas, The Classy Closet, Stirrup Queen's Crème de la Crème, MomTV, and Bridges

Facebook Id: Melissa Veete-Denton

Twitter Id: @FullCircle_Mel

Approximate # of followers: 900

How many moms do you typically interact with during the week offline? Hundreds ... I work full-time outside of our home.

Offline Involvements: We are also involved with rescue and foster dogs for a national group, in addition to our own 6 canines. Yes, we're nuts. As a certified fost/adopt mommy, I volunteer working booths for our county at local events to help raise awareness for our children in need. The goal is to recruit possible foster parents or respite care providers. I answer questions and chat about our amazing experiences (not giving specific case information, of course!).

What's the best way for companies to reach you as an influencer or as a mom? Email: adoptionangles.momtv@gmail.com

Are there companies who you feel are doing a great job connecting with moms? Kimochis, Build A Bear, Incredibeds and SkinCareRX

How do you define influence among moms? Creating big change lead by passionate women. Never mess with a mom on a mission!

How do you feel you influence moms online? With simple honesty, I think the mere act of sharing our journey and telling it "like it is," is very powerful. Fostering to adopt is not butterflies and warm fuzzies all the time, but our triumphs and joys outweigh the hard times. My readers/viewers laugh and cry with us, they fall in love with children whose names and faces they'll never know. They pray for the children's safety and well-being. Most importantly, they see for themselves that our children in the system are not hopeless and can blossom when provided the right environment. The bottom line? The beautiful children that come and go from our lives are the real influencers. I am just the one honored to share with others our experiences as best I can.

Is there one moment when you realized you were impacting the life/lives of others? The first time I got an email from a reader letting me know they were inspired to "jump off the fence" and start their own adoption journey. That was awesome!

Final words: Naysayers beware: we are a force to be reckoned with. Not only are we smart, tech savvy, and love our family deeply—we've got friends worldwide that have our backs.

Name: Niki DiSilvio

Children: One, age 5

Hometown: Sicklerville, NJ

Websites or Blogs you own: Free 2 Be Frugal http://www.free2befrugal.com

Approximate audience size: 1,500

Twitter Id: @Free2BFrugal

Approximate # of followers: 190

Online Involvements and associations: One2One Network, Mom Select, Team Mom, Book Sneeze blogger, Tyndale Book blogger, My Blog Spark, SheSpeaks, Vocalpoint, Pssst..., MyGetTogether (general mills), All You Reality Checker, Kraft First Taste

Are there companies who you feel are doing a great job connecting with moms? Pampers, Huggies

How do you define influence among moms? Becoming a mom is like entering this secret club ... this whole world exists that you never even knew about when you were a young single or newlywed ... moms join forces to share information about issues and talk about absolutely everything at those playdates, at the pediatrician office waiting room, at the swingset ....

How do you feel you influence moms online? I share with moms to tell them how to save money (because raising a kiddo is $$$) and how to be a smart consumer, an educated shopper.

How do you feel you influence moms offline? Is it more than chatting in the carpool line? You just never know who you meet in the course of a week. Moms are everywhere and even people of higher celebrity are moms, too. I was recently at a MOPS meeting and was chatting to this lady who was asking about my blog (she heard about it from an acquaintance) and here she turns out to be the former Miss New Jersey. If one mom tells one person about something they love (be it a doctor, a product, a play place) then that person takes it back to their main group of mom friends, and the friends spread it. That's a whole lot of communication (and power!).

How can companies best support your business or mission as a mom? I love that so many moms are able to check out the newest products, especially bloggers. I mean, doctor recommended products are nice, but a mom-approved product? Now THAT is one that I want to buy! Some businessman or doctor isn't the person who has stayed up all night with a sick, cranky baby or tried to feed a finicky toddler. A mom does those things. So a mom KNOWS what will work and what doesn't.

What motivates you to tell other moms (good or bad) about a company, brand or product? I think we all look back at those early days of being a mom and how we felt as if we had no idea what we were doing. How could you NOT want to pay it forward? I see those frazzled moms in the stores, at the park, and I just want to help them and let them know there's a light at the end of the tunnel. There's a book, or a group, or a product, or something that will make life easier so that they can simply enjoy their calling—their children.

How do you feel companies can best connect with moms, particularly those who are influencers? Surveys are cool, blog reviews and giveaways are great, too. But there is nothing that can compare to getting moms together! We love to talk and talk and talk. And a group of ladies (especially moms) can cover so much ground, so many topics in an hour's time.

Final words: Moms definitely influence every area. When a mom wants to be heard the sky is the limit. We will find other moms and we will join together for a cause.

Name: Lisa Druxman

Children: Two, ages 9 and 5

Hometown: San Diego CA

Company Name(s): Stroller Strides

Short description of business: Stroller Strides is one of the fastest growing franchises in the nation. We offer fitness classes for moms at any stage of motherhood. Stroller Strides was one of those "ah-ha moments" in life. I was a new mom on maternity leave and every moment was precious to me. I loved working in the fitness industry but did not want to go back to work full-time in a traditional capacity. Unfortunately, I could not afford to be a stay-at-home mom. So while working out with my son, I realized that I could help other moms get back into shape if I put a class together. This would help me, too, because I did not know any new moms and was looking for a way to connect. I came up with the name on that very walk. I started with just a few moms in my local neighborhood and word soon spread and we grew quickly from there. Just after starting that first class, we started getting requests for classes all over San Diego, so we kept adding more. By the end of the first year, we had over 12 classes and 1,000 moms participating in San Diego. During that first year, we got requests for classes all over the country. At the time, I had no idea how I would accomplish that one. Then one of my instructors said that she was moving and wanted to start classes in her new town. I agreed and gave her all the plans to run her own classes. She was a hit. We then decided to release 10 "beta" locations across the country to see how it would work in other cities. We learned a lot, tweaked a few things, and then they were a hit. We hired attorneys, worked with consultants and joined the International Franchise Association. We are now franchised across the country and have over 300 franchisees.

Location of business: Corporate office is in San Marcos but we have 1,200 locations nationwide.

Websites or Blogs you own: Stroller Strides www.strollerstrides.com, www.lisadruxman.com, Body Back Workout www.bodybackworkout.com.

Approximate audience size: 65,000

Websites or blogs you contribute to: www.strollerstrides.com/blog, www.drgreene.com

Facebook Id: Lisa Druxman and Stroller Strides

Twitter Id: @LisaDruxman

Approximate # of followers: 2,000

Online Involvements and associations: Healthy Child, Healthy World, Dr.Greene.com, Pregnancy Awareness Month.com

How many moms do you typically interact with during the week offline? 100

Offline Involvements: Stroller Strides, Fit4Baby, Body Back, volunteering as ambassador for collaboration with Healthy Child Healthy World and Jamie Oliver's Food Revolution

How is the best way to work with you and your company? There are so many opportunities, we do everything from sampling to special events. We are very good at creating custom opportunities that match the company. For instance a diaper derby was a fit for Pampers. We created the LUNA Moms Club with Luna bar. The best thing is to reach out to our marketing director at marketing@strollerstrides.com. Not all companies are a fit. Our customers trust us to promote/endorse companies that are like-minded with us. We look for healthy, eco-friendly companies whenever possible.

What do you think is the biggest mistake companies make in trying to work with moms? I think companies are mistaken to make blanket assumptions about all moms being the same. A working mom has very different needs than a stay-at-home mom, for instance. We don't want to be patronized. We want companies to value all that we do and all the balls that we juggle.

Are there companies who you feel are doing a great job connecting with moms? I'm always a fan of Disney and how they keep up with the times and communicating to moms, from blogs, to Twitter, to podcasts.

How do you feel you influence moms online? I think I influence moms because I share my real life experiences. They see me ask questions, share products and companies that I like, and they see that I don't endorse just anything that comes my way.

How do you feel you influence moms offline? Is it more than chatting in the carpool line? Moms are always asking each other (myself included) for referrals for companies, doctors, etc. It happens at playdates, moms nights out, and at workouts. Last week, I put out a tweet asking for a referral for a doctor. I have trusted sources who, if they point me in a certain direction, I will go without question.

How can companies best support your business or mission as a mom? My mission is to raise healthy moms so that they can raise healthy children. We do not feel the need to be the expert in all things. If companies feel they can help support that mission, we want to work with them!

What motivates you to tell other moms (good or bad) about a company, brand or product? I think there are lots of good companies but very few great ones. So, any time I encounter a great product or great service, I want to tell people about it.

How do you feel companies can best connect with moms, particularly those who are influencers? Reach out. Get creative and think about how potential customers can experience your product. I get lots of companies who send us sample products. We cannot and do not promote each that is sent. However, sometimes it's a great way for us to experience something new.

Final words: I believe there is great power when moms come together for a cause. While one cause may seem too overwhelming for a single mom, it is easily achievable when taken on by a team of moms. I think all moms should realize their influence and power and get together to speak out about their beliefs.

Name: Melanie Edwards

Children: Two, ages 5 and baby expected Dec. 2010
Hometown: Orlando, FL

Company Name(s): Ella Media & ModernMami.com

Short description of business: Ella Media provides digital marketing and consulting services for large brands, small businesses, and social media-savvy women. The goal of Ella Media is to connect businesses with today's digital Latina to create valuable partnerships and social media campaigns. Ella Media launched in September 2010. More and more brands are leveraging the reach of social media Latinas. Brands and the PR agencies representing them are interested in marketing to Latinas and many times look to our community for help in doing so. With the continually growing digital Latina community, it was the perfect time for Ella Media to provide a much-needed service.

Websites or Blogs you own: Modern Mami http://www.modernmami.com; 40 weeks + Modern Mami http://40weeks.modernmami.com; Ella Media http://www.ellamedia.com/blog

Approximate audience size: 5,500 monthly unique visitors and 7500 monthly page views.

Facebook Id: ModernMami.com

Twitter Id: @modernmami

Approximate # of followers: 7,000+

Online Involvements and associations: Brand ambassador for a variety of brands, including Kellogg's, General Mills/Qué Rica Vida, and Vme TV.

What's the best way for companies to reach you as an influencer or as a mom? Email: melanie@modernmami.com

What do you think is the biggest mistake companies make in trying to work with moms? A lot of times moms are viewed as one big market or niche. The reality is that there is a vast variety of parenting styles, needs, and women within the mom community. Not all moms are interested in the same products, topics, and information.

Are there companies who you feel are doing a great job connecting with moms? Kellogg's and General Mills' Qué Rica Vida

How do you feel companies can best connect with moms, particularly those who are

influencers? Creating a connection, dialogue, or relationship via company representatives is key to engaging with moms. We have many resources at our disposal, and providing one-way information or messages via traditional press releases or advertising is not as effective as personally reaching out to moms.

Name: Erika Engberg

Children: Three, ages 4, 2, and 1

Hometown: Colorado Springs, CO

Company Name(s): Simply Cute

Short description of business: We are a new and used online clothing resale store carrying brand names such as Gymboree, Janie and Jack, Crazy 8, The Children's Place, Gap, and Old Navy. We also carry handmade items such as hair bows, décor, etc., for little kids. We started around the beginning of 2010 and were mainly motivated by a love of resale and a love of crafting. Wanting to make a little extra spending money to help out of family of 7 (with the two stepchildren) that was relying on only one income, I decided to open my own online shop.

Websites or Blogs you own: Simply Cute Kids http://www.simplycutekids.blogspot.com

Facebook Id: Simply Cute

Approximate # of followers: 70

How is the best way to work with you and your company? Email simplycutekids@rocketmail.com

What do you think is the biggest mistake companies make in trying to work with moms? I think that companies don't do a good job of building a relationship with their clients.

How do you feel you influence moms offline? Is it more than chatting in the carpool line? I can't tell you how many people would have never given a second thought to couponing until they saw my cart loads of groceries and saw me pay only 1/3 the regular cost! It's amazing when people are looking at you in awe and you can show them that it really isn't that hard and you can teach them to save money as well.

How can companies best support your business or mission as a mom? To keep their products and services kid-friendly and kid-safe and to really promote the quality of "mom and me" time. To keep their products reasonably priced so that moms everywhere can enjoy them and benefit from them. It really depends on the company, I guess, but remembering that their audience is moms is the first step.

How do you feel companies can best connect with moms, particularly those who are influencers? Offering the opportunity to try their product is huge because then the mom will talk it up (word of mouth) and that really grabs attention. Offering great deals and discounts on the product so that the mom has a chance to get it or try it because again, it is word of mouth that goes farther than anything else!

Final words: I would really like to see more home schooling moms out there influencing the world! There is such a negative view of home school in society and I deal with it on a constant basis since I home school my own children. Moms need to be out there proving to the world why it works, why it isn't just a destiny to ruin your kids' self-esteem and social life, and that home schooled kids have the same advantages as any other.

Name: Melissa Erickson

Children: Three, ages 14, 12, and 11

Hometown: Madison, WI

Company Name(s): Your Fun Family

Short description of business: Your Fun Family is your source for all things family. Our goal is to help families find fun ways to spend time together and make memories that will last a lifetime. We also have webhosting and consult in social media marketing. I started the original website in 2008. As I shared with my daughters things that I loved doing as a child, I realized that many families get trapped in a busy lifestyle and they do not find the time to pass these things on to their children. I hoped to inspire a few families to set aside the time to pass things on to their children and make some great memories.

Websites or Blogs you own: Your Fun Family http://yourfunfamily.com, Your Fun Family blog http://yourfunfamily.blogspot.com, Erickson Duoservers http://erickson.duoservers.com

Approximate audience size: 7,000

Facebook Id: Melissa Erickson

Twitter Id: @YourFunFamily

Approximate # of followers: 1,500

Online Involvements and associations: Brand Ambassador for The View television show, a Soft Scrub Club Captain, an Event Chaser, Team Mom, Music Moms, Book Review Blogger for Thomas Nelson Publishing, and I am currently working with Wet Ones to promote their new Wet Ones Healthy Hands Zone. I do frequent product reviews and giveaways for many brands in addition to working with CSN, MyBlogSpark, and UPrinting on a monthly basis. I attended Baking With Betty which was an all expense paid blogger event at the General Mills headquarters. I will also be attending an all expense paid blogger event for Crayola in NYC .

How many moms do you typically interact with during the week offline? 200

Offline Involvements: I am very involved at my children's schools and in the community. My daughters are in band, choir, Math Meet, Art Club, Battle of the Books, and Student Action Committee.

What's the best way for companies to reach you as an influencer or as a mom? Email: melissa@yourfunfamily.com

Are there companies who you feel are doing a great job connecting with moms? CSN, General Mills, and Crayola (through MyBlogSpark). CSN allows me to pick what I review. As a mom, I know what moms would be interested in seeing. MyBlogSpark realizes that the combination of a review and giveaway creates the best ROI.

How do you define influence among moms? Moms have the weight of the whole family resting on their shoulders. They are overworked and underpaid, but at the end of the day it is all worth it. A mom looks at ads by actresses and athletes but there is no connection. These are people that she has nothing in common with. They do not know her life and her struggles. A mom wants to hear from another mom, someone who is more real to her, someone who has the same needs as she does.

How do you feel you influence moms offline? Is it more than chatting in the carpool line? I have found that people come to me for advice on what to buy since they figure I know more about the different brands.

Final words: Moms are building the future every day. They are running their homes and creating core values in tomorrow's decision makers. They influence every aspect of life and they want to hear from people they respect, especially other moms.

Name: Dr. Yakini Etheridge

Children: Two, 21 months and 11 weeks (both boys)

Hometown: New York, NY

Short Description of business: My blog was initially created as a way for family/friends (who live out of town) to stay abreast of my journey into motherhood. It has since expanded into a place where I also review products. I love helping other moms cut out all the guess work by showing them what's out there, how it can benefit their family, and whether it's worth spending their hard earned money to buy it or not.

Websites or Blogs you own: The Prissy Mommy Chronicles www.prissymommy.com, The Prissy Mommy Reviews & Giveaways www.prissymommy.com/pr

Approximate audience size: 540 subscribed readers

Websites or blogs you contribute to: Mom Fuse, Noir Mommies, My Brown Baby, Bellyitch, and A Lil' Butter

Facebook Id: The Prissy Mommy Life

Approximate # of followers: 2,000

Twitter Id: @ThePrissyMommy

Approximate # of followers: 1,840

Online Involvements and associations: Snapfish Selects VIP Program, Mom Blogger with Washington FAMILY Magazine

How many moms do you typically interact with during the week offline? 20-25 daily

Offline Involvements: I'm a member of Delta Sigma Theta Sorority, Inc. Also, I work full time at a hospital. I'm the psychologist on a multidisciplinary treatment team that consists of a nurse, social worker, psychiatrist, physician, occupational therapist, recreational therapist, and psychologist (me). These are primarily moms and we interact and converse daily. I'm an active member of the Board of Directors for my sons' daycare.

What's the best way for companies to reach you as an influencer or as a mom? By email at mochatini@gmail.com

What do you think is the biggest mistake companies make in trying to work with moms? 1) Not including enough moms of color in some of their events/opportunities, and 2) Making certain opportunities only available to moms who are home during the day.

Are there companies who you feel are doing a great job connecting with moms? Build-A-Bear (always active throughout the seasons), Unilver (especially the Dove self-esteem/beauty campaigns), Pampers

How do you feel you influence moms offline? Is it more than chatting in the carpool line? Most of my influence happens at work or the daycare board meeting. Now that all my co-workers know that I'm a blogger who reviews products, they are always curious to know what the latest, hottest product is for themselves or their kids. Many people aren't familiar with blogging or social media (especially my older coworkers) but they have learned a lot from me about it, and through different experiences I've shared with them they've come to respect it a great deal. They see me as a credible source, and the fact that various companies want to work with me seems to further validate me in their eyes. So when I suggest something in a meeting, it becomes the focus of conversation and everyone is eager to try it out with their family. They often come back and give me feedback about what they've tried, based on something I may have recommended or spoken about (even casually).

How can companies best support your business or mission as a mom? To continue to be open to working with a mom who is also a full-time, professional working woman, as most of my offline networking/outreach is done in that setting. Specifically, I think companies should consider having more events in the evening, since every "mom blogger" isn't a stay-/work-at-home mom. I miss a lot of really great events that I know my readers would have loved to learn about, because they take place during time slots that just don't work for me (*i.e.*, 11 a.m.–1 p.m. is a popular mom blogger event time slot). My maternity leave was so great for the simple reason that I've been able to attend many of those daytime events. But now that has ended, and I'm disappointed that once again I'll be feeling out of the loop. In the end, it's really my readers who miss out most, because I can't share with them.

Name: Dian Farmer

Children: Four, ages 28, 26, 20, and 13

Hometown: Arlington, TX

Company Name(s): HouseMenders Of Texas

Short description of business: HouseMenders of Texas began in 2002 to help our family finances. My husband had a full-time job, we were also volunteer youth pastors at our church at that time, and I was looking for a way to contribute monetarily. My brother began the business in New Mexico and helped guide me to begin the same business. After 4 years, my husband was able to quit his full-time job and come home and run the "family" business. I then moved on to a full-time eBay business and finally to my current project—my website—Grocery Shop For FREE.

Websites or Blogs you own: Grocery Shop For FREE http://www.GroceryShopForFREE.com

Websites or blogs you contribute to: Inexpensively

Facebook Id: Grocery Shop For FREE

Twitter Id: @GroceryShopFREE, @CheckThisOutNow

Approximate # of followers: 5,540

Online Involvements and associations: Inexpensively, VocalPoint, She Speaks, Role Mommy

How do you feel you influence moms online? I share thoughts and ideas and conclusions and hope that I give enough information that they can make an informed choice.

How do you feel you influence moms offline? Is it more than chatting in the carpool line? As a pastor's wife I have an entirely different opportunity to influence moms offline. I take both online and offline opportunities very seriously.

How can companies best support your business or mission as a mom? Again, respect what "power we wield" within the community. Treat us with respect and we are more than willing to help you with your goals as long as we feel heard and respected.

How do you feel companies can best connect with moms, particularly those who are influencers? Reach out–Twitter or email and let us talk to you. I personally LOVE being able to reach a PR person by Twitter or email when a Customer Service line isn't answering my questions or returning my calls. I LOVE that I can reach out and get answers!

Name: Amy Filip

Children: Two, ages 3 and 1

Hometown: Bolingbrook, IL

Company Name(s): Anchor Insurance

Websites or blogs you contribute to: Facebook Mom Groups, Myspace Mom Groups, BabyCenter Groups

Facebook Id: Amy Filip

Twitter Id: @Peachy4995

Approximate # of followers: 30

Online Involvements and associations: Mom groups mostly, political activist groups, cooking groups

What's the best way for companies to reach you as an influencer or as a mom? I usually look at companies or opportunities that offer me some sort of reward for participating. I spend a lot of time looking at things online, so even point rewards are a nice motivator for me to use a certain company.

How is the best way to work with you and your company? Email: peachy4995@yahoo.com

How can companies best support your business or mission as a mom? I think companies can support me as a mom by recognizing how to contact me. I prefer email because my phone time is limited and I like to handle most things after my kids have gone to bed late at night when most companies would be closed. I think that companies need to realize that we are not all soccer moms. I'm a part-time worker and full-time mom, so I have different priorities than just a SAHM.

What motivates you to tell other moms (good or bad) about a company, brand or product? I tend to tell people more often when a company wrongs me, but I am trying to also spread good reviews as well. I find that if it's something child related, my mom friends really do need to know, so that they don't make the same mistakes that I do, or can make good choices like I have. With child-related products, even if a child's safety and health are not involved, their emotions are.

Name: Tonya Filleman

Children: Four, ages 11, 9, 6 and 2

Hometown: Omaha, NE

Company Name(s): My "business" is called Pleasantly Piano.

Short description of business: February 2009. I started it because I LOVE music and everything about it. I want others to experience the joy that music can bring. I have no exit strategy other than referring them to other teachers should I decide to quit.

Websites or Blogs you own: Nebraska Hockey Mom
www.nebraskahockeymom.blogspot.com,
Nebraska Filleman's www.nebraskafillemans.blogspot.com,
Pleasantly Piano www.pleasantlypiano.blogspot.com

Approximate audience size: A little over 125 are subscribed or follow...but I get MANY hits per day.

Facebook Id: Tonya Stutzman Filleman

Twitter Id: @Nefillemans

Approximate # of followers: 40+

Online Involvements and associations: Mom Select

Offline Involvements: Bible Study and Mops child care coordinator, school PTO, headhunter for a financial advisor, Junior High Leader at our church, I also am a Susan G. Komen speaker of breast cancer dangers, delivery of food, etc., for our Open Door Mission.

What do you think is the biggest mistake companies make in trying to work with moms? Assuming that if they are a stay-at-home mom they have all the time in the world. That is SO untrue. I have less time now than when I worked full time. Life is CRAZY busy ... and anything that will make life easier is wonderful in my book.

Are there companies who you feel are doing a great job connecting with moms? Mops International, Mom Select.

Is there one moment when you realized you were impacting the life/lives of others? When my mom died I was asked to write a book and also to be a speaker about Breast Cancer. It was then that I realized that my blogging about my mom's horrible disease was helping others.

How can companies best support your business or mission as a mom? With free products to review, or free handouts to give to other moms regarding something important in their lives, such as breast cancer or raising children.

What motivates you to tell other moms (good or bad) about a company, brand or product? I just always tell others ... whether they ask or not. I won't hold back if it is negative, and the positive speaks for itself. I think making a life easier for moms is really important, so if I find a product that will do that, I will let others know. Likewise, if I find a product that will make their life more difficult, I will let them know that, too.

How do you feel companies can best connect with moms, particularly those who are influencers? Free product reviews ... even if they don't have a blog. Many moms are at least on Facebook, or some sort of social media. Find thank-you opportunities: moms LOVE to be thanked ... even if it is just an email, any small token is much appreciated.

Final words: I wish that more moms would take a stand on voting. So many of us are stuck at home day in and day out and we watch cartoons ... not the news. We need to be better informed, though, and we need to go out and vote because all the changes being made are going to effect the moms even more than some others. An example is the health care bill that will increase our premiums. We are one-income families ... and now we have to pay MORE for insurance and get LESS care. It makes LITTLE to NO sense. We need to be better informed and take a stand!

Name: Laura (aka Lolli) Franklin

Children: Five, ages 14, 11, 9½, 7, and 5

Hometown: Gaithersburg, MD

Company Name(s): Simply You Photos

Short description of business: I am a one-woman custom photography studio, specializing in newborns all the way to weddings and back full circle. I started my photography company, slowly at first, in the beginning of 2008. I started taking pictures of friends and family and slowly expanded to their friends and family members, until it has grown to a very successful home business for me.

Websites or Blogs you own: Better in Bulk http://betterinbulk.net/

Approximate audience size: 10,000 readers per month

Facebook Id: Better in Bulk

Twitter Id: @1momof5

Approximate # of followers: 5,320

Online Involvements and associations: Faculty mom for the Pepperidge Farms Fishful Thinking ambassador program, Genesis Today VIP Pit Crew blogger, Aquafina Moms, Yoursphere Ambassador mom

How many moms do you typically interact with during the week offline? 20

Offline Involvements: Book club, church youth program (week nights), PTA/volunteering at school, Sunday church teaching.

How is the best way to work with you and your company? Social media and more traditional "word of mouth" have been the most successful for me. The majority of my business comes from Facebook.

Are there companies who you feel are doing a great job connecting with moms? I think Pepperidge Farm has done a great job connecting with moms. I'm also impressed with the things that Disney and Walmart have done.

How do you define influence among moms? I think influence is a balance between reach and trust. It doesn't matter how many people hear your words if there is no trust present. However, a small handful of people who hear a message from a trusted friend will have a long-term impact.

What motivates you to tell other moms (good or bad) about a company, brand or product? I will typically get into conversations about products when I am asked directly about them (for instance, if someone has read my review and wants more information or if a person sees me using a product) as well as when I hear someone talking about a product or expressing a need that might be helped by a product I've tried or a brand I've worked with.

How do you feel companies can best connect with moms, particularly those who are influencers? I think that companies need to involve more moms in long-term conversations and projects versus one-stop reviews or sponsored posts. The more time I've spent as a Faculty Mom for Fishful Thinking, the more of an asset I feel I am to the company, and the more I can give back.

Name: Sandra Frawley

Children: Two, ages 10 and 6

Hometown: Greenwood Lake, New York

Company Name(s): babybindle (The Babybindle Company, LLC)

Short description of business: babybindle is a manufacturer of simple, affordable and modern diaper bags. Our launching product, the SeatPak, won the 2010 Huggies® MomInspired™ Grant Award. The SeatPak attaches to the handle of a car seat, eliminating the need for a traditional diaper bag. Our Diapurse Collection, which will be launched in the spring of 2011, simplifies the diaper bag. The purse/diaper bag-in-one eliminates the need to carry two bags. They are affordable yet stylish for the busy mom or dad. babybindle was born in September 2010 with $15,000 seed money from the 2010 Huggies® MomInspired™ Grant Program. With an invention, a grant and a dream, I launched my company babybindle with a mission in mind: to be the #1 manufacturer of diaper bags in the United States and abroad.

Websites or Blogs you own: babybindle www.babybindle.com

Twitter Id: @babybindle

Approximate # of followers: 239 & growing

Biggest mistake companies make when working with moms: Not realizing what a force mothers are. With all the networking via social sites, church mommy groups, you name it, there is usually a mom there who can influence other mothers. A few mothers I know do not have Twitter or Facebook accounts, yet influence other mothers via playgroups, music classes or on the playground.

One moment when I realized I was impacting the lives of others: By following my dreams I inspired others to do the same. A few have asked for advice and help finding their own road to the beginning of their own journey. Starting my own company has given me a confidence that shows in the way I connect with people, and inspires others to have confidence in themselves. I have also realized that by doing, I have become a role model for other moms and, most importantly, for my children.

Name: Alaina Frederick

Children: Three, ages 7, 5, and 3 (all boys)

Hometown: Pittsburgh, PA

Company Name(s): Dinker & Giggles

Short description of business: My main passion is Dinker & Giggles which I first started in September 2005 after catching the "cloth diaper bug." Dinker & Giggles has changed many times since it began. We are currently helping families raise their young "stinkers" into tomorrow's gentlemen with God and Mother Nature in mind. Having only boys, I knew how hard it was to find cute items for boys. I continue to have a passion for letting families know about great places for quality boy products as well as helping families introduce God and environmental issues in ways that make it fun for all involved.

Websites or Blogs you own: Dinker & Giggles http://dinkerandgiggles.com; Alaina Frederick http://alainafrederick.com

Approximate audience size: 3,200

Websites or blogs you contribute to: The M.O.B. Society

Facebook Id: Alaina Fuller Frederick; Dinker and Giggles

Approximate # of followers: 1,200

Twitter Id: @AlainaFrederick

Approximate # of followers: 2,970

Offline Involvements: MOPS, SEAPC

What's the best way for companies to reach you as an influencer or as a mom? The best way to reach me is via email, alaina@alainafrederick.com. I have a horrible habit of checking it every ten minutes!

How do you feel you influence moms online? I believe that moms know that I will only accept the best for my children. Having three boys and raising them purely on trial and error, I have learned what works and what doesn't. Moms know they can trust me, as I never do anything just solely based on money or free products, but only because I have a love for what I talk about.

How do you feel you influence moms offline? Is it more than chatting in the carpool line? Many moms know what I do online and the same rings true when chatting offline. Typically it's over a roll of Sushi and it's a time of bonding and sharing our "oh, crap" moments.

How can companies best support your business or mission as a mom? I'd love for companies that I know and trust to help me get more training. Things like affiliate training workshops and blogging conferences would be ideal to further my talents. In addition to this, by not "dumbing down" their materials and instead treating us like the educated and knowledgeable people we are.

How do you feel companies can best connect with moms, particularly those who are influencers? Reaching out via Facebook and Twitter is one of the quickest ways to strike up a conversation. Companies should make sure they are actively checking their @ and DM messages for positive and negative remarks. When it takes a company two weeks to reply to a question it really gets on my nerves. You don't want to make an influential mother angry.

Name: Emily Freelove

Children: Three, ages 16, 6, and 3

Hometown: Drummonds, TN

Company Name(s): Saving with a Plan

Short description of business: Life Coach

Websites or Blogs you own: Saving with a Plan www.savingwithaplan.com

Approximate audience size: 3000 monthly

Websites or blogs you contribute to: Viewpoints, raising Homemakers, My total Money makeover

Facebook Id: Emily SavingwithaPlan

Online Involvements and associations: Google Affiliate, CARE volunteer, Viewpoints

How many moms do you typically interact with during the week offline? 25

Offline Involvements: FPU Class, CARE volunteer, Angel Food Volunteer

What's the best way for companies to reach you as an influencer or as a mom? Email at savingwithaplan@gmail.com

How do you define influence among moms? Knowledge and a Voice is all you need to influence.

How can companies best support your business or mission as a mom? By providing my blog with products for giveaways and promotions.

Name: Natalie Gahrmann

Children: Two, ages 16 and 13

Hometown: Hillsborough, NJ

Company Name(s): The Priority Pro; N-R-G Coaching Associates

Short description of business: International expert who empowers professional women to ignite their passion, demonstrate personal leadership and exude greater confidence. This is instinctively applied through 1-1 coaching, workshops and keynote speaking. I launched Personal Best coaching company following the birth of my daughter in 1997 after accepting a voluntary termination package and enrolling in a professional training program for coaches. I then grew and evolved the company over the years. In 2002, I added professional speaking after publishing *Succeeding as a Super Busy Parent* and contributing expertise at several websites and resources for working mothers. I changed the name of my business to N-R-G Coaching Associates in 2003 when the business and resources were brought online. The mission today is to continue empowering Super Busy people by helping them develop strategies, support and structures that allow them to be their best personally and professionally.

Websites or Blogs you own: The Priority Pro www.theprioritypro.com www.nrgcoaching.com http://www.theprioritypro.com/resources/blog/; Succeeding as a Super Busy Parent www.superbusyparent.com;

Approximate audience size: 2,000

How many moms do you typically interact with during the week offline? 100+

What's the best way for companies to reach you as an influencer or as a mom? Email: natalie@theprioritypro.com

What do you think is the biggest mistake companies make in trying to work with moms? They make it too difficult or time-consuming for busy moms to gain personal benefit from their product or service.

How do you feel you influence moms online? I supply resources, tools and information in a practical and timely fashion that's easily accessible and simple to navigate.

Is there one moment when you realized you were impacting the life/lives of others? There have been several poignant moments when I've received powerful feedback from those whose lives I've had the privilege and opportunity to touch. What stands out for me is the collection of emails I received from my e-newsletter readers about how they apply the content , feedback and testimonials from coaching and speaking clients, and when readers asked me to publish a book with my tips and resources.

How do you feel you influence moms offline? Is it more than chatting in the carpool line? I motivate and empower moms everywhere I go through my patience, calm nature, positive attitude, and willingness to help. I volunteer within the community regularly where I know I can make a difference, including in the classroom where I've taught self-esteem, anti-bullying, and respect to students in grades 1-8. I am a role model (most of the time!) for living a conscious and balanced life based on my priorities.

How can companies best support your business or mission as a mom? Invite me to contribute to their companies through keynote speaking, workshops and articles in their print or online resources; sponsor events in the community where I can contribute my expertise; ask me to contribute to panels, advisory boards, be a brand ambassador or spokesperson; link to my articles and resources; request my expertise for your customer newsletters or online.

How do you feel companies can best connect with moms, particularly those who are influencers? Share your product with moms and let them experience it in a positive way!

Final word: Moms are the primary decision-makers for most things within the household so treat them with the respect they deserve!

Name: Cara Gawlik

Children: Two, ages 4 and 5 (both boys)

Hometown: San Antonio TX

Company Name(s): Blog: The Life Of A Coast Guard Wife

Short description of business: I mainly have a review/giveaway blog, letting others know about wonderful products I find. I also post about the crazy Coast Guard life.

Websites or Blogs you own: The Life Of A Coast Guard Wife http://thelifeofacoastguardwife.blogspot.com/

Approximate audience size: 569 followers

Facebook Id: The Life of a Coast Guard Wife

Approximate # of followers: 240

Twitter Id: @USCGWifey

Approximate # of followers: 780

Online Involvements and associations: Mom Bloggers Club, CSN preferred blogger

Offline Involvements: I am a proud soccer mom! I am about to start volunteering at the local animal shelter.

What's the best way for companies to reach you as an influencer or as a mom? USCGWifey@gmail.com

How do you define influence among moms? I believe all of us influence one another. Whether it is through product reviews, recipes, or advice about kids, we can all learn from each other!

Is there one moment when you realized you were impacting the life/lives of others? Every time I post a review and someone leaves a comment saying "Thank you for the awesome review."

Final words: Moms are strong by nature! There are some out there that think all we are good at is cooking and cleaning. That is so far from the truth! We can do anything we put our minds to. And the word of mouth from one mom to another is a very powerful thing that spreads like wild fire. I am a survivor from an abusive relationship. I know first hand how strong a mother is.

Name: Christie Glascoe Crowder

Children: Two, ages 6 and 3

Hometown: Atlanta, GA

Company Name(s): The BlogRollers Media

Short description of business: The BlogRollers Media specializes in creating unique and entertaining consumer experiences using multiple social media platforms in conjunction with in-person events to create awareness and promote brand loyalty. The majority of our experiences involve a physical activity, challenges, contests, and interactive social media components. The participants always include a diverse group of influential bloggers and journalists who (as part of their requirement to participate) chronicle their experiences on their blogs, online communities, publications, Twitter, Facebook, YouTube, and more. When we invite companies to partner with us, our goal is to match our program with the company's initiatives and marketing objectives to make the entire experience a win-win for everyone involved!

The BlogRollers Media was started on April 6, 2009, when Lorraine Robertson (AskWifey) and I had an idea to take a road trip to the 2009 BlogHer Conference. The original intent was to have fun while blogging, vlogging, and tweeting about our adventures on the road. We had no idea we were embarking on something BIG! Adding contests and giveaways as well as interactive live streaming video and live internet radio broadcasts caught the attention of bloggers and brands alike. The popularity of The BlogRollers increased our level of influence (individually and collectively) making us valuable to brands that use bloggers to market and spread their message. We are often asked to participate in, and/or to create digital media outreach campaigns for businesses. What began as a girlfriends' getaway is now a full-blown brand for social media marketing. We are all about promoting the power of bloggers and our impact on the economy and social media at large.

Websites or Blogs you own: Inside The ChatterBox http://christiecrowder, Yeah, Write! http://theyeahwriteblog.blogspot.com, The BlogRollers (http://theblogrollers.com)

Approximate audience size: 3,000 (subscribers/visitors)

Websites or blogs you contribute to: www.HybridMom.com and www.TypeTrigger.com

Facebook Id: Christie Glascoe Crowder, ChatterBox Christie Live and The BlogRollers

Twitter Id: @chatterboxcgc

Approximate # of followers: 4,700

Online Involvements and associations: Disney African-American Mom Bloggers, Heart of Haiti Ambassador, Lifetime Moms Affiliate, Child Hunger Ends Here Blogger Correspondent, BarkWorld Expo Conference Education Committee, AllConnect Advisory Panel

Offline Community Service: Food drives, clothing drives, and other fundraisers through my daughter's school. This summer I took a cross-country road trip from Atlanta to Albuquerque. Along the way we stopped in various cities doing social projects like volunteering at a food bank, helping to rebuild a home destroyed by Katrina, and planting vegetables on a farm for autistic women.

What's the best way for companies to reach you as an influencer or as a mom? Email is the best way to reach me and please don't address it "dear mom blogger." Try to convince me that you really have read my blog(s) and that you do truly in fact see synergies with my content, my audience, and your product.

What do you think is the biggest mistake companies make in trying to work with moms? From my experience, it is insulting our intelligence. Companies and PR firms apparently forget that most of us had "lives" before becoming mothers... before becoming bloggers. We were managers, executives, lawyers, doctors, accountants, teachers, administrators, etc. We worked in sales, marketing, and public relations. We worked in nonprofits, private sector, and government. Some of us are still in the corporate game. Some of us have hung our own shingle. Granted we all are plagued with "mommy-brain," but we haven't completely lost all of our past intelligence or experience. Don't assume a blogging mom is a desperate housewife with a little hobby. A blogging mom's conversation about your brand could reach farther and therefore have a larger, more measureable impact than that ad you just placed in a major magazine...don't assume she's not worth more than a product sample. Don't assume that your product sample is the only acceptable form of compensation... if she talked about your product for an hour, she worked; which brings me to another mistake that is kind of a spin off of this one. I affectionately call it "getting pimped": when you work with a brand once and they love you and love your ideas, so they regularly "pimp" you for your knowledge, expertise, and ideas...only you don't realize it until it's too late. The rep makes friends with you and has casual conversations with you and is asking your expertise on the sly. Next thing you know, the little "brainstorm" you had is now some full-blown marketing initiative and you have received ZERO credit and worse...ZERO compensation. What's even worse than that, is when they have bloggers participate in the initiative and you are not one of them! (Yes, I have had that happen to me.) With brands/reps I have a good relationship with, I don't mind "throwing a bone" every once in a while, but I've learned my lesson the hard way. I know when I'm starting to get "pimped" and I nip it in the bud. I have to politely remind them that this is in fact my job.

Oh, last thing ... I HATE when I get a form-email with a press release asking me to write about something that I have never seen or tried and tell my readers how great it is. I'm not going to write about anything I haven't tried for myself. They always end it with "If you need any more copy or images for your post, please let me know. I'll be happy to send it." Um, how about the product?

How do you define influence among moms? That's a hard one. I'm starting to hate the word influence. It is getting overused and the meaning is muddy. On the flip side, I feel that more of the true meaning of influence is coming out more than before but it's kind of too little, too late. When I first got started, it was a numbers game. Stats, comments, and followers. You lived or died by them. Along with the numbers, it was all about the "brand badges" you wore ... Walmart Moms, "This" Mom, "That" Mom, etc. Or what brand "trip" you got to go on. What private parties you were invited to at BlogHer. It was almost like you could give a crap about the brand in real life, but you wanted the involvement to enhance your supposed influence. It was a high-school popularity contest. Then (finally) the game changed as it was more about the person, the voice, the content ... the quality of the blog/blogger than the numbers associated. How I would define influence is that along with the personality, the voice, the content, and the quality, is also passion and integrity. If we choose to get involved with a brand, it's not as another "check-in" to get a new "badge." It should be because we believe in the company, the product, what it means to us personally, culturally, globally, etc., and we want to make an impact in the future development/success. I know I pretty much answered this from a blogger influence perspective but the same could go with a non-blogger.

How do you feel you influence moms offline? Is it more than chatting in the carpool line? Yes, definitely. At play dates and birthday parties. Not many of my offline mom friends are on the internet as much as me so they often ask me what I've seen about certain brands or products. Or they may ask me to find out because most likely I can find it more quickly than they could. Many of them have been inspired to start writing or blogging since knowing me.

How can companies best support your business or mission as a mom? Hire me! Just kidding (but not really). Um, I think by taking into consideration the things I've mentioned above.

What motivates you to tell other moms (good or bad) about a company, brand or product? When it's really really really good ... or when it's really really really bad. How it affects me on a personal level is what makes me talk about it.

Final words: The hand that rocks the cradle rules the world and if Mama ain't happy, nobody's happy! The sooner everybody realizes that, we'll all be fine.

Name: Molly Gold

Children: Three, ages 15, 13, and 7

Hometown: Apex, NC

Company Name(s): GO MOM!® Inc.

Short description of business: GO MOM!® Inc is the every Mom brand, offering useful scheduling and organizing video tutorials, solutions, and time management products. We promise to help Moms make positive mothering a daily reality by educating them how to Schedule. Organize. Grow.® and create personalized solutions to improve the chaos in their everyday lives. The company is a nationally recognized Lifestyle Media Expert in Family Time Management and Home Organization. GO MOM!® Inc was launched in 2000 with the idea to create a day planner designed completely with a mom's perspective first, including everything she needed to manage her busy family no matter her work status or stage of her family's growth. I was a meeting planner pre-kids and spent countless hours and more than $500 trying to piece together the perfect planner before I decided it was time to make my own. I knew the mundane details of home management and family care didn't need to be my center, but merely the necessary background to my daily work of raising and enjoying the family my husband and I were now creating. GO MOM!® will offer useful scheduling and organizing video tutorials, solutions, and time management products. We promise to help moms make positive mothering a daily reality by educating them how to Schedule. Organize. Grow.® and create personalized solutions to improve the chaos in their everyday lives.

Websites or Blogs you own: GO MOM!® Inc. www.GOMOMINC.com

Approximate audience size: Monthly page views = 60,000; 6,000 Unique

Websites or blogs you contribute to: 2011 Babycenter Momformation Guest Blogger Network, Primrose Schools Friends of Dr. Z

Facebook Id: GO MOM!

Twitter Id: @MyGOMOM

Approximate # of followers: 4,000

Online Involvements and associations: Day-Timer, The Stow Company, and Build-A-Bear, Mom Select, Global Influence, Mom Blogger Club, The Motherhood, Clever Girls Collective, Collective Bias

How many moms do you typically interact with during the week offline? 25-50

Offline Involvements: Triangle Community Church, NC NAPO, PTA for highschool, middle school, and elementary school

Is there one moment when you realized you were impacting the life/lives of others? One particularly touching story unfolded when our GO MOM!® Planner was widely available at Target stores but not yet sold online. At that time, it was manufactured by Mead Westvaco and was just one sku, set on the shelf with no explanation in the middle of a group of products under another brand name. It took off like wild fire reaching tens of thousands of moms nationwide. A mom in western Nebraska called me in tears, not able to find it in her home town. She said it was the Bible that held her family together during her father's ongoing battle with cancer and without it, she would be utterly lost. In that moment I knew that this idea was truly not of my own, but a blessing and responsibility, and that I had to make certain it would grow for countless women and families I'll never know.

What motivates you to tell other moms (good or bad) about a company, brand or product? I share about companies, brands and products when their customer service is stellar, their team is personable, empowered to resolve any issues, and their policies are fair. I also love a company, brand, or product that offers me a solution on some level that meets me where I am in my journey as a mom. The conversation has to be relevant and grounded in reality, not celebrity, expertise, not the bandwagon of the crowd, and integrity. Authenticity is everything and therefore, as a fellow brand owner, I try hard not to be negative; rather, when there are challenges, give the benefit of the doubt that the right thing will happen, and when it does, praise that experience as best I can.

Final words: Mothers are the past, present and future of the world because qualified or not, they have the monumental task of raising a generation of children to be educationally engaged, open-minded, politically astute, economically competent, intellectually inspired, artistically respectful, and spiritually moral. That is all.

Name: Stacie Gorkow

Chidlren: Three, ages 10, 9, and 5

Hometown: Van Horne, Iowa

Company Name(s): Sincerely Stacie

Short description of business: A blog where I can share things about my life, my thoughts, my ideas, some inspiration, and some reviews/giveaways of products that have benefited my life and my family's life. I started my blog in December 2007 because I wanted a way to reach other women and have a way to write about my life, and share my experiences with them. Then after seeing that there was an opportunity to provide a service of reviewing products, I jumped at it. I would never review a product that wouldn't benefit my family or me. I also wouldn't review something that didn't meet up with my values.

Websites or Blogs you own: http://SincerelyStacie.blogspot.com

Facebook Id: Stacie Gorkow

Online Involvements and associations: SheKnows.com, MomCentral, CSN Stores, The View Ambassador, Big Idea Ambassador, MomSelect, ParkerPROnline, Energizer/Build-A-Bear, Kraft First Taste, Blog with Integrity, Momblogs, Sheblogs, Picket Fence Blogs, BlogFrog

How many moms do you typically interact with during the week offline? 50

Offline Involvements: Book club, Chair of Church Circle, Bible Study, Young Couples Group, run After-School program at church, teach Storytime for preschoolers at the library, Hospice volunteer

What do you think is the biggest mistake companies make in trying to work with moms? Not realizing that we may not like their product. Just because I am a mom, you can't assume I will love the product; be prepared to hear why I wasn't happy with it. That doesn't mean I won't like another product of yours. I just didn't have good luck with this particular one.

Are there companies who you feel are doing a great job connecting with moms? I have had great relationships with CSN Stores, Energizer/Build-A-Bear and Kraft. I think Pillsbury, Betty Crocker, Martha Stewart Real Simple, Disney, Fisher Price, etc., could do better at reaching out to moms.

Is there one moment when you realized you were impacting the life/lives of others? When I heard from people in my small town who I had no idea were reading my blog every day. They would stop me on the street and say, "I went out and bought that product," or, "I loved your inspiration today," or, "That story about your kids was funny and made my day." When I realized people were looking forward to my posts, it made me think more about my writing.

How do you feel companies can best connect with moms, particularly those who are influencers? By providing us with samples to try and review. By offering a giveaway. Readers are more interested in reading the review if there is a giveaway in return.

Final words: Moms have lots of power in today's society. I am especially interested in the new TV show THE TALK because it is a group of moms (with kids of all ages) who get together and discuss life and the world we are in. I do believe that I look at the world differently because I am a mom. When I was single, I thought about how the world would affect me, but now, I am seeing the world through the eyes of my children. How do I want to expose them to things, how do I want to share experiences with them, what kind of filter do I need to use with them and what they see and hear?

Name: Robin Gorman Newman

Children: One, age 7

Hometown: Great Neck, NY

Company Name(s): Motherhood Later ... Than Sooner

Short description of business: Motherhood Later ... Than Sooner, founded by Robin Gorman Newman, is an international organization devoted to those parenting later in life. If you became a mom for the first time, or again, at age 35+, they welcome your participation. Their mission is to inform, empower and connect "later" mothers through their site, blog, newsletter, learning opportunities, online communities and in-person events through chapters worldwide for moms and families. The mission of Motherhood Later ... Than Sooner is to inform, empower and connect midlife moms, so they know they're not alone, both on and offline. It launched as a website in 2006.

Websites or Blogs you own: Motherhood Later ... Than Sooner http://www.MotherhoodLater.com

Approximate audience size: 25,000+ visitors/month to date to the site. Additionally, we have chapters worldwide, newsletter subscribers and multiple online communities. I don't have an accurate tally of all these members, but it's over 5,000.

Facebook Id: Motherhood Later Than Sooner and Robin G Newman

Twitter Id: @rgnewman

Approximate # of followers: 1,500 at present ... and growing

What's the best way for companies to reach you as an influencer or as a mom? Email robin@motherhoodlater.com

How is the best way to work with you and your company? I am a former Vice President with a PR firm in Manhattan and have my own practice, RGN Communications. I have an MBA in Marketing and 20+ years PR experience in a wide array of industries, including targeting the parenting market. I'd welcome the opportunity to work with companies to help generate buzz for their brand. We offer sponsorship opportunities on MotherhoodLater.com, and we're opening to partnering on an event level with companies and other mompreneurs.

Is there one moment when you realized you were impacting the life/lives of others? Whenever I received a heartfelt email from a later mom who was grateful to have found us because she then knew she wasn't alone. And, I continue to receive notes like that, even from later dads.

How can companies best support your business or mission as a mom? We welcome sponsors and advertisers and offer affordable rates through social networking, our site, newsletters, regional chapters, etc. We would welcome an investor and/or business partner, so we can continue our endeavors to serve later moms. Our mom demographic is a desirable one since those parenting later in life typically have higher spending power because they're older and have worked longer. This is appealing to marketers.

What motivates you to tell other moms (good or bad) about a company, brand or product? It resonates with me on a gut level. It helps if the company's message is "feel good" and if they are genuine in their efforts to enhance the lives of families and ideally to give back and do good in the world and not just make a profit.

Name: Linda Grant

Children: One, age 7

Hometown: New York, NY

Company Name(s): my NY employee.com and NYC Single Mom

Short description of business: mynyemployee.com provides small businesses that travel to NYC on a regular basis with NY based employees on a short term basis. NYCsinglemom.com details the parenting tales of a single mom in NYC. I launched my site http://www.nycsinglemom.com after being laid off from a marketing position at a large financial services company. The reason for starting this site was that even though I had been in marketing for 20 years, I knew nothing about blogging, Twitter and Facebook. This was a way for me to learn firsthand about social media so that I could stay sharp within my field.

Websites or Blogs you own: NYC Single Mom http://www.nycsinglemom.com, NYC Single Mom Reviews http://www.nycsinglemomreviews.com and my NY employee.com http://www.mynyemployee.com

Approximate audience size: 3,000/month

Websites or blogs you contribute to: I contribute to travelingmom.com, nymetropolista.com.

Facebook Id: New York City Single Mom

Twitter Id: @NYCSINGLEMOM

Approximate # of followers: 3,030

Online Involvements and associations: KIDS CLUB 13 AMBASSADOR—PBS

What do you think is the biggest mistake companies make in trying to work with? Treating us all the same: women from the south are different from women of the west.

Is there one moment when you realized you were impacting the life/lives of others? When a reader said, "You give me hope that I can be a single mom and adopt."

What motivates you to tell other moms (good or bad) about a company, brand or product? If I have a good experience with a brand, I want to shout it from the rooftops.

How do you feel companies can best connect with moms, particularly those who are influencers? Smaller intimate gatherings so we can really learn about the products.

Name: Natalie Green

Children: One, age 9 months

Hometown: Lansing, Illinois

Company Name(s): Stellar Therapy Services

Short description of business: Stellar Therapy Services focuses on physical, occupational, and speech therapy. I started my blog in January 2008 after suffering a miscarriage the previous month. I began blogging about my weight loss, and then through our struggles to conceive again. It took us ten cycles but we did get pregnant. I blogged through my pregnancy and I now blog about my adventures as mom to a 9-month-old girl. My mission has always been to touch other women with my story and to give them hope for their futures as mothers. Now, I hope to entertain people who read my blog with funny stories, and touch them with heartfelt letters to my daughter.

Websites or Blogs you own: Mommy Boots http://mommyboots.com

Approximate audience size: 1,500+

Twitter Id: @mommyboots

Approximate # of followers: 790

Online Involvements and associations: Mom Bloggers Club, Twittermoms, Eden Fantasys, Clever Girls Collective, PTPA

What's the best way for companies to reach you as an influencer or as a mom? Through a thought-out, personalized email: nagreen84@gmail.com

What do you think is the biggest mistake companies make in trying to work with moms? Not being personal enough and treating moms like every other blogger; also trying to take advantage of them, their writing and their blog space.

Are there companies who you feel are doing a great job connecting with moms? One of my favorite companies that I've worked with is Earth Mama, Angel Baby.

Is there one moment when you realized you were impacting the life/lives of others? I had three women, who I went to high school with, come forward and thank me for writing so candidly about my struggles in conceiving. They, too, were struggling and thought they were all alone.

How can companies best support your business or mission as a mom? Spreading the word about my blog, offering new opportunities to try new products so I can share them with my online and offline mom friends.

What motivates you to tell other moms (good or bad) about a company, brand or product? I usually brag when I find a product that I am absolutely in love with. If I have a particularly bad experience with a company, I tell my fellow mom bloggers to stay away.

How do you feel companies can best connect with moms, particularly those who are influencers? By taking the time to actually read their blog and reach out to them in a personal manner.

Final words: Mothers are superheroes!

Name: Melissa Gregg

Children: Three, ages 11, 7, and 15 months

Hometown: Lanoka Harbor NJ

Company Name(s): design 36

Short description of business: I started my business September 2010. My mission is to better enhance my children's lives. The business is geared toward decorating design and decor renovations.

Websites or Blogs you own: Saveatunities www.saveatunities.com; design36 www.design36.biz; http://www.designthirtysix.blogspot.com

Websites or blogs you contribute to: www.saveatunities.com, www.design36.biz, http://www.designthirtysix.blogspot.com, www.pmheatingcooling.com, and http://www.pmheatingcooling.blogspot.com

Facebook Id: melissalyngregg, saveatunity, and design36

Twitter Id: @saveatunity, @designthirtysix

Approximate # of followers: 800

Online Involvements and associations: Barefoot Books Ambassador, operationnice.com, Society of Socialpreneurs, Today Moms, Mothersclick, Collective Bias, Renegade Moms, Global Influence, Business 2 Blogger, MomSelect, Mom Blog Network, Mom Relations, Mombit, momsrising.org, Parker PR, Publish America, Mommy PR, Bloggers Connection, Blogger Black Book, Bloggy Mom, Mom Fuse Pop, Green & Clean Mom, Helium, ezinearticles, and The Review Place

Offline Involvements: Church, PTA and PTO functions, Cookies for Kids Cancer, American Heart Association

What's the best way for companies to reach you as an influencer or as a mom? Email: saveatunity@gmail.com

Are there companies who you feel are doing a great job connecting with moms? Truvia, Barber Foods

Final words: Moms influence everything because of the old saying, "if mom's not happy nobody is happy." We all know what it takes to lead our family to success in every aspect and will voice our opinions to get the job done.

Name: Kim Grenon

Children: Two, ages 8 and 5

Hometown: Rochester, NH

Company Name(s): Mommycosm, LLC

Short description of business: I started blogging at Mommycosm in 2007 as a research project for work. I was rocking my SAHM gig when an ex-employer offered me a web research opportunity. I could work solely from home ... in my pjs at midnight if I wanted. I distinctly remember my boss outlining one of the first projects. He wanted me to gather lots of information about top blogs. I remember asking "Um, what's a blog?!" He assigned me the task to set one up from scratch to see how it is done. So, I did. I set up Mommycosm. Task accomplished and we all moved on. Right? Not so much. I enjoyed blogging so much, I continued on my own time. When my boss decided to close doors in April of 2010, I decided to transition my blog from hobby to business. I launched Mommycosm, LLC and started offering my services as a brand ambassador and freelance writer. My live web show, Mommycosm Reviews, was launched later that fall.

Websites or Blogs you own: Mommycosm www.mommycosm.com

Approximate audience size: 35,000 views /month

Websites or blogs you contribute to: Mom It Forward and Lady Bloggers Society, Hoping to contribute more in 2011

Facebook Id: Mommycosm

Twitter Id: @Mommycosm

Approximate # of followers: 1,100+

Online Involvements and associations: I am a Boston Parent Blogger, TwitterMom, Member of Mom Central, Mom Select, The Motherhood, Mom Spark Media, and One2One Network. I have done brand ambassador work for: Energizer, Cotton, Ford, and Eden Fantasys.

How many moms do you typically interact with during the week offline? 10-20

Offline Involvements: I coach high school softball as well as my daughter's youth softball teams; I am a member of the National Marrow Donor Program and donated stem cells in 2007.

What's the best way for companies to reach you as an influencer or as a mom? Email: themommy@mommycosm.com

What do you think is the biggest mistake companies make in trying to work with moms? Companies need to realize that moms can't pay the mortgage with product. Sure, free stuff is great ... but if moms are going to devote the proper amount of time to deliver quality content consistently, they need to be paid in real money.

Are there companies who you feel are doing a great job connecting with moms? Energizer, Wendy's, Mabel's Labels, LeapFrog, to name just a few

Is there one moment when you realized you were impacting the life/lives of others? There is no one major moment. There are many small moments ... from a reader commenting back that they feel less alone, to a softball player smiling after getting that big hit after we've worked hard on her swing ... to my daughter standing fearlessly on stage. Ok, if I had to name one, it would be the time I quit coaching. I had to walk away from a difficult situation at a school I loved. I didn't want to associate myself with other people having a negative influence. I wasn't sure the girls understood my intentions. I wondered if they simply thought I abandoned them, until I got an email from a player thanking me and telling me she understood ...

and that she hoped to be like me one day. She has since gone on to earn a Division 1 scholarship for college. Talk about validation. Wow.

How can companies best support your business or mission as a mom? I would love to be able to continue promoting quality companies to my online and offline network of moms. They can best support me by hiring me as a brand ambassador, spokes Mom, correspondent.

How do you feel companies can best connect with moms, particularly those who are influencers? I think companies are starting to reach moms where they are communicating: on social media. Come to our playing field. Engage in our discussions. Find out what you can do for us before asking us to do for you. Build relationships, not just numbers. A loyal, devoted mom in your back pocket is priceless.

Name: Apryl Griffith

Children: Three, ages 5 ½ (twin girls) and 2 ½

Hometown: Big Bear City, CA

Short description of business: I created this blog in June 2009 when I discovered the amount of money I was saving using coupons. I wanted everyone to know how simple it can be to use a coupon.

Websites or Blogs you own: Christian Clippers - Spending God's Money Wisely http://christianclippers.com

Approximate audience size: 25,000 Monthly page views, 12,000 unique visitors

Facebook Id: Christian Clippers

Twitter Id: @christianclippe

Approximate # of followers: 1,600

Online Involvements and associations: Mom Bloggers Club, Moms Select, The Mom Blogs, Mom Blog Network, Mom Central, The Product Review Place, Business 2 Blogger, MyBlogSpark, BzzAgent, One2One Network, Moms Connect, Pitch It To Me, Christian Stay At Homes, Top Mommy Blog

How many moms do you typically interact with during the week offline? 40

Is there one moment when you realized you were impacting the life/lives of others? Yes, it's when people are so excited to tell me how much they saved.

What motivates you to tell other moms (good or bad) about a company, brand or product? I like to do giveaways and reviews. I tell other moms my experience with the products.

Name: Kimberly Grisham

Children: Two, ages 2 and 5 months

Hometown: Salt Lake City, UT

Company Name(s): EcoGlo Minerals

Short description of business: All of our makeup is 100% natural. EcoGlo's mineral makeup is a healthy alternative for flawless looking skin. With EcoGlo's all natural and long-lasting mineral makeup, you will have cleaner, flawless looking skin and coverage that persists through the day. Our mineral makeup is super light and feels completely natural, and it will never clog your pores since it is free of oils, silicone and waxes. In fact, it contains some ingredients that actually help the negative effects of acne and rosacea. My company started in 2007. My son was playing with one of my makeup brushes and broke out in a horrible rash. This made me question what was in my makeup to cause such a reaction. I researched online and discovered natural mineral cosmetics. I spent a lot of time creating recipes to contain only ingredients that were good for one's skin. My mission is to stay as natural as possible with my cosmetics line.

Websites or Blogs you own: EcoGlo Minerals http://www.ecoglominerals.com

Facebook Id: EcoGlo Minerals

Twitter Id: @ecoglominerals

Approximate # of followers: 810

Are there companies who you feel are doing a great job connecting with moms? Any company that uses social media to interact with and ask moms their opinions is doing a terrific job. It shows that the company knows that moms are the largest group of consumers and the company wants their input.

How do you define influence among moms? I define influence among moms as anything that makes another mom stop and think. Once that happens, a change usually occurs within the mom to be better, do better.

How can companies best support your business or mission as a mom? Go natural! There are a few companies that are marketing the natural/eco-friendly side of the spectrum which raises awareness about a better way of life (chemical free). Any company that is truly free of chemically laden products helps spread the word that there are better choices out there.

How do you feel companies can best connect with moms, particularly those who are influencers? Listen. Ask questions. Get out there and use social media to your advantage. Ask moms what they like, what they don't like, what they would change, and then DO IT. Moms will catch on to this and stay with those companies that listen and do.

Name: Maricris Guadagna

Children: One, age 6

Hometown: Charlotte, NC

Company Name(s): Lake Norman Tai Chi Center (co-owner}

Short description of business: A Martial Arts School teaching authentic, traditional Tai Chi, Qigong, yoga and meditation dedicated to a healthy lifestyle and physical wellness for all ages. It was established January of 2010. I co-founded it with my husband in support of his passion for the arts and also a way of making it into our primary income source.

Websites or Blogs you own: Zensible Mama http://zenforyou.dalefg.net/

Approximate audience size: 8,000 – 10,000

Websites or blogs you contribute to: Working Mother, Zensible Mama, Blog Critics, Charlotte Moms Like Me, and Moms of Charlotte

Facebook Id: MaricrisMMG

Twitter Id: @MaricrisG

Approximate # of followers: 2,250

Online Involvements and associations: Ocean Isle Inn Momblogger, Rice Krispies Brand Ambassador, Soft Scrub Club Captain, Mabel Label Buzz Mama, Hebrew National Better-than-a-picnic Picnic host, Disney Social Media Mom, Moms Meet Ambassador, More than 11 Moms, Charlotte Moms Like Me, Moms of Charlotte, Moms Meet, Media Egg Mom Panel, Bit Moms etc.

How many moms do you typically interact with during the week offline? 10-100, I work in a martial arts school with 300 students adults/kids combined.

Offline Involvements: Local Moms Meet, Recently coordinated/established a play-date group in the neighborhood to connect moms and their kids, Birthday Blessings, Kickathon

What's the best way for companies to reach you as an influencer or as a mom? Via email, criska826@gmail.com or Twitter

How do you feel you influence moms online? When our relationship goes beyond online and transcends offline. Also having a sense of authority on a certain topic and I get positive reactions to it and persuade them to try a specific suggestion.

How can companies best support your business or mission as a mom? It's more of a respect and the freedom to speak what we think of their brand and to partner with us not just by product reviews and the like, but more so with projects that can help us tap into our potentials.

Final words: Moms as women should be given the same opportunity and pay grade as our male counterparts, especially in the workforce. We're hardworking, smart, educated and do a lot to raise a family. We deserve a fighting chance!

Name: Renee Hall

Children: Two, ages 13 and 6 (both boys)

City and home state: Stanley, NC

Short description of business: I started Giveaways with Grace on October 29, 2010, because I had lost my teaching position due to the economy. As a new stay-at-home mom, I needed something to keep me busy. I have always liked trying new products and I LOVE giving my opinion to people, whether they want it or not. I thought this would be a great opportunity for me.

Websites or Blogs you own: http://giveawayswithgrace.blogspot.com/ and http://memoirs-of-a-fat-chick.blogspot.com/

Approximate audience size: 90 followers

Facebook Id: Giveaways with Grace

Twitter Id: @gracegives and @FatChickRSexy

Approximate # of followers: 130 followers

Online Involvements and associations: Bzz Agent, Sheblogs.org, SITS, Review Maven

How many moms do you typically interact with during the week offline? 20

Offline Involvements: Volunteer at my sons' school, PTA, School Clean Up, Town Clean Up

What's the best way for companies to reach you as an influencer or as a mom? giveawayswithgrace@yahoo.com

What do you think is the biggest mistake companies make in trying to work with moms? They are too pushy and sometimes are not sensitive to the fact that we are mothers. We do not like to be talked down to. Just because we are stay-at-home moms does not mean we do not work. When discussing our children, please remember that they are our world!

How do you feel you influence moms offline? Is it more than chatting in the carpool line? I love to chat with parents and I am always letting them know about new products I have found or tried out. I have also had a few parties to promote products like Chex Mix. I love doing this, because moms can come over and relax in my home and we can talk about awesome stuff.

How can company's best support your business or mission as a mom? Provide us with samples. Samples are great, because a lot of moms do not want to spend money on something unless they know that it works. If we try something and like it we will buy it. Cater to our children. We love that!

Final words: The one thing that I have discovered since blogging is that moms are a community, we are family that looks out for one another. We want what's best for our kids, our neighbor's kids, and everybody else's kids. We are a close-knit community that shares everything we know. I have never been part of such a loving supportive group, until now.

Name: Rachel Hamrick

Children: Three, ages 6, 5, and 3 (all boys)

Hometown: Arlington, VA

Company Name: On the Fly Fitness

Short description of business: I help people (mostly moms) find ways to fit fitness and healthy eating into their lives. I work with my clients to design exercise and eating plans that fit their specific needs and lifestyles. I started my fitness coaching business in the spring of 2009. My motivation in starting the business was that I gained a ton of weight when I had my kids and was looking for someone who had been through it before and could help me figure out how I could get fit and healthy again while taking into account my new busy life with kids. I was lucky enough to find some at-home workout DVDs that helped me lose 70+ pounds and I wanted to pay it forward. The mission of my business is to show moms that time is not an excuse or an impediment to being fit and healthy.

Websites or Blogs you own: On the Fly Fitness www.ontheflyfitness.com; Beach Body Coach www.fitrh72.com

Websites or blogs you contribute to: Bloggy Moms, Bookieboo, I have also guest blogged on a few other mommy blogs.

Facebook Id: Rachel Hamrick

Approximate # of followers: 750

Twitter Id: @rhamrick

Approximate # of followers: 600

How many moms do you typically interact with during the week offline? 30-40

Offline Involvements: Several moms' groups, Business Networking International, a weekly fit club, PTA; volunteer at the local women's shelter and at my kids' schools

What's the best way for companies to reach you as an influencer or as a mom? Through Facebook, Twitter or my website www.ontheflyfitness.com

What do you think is the biggest mistake companies make in trying to work with moms? Assuming that we all think and/or act in a particular way instead of viewing us/marketing to us as individuals with individual needs. Also, I think sometimes companies assume that their mom demographic has to fit into either the "stay-at-home" or the "working" mom box, when, in reality, many of us are living lives somewhere in the middle.

Is there one moment when you realized you were impacting the life/lives of others? The first letter I ever got from a woman who had been able to lose 35 pounds and stop taking some medication because of the program I helped her design was an amazing moment for me and the reason I started my business in the first place.

What motivates you to tell other moms (good or bad) about a company, brand or product? If I have tried it and it makes my life easier in some way or it's something I believe in because it has worked for me, then I will tell everyone who will listen about it. And I will also tell people if I don't like something or it doesn't work.

How do you feel companies can best connect with moms, particularly those who are influencers? I don't think there is a "best" way to connect. For me, if a company has integrity, has a good product or service that will make my life easier and/or better and treats me as the unique, smart and saavy person that I am then I am happy!

Name: Leanne Heilman

Children: Two, ages 2 and a newborn

Hometown: Seattle, WA

Company Name(s): Rave and Review

Short description of business: Rave and Review is all about honest and in-depth reviews for the stuff families use. When our first child was born, my husband and I searched everywhere for the best gear for our growing family; it was important to us to have quality gear that could last through multiple children as well as items that were very practical with our on-the-go lifestyle. What we found was that other parents were looking for this same exact thing and that every time we went out with our new gear we were bombarded with questions from other parents. We were happy to hand out product information and tell other parents where to purchase, but it was hard to carry around the information for all the products we had found. I got the idea in 2008 to start a website that featured all the products we were using and then we could simply direct the moms and dads we met around town, or while traveling, to the website to find the products they were looking for. What I didn't anticipate was that parents, grandparents and more would find Rave and Review online and our site would become so popular amongst readers we had never met in person. Now a good deal of our influence is online, something I never would have guessed when I first started the site.

Websites or Blogs you own: Rave and Review www.raveandreview.com

Approximate audience size: 35,000 + monthly

Websites or blogs you contribute to: Traveling Mom, Mama Buzz, An Island Life, Family Review Network, Parent Reviewers, and Mommy PR

Twitter Id: @raveandreview

Approximate # of followers: 3,200

Online Involvements and associations: Infantino Test Mom (ambassador), Mom Central Reviewer, Mom Blogger's Club Reviewer, PTPA Panel of Moms, Traveling Mom contributor, Mama Buzz contributor, An Island Life contributor, Family Review Network reviewer, Parent Reviewers reviewer, Mommy PR contributor

How many moms do you typically interact with during the week offline? 50+

What do you think is the biggest mistake companies make in trying to work with moms? Undervaluing the work that they do: writing may seem like an easy living, but if you really want to become successful you need to see each and every post as part of your brand and perfect it as such. This means long hours at the computer researching, writing, and editing. My hope is that eventually all mom bloggers will be paid accordingly, but right now that certainly is not the case and I get many emails each week asking me to dedicate my time and energy to building others' sites—for free.

Are there companies who you feel are doing a great job connecting with moms? Absolutely! I have had such great experiences with brands such as Step2, Infantino, Maukilo, Hoover, Pampers, Corolle, Steiff, HABA, Playmobil, SodaStream, Hasbro and many, many more. There are really too many to list.

How do you define influence among moms? Someone that other moms trust and turn to for advice.

Is there one moment when you realized you were impacting the life/lives of others? I will never forget that first email from a reader who was asking for advice for an overseas trip with a small baby and she had read about all of our adventures with our daughter while traveling in Europe. I loved helping her select all the gear we had found essential in our travels and giving her advice for her specific situation. Twenty-plus emails later, I knew that I not only had a reader for life, I had also made a good friend.

How do you feel you influence moms offline? Is it more than chatting in the carpool line? I love to help moms wherever I meet them, which means I am the go-to-gal for anyone looking to make a big purchase. I have a group of 100+ moms who reach out to me whenever they are looking to find a specific product and I love that I can offer so much feedback. Nothing is more rewarding that introducing a mom to a brand and then hearing her introduce another mom to it after she has used it for a while.

How do you feel companies can best connect with moms, particularly those who are influencers? By reaching out to them and introducing themselves—I have made so many connections with companies and PR firms and in the process have made so many friends!

Final words: Really, the reach of moms cannot be fully defined because moms today are on the move. They are the first users of many products and services and they are the first in line to try out the newest technology, so it makes sense that they should be making waves both online and off. I think the future of mom blogging and mom influencing is bright and limitless!

Name: Dawn Heinold

Children: Two, ages 8 and 7

Hometown: Wayne ,New Jersey

Company Name(s): in the process of getting L.L.C./ Fitness Mama LLC

Short description of business: Fitness-based company for fitness modeling,fitness products,dvds and all Fitness Mama-related projects. I am currently starting a business for fitness-related purposes. I plan to personally train people, and get involved in various fitness products and dvds.

Websites or blogs you contribute to: MOMTV and The Real Mom TV

Facebook Id: Dawn O'Reilly Heinold

Online Involvements and associations: MomTV and RMTV currently

How many moms do you typically interact with during the week offline? About 500 moms each week through various fitness classes I teach. I interact and motivate many mothers each day "live" during fitness workouts. I inspire and motivate each and every mom.

Offline Involvements: PTO at the local elementary school, Pines Lake Elementary. I am chairperson of New Comers committee on the PTO 4 years. I do ice cream socials and kindergarten orientation each year. It is very rewarding. Involvement in the community and school is important to me. I am a Brownie Leader to 16 girls at the school. I am part of a team of instructors at La Fitness in Wayne, New Jersey. I am coach to a Boys and Girls club in Wayne New Jersey. I coach Boys' soccer, Girls' soccer and softball. I help with fundraisers for the elementary school and support women's groups.

What's the best way for companies to reach you as an influencer or as a mom? Email dawn19@optonline.net and fitnessmama@optonline.net

What do you think is the biggest mistake companies make in trying to work with moms? The biggest mistake companies make is trying to connect with REAL moms but are not using REAL MOMS to represent the product: moms who cook, clean, WORK, coach and lead by example. Companies need to connect with moms who relate to their products and use them. Moms are always looking for new products and information to help them and their family, but they will only purchase products they can relate to and that work for them.

Are there companies who you feel are doing a great job connecting with moms? I think Babycenter connects well with moms who are expecting. MomTV also connects well with real moms and helps them all by giving them valuable information from other real mothers and real people, with a good result. Some talk shows also do a great job connecting with all moms by giving them information and advice.

How do you feel you influence moms online? I influence moms online by hosting a mom-based TV show off the net each week on RMTV and MOMTV called Get Fit Friday. I reach out to all moms who need a push and an honest trainer to help them achieve the mind and body they so desire. I teach them about being healthy; I give them nutrition information and fitness workouts for all levels. I help to inspire them all to get healthier and happier through fitness and diet. I motivate and captivate each and every person, and strive to give them all valuable information and fitness workouts so that they can become a healthier and happier Mom!

How do you feel companies can best connect with moms, particularly those who are influencers? Companies should have real mothers on their products, commercials, print ads, etc. They should relate to all moms out there, ones who work and the stay-at-home moms, too; moms with high income in their household and moms with very little income. We are all moms and they should reach out to influencers because they are the ones the moms trust and listen carefully to! That is a fact.

Final words: Moms should appreciate that being a mother is the most rewarding thing that will ever come their way. I think that by being socially active, educating themselves on motherhood, getting involved in groups and discussions and getting involved in their children's school and sports/activities is best! Being in contact with a mom face to face is real, genuine and rewarding. We can all learn by setting the example. We should spend time educating ourselves on what we don't know, and should want to be better each and every day we exist. We all need to help each other in any way possible. I believe that I inspire many women and I am a role model to many mothers in life. What I do is truly rewarding, and I enjoy helping each and every mom however I can, each and every day. Being a mom, and a Mom Influencer, is so rewarding. I am a mom that others can count on, lean on and learn from. I love being a MOM!

Name: Paula Herrmann

Children: Four, ages 15, 13, 8, and 6

Hometown state: Racine, WI

Company Name(s): Just Add Kids

Short description of business: Just Add Kids is a regional resource highlighting kid-oriented, family-friendly activities and events. The product mix consists of website, weekly e-newsletter, social network sites and special events. Just Add Kids was launched in October 2009. In August of 2009 I lost my employment due to workforce reduction at a large media conglomerate. I had been an advertising sales executive for a regional parenting resource (monthly print with special supplement publications, website, and special events). As a sales rep out in the field, I had communicated holes (areas of under-deliverance, or rather, missed opportunities), and plugging those holes inspired the Just Add Kids mission and business model. The Just Add Kids mission is to provide the most complete and up-to-date resource for kid-oriented, family-friendly activities and events; connecting SE Wisconsin families that have children 0-18 (where they are, whether on their mobile devices, computers, or face-to-face) with those businesses and organizations that serve them. Right now I am living the life of a mom in need of easily accessible information. I am purposeful in the brand name and logo...it will not limit expansion on many levels (geographical reach and product mix).

Website or Blogs you own: Just Add Kids www.JustAddKidsOnline.net, www.JAKChat.wordpress.com

Facebook Id: Just Add Kids

Twitter Id: @JustAddKids

Approximate # of followers: 150

How many moms do you typically interact with during the week offline? 25

Offline Involvements: Synergy productivity group (5 business women, 1 productivity coach), weekly Bible Study. Volunteer for kids' school and their sports/extra-curricular activities/homeless meals. At this time, my focus is on my faith, family, business, friends, health (in that order). When my children are grown, I will look at becoming active in professional and/or charitable organizations that fit my life's purpose.

What's the best way for companies to reach you as an influencer or as a mom? Email: paula@justaddkidsonline.net

What do you think is the biggest mistake companies make in trying to work with moms? In my experience, many smaller companies (1 outlet, not national) market at moms, and not with moms. Branding is important, yet engaging moms with the brand is essential.

Is there one moment when you realized you were impacting the life/lives of others? Losing employment was not as difficult from the emotional standpoint for me. The timing was right, and quite honestly, I needed the kick in the butt. I was unsatisfied representing a product I lost belief in, however the financial security kept me there. I work very hard to deliver the best product to Just Add Kids/JAK family audience, and likewise, take very seriously being a great steward of the money my customers/advertisers invest in me/Just Add Kids. I recall a moment at the bank drive-through, depositing a measly $60 check in my business account, feeling a bit beaten up ("All this work for $60?" I thought). The teller asked me "What's Just Add Kids?" As I started to describe to her (my 15-second commercial) Just Add Kids, I felt such a great sense of pride. I LOVE DOING WHAT I DO! AND I LOVE TO TALK TO PEOPLE ABOUT IT! I LOVE THEIR INTERESTED, SUPPORTING RESPONSES! It's the little, unsolicited comments on Facebook, or an email, or a smile on a mom's face that make all the difference. I am making a positive impact with JAK.

How can companies best support your business or mission as a mom? Take notice of the important market (extremely targeted, defined) that Just Add Kids serves. If they want to get their message to this market, utilize JAK with advertising, sponsorship! Support the JAK mission.

What motivates you to tell other moms (good or bad) about a company, brand or product? If it's a good product, with a great honest company behind it, I enjoy sharing that with others that can benefit. I tend to think that businesses that run with money as their first priority have their priorities wrong. If a company is misleading in any way, their actions don't reflect their message. I avoid them. If I've had a negative experience, I will let the company know my issue, and give them an opportunity to fix the issue. I don't publicly rat on a product, service, or company.

How do you feel companies can best connect with moms, particularly those who are influencers? Engage with them, where they want to be engaged. Not where the company thinks they want to engage.

Final words: I am enjoying watching Sarah Palin. How she came on the scene a couple of years ago, how she handled such public criticism of her and her family, how she makes mistakes and addresses them, how she influences, how she ticks people off, where she'll end up. I feel she stands tall on the things she believes in and will not cave, even though she has a lot of people that don't believe in the same ideals as she does. I don't care for how she bashes people, but she gets it back tenfold. Interesting.

Name: Brenda Hess

Children: Five, ages 22, 20, 16, 4, 2

Hometown: Harrisburg, PA

Websites or Blogs you own: Shoestring Muse http://shoestringmuse.blogspot.com/

Websites or blogs you contribute to: freestufftimes.com, swagbucks.com, Babycenter.com

Facebook Id: Brenda Hess

Approximate # of followers: 1140

Twitter Id: @brnd1968

Approximate # of followers: 100+

Online Involvements and associations: Bzzagent, Momselect, Momcentral, Houseparty.com, Pssst, Kraft First Taste

How many moms do you typically interact with during the week offline? 15-20

What's the best way for companies to reach you as an influencer or as a mom? Via emai: brnd1968@aol.com or Facebook.

How do you feel you influence moms online? I would say I influence moms online by just sharing my experiences—good AND bad. Maybe someone will read a comment I make about a product or service (GOOD or BAD) and decide purely on what they read whether or not to try it. Maybe another mom will read about my trials and errors with my own children and decide that it is indeed OK to use the HELL out of a certain movie or children's channel in order to get some MUCH needed "ME" time. Perhaps, when I do a word of mouth marketing campaign, another mom will be introduced to a brand they had previously never used and fall in LOVE.

How do you feel you influence moms offline? Is it more than chatting in the carpool line? Absolutely it's more than chatting in the carpool line! It's moms seeing other moms in the grocery aisle and conversing on different brands. It's about moms telling other moms what works for them, and their experience with a particular product. It's about recommending to people you know and run into frequently who/what services to use AND stay away from. It's about me wearing my FAVORITE baby wrap and three different women approaching me and asking me where I purchased it. It's about having an AWESOME hair day (TRUST me ... as a busy mom of preschoolers, that doesn't happen too often!) and having several people asking me where I get my hair cut and sending business to my favorite hairdresser.

How can companies best support your business or mission as a mom? By listening! We are not just moms who do nothing but get together and gossip or talk about potty training techniques ... there is SO much that concerns us (product safety and quality being HIGH on the list!!) regarding our children and families. Also, don't dismiss me (or give me a canned response) when I have a concern ... it really sours me on the company's product/service.

How do you feel companies can best connect with moms, particularly those who are influencers? Again, I say—just listen. They could use actual moms more in product development ... instead of having people who can "guess" with statistics on what would sell, how about using moms? They are your BEST gauge on what MOMS would buy and use. You can damn well bet that a real mom would be telling Mattel to STOP it with sewing Barbie's EFFING hair to the EFFING package already! Seriously! And do those toys REALLY need all that plastic coated wire tying it in 125 different places to the packaging and twisted by some unholy force so that it is beyond unwrapping—so we have to find the scissors (but since we can never seem to find the "good" scissors, we are forced to use the blunt tips from the art box) to just cut those EMM EFFERS?

Last words: Moms are in every walk of life, and in every socioeconomic bracket. I am seeing more and more that the higher your household income bracket is, the more likely a company is to even want your opinion on their product. I understand that the higher income brackets are more likely to purchase/use certain brands, but what about trying to engage moms in the lower income brackets? I have been in several income brackets in my lifetime, and there are MANY brands that I refuse to compromise on because of their quality, no matter WHAT my economic situation has been. I think moms are pretty much the silent (and most underrated) backbone of our society. Just look at who shows up at most PTA meetings. Just look at who comprises most of any of the "booster" clubs in any high school. Just look at who is accompanying their child to doctor appointments. Just look at who is doing the grocery shopping. Just look at who is blogging. Just walk down any street in the early evenings and see how many times you will hear from a dad "Well, what did your mom say?" or "Better clear it with Mom first." Just look at who is preparing most of the family meals, wiping the most butts (and noses). I could go on and on, but you get the gist.

Name: Stephanie Hess

Children: One son, age 3

Hometown: Hartford City, IN

Company Name(s): BargainFun

Short description of business: Tips on saving money, making money online and coupons. I also share product reviews and giveaways. I love sharing great deals and products with my readers, if I can help even one person save some money.

Websites or Blogs you own: Bargain Fun http://bargainfun.net

Approximate audience size: I've had over 100,000 page views

Facebook Id: Steph Bargainfun

Twitter Id: @bargainfunl

Approximate # of followers: 650

What's the best way for companies to reach you as an influencer or as a mom? Email: bargainfunl@yahoo.com

What do you think is the biggest mistake companies make in trying to work with moms? I just don't think they do it enough.

Are there companies who you feel are doing a great job connecting with moms? Yes, Hasbro is one of them.

How do you feel you influence moms online? I love sharing reviews and giveaways.

Name: Amy Hilbrich Davis

Children and ages: Seven, ages 18, 16 ½, 15, 13 ½, 10, 8, and 6

Hometown: Stilwell, KS

Company Name(s): Inspiring Moms

Short description of business: Inspiring Moms is dedicated to enriching and improving the lives of moms and their families. We provide professional development for motherhood. Our work life programs provide strategies, tools, and best practices to guide mothers towards achieving greater balance, success, and happiness. The foundation of our program is the Balance MAP; an online tool that provides over 63 million unique versions of action plans to help mothers achieve success in their family life. Research and development of Inspiring Moms began in 2006 and the program was created in 2007. Seminars and workshops to confirm and perfect our program were done in '08 and '09. The Balance MAP product was launched in 2010. Our motivation was and still is to enrich and improve the lives of mothers and their families. As a new mom, I recognized that for me to be and feel successful at managing all the demands of motherhood I needed development—I needed more than my instincts. I realized that when I approached motherhood as if it was a profession, and found training and development for those areas where I didn't feel strong, I felt more efficient and became more effective. With that confidence came an increase in my happiness and fulfillment. It became clear to me as our family grew, that my success and happiness was an indicator of my family's happiness. As we developed our company and did the research on personal and family wellness, our hunch and my personal experience was confirmed. A happy and fulfilled mother raises a thriving family. It is my mission to help each mom and her family achieve their definition of happy and fulfilled. We do not anticipate exiting in the near future. We are by design, self-funded, yet would entertain merging with a strategic partner who is also dedicated to helping families thrive. We see our company as a catalyst for improving the lives of today's and tomorrow's parents. We plan to create a new paradigm around parenting.

Websites or Blogs you own: Inspiring Moms www.inspiringmoms.com

Approximate audience size: Forty million women with children under 18 years

Websites or blogs you contribute to: Cozi.com, trueconfessions.com, hannahkeeley.com, lynnekenney.com, and cvworkingfamilies.org.

Facebook Id: inspiring Moms

Twitter Id: @inspiringmoms

Approximate # of followers: 7,200

How many moms do you typically interact with during the week offline? Depending on whether I am presenting to corporations or not, I interact and support hundreds of moms in person weekly through keynotes, workshops, and one-on-one coaching.

Offline Involvements: I have just recently aligned with Corporate Voices to help improve the lives of working families. I am anxious to provide Inspiring Moms and the Balance MAP to those corporations who are dedicated to helping their working mothers and their families thrive. Our program provides ongoing training and development. 2011 will be a huge year of growth for Inspiring Moms in corporate America as we just launched the Balance MAP and presented it at the Working Mother Media Work Life Congress in NYC in October 2010.

What's the best way for companies to reach you as an influencer or as a mom? Email: amy@inspiringmoms.com

How is the best way to work with you and your company? The Balance MAP is the foundation for both our b2b and consumer program. It is our online tool that recently won a 2010 Huggies® MomInspired™ Grant for its ability to make the lives of parents easier and more enjoyable. The Balance MAP helps moms take control of and organize their busy lives. All it requires is 15 minutes to complete an online confidential questionnaire.

What do you think is the biggest mistake companies make in trying to work with moms? Mothers juggle an enormous amount of demands each day with little end in sight. When companies affirm mothers by recognizing everything on their plate, they feel appreciated and will reward those companies that treat them with respect and understanding. Those companies that help them manage will be rewarded with their time, attention, and business.

Are there companies who you feel are doing a great job connecting with moms? Obviously, Kimberly Clark has done a phenomenal job by reaching out to moms. The Huggies® MomInspired™ Grant program is ingenious and sends a powerful message that KC cares about the needs of moms and their families. They make it clear that they want to support moms on their journey, both as entrepreneurs and mothers. They are making a difference for millions of moms all over the world!

How do you feel you influence moms online? Motherhood is hard—physically, mentally, and emotionally. Most moms judge themselves and feel judged by others at how well they manage the demands of raising a family. As a mom and family expert, I want to share my expertise to make the lives of moms easier and more fulfilling, which means it will be more fun. And when a mom has fun, so do her kids. I want moms to know that there is no "one way" to achieve balance, success, and happiness, but each mom has her way. I want moms to know how much they matter to the equation of a happy family. I want to elevate how they treat themselves while they are raising their families.

How do you feel you influence moms offline? Is it more than chatting in the carpool line? Reaching out and connecting with other moms is important, but it's more than that. It's HOW you talk to other moms. My attitude and how I encourage other moms makes a difference—it matters. I believe that every one of us is doing our best to raise our families—I really do. We only know what we know. I have always tried to share what is working for me as I raise my kids—even before Inspiring Moms. By sharing those specific techniques or strategies that I have implemented over the years which work (and those that don't), I am enhancing the life of one mom and her family. Now that I am a mom and family expert and my company is dedicated to helping parents be satisfied and fulfilled at managing the demands of raising a family, I not only share how to do it, but I share why it's important, and with the help of the Balance MAP, I help parents focus in on where to begin. Each of us has strengths or areas of our life where we feel really confident, and areas where we wish we were stronger—that's life. None of us is as strong as all of us!

How can companies best support your business or mission as a mom? Companies can support Inspiring Moms by hiring us to provide employee engagement programs. Ultimately, when companies support their working mothers/fathers, they support us. We provide employee engagement programs designed to impact and enhance the family experience. We have a suite of offerings to meet the needs of any size organization. Research confirms that when a mother feels in control and satisfied at home, she comes to work more focused, engaged, and productive. In short, we begin by providing the Balance MAP to every mother (fathers will be added in 3/2011) and then armed with their customized action plan, our program continues to strengthen each parent with ongoing development. Companies receive a bird's eye view of the strengths and challenges of their working parents through our Pulse Report. Companies gain a crystal clear understanding of where to assign their resources as an organization, based upon where their working mothers/fathers feel concern or confident.

How do you feel companies can best connect with moms, particularly those who are influencers? Social media provides the perfect backdrop for easily connecting with mom influencers, yet, without question, the most jaw-dropping service happens offline. I love to see an online connection be taken offline. A powerful and recent example happened to me just days ago. I had an amazing customer service experience with Zappos.com. The customer rep was beyond helpful, kind, funny, and made me feel like I wasn't lame for returning a pair of boots a year later. The day after our talk, I received a hand written thank you note from that customer loyalty rep along with two books. It's that experience which affirmed my practices at Inspiring Moms and one that has lead to a relationship with a company (Zappos) whom I think is "best in class" of customer service. This exchange has resulted in brand loyalty (I have pledged to buy my shoes only with Zappos). Bottom line, It's that attention to detail, that little extra that shows an investment in time and energy which impresses me the most. All it takes is a hand-written thank-you note to send a powerful message.

Final Words: Katherine Ellison writes about the bounty of benefits that accompany motherhood in her book, *The Mommy Brain*. Put simply, we become smarter, better multi-taskers, higher EQ, and better communicators, as moms. What does that mean to our sphere of influence? It means that we have the power to create change for ourselves and our families across the globe. Together we can create a virtuous cycle where mother supports mother and company supports company, and government supports government to make the lives of families healthier, happier and more successful. None of us is as strong as all of us!

Name: Deana Hipwell

Children: One, age 4

Hometown: Winston Salem, NC

Company Name(s): Frugal Homeschooling Mom

Short description of business: Helping homeschooling families who are living on stretched budgets. There are so many families who have chosen to teach their children at home instead of sending them to public school or private school, and one parent (usually the mother) doesn't work in order to do so. So these families are living off one income, and I encourage and support them in those efforts. I began blogging in March of 2009 when we first decided we were going to homeschool. I was passionate about it and was learning a lot about it and wanted to share and talk about what I was planning. I had read several really great blogs and decided it would be a fun thing to write about my passions and have people that actually liked listening to (reading) what I had to say. I was also getting really good at couponing strategies, and decided to blend my two interests together into an informative and encouraging site for those to visit who had the same interests. My mission is helping others to live an abundant life on a not-so-abundant budget.

Websites or Blogs you own: www.TheFrugalHomeschoolingMom.com

Approximate audience size: I have about 3,000 site views per month

Facebook Id: Frugal Homeschooling Mom

Twitter Id: @tfhsm

Approximate # of followers: 603

How many moms do you typically interact with during the week offline? 20-30

Offline Involvements: I attend church, I am involved in four local homeschool groups, with combined memberships of over 2,000 families. I am also involved in small community groups as well. I coach women on how to shop with coupons, for free. Someone coached me for free, and I'm so thankful she did, so I pass it on to others.

What's the best way for companies to reach you as an influencer or as a mom? By email: thefrugalhomeschoolingmom@gmail.com

What do you think is the biggest mistake companies make in trying to work with moms? Giving strict deadlines. Moms sometimes have trouble meeting them if they're busy with little ones. In my business, blogging, many moms are "working from home" (blogging) just so that they can stay at home and not have to work outside the home. Their priority is their children/family, and work comes second. A deadline is a joke—we'll get to it when we can, and if you want to work with us, you'll understand that and not push us. One time I had an advertiser give me a deadline after I had told him my reasonable time frame, and I just knew I wouldn't be able to meet it. He was nice and we worked together anyway.

How do you define influence among moms? It means a built-up amount of trust, based on a relationship or friendship. Nothing one mom says to another will matter if there is no trust built up in their friendship.

How do you feel you influence moms online? I hope that I influence them to be confident in their choices, no matter what choices they make for themselves. I'm not out to tell them what to do; rather I want to give them the knowledge they need to make their own decisions about what's right for them. I put the information out there for them to read, about homeschooling, and about saving money, and if they find something useful, then great!

How do you feel you influence moms offline? Is it more than chatting in the carpool line? I influence other moms by living a life that's a little different, that causes them to ask questions, and I find myself teaching others fairly often, and answering whys, whats and hows about what I do.

Name: Natalie Hoage

Children: Three, ages 3, and 1 (twins)

Hometown: Corona, CA

Websites or Blogs you own: Mommy of a Monster and Twins http://www.mommyofamonster.com

Websites or blogs you contribute to: Our Mommyhood http://www.ourmommyhood.com

Twitter Id: @mommyofamonster

Approximate # of followers: 2,600

What's the best way for companies to reach you as an influencer or as a mom? Via email at natalieblogs@hotmail.com or Twitter ... if companies are searching for mom bloggers and influencers, I think both of those avenues are the best way to do it. It tells the company the mom is already open to being contacted and open to working with new companies/brands.

What do you think is the biggest mistake companies make in trying to work with moms? They assume that we don't have a strong educational and/or business background (I have a bachelor's degree in business, and started my MBA. I also worked in management for several years in both accounting and HR).

Are there companies who you feel are doing a great job connecting with moms? Boogie Wipes, Disney, Nickelodeon

How do you feel you influence moms online? Via Twitter. And on my blog by posting about "mommy must haves" and doing product reviews. Also, if I find a product/service that is a time and/or money saver, I share it.

How can companies best support your business or mission as a mom? ASK US what we want and need! Get us involved in testing products. Surveys. Brand Ambassadors. Knowing and understanding how we can help spread the word about their products/services. Not taking us for granted because we're "just moms."

What motivates you to tell other moms (good or bad) about a company, brand or product? If I have a positive or negative strong reaction, I share. If I think my opinion or experience will help others, I share. If I want to know how others feel about a company, brand, or product, I start a conversation on Facebook, Twitter, or Blog Frog.

How do you feel companies can best connect with moms, particularly those who are

influencers? Twitter! Also, through mommy blogs, Facebook, and of course word-of-mouth recommendations. I know that when I am asked to review a product, after I review it I always tell the company that I know a few other moms that might be interested in their product.

Final words: With social media becoming the new wave of marketing and advertising, I think companies should really get into contact with moms who know and understand this avenue. If a company is "old school" or remains in the dark about social media, they will lose a huge amount of money and quite possibly new customers simply by ignoring the way so many of us want to be communicated with and contacted through.

Name: Lauren Hochreiter

Children: Two, ages 7 and 4

Hometown: Port Richey, FL

Short description of business: 4BabyAndMom started out as a small business online selling hand-made clothing, accessories and toys that I made in my spare time. I also sold beauty products and pocketbooks that I created for moms. After the CPSIA laws came out, I decided to close my shop because of the grey areas of the laws. When I find a product I love, I share it with everyone. Some of my online mom friends started their blogs around the same time, and with their suggestions, I switched my small business to a blog, and 4BabyAndMom officially started in November of 2008. Since then, we've been booming, and I could not have asked for more. In 2009, another mom joined the 4BabyAndMom team and we've been growing ever since.

Websites or Blogs you own: 4 Baby And Mom www.4BabyAndMom.com

Approximate audience size: 3,000 unique/month

Websites or blogs you contribute to: I participate in several message boards, forums, networks and things geared toward parenting, blogging or reviews, *i.e.*, Mamasphere.com, The Product Review Place, etc. I also have an article that was published on Mommie911.com on 1/30/09.

Twitter Id: @4BabyAndMom

Approximate # of followers: 1,910

Online Involvements and associations: Mom Select, OnetoOne Network, Mom Central, Team Mom, Soft Scrub Captain, The View Ambassador, The Product Review Place.

How many moms do you typically interact with during the week offline? Offline I interact with about 25-50 moms weekly.

Offline Involvements: I belong to two elementary school PTAs, SAC (School Advisory Committee), Parent Involvement Committee, Policy Council, and volunteer at both elementary schools, as well.

Offline Community Service: I volunteer at both of my children's elementary schools, in the classroom, and in the community.

What do you think is the biggest mistake companies make in trying to work with moms? Underselling the Mom Factor. Moms are the most influential consumer to date. Word of mouth marketing is always the best, but many companies try to undersell and undervalue the moms they work with. I also hate when a company doesn't take the time to get to know the moms they contact ... writing an impersonal, "Hello Blogger!" letter and then telling me you like what I write about really frustrates me. If you are contacting me, trying to sell me your company and product, then look through a few of my pages and scroll to the bottom of my post so at least you know my name. Companies pay for advertising, but often feel that they can just ask a mom to talk or write about their product, service or program without a cost. It takes time out of our days to write about their company, and we should feel taken care of, in that sense. When I started out, I asked for only the product to review as compensation for my time. As my blog expanded, I started charging minimal fees for certain components, or specific articles. I lost several of my connections because they refused to pay even a minimal fee. My time is valuable, even more so because I am a mom who wears many hats.

Are there companies who you feel are doing a great job connecting with moms? Absolutely! There are many companies that I work with (HIT Entertainment, Foot Locker, Three Peas Co., Jump Start, Sea World, and Soft Scrub to name a few) that I never have to worry about. Last year, we took in a foster child; I had a company contact message me to see how everything was going. I wrote for that company several months prior, but their message showed me that not only did they follow my blog, but that they cared about their bloggers.

How do you define influence among moms? We put our hearts into everything that we do, and our audience recognizes it. We are truthful in our reviews and don't overly romanticize a product. My kids are super hard on their toys, their clothes and their opinions. I have no problem in contacting a company and telling them, "We thought we'd really love your product, but it's just not right for our family. Here's what we suggest you might change ...." The clients we work with value our opinion and thankfully, we rarely encounter a product we genuinely dislike 100%. Moms we are in touch with (online and offline) know that if they ask our opinion, they're going to get it, and that they can trust that no matter what our experience is or was—that it's the truth. So back to the question, "How do I define influence among moms?"—by trust and truthfulness.

How do you feel you influence moms offline? Is it more than chatting in the carpool line? Sometimes the most amount of magic happens in the carpool line! Standing, waiting for my child to get out of school has introduced me to many people in my community I would have never met if I wasn't there. I've made many good friends through that, and since diving into all of my extra-curricular activities (PTA, SAC, Policy Council, Parent Involvement Committee) I feel that I've been better able to influence my peers in person. I've become more resourceful and have taken that knowledge with me to workshops, meetings and get-togethers. The moms I talk with trust me from the get-go, whether it's in the shopping aisle, car loop, or at a school function. I do notice more when I personally influence people offline, but that's all part of the heart I put into helping people, the face-to-face contact, and the instant reaction and satisfaction.

How can companies best support your business or mission as a mom? By supporting us, encouraging us, helping us. Don't be afraid to invest in a mom, be honest with a mom, and loyal to a mom. If you like what we did, tell us. If there's a problem, tell us. Treat us like you would your own mother.

How do you feel companies can best connect with moms, particularly those who are influencers? Blog hop, take a day to really read some articles, reviews, and pictures. See what your mom influencer/blogger is all about. Learn their names, (most of us have them on our profile or contact us page, if not at the bottom of our posts), and what they're into. Click their network buttons, or other blogs they follow. Chances are they are similar in their likes and dislikes and you may meet new people. Put yourself out there, offer product and compensation, and make us feel valuable as influencers. Highlight our reviews or blogs on your company website, newsletter, blog, or Facebook fan page. Work with us, in a "one hand washes the other" type commitment.

Final words: Moms and their influence are economically resilient. Whether they are looking to scrimp and save, or splurge on the best of the best, moms will take the opinion of other moms and their friends over the opinion of an advertiser, advertisement, or sales person.

Name: Stacey Hoffer Weckstein

Children: Two, ages 7 and 5

Hometown: Evanston, IL

Company Name(s): Inspiring Social Media

Short description of business: A place where social media and personal growth connect. I started Inspiring Social Media in December of 2009 to help inspiring women in the personal growth industry share their voices in the world of social media. In July of 2010, I built the Inspiring Social Media Moms Network for social media for people who want to both be inspired and inspire others. This network of moms participates in engaging personal growth social media campaigns, and reviews products that are good for them (body, mind, and spirit). The mission of this mom's network is to use our influence to inspire the world.

Overall, Inspiring Social Media creates custom social media campaigns for inspiring personal growth companies, entrepreneurs, authors, life coaches, artists, and spas. When my clients partner with me, they are able to focus more on what they are truly passionate about while I make it more user-friendly to engage and connect with their clients, customers, and fans.

Websites or Blogs you own: Mom Renewal http://momrenewal.com, Inspiring Social Media http://www.inspiringsocialmedia.com and Still Look Pregnant http://www.stilllookpregnant.com

Approximate audience size: 4,500 unique visitors a month

Websites or blogs you contribute to: http://thechicagomoms.com, http://technorati.com/women (starting soon), http://www.thebalancingact.com/blogs

Facebook Id: Mom Renewal

Twitter Id: @MomRenewal

Approximate # of followers: 4,725 Twitter followers

What's the best way for companies to reach you as an influencer or as a mom? Email: Stacey@MomRenewal.com

Are there companies who you feel are doing a great job connecting with moms? Chevrolet, Mabels Labels, Hewlett Packard

How do you define influence among moms? I think influence has to do with how bloggers use different social media platforms, how often they are using social media, who they are connecting with online, and how many people engage with them online. I think numbers are important but influence is so much more than just numbers. I think a blogger who truly engages and connects with 4000 Twitter followers has more influence than someone who has 40,000 Twitter followers but lacks the ability to authentically engage and connect with their audience. I think influence has to do with trust, engagement, and authenticity.

How do you feel you influence moms online? I believe my greatest gift to moms online is when I'm influencing them to put themselves back onto their priority lists and practice self-care. There are many ways to do this and there are many brands that can support this mission. Working with brands to support moms is a win-win-win situation for brands, online moms, and me.

Is there one moment when you realized you were impacting the life/lives of others? There were many moments when I knew I was impacting the lives of others when I was leading the social media efforts of the Inner Mean Girl 40 Day Cleanse. We received over 100 blog posts from moms around the country who stood up to their inner mean girls and began embracing their inner wisdom instead. That type of influence is priceless, but their positive energy helped influence their readers, their offline friends, and their children.

What motivates you to tell other moms (good or bad) about a company, brand or product?
I am inspired to tell other moms about a company, brand, or product when:
I know more about the people behind the brand; I feel as if the people behind the brand understand the needs of modern day moms; I see the people behind the brand supporting moms; I see the people behind the brand authentically engaging with moms and not just marketing to them.

How do you feel companies can best connect with moms, particularly those who are influencers? Build true relationships with social media moms. Pay social media moms as freelance consultants and/or spokeswomen. Ask social media moms how you can best support them.

Name: Linda Hughes

Children: One, age 23

Hometown: Chicago, IL

Company Name(s): Monkey Bizness

Short description of business: Handmade eco-friendly products for babies, children, and moms. I've always been an avid crafter: candle making, soaps, crocheting, and sewing. And I like to use my skills to help others in need as well. When hurricane Katrina hit years ago, watching the news and seeing children being homeless and not even having one toy to comfort them was heartbreaking to me.

So I set in motion a plan. I started making up sock monkey dolls and shipping them to shelters in the affected areas for the children. I started emailing my girlfriends that live in different states and told them about my plight. They were excited to be part of this and joined in and mailed me material, socks, etc.

In return for my friends' unselfish acts in helping me out, I asked them if they had a person they wanted to honor. The monkeys were all given names in memory of a loved one. I thought it was a great way to touch people's lives all the way around, have it come full circle.

Since then I have kept up the tradition of making these, and attach name tags to most of the monkeys. I donate to hospitals, shelters, etc. Then the requests started coming in, people wanted to buy them. So I decided to keep going at it, and offer to sell these to people.

I am amazed that something I did with the true intention of helping others has turned into a home business, and has expanded my product line. I feel very blessed that I have a chance to make a go of this. I put a lot of time and care into making each item and they are all unique and handmade which makes each one a little different looking but with their own flair. They truly are a passion of mine and a labor of love.

I just know that when you do something you love it shows, in your product, in your attitude, and how you view life.

Websites or Blogs you own: Monkey Bizness http://Hyenacart.com/Monkeybizness, http://monkeybiznessl.blogspot.com/

Websites or blogs you contribute to: http://www.cafemom.com/group/108910, http://www.carewear.org/, http://www.orgsites.com/il/projectlinuschicago/

Facebook Id: Linda Hughes

Online Involvements and associations: Admin of Circle of Hope on cafemom.com http://www.cafemom.com/group/108910

What do you think is the biggest mistake companies make in trying to work with moms? Don't push products on people. Do take time to say thank you.

Are there companies who you feel are doing a great job connecting with moms? Mom Select

How do you feel you influence moms online? I help low-income moms in need and ship them items to help them. I offer an ear to anyone who needs someone to listen. I help people to be more frugal by offering suggestions, and eco-friendly ways.

How do you feel companies can best connect with moms, particularly those who are influencers? Discuss the companies; make it friendly and welcoming, but not pushy.

Final words: I think moms want to connect with other moms, to get advice, tips, and understanding from one another, etc.

Name: Melissa Jennings and Shelley King Steimer

Children and ages: Melissa has one, age 5 and Shelley has two, ages 4 and 3

Hometown: Independence, KY—Melissa and Walton, KY—Shelley

Company Name(s): MJennings Designs, LLC—Stockpiling Moms and Stockpiling Dads

Short description of business: We co-own a Frugal Mom Blog called Stockpiling Moms. It's a guide to frugal living. We feature money-saving deals, frugal recipes, menu planning and much more! We started Stockpiling Moms on December 12, 2009. We are friends who met through Guatemalan Adoption. We left our careers to stay home with our children and because of the tough economy started stockpiling. We wanted to help others so we started our blog. We are an LLC.

Websites or Blogs you own: Stockpiling Moms http://www.stockpilingmoms.com and Stockpiling Dads http://www.stockpilingdads.com

Approximate audience size: 32,030 unique visitors a month and 4,000 page views a day.

Websites or blogs you contribute to: My Mommy Manuel, http://mymommymanual.com/ —Melissa is a Mommy Expert, Cincinnati.com—Bloggers Network http://cincinnati.com/blogs/cincymoms/2010/09/01/check-out-the-new-cincy-moms-blog-network/ Blog Frog—Frugal Living Community Leader—November 2010, Crazy Coupon Mommy—Kroger and Meijer Deals, MoJo Savings—Kroger

Deal Seeker, Our Kroger and Meijer matchups are on a total of 15 blogs.

Facebook Id: Stockpiling Moms

Twitter Id: @stockpilingmoms

Approximate # of followers: 1,580

Online Involvements and associations: Aquafina Flavorsplash Mom, Kaplan Tutoring Test Drive Program.

How many moms do you typically interact with during the week offline? 100

What's the best way for companies to reach you as an influencer or as a mom? Email: stockpilingmoms@fuse.net or on Twitter @stockpilingmoms

What do you think is the biggest mistake companies make in trying to work with moms? If they are not taking Moms seriously and Mom Bloggers as brand ambassadors they are making a major mistake. Social media is HUGE.

Are there companies who you feel are doing a great job connecting with moms? Those brands that are doing a great job: Aquafina, all brands working with House Party including Wii, Jello, Tombstone, and many more. Country Bob's is doing a great job!

How do you feel you influence moms offline? Is it more than chatting in the carpool line? I am serving as the Holiday Shop Chairperson for our PTO. I am able to make a difference in the budget by showing them how to strategically use coupons.

How can companies best support your business or mission as a mom? They can network with moms in the form of paid posts, reviews, giveaways and can form partnerships that help us both succeed.

How do you feel companies can best connect with moms, particularly those who are influencers? Reach out and see if there is a connection; if so, develop a more lasting partnership.

Final words: I like that we are able to teach consumers to save thousands of dollars per year in addition to being able to give back to the community by stockpiling. Economically we are making a difference in people's lives through stockpiling.

Name: Bryana Jordan

Children: Two, 6 and 3 (both boys)

Hometown: South Dayton, NY

Company Name(s): Coupons On Caffeine

Short description of business: Finding bargains for my family and others to live rich without spending. Started late Aug of 2010. I was motivated because I was seeing a lot of people cutting back with the economy going the way it was. People losing jobs and not being able to find them were scaling back in big ways. This was the time I decided to get out of the military after 9 years. Being on deployments and away from my boys was just very hard for me. I noticed people were not going out as much, and I heard over and over, I can't afford to do that right now. People were almost strapped to their lack of income. I realized that people were eating out less, buying generic items, and scaling down on "fun" spending, but they were not happy about it. That's when I realized that people are saving money the way their grandparents may have when they were growing up. With online shopping, collective buying sites, stores that double and even triple coupons at times, people can learn to save in all new ways. I wanted to share with people the idea that just because you live on a limited budget, does not mean that you eat noodles every night, never go out and never splurge on yourself. It's about splurging frugally!

Websites or Blogs you own: Coupons on Caffeine http://www.couponsoncaffeine.com

Websites or blogs you contribute to: http://kingdomfirstmom.com

Twitter Id: @Qponsncaffeine

Online Involvements and associations: Viewpoints

What's the best way for companies to reach you as an influencer or as a mom? Honestly as a mom, I don't normally try something until I have seen it. Until someone else has raved about it, I'm very leery about buying a new product. Today's market has so much to choose from. It seems like every time you think, "OK I'm going to buy that" a new "improved" version comes out and now I want to wait again to see how that product pans out. As an influencer I want to try it first. I would never recommend something to a parent that I didn't believe in myself.

What do you think is the biggest mistake companies make in trying to work with moms? When working with moms companies expect a good review. In some cases it is true. A company may have a great product, and that warrants a nice review. However, it is not a product that they would have a "need" for. Some products seem very excessive in the market place. They may be good products, but there is no real "need."

How do you define influence among moms? Influence with moms in person comes naturally. It's not forced. A topic comes up and you remember "Oh, when my kid was young we loved that toy." The conversation flows and the mom trusts you as a person, and trusts your opinion even if you only met 5 minutes ago.

Is there one moment when you realized you were impacting the life/lives of others? Yes! I saw a woman at a store, with her boy and she was putting back some items as they were "too much right now." We started talking, I gave her my card for my web page and didn't think anything of it. About a week later, the woman saw me again in Target, where she was getting a prescription filled. She yelled out "Hey wait, don't go anywhere, just wait." I could see she was torn between coming to see me and finishing her prescription. So I waited for a second, not knowing that this was the woman I talked to a week ago. She came over and HUGGED me. Right there in Target. Then explained she was on my site for an hour the day I gave her my card. She was so happy and grateful that I almost cried. It was amazing to know that I was helping someone like that!

How do you feel companies can best connect with moms, particularly those who are influencers? People who are influencers are naturally outgoing. They LIKE to talk to people, strike up conversations, etc. Events are always something that go over well, such as events that they can take their children to (if it is for the kids), and introduce them to the product. Moms like to be social, so getting a group together will only result in good things.

Final Words: More and more parents are staying at home. This is going to be a large shift in buying. I don't see the economy getting any better; I see more stay-at-home parents because they can't afford day care. Moms that grew up in the 80s were never taught how to be a stay-at-home mom. Many of these moms have degrees and don't know how to cook, clean, etc., so they look to others. The only way they know is their grandma's way of being a stay-at-home mom. I think being a stay-at-home mom is NOT the way it was, it has shifted; but people don't know HOW it's shifted and are struggling with this.

For example, what gets out a stain? Well back when Grandma was a kid, all you had was bleach. BUT go to the store now, and there are 100s of cleaning products all saying it will get that stain out. What do you do? You ask a friend, "Hey what do you use for XYZ?" (And you don't ask on the phone, you send a text). Or you ask the mom standing next to you in the store, or when you drop the kids off at school the next day you ask the mom that always has nice clothes for her kids. They ask other moms, because there is no one else TO ask.

Name: Cecily Kellogg

Children: One, age 4

Hometown: Philadelphia, PA

Company Name(s): CecilyKellogg.com

Short Description of business: launched in 2007, when daughter was a year old, so that I could work from home.

Websites or Blogs you own: www.CecilyKellogg.com, www.CecilyK.com, www.UppercaseWoman.com

Approximate audience size: 80,000 pageviews a month

Websites or blogs you contribute to: editor at Aiming Low

Facebook Id: Cecily Kellogg

Approximate # of followers: 2,500

Twitter Id: @CecilyK

Approximate # of followers: 37,500

What's the best way for companies to reach you as an influencer or as a mom? Email me.

What do you think is the biggest mistake companies make in trying to work with moms? Not researching their sites before pitching.

How do you define influence among moms? Really, really depends. A mom may have a small readership but be highly influential with that group. I have a large readership but I'm not sure how influential I am.

How do you feel you influence moms online? Remember the Amazon pedophile book? Yeah. I pretty much broke that story (although Angie from A Whole Lot of Nothing told me about it first, I was retweeted some 1,500 times).

How can companies best support your business or mission as a mom? Buy ads on my blog.

Name: Alicia Kirby

Children: Three, ages 6, 3, 1

Hometown: Elgin, MN

Websites or Blogs you own: The Mama Report http://themamareport.com/

Approximate audience size: 8,000

Websites or blogs you contribute to: Money Saving Mom

Twitter Id: @themamareport

Approximate # of followers: 50

Brief history of your company: It began in September 2010. My mission is to connect with other moms, review products and establish a voice on the web.

What's the best way for companies to reach you as an influencer or as a mom? Through email: themamareport@gmail.com

Name: Sherrelle Kirkland-Andrews

Children: Two, ages 15 and 9

Hometown: Atlanta, GA

Websites or Blogs you own: Funki Diva Girl Funkidivagirl.com

Facebook Id: Funkidivagirl and Chilidawgdog.

Twitter Id: @Funkidivagirl

Approximate # of followers: 1860 at this time

Offline Involvements: Mocha Moms

What do you think is the biggest mistake companies make in trying to work with moms? Putting everyone in the same bucket and labeling them all as "mom bloggers." There are so many ways of writing a blog and companies need to be aware and do their homework on a blog/website before approaching the owner. While some bloggers are strictly review bloggers, others are better at writing stories around the brand. Lifestyle blogs (like mine) are just as influential as so-called "mommy blogs."

Are there companies who you feel are doing a great job connecting with moms? Disney World; they treat bloggers with respect.

How do you feel you influence moms online? By being transparent and authentic. I think moms listen to me because I tell the truth. I have proved through many blog posts that I am a complex individual—just like they are—and I am relatable and touchable.

Is there one moment when you realized you were impacting the life/lives of others? My website name came from my email address. I was a frequent contributor to my neighborhood email loop and one day someone—who I didn't know—stopped me on the street when they heard my (real) name and said, "Aren't you Funkidivagirl? I recognize your real name connected to your email address. You send out good information."

What motivates you to tell other moms (good or bad) about a company, brand or product? My motto is: why reinvent the wheel? If I can save you money, time or energy, then great. Or if I can tell you about something that will make your life easier/better/more fun/healthier, then I love to share that information.

Name: Angie Knutson

Children: Four, ages 10,,8,,6, and 2

Hometown: Richmond, VA

Short description of business: I started My Four Monkeys blog in 2009 as a way to spread the word about our favorite products, the products we use for playtime, schooltime, relaxing time, cleaning time, and more. My Four Monkeys was birthed as a resource for parents.

Websites or Blogs you own: My Four Monkeys http://www.myfourmonkeys.com/

Approximate audience size: 3,000

Websites or blogs you contribute to: www.MyFourMonkeys.com

Twitter Id: @MyFourMonkeys

Approximate # of followers: 4,600

Online Involvements and associations: Social Media Manager for Double Duty Divas, Tommy Mommy for Thomas Nelson Publishers, Mabel's Labels BuzzMama, Mom Bloggers Club Reviewer, MomSpark Media Member, One2One Network Member, PBS Sprout Band of Bloggers

Offline Involvements: Homeschool groups and Various Church Ministries

What's the best way for companies to reach you as an influencer or as a mom? via email: (angie@myfourmonkeys.com) or via Twitter: (twitter.com/MyFourMonkeys)

What do you think is the biggest mistake companies make in trying to work with moms? Not placing enough value on the time and effort it takes to do what we do.

Name: Maura Kopulos

Children: Four, ages 6, 4, and 2 (twins)

Hometown: Woodstock, IL

Company Name(s): ZYNKS for drinks

Short description of business: ZYNKS for drinks are fun drink identifiers for cups, cans, water bottles, juice boxes, beer bottles, sports drinks and more. ZYNKS for drinks was started in January of 2007, about four years ago. The idea came to life when we were at a friend's BBQ and my oldest son came running up to me asking me if I knew which drink was his. I looked at the other moms I was talking to and we all shrugged our shoulders as we looked at the sea of juice boxes on the table.

A few months into playing around with the idea, I saw a show on TV that was running a contest for the NEXT BIG IDEA in the Chicago area. I knew I could get my product to the point where I could present it to the panel and so that became my focus.

My exit strategy was always to either sell the company or license it when it was ready. Six months ago, I was able to sign rights over to a company that is now licensing my product to many retailers that I was not able to penetrate.

Websites or Blogs you own: ZYNKS for Drinks www.zynks4drinks.com, www.zynks.com, www.shop.zynks.com, blog.zynks.com,

Websites or blogs you contribute to: www.blog.zynks.com

Facebook Id: ZYNKS for drinks

How many moms do you typically interact with during the week offline? 50-75+

Offline Involvements: Book Club, Bible Study, Coop, Cub Scouts (son), Lego Club (son), soccer (daughter and son), running group, Home School group, Home School social group, and volunteer driver for Meals on Wheels

What's the best way for companies to reach you as an influencer or as a mom? Email: Maura@zynks.com

Are there companies who you feel are doing a great job connecting with moms? I really do feel that bsmmedia.com does a terrific job!

How do you feel you influence moms online? I have had a lot of people comment and write to me regarding my product and blog. They really love to read the blog and I find that they relate to it because I don't pretend to know exactly what I am doing. My degrees are totally unrelated with what I am doing with my business. I am just someone who had an idea and I muddle through it and in the end, I get the job done. I am not saying that I don't appreciate advice by the experts by any means; I am just saying that I think that others find me approachable because I am a little more humble.

Is there one moment when you realized you were impacting the life/lives of others? I know I have inspired many other moms, who have had ideas, to do something with them. I have talked with many moms about what steps to take next and where to find the resources available. I try to help them learn from my mistakes.

Name: Trish Kratka

Children: Three, ages 16, 11, and 6

Hometown: Belfast, ME

Company Name(s): Kratka Photography

Short description of business: Stock photos as well as photo sessions

Websites or Blogs you own: I am Succeeding www.iamsucceeding.com and Kratka Photography www.kratkaphotography.com

Approximate audience size: 5,000

Websites or blogs you contribute to: http://journeyofhearts.wordpress.com/

Twitter Id: @IamSucceeding

Approximate # of followers: 2,300

How many moms do you typically interact with during the week offline? 25+

What's the best way for companies to reach you as an influencer or as a mom? Email: iamsucceeding@gmail.com

What do you think is the biggest mistake companies make in trying to work with moms? Asking them to work for free.

How do you define influence among moms? Being genuine and honest in dealings, no matter how hard it may be.

What motivates you to tell other moms (good or bad) about a company, brand or product? Consumers are the best test of a product and company and the best spokespersons a company can have.

How do you feel companies can best connect with moms, particularly those who are influencers? Respect again, speak to them as equals, not down to them.

Name: Karen Kripalani

Children: Two, ages 2 and 7 months (both girls)

Hometown: Encinitas, CA

Company Name(s): Oceanhouse Media www.oceanhousemedia.com

Short description of business: Oceanhouse Media builds apps for mobile devices (smartphones, tablets, etc.) that uplift, educate and inspire. Currently we develop for Apple and Android devices, with more to come. We are especially known for our children's products such as Dr. Seuss, Rudolph the Red Nosed-Reindeer, Little Critter, Tacky the Penguin and Berenstain Bears digital omBooks™. We also make apps for Hay House's best-selling self-improvement authors and speakers (Wayne Dyer, Louise Hay, Deepak Chopra, etc.).

My husband was laid off in January 2009, just six weeks after our first child was born. Scary times. We were both intensely motivated. He had been talking about starting his own company for quite some time and we both believed that God was just giving him a good kick in the pants to start making things happen. One week later we had decided on a company name, bought our URL and incorporated. Our mission is to Create Apps That Uplift, Educate and Inspire. I manage the marketing and public relations efforts. I also direct talent for the company when we do voiceover sessions. We do not have an exit strategy at this time, as we believe that we can do this for many years to come.

Our boiler plate is: Oceanhouse Media, Inc. is an iPhone, iPod Touch and iPad app development company founded in early 2009 by husband and wife team, Karen and Michel Kripalani, former CEO of Presto Studios and Director of Business Development at Autodesk. The team is comprised of developers with decades of experience, primarily from the videogame business, that now share a common purpose to uplift, educate and inspire through technology. Currently, Oceanhouse Media has over 120 apps on the App Store, including nine hitting #1. The company's corporate mantra is "Creativity with Purpose." www.oceanhouse-media.com

Websites or Blogs you own: Oceanhouse Media www.oceanhousemedia.com and Karen Kripalani Photography www.KarenKripalani.com

Approximate audience size: Worldwide. Our apps are available in over 80 countries. During our first two years of business we've sold one million individual apps.

Facebook Id: Oceanhouse Media

Twitter Id: @OceanhouseMedia

Approximate # of followers: 600

Online Involvements and associations: We have won multiple awards from Parent's Choice Awards and Children's Technology Review. Additionally, we are members of an online community called Moms With Apps (www.MomsWithApps.com).

How many moms do you typically interact with during the week offline? I lead two playgroups that I started, one for my first daughter with 50 (14 of whom I see regularly) moms in it and one for moms of two with about 16 moms in it. I meet up with each weekly. Sometimes I see everyone and sometimes only a few. I also take my older daughter to two mommy and me classes weekly.

Offline Involvements: My husband is a member of Entrepreneur's Organization (http://eoaccess.eonetwork.org/) and I will be joining their Spousal Forum soon. We are actively involved with UCSD and more specifically, the UCSD Libraries. Last Christmas, I got the moms together to make boxed presents with our kids that would be sent to underprivileged children around the world through Operation Christmas Child (Samaritan's Purse). Traditionally, I also visit the children's hospital at Christmas time to bring gifts to the kids in the cancer wing. For years in the past, I volunteered with Camp Ronald McDonald for Goodtimes, a camp for children with cancer, as a camp counselor; was a camp counselor for Casa Colina, a watersports camp for the disabled; gave out food to the homeless with Hand To Hand; and traveled to India as an ambassador representing Los Angeles and the film industry through the Rotary Club.

What's the best way for companies to reach you as an influencer or as a mom? Email: kk@oceanhousemedia.com

How is the best way to work with you and your company? We're always looking for great co-marketing ideas, especially ones that use social media. We are always searching for ways to build our mailing list and Facebook and Twitter followers.

How do you feel you influence moms online? Our goal is to offer parents quality, enlightening entertainment that uplifts, educates and inspires. Many of the series we have licensed, such as Dr. Seuss and Berenstain Bears, bring adults those warm fuzzy feelings they had when they were a kid reading a book with their mom or dad. Now, instead of physical books and large shelves storing all of those bulky books, kids can pick from a whole library that is always at their fingertips. As they decide what to read each night before bed, parents can sit down with them on their lap and cozy up to a bedtime story on the iPad. They can also learn to read and build vocabulary with highlighting words and interactive pop-up features that traditional books don't offer. And, when stuck with antsy kids waiting at the doctor's office, in the car or in line at the grocery store, what parent doesn't love being able to hand a child an iPhone with an educational and entertaining story on it from a company that they trust has their kid's best interests at hand, like Oceanhouse Media? As head of marketing and PR it is my goal to spread the word to moms (and dads!) about these quality products and to help spread positive learning not only across America, but also globally.

How do you feel you influence moms offline? Is it more than chatting in the carpool line? I like to think of myself as a connector. I have built many women's circles that have brought women together in community for years. I have three younger sisters and love to surround myself with women. Starting my playgroups was the natural progression and I knew I would form deep and lasting relationships with women who were going through the same life experience as I am at this time. They are the people that I can lean on when I am sleep deprived, my kids are sick and whining, I'm mile-high in poopy diapers or I've had an "I'm a terrible mother" day. They are also the ones that I want to celebrate life's little, wonderful moments with, too. They watch my silly videos of my daughter singing opera, listen to me gush about the baby getting her first tooth and help me plan birthday parties. In short, I strive to bring people together, to be a connector and I like to think that I am a positive influence on moms in my offline community ... and with my business I hope that positivity stretches to families worldwide.

Name: Tiffany Lamb

Children: Two, ages 3 and 6 months

Hometown: Los Angeles, CA

Company Name(s): Organic Parenthood

Short description of business: I write a blog in which I talk about the adventures of parenting in an eco-friendly way, living life as a stay-at-home mom in a family with limited income.

Websites or Blogs you own: Organic Parenthood
http://www.organicparenthood.com

Approximate audience size: 500

Websites or blogs you contribute to: Examiner.com as the "West LA Stay at Home Moms Examiner"

Twitter Id: @OrPaBLOG

Approximate # of followers: 320

How do you feel you influence moms online? I write in my blog, and tweet about my parenting adventures and all it entails. I am very open to responding to people's emails and questions about the things I use, the way I do things, or what I believe.

Is there one moment when you realized you were impacting the life/lives of others? I cannot pinpoint the moment, but I realized fairly soon after baby wearing my son that I was exposing people to an idea they never knew about. So many, many people have stopped me to talk about my slings or my wraps: moms, future moms, family and friends of moms. It's truly amazing.

How can companies best support your business or mission as a mom? My mission is to share the trials and tribulations of a stay-at-home mom (perhaps more on the lower financial scale) with others who need a laugh, a bit of hope or someone to relate to. I do this through my blog, so any company who would support my blog would also support my mission.

How do you feel companies can best connect with moms, particularly those who are influencers? Having an email list that sends out emails (but not too many) talking about opportunites to connect influencing moms with companies. The idea of hosting a party to talk about products is an excellent way to bring moms together who will also later tell of the product to others they know.

Final words: I feel like a lot of moms and companies aim their information at the common middle class family. The truth really is that there are a lot of families living in low income situations that can only partially benefit from much of the information out there. Not to mention, they end up feeling like they are alone as not many people are quick to talk about being without enough money all the time. I don't feel anyone should ENDORSE being broke, but sometimes families are stuck doing their best to get by and go through periods of time where they do not have a lot of money. It would be nice to have more influencing moms to talk about THOSE situations and relate on that level.

Name: Dina Lettre

Children: Two, ages 6 and 2

Hometown: Kennesaw, GA

Websites or Blogs you own: 4 Lettre Words/ http://lettrefamily.blogspot.com/

Approximate audience size: 3,000 page loads a month

Online Involvements and associations: CSN preferred blogger and I do book reviews for many companies

How many moms do you typically interact with during the week offline? 20-30

Offline Involvements: Local Moms Group, 1st grade room mom, sports, Cub Scouts, church volunteer

What do you think is the biggest mistake companies make in trying to work with moms? Doubting his/her intelligence/ability!

How do you feel you influence moms online? I stay positive online and off so that carries over in my posts and comments on other blogs. I'm also 100% honest.

How do you feel you influence moms offline? Is it more than chatting in the carpool line? I'm room-mom for my 6-year old and try to bring a lot of fun into the classroom. It's rewarding because our school has many impoverished children/ families. The same can be said for our church. My entire family volunteers at as many things as possible. We have a wonderful community outreach program. It brings tears and smiles.

What motivates you to tell other moms (good or bad) about a company, brand or product? I'm more about quality/appeal than price, plus I love a great "experience," whether that's an email or customer service contact.

Final words: Since moms have so many vested interests in the future, it only makes sense that companies would come to them with questions/suggestions and for support; whether that be auto makers or pasta makers. We have the answers.

Name: Rebecca Levey

Children: Two, age 8 (both girls)

Hometown: New York, NY

Company Name(s): Beccarama.com and The Blogging Angels

Short description of business: Beccarama is a blog about parenting, culture, education, tech, and all things NYC. The Blogging Angels is a weekly podcast about social media and the blogosphere. KidzVuz.com, which launcheds in January 2011, is a review site by tweens for tweens where tweens submit their own video reviews on the products and media they love (or don't).

My blog began as a means for me to get back into writing after staying at home with my twin daughters for their first 5 years. I started it in April of 2008 after beginning to write for nycmomsblog.com. My motivation was to find my creative voice again and figure out how I could write as a mom not just as a woman. I never anticipated the growth or community that followed. Through my blog I met the women with whom I started the Blogging Angels podcast. I knew I wanted to start a weekly conversation with smart like-minded bloggers that would bring the topics we talked about amongst ourselves to a wider audience. The mission for the Blogging Angels is to educate beginning bloggers and other more established bloggers on how to build their brand, work with companies, monetize their blogs and also to give a voice to women about the blogosphere and social media. My exit strategy is to become part of a larger media group as a podcast that adds to their roster about tech or business. The only exit strategy for Beccarama.com, my personal blog, is to continually evolve and grow—not to exit, but to find new doors in new directions.

Websites or Blogs you own: www.Beccarama.com, www.BloggingAngels.com and www.KidzVuz.com

Approximate audience size: 5,000

Websites or blogs you contribute to: Social Media Editor: Mom Blog Magazine; contributing regular blogger: Westsideindependent.com, Yahoo!Motherboard, Yahoo!Shine, CBSTV NY local, Technorati Women's Channel, NYCmomsblog (now defunct)

Facebook Id: Rebecca Levey

Twitter Id: @beccasara

Approximate # of followers: 1,650

Online Involvements and associations: Yahoo! Motherboard, Microsoft Windows Live blogger, Social Media Editor—MomBlog Magazine

How many moms do you typically interact with during the week offline? 200-800 or more if we are having school-wide fundraising events.

Offline Involvements: President of PTA at PS 87 (1,000 students) K-5 school on the Upper West Side of Manhattan

Are there companies who you feel are doing a great job connecting with moms? I love Mabels Labels and their very personal strategy as well as their fundraising efforts for schools. I think Microsoft is doing a good job reaching out to moms by approaching them about tech and organization without talking down to them. I do wish more tech companies would look at moms beyond the "color and style" aspects. Also, entertainment companies need to realize that moms don't just want to see "chick" flicks and TV.

How do you feel you influence moms online? I am always shocked and flattered when someone comes up to me at a party or DMs me on Twitter to let me know that something I wrote or said affected them and stuck with them. I think my writing is personal but approachable and I never, ever write about products or events that I don't believe in. I don't do straight up product reviews–I tell a story and if a product made its way into my life in an authentic way I will write from that point of view. On the Blogging Angels I have a very distinct and engaged voice with my cohosts. This podcast has reached into the social media mom community in a rich and direct way. I hear from listeners daily about how a podcast made them try a new site or service, made them think, or just got them laughing. I also hear from PR people who feel that they are getting the inside scoop from bloggers and answers to questions that they always wanted to ask but didn't know how. That's a great thing to hear! As Social Media Editor for MomBlog Magazine I reach mombloggers who are looking for tools and ideas they can use to increase their own social media presence. I also discuss what is going on in the space and how mombloggers can use their influence in positive and powerful ways.

How do you feel you influence moms offline? Is it more than chatting in the carpool line? I write a weekly column in my school's "BackPack News," our weekly newsletter that goes home to our 900 families every week. In that column I talk about our school, education goals, PTA goals and budgets and try to motivate parents to get involved. I oversee 28 committees, a fundraising machine that raises over 600K/year to support our programs and speak about our school to delegations from abroad and other parents in Manhattan going through the public school admissions process for the first time. As a writer about local NYC events, I am also a source of information about all the goings on in the city and try to constantly connect parents and events and local businesses.

How can companies best support your business or mission as a mom? By supporting education, companies are supporting me as a mom. Through fundraising efforts, real dialog and donations, companies show me that my priorities are their priorities. For my business I look to companies who want to support my writing and my podcast–that means sponsorship to conferences, recording sponsorship of the The Blogging Angels podcast or real information sessions and services I can use for my blogs.

How do you feel companies can best connect with moms, particularly those who are influencers? Be genuine, be respectful. Offer real compensation, either as monetary or in services or experiences. Open a dialog and take the time to build a relationship. They shouldn't approach "everyone." Not all bloggers are good fits for all products. Move beyond the statistics and don't take the lazy way out of just reading "top" whatever lists that mean nothing. Look for quality writing. Read the blog. Connect with me because you like what I have to say and how I say it.

Final words: I think moms will always be the key deciders in their families on product purchases, food preparation, travel, clothing, etc. But where I really think moms have more influence than ever is online in communities they build every day. For me one of my key forms of influence is on my daughters' approach to technology and how they are learning to navigate social media and online communities aimed at them. Worlds like Club Penguin or Fantage are just the beginning for them as they learn to safely chat, maintain privacy, stay away from and report cyberbullies and build their digital footprint. These are tools they will need to use now that their world is both on and offline and I think that as a mom this is where I can help influence their decisions now so that they make good virtual decisions later. Technology is going to be more and more integrated into the home and as long as moms remain the primary keepers of the home they will have the power to shape their children's online experiences.

Name: Heather Lopez

Children: Two, ages 4 and 2

Hometown: Ft. Lauderdale, FL

Company Name(s): Heather Lopez Enterprises, parent company to: Happy and Healthy Mom.Com, the Super Mom Entrepreneur Conference & Expo, the Bloggin' Mamas Conference & Cruise, Become Better Brands, and WAHM Kiddie Swap

Short description of business: Heather Lopez Enterprises helps businesses and brands connect to their consumer through social media, branding, marketing, public relations, and events. We specialize in working with small business owners, entrepreneurs, and moms.

I started Happy and Healthy Mom.Com in August 2009 while sitting in my son's hospital room. He and my daughter were both hospitalized for having RSV they contracted in daycare. My daughter also had pneumonia and my son was in intensive care because he was only three months old. I knew I needed to take them out of daycare and that I needed to stop making other people rich without doing it for myself first. After numerous projects, events, websites, etc., I am finally launching the real overall business, Heather Lopez Enterprises, on 12/1/10. I have been taking business classes and got my first small business loan. All of my avenues now lead to an intersection where I can direct businesses who are trying to work with me. The name of the business also incorporates my personal brand that I have begun developing over the last year. Heather Lopez Enterprises is a B2B helping to connect B2Cs via social media, branding, marketing, p.r. and events. There is no exit strategy as it is an umbrella company. I can stop, sell, or expand divisions underneath it, but am not considering selling the overall business.

Websites or Blogs you own: http://www.heatherlopezenterprises.com http://www.happyandhealthymom.com http://www.supermompreneur.com http://www.bloggmamascruise.com http://www.becomebetterbrands.com http://wahmkiddieswap.ning.com

Approximate audience size: 6K

Facebook Id: Heather Lopez, Heather Lopez Enterprises, Happy and Helathy Mom, Super Mom Entrepreneur, Bloggin Mamas, Become Better Brands

Approximate # of followers: 2100 friends and fans

Twitter Id: @HeLoEnterprises @HAHMom @supermompreneur @blogginmamas @wherebrandsgo

Approximate # of followers: 5300

Online Involvements and associations: The Mom Entrepreneur Ambassador, Question Moms Expert, The View Brand Ambassador, TwitterMoms Elite Member

How many moms do you typically interact with during the week offline? I make weekly visits to various play cafes, family events, and mom groups.

Offline Involvements: BizMoms Chapter Leader, Florida Association of Nonprofit Organizations, South Florida Chamber of Commerce, Broward County Chamber of Commerce, & South Florida Women's Chamber of Commerce, Vice President on the Board of the Super Swimmers Foundation, a 501 c 3. Serve as a volunteer consultant for the Florida Association of Nonprofit Organizations.

What's the best way for companies to reach you as an influencer or as a mom? As an influencer, they should not assume that I will market them to other moms for free. My time is valuable and I have spent a lot of time building my reputation, so it is important that I am valued and compensated for my efforts to promote them to my followers. As a mom, I think that social media is a great way to reach me, though a recent marketing study shows that moms find out about products and services through search engines first, emails second, product review sites third, and so on. Social media isn't currently ranked as high on the list, though search engines are influenced by what takes place in social media.

Are there companies who you feel are doing a great job connecting with moms? Earth Mama Angel Baby, Disney, Huggies, Little Tikes, Proctor & Gamble

How do you define influence among moms? The ability to propel other moms to take an action. Not just share information, but actually utilize that information to make informed purchases and decisions.

How do you feel you influence moms online? Because I do offline events, I have a strong influence on moms both locally and even nationally as I have done events in other states. I even had a mom do an event using Happy and Healthy Mom without me physically being at the event, but had hundreds of attendees.

How can companies best support your business or mission as a mom? Larger companies can sponsor my events that help small business owners, entrepreneurs, and moms to learn how to create their own financial freedoms. For mom entrepreneurs, I also offer a grant fund that could use sponsors to help moms start and grow businesses.

Final words: Women-owned businesses are becoming a larger percentage of businesses in the world, and of those, mom-owned businesses are growing at the fastest rate. The tough economy leaves room for entrepreneurs to flourish, and the at-home moms who might have lost their jobs or can't afford outside childcare are beginning to get creative in order to develop their own self-sustaining businesses. Politically, women are starting to take on roles that were normally closed off to them. People are starting to realize that women are not as weak as they are characterized to be and in fact can make great problem solvers, mediators, collaborators, and leaders. Moms control the household funds, which means that reaching moms is a necessary step in gaining customers. Even if the product might not appeal to a mom personally, she will buy it if she thinks it will appeal to her husband, kids, family, or friends. This means that niche marketing should always account for including moms who have relationships to people in the target market. For instance, a toy might be geared towards kids and the company chooses to air the commercial during their cartoons in hopes that they will beg their mom to buy it for them. Well, have the companies also thought about reaching out to the mom when she might be watching TV, visiting a website, etc.?

That is just an obvious example, but the thought can be applied to other types of businesses. "Build a strong mom following, build your brand."

Name: Jazerai Lord

Children: Two, ages 8 and 3

Hometown: Los Angeles, Ca

Company Name(s): www.nerdlike.com

Short description of business: NerdLike.com caters to the urban sophisticate, bridging the gap between hip and hipster. NerdLike was started by my partner, Jacques, and me, in an effort to house all the gadgets, videos, reviews and quirky news that we couldn't find in one online space. There are very few sites that mix urban culture with geekdom, as it is often frowned up. Hence the name, Nerd "like." Our mission is to reach that community, bringing together a band of misfits.

Websites or Blogs you own: www.nerdlike.com also www.nerdlikejazzy.com

Approximate audience size: 80,000 visitors monthly

Websites or blogs you contribute to: www.kicksonfire.com the #1 ranked online sneaker magazine in the world. www.StyleEngine.com Is a sister site to Kicksonfire, featuring mens streetwear fashion. www.Patch.com

Facebook Id: www.facebook.com/nerdlike also www.facebook.com/jazerai

Twitter Id: jazzyrae

Approximate # of followers: 2,615

How many moms do you typically interact with during the week offline? 20-25

Offline Involvements: PTSA, room mom for my 3rd grader's class, Team Manager for his track team, event coordinator for local events, room mom for my preschooler's class, website consultant, previous work with the Girl Scouts of LA

What's the best way for companies to reach you as an influencer or as a mom? The best way for companies to reach moms is to just be real. Be honest. Recognize that moms are women first, and our lives don't always revolve around our children. We actually have interests ... personalities.

What do you think is the biggest mistake companies make in trying to work with moms? The biggest mistake that companies make is treating us as if we are Susy Homemakers. Sometimes, companies act as if we have no business sense, or common sense for that matter. As I said before, we are women first. We have the ability to run businesses and dominate this industry.

How do you feel you influence moms offline? Is it more than chatting in the carpool line? Most of the moms I come across through my son's school aren't too internet saavy. I have worked with a lot of them one-on-one to help them use social media to develop their own talents, whether it be art, web design, Etsy shops, etc. I've even helped someone start their own personal shopping business!

What motivates you to tell other moms (good or bad) about a company, brand or product? I want to give moms exactly what I want to see: thorough and honest reviews and opinions. I don't believe in pay-for-posts, or giving fluffy reviews for free products. Moms and consumers in general deserve to know the truth about what they are spending their money on, whether good or bad.

Name: Kelly Loubet

Children: Two, ages 6 and 5 (both girls)

Hometown: Phoenix, AZ

Company Name(s): Everyday Childhood

Short description of business: Everyday Childhood encompasses my blog, Twitter, and MomTV presence. I consider myself a speaker, writer, and promoter of good things. Childhood began as an independent clothing design firm and has grown into a new media outlet. Now branded Everyday Childhood, the blog shares recommendations of new products, travel locations, and all things good. I also consider my Twitter presence and my MomTV show to be a part of the influence that is Everyday Childhood.

Websites or Blogs you own: Everyday Childhood http://everydaychildhood.com/ and momtv.com/everyday-childhood

Approximate audience size: I don't keep track. It gives me anxiety. My last campaign with Lexus reached 60,000 readers and made 500,000 impressions over a two day period (according to the report).

Websites or blogs you contribute to: I contribute weekly to MomTV. I also contribute on occasion to Type A Parent.

Facebook Id: Kelly Loubet

Twitter Id: @childhood

Approximate # of followers: 4,600 and growing

Online Involvements and associations: I am the President of the Arizona Chapter of Mom It Forward. I'm a proud MomTV weekly show host. I'm also a paid Community Leader for Collective Bias. Currently, I am the Social Media Community Manager for The UPS Store through Collective Bias.

How many moms do you typically interact with during the week offline? I host a live offline event monthly in Arizona. Typically 30-100 moms will show up to these events.

Offline Involvements: Mom It Forward offline events that are tied to a community service, Room Mom at my child's school, involved in JDRF (my daughter Allison has Type 1 diabetes)

What's the best way for companies to reach you as an influencer or as a mom? Email: kellyloubet@gmail.com

What do you think is the biggest mistake companies make in trying to work with moms? I think that companies need to do their homework a little bit better when finding a mom to work with. Companies are used to moms who work for free or for very little valuable compensation. The responsibility for showing their worth falls on the moms ... but in the end ... I tell companies that they truly get what they pay for.

Are there companies who you feel are doing a great job connecting with moms? Companies like Disney, who organizes things for moms are doing well in the mom world. The Goldfish branded Fishful Thinking had a wonderful campaign. Build-a-Bear works wonderfully with moms. Open Sky, a platform for sellers, has been very open to the Mom community. To be honest I could list dozens of brands who get it that moms are key influencers. It's how they go about reaching them that makes the difference. Buying the same "popular" moms over and over again on recycled campaigns doesn't spread the word. Brands need to broaden their range and take a chance on some lesser known, bright, moms out there.

Is there one moment when you realized you were impacting the life/lives of others? There have been many moments like this ... but more recently ... I was bitten on the face by a dog this year. The whole experience was devastating to me, mostly because I was supposed to be broadcasting live in New York from BlogHer, at a number of events, for MomTV. How was I supposed to broadcast when I looked like that? But I pulled myself together and I did it anyway. I continued doing my regular show as well in the following weeks. A couple of months later, I received a comment on my blog, thanking me for my strength and courage. Apparently, one of my viewers had a tween daughter who was also recently bitten by a dog on the face. She was fearful of returning to school and worried about what people would say. She watched my show weekly with her mother and saw how I was putting myself out there in front of all these people, even with my left cheek all torn to pieces. I had helped this young girl to feel better about her appearance just by doing what I always do. This is a moment I will never forget.

How do you feel you influence moms offline? Is it more than chatting in the carpool line? Offline, I host monthly events for moms to get out of the house and do something of importance in their community. I love to do these events! Many of these moms don't get out of their homes socially unless it's to come to one of my events. I don't do it for profit. In fact, I don't make any money at all doing it. I do it to help my community.

How can companies best support your business or mission as a mom? Companies can get behind a cause I'm supporting by sponsoring an event. They get their names out there in public at a live event as well as online through blog posts, tweets, and MomTV.

Final words: My biggest concern as an influencer is that we don't lose sight of why we're influencing. We are to be sharing our genuine experiences to benefit others ... not just sharing for the sake of a few dollars.

Name: Misty Lowe

Children: One, age 1

Hometown: Knoxville, TN

Company Name(s): pixie kisses

Short description of business: I make handmade soy candles that are earth friendly, and smell wonderful, too. It started in 2010, when I was laid off and needed a way to take care of my son and me. I wanted to make something I would love and was worth the money you pay.

Websites or Blogs you own: Rowans Mom http://rowansmom1127.livejournal.com/, http://pixiekisses.co.cc/

Twitter Id: @rowansmom1127

Online Involvements and associations: Kraft, General Mills Psst, Chickadviser, Frog Blog, Moms Meet, Mom Blogs, She Speaks, one2one, Blog Spark

How do you feel you influence moms online? I support them, by posting product reviews so that they don't waste their money on things that just don't work or are a flop. I also help by finding things they love for free. A lot of them even email and IM me and talk one on one.

How can companies best support your business or mission as a mom? Make their products more available to mom reviewers, so that they can be talked about.

Gear them toward moms and kids, make them a must have.

How do you feel companies can best connect with moms, particularly those who are influencers? Offer them the chance to see and use it before anyone else. If we like something we won't stop talking about to everyone, and we want everyone to get one—that's just how we are.

Final words: I think that the web has made it easier for us to connect and open up about our lives and everyday buys: if we find a good sale you know we are going to twitter.

Name: Dr. Sarah Manongdo-Joya

Children: One, age 8 ½ months

Hometown: Chicago, IL

Company Name(s): Budget Wedding Centerpieces, Inc.

Short description of business: I sell affordable yet elegant silk bridal and bridesmaid bouquets and party/special event centerpieces under $10 each. Including for wedding rehearsals, birthday parties, corporate events, church events, and baby showers, etc., I sell close to wholesale prices since I do not need a brick and mortar store. I have been selling odds and ends as "sarspinay" http://shop.ebay.com/merchant/sarspinay on eBay since 1998, making money on the side as a student entrepreneur. The idea came to me to sell wedding centerpieces on eBay after planning my own 2005 "big fat eBay wedding" and cowriting a book about the process entitled *How to Buy Everything for Your Wedding on eBay ... and Save a Fortune!* published by McGraw-Hill in April 2005. My eBay profits were on the rise, and I decided to automate the ordering process and expand by making the website www.budgetweddingcenterpieces.com in 2007 and incorporating in 2009. The beauty of running an online business is the availability to process orders anytime, anywhere you have an Internet connection. I still had orders to process for customers the morning of my wedding day, and also the day I was giving birth! I also run the website www.saveafortuneonyourwedding.com that details the press coverage of my book, including TV, radio, newspaper, and magazine coverage. I was also featured on TV to promote www.swaptree.com to save money by swapping books, DVDs and music online. I document how to start your own business website online for free or very little money at http://sarahjoya.blogspot.com

Websites or Blogs you own: Budget Wedding Centerpieces http://www.budgetweddingcenterpieces.com, http://www.saveafortuneonyourwedding.com, Sarah Joya http://www.SarahJoya.com; http://sarahjoya.blogspot.com;http://shop.ebay.com/merchant/sarspinay

Facebook Id: Sarah Manongdo-Joya

Online Involvements and associations: Inventive Advance Insights—contact lens research survey panelist as a doctor of optometry; My blog: http://sarahjoya.blogspot.com; eBay merchant "sarspinay"

Offline Involvements: National Board of Examiners in Optometry Clinical Station Examiner 2009-2010, Holy Name Cathedral Mom's Group

What's the best way for companies to reach you as an influencer or as a mom? Email: smanong@hotmail.com or Facebook

What do you think is the biggest mistake companies make in trying to work with moms? Companies often forget that time is just as valuable to moms as getting a great deal and saving money. If the product takes too long to be delivered, chances are moms won't want to purchase it. Also testimonials are very important to moms and the ability to leave feedback is essential.

Are there companies who you feel are doing a great job connecting with moms? Diapers.com, Babiesrus.com, Parenting Magazine, Babycenter.com

How do you feel you influence moms online? By setting an example: being a full-time working mom plus having an online business on the side. Also my websites are all about saving money and time.

Is there one moment when you realized you were impacting the life/lives of others? The first time I received my first (unsolicited) photo testimonial (a bride thanking me for making her wedding flowers affordable and beautiful) I was overwhelmed. I decided to include a section on my website of picture testimonials to share my joy with others.

What motivates you to tell other moms (good or bad) about a company, brand or product? If I feel that the product has somehow improved my life like no other product has before, or has solved a unique problem, I then tell other moms about the product.

Final words: I feel that moms are the number one target audience that companies should target if they want their product(s) to do well. We moms usually make the purchasing decision from something as major as an automobile or home to something as small as diaper rash cream. There should be discounts for moms with multiple children, multiple jobs, etc.

Name: Lynette Mattke

Children: Three, ages 16, 13, and 10

Hometown: Silver Spring, MD

Company Name(s): PicPocket Books

Short description of business: PicPocket Books publishes quality children's picture books to the iPhone and iPad as apps. We aim to maintain all the positive qualities and benefits of traditional books while increasing the level of engagement and the opportunities for learning with a digital platform. I founded PicPocket Books in January 2009. I wanted to give parents and their kids the option of having picture books on their mobile devices—not only games and movies. Books on the iPhone or iPad are an excellent option when it comes to screen time because reading a book, whether on a screen or in print—has educational, mind-opening benefits such as increasing vocabulary and improving focus and expanding horizons.

Websites or Blogs you own: PicPocket Books www.picpocketbooks.com, blog: www.picpocketbooks.com/blog/

Approximate audience size: 50-100 hits a day

Websites or blogs you contribute to: MomsWithApps www.momswithapps.com

Facebook Id: PicPocket Books

Twitter Id: @picpocketbooks

Approximate # of followers: 1,300

Online Involvements and associations: Huggies MomInspired, MomsWithApps

What do you think is the biggest mistake companies make in trying to work with moms? I think it is a big mistake when companies are just concerned about delivering their message, but don't value moms' voices and seek out their input.

Are there companies who you feel are doing a great job connecting with moms? Huggies, Toyota, Pottery Barn, Athleta

How do you feel you influence moms offline? Is it more than chatting in the carpool line? My entrepreneurial experience is something that I notice other moms are really interested in, and they have a lot of questions about different aspects of running a business. Moms ask me about employment opportunities, advice about starting businesses, and I get a lot of people who want to talk to me and ask questions about my areas of expertise—publishing and writing for children.

What motivates you to tell other moms (good or bad) about a company, brand, or product? Personal attention and great customer service always gets my attention, as well as quality, especially "green" or environmentally conscious products.

How do you feel companies can best connect with moms, particularly those who are influencers? Hosting seminars or conferences for mom entrepreneurs that include company spokespeople, on general family-friendly topics—such as healthy lifestyles, literacy, media, education, play, etc.

Name: Michele McGraw

Children: Four, ages 14, 12, 8, and 6

Hometown: Chantilly, VA

Company Name(s): Mom Geek Media

Short description of business: Freelance Technology Blogger, started in 2007 when more than just my mom read my blog and I realized I was a business, so I decided to make it official.

Websites or Blogs you own: Mom Geek Media http://momgeekmedia.com, Scraps of My Geek Life http://scrapsofmygeeklife.com, Project 365 Geek http://project365geek.com

Approximate audience size: 4,000

Facebook Id: Michele Rasner McGraw

Twitter Id: @scrappinmichele

Approximate # of followers: 9,800

Online Involvements and associations: Yahoo! Mother Board, AMD Mom, BitMom

How many moms do you typically interact with during the week offline? 50

Offline Involvements: PTA, Local Mom Blogger Group

What's the best way for companies to reach you as an influencer or as a mom? Email: Michele@momgeekmedia.com

What do you think is the biggest mistake companies make in trying to work with moms? They don't treat us like a business. We should be treated the same as any other consultant or business they deal with.

Are there companies who you feel are doing a great job connecting with moms? I'm a little biased because of the companies I've worked with, but I think both Yahoo! and AMD have done an awesome job. Kodak is another one that I have been watching and really am impressed with.

How do you feel you influence moms online? By being myself. I don't write or say anything online that I wouldn't say to my offline friends. I'm open and honest and I care.

What motivates you to tell other moms (good or bad) about a company, brand or product? I won't talk about anything that I haven't tried myself and that I don't love. If I have an excellent experience with a company or brand I'll talk about it. If I have a horrible experience and I feel that others should know, then I'll talk about it. But I don't want to talk negatively about a company or brand just for the sake of it. I would do it hoping to bring change.

How do you feel companies can best connect with moms, particularly those who are influencers? By being where we are: Facebook, Twitter, our blogs, our communities. Treating us like businesses and really understanding our needs. Listen because we are always willing to give opinions, but don't ask just because it's the thing to do. Listen because you want to know.

Name: Tiffany Merritt

Children: One, age 14 months

Hometown: Chattanooga, TN

Websites or Blogs you own: Stuff Parents Need
http://stuffparentsneed.blogspot.com

Approximate audience size: 1,320

Facebook Id: Stuff Parents Need

Twitter Id: @Tiffanyblogs

Approximate # of followers: 1,100

Offline Involvements: MOPS group member, Junior League of Chattanooga

What do you think is the biggest mistake companies make in trying to work with moms? It drives me bonkers when companies essentially ask for free advertising in exchange for a small sample of their product or no product to review, at all. Product reviews do not write themselves, so you are not giving us something for free! I also don't feel that I can write about the merits of a product and have any integrity if I have not personally used it. Bloggers work very hard to establish trust with their readers, and the vast majority of us (even the review-focused blogs) are not trying to get something for nothing. We are bringing something of great value to the table by writing a personal and thoughtfully crafted review of your product, and we are sharing that with a group of people who trust us and take our opinions seriously. Please don't underestimate the value this has!

How do you define influence among moms? Influence means that you are able to get a mom to stop for a moment and seriously consider what you are saying. Your words have weight to her, even if she decides that she doesn't agree with you. Influence means that you are able to engage another mom in meaningful conversation or in meaningful consideration of an idea or even of a product.

How do you feel you influence moms online? I am a review blogger, so my influence is largely based on giving my honest opinions about products that I test out. Many of my readers have told me that they have purchased products based on my recommendations, because they trust me. Since I know other moms out there are counting on me to be honest about my experience with products, I take writing my reviews very seriously and give them careful thought. When I read reviews of products that other moms write, I expect and hope that they are doing the same (and the blogs that I continue to read for a longer period of the time are the ones that actually do that!).

Is there one moment when you realized you were impacting the life/lives of others? I have had other moms tell me that they have made purchasing decisions based on my reviews, and that was really amazing for me to hear. Most of us have limited resources and there are SO many choices for products in every category. I knew that my words carried weight when I started hearing that other people were taking my advice on which products to consider, and those to leave behind.

Another moment is when my younger sister told me that when she gets married and has a child, she will use cloth diapers. She said, "I've watched and read about you doing it, and I think it sounds like a great idea." We come from a family and a community where cloth diapering is still VERY weird, so I was overjoyed to hear that I had that kind of an impact!

How can companies best support your business or mission as a mom? As a mommy blogger, I think VERY highly of those companies who are supporting other bloggers and reaching out to us in a much more personal way. The blogosphere is such an amazing place for moms to get together and talk about all sorts of issues, and not feel alone in the midst of a joyful, but also quite alienating, season of our lives. When a company seeks to meet us where we are, listens to our concerns, and develops products that we TRULY need, they've got my attention, and likely my business.

What motivates you to tell other moms (good or bad) about a company, brand or product? I'm motivated to talk about any product that makes my life a little less hectic and a lot more fun as a new parent! Conversely, if a product does the complete opposite of that (especially when I thought it would make life easier and more fun) I want to tell moms about that experience, as well, so that they can steer clear.

How do you feel companies can best connect with moms, particularly those who are influencers? I think that forming a relationship with the mom influencers out there is ideal. I love when I have the opportunity to work with a company multiple times, and feature them in different ways on my blog (perhaps a review, a give-away, but also an interview or a promotion of a great thing they are doing for a nonprofit). Not everything has to be about making a sale. It also needs to be about getting to know the people behind the company, and the reason the company exists beyond making a profit. When I get to know a company on that more intimate level, a real sense of trust forms, and I share that with my readers. As a mom, when I read about a company like that, it makes me want to spend my dollars with them.

Name: Denene Millner

Children: Three, ages 18, 11, and 8

Hometown: Snellville, GA

Company Name(s): Chilmill Publishing, Inc.; MyBrownBaby

Short description of business: Chilmill Publishing, Inc. is a multi-media publishing firm that oversees various media projects, including authoring and ghostwriting books and freelance articles; public speaking; and social media consultation, freelancing and blogging. My husband and I founded Chilmill Publishing, Inc., in 1994. It was founded to distinguish our business as authors from our day jobs as journalists—he worked as an education reporter for the Star-Ledger of Newark; I worked as a political and then entertainment journalist for The New York Daily News, then later as an editor for Honey magazine and Parenting magazine. Through the company, we authored six books together; in addition, I've authored or coauthored 13 more—fiction, non-fiction, adult, teen, and children's picture books. I've also freelanced for a plethora of publications, including Essence, Health, Heart & Soul, Parenting, Ebony, and more. Later, after successfully penning an advice column for Parenting magazine (a position I've had—and continue to have—for almost seven years), I began to explore journalism through social media and founded MyBrownBaby as the conduit to that fascinating world. MyBrownBaby was created to give voice to mothers of color who rarely, if ever, are invited to participate in the national parenting debate. My hope was that MyBrownBaby would give voice to the fears, frustrations, joys and beauty of parenting children of color and help bridge what seems to be a divide between the ways moms of color raise their children versus the way mainstream media portrays motherhood. Through MyBrownBaby, moms of color have found a voice and are being acknowledged, particularly in the realm of social media. I'm very proud of that.

Websites or Blogs you own: www.mybrownbaby.com (currently, it's located at www.mybrownbaby.blogspot.com, but the site is being redesigned and moved to .com.)

Approximate audience size: 2500 subscribers

Websites or blogs you contribute to: www.Parenting.com; www.dove.com; www.dontfretthesweat.com

Facebook Id: Denene Millner

Twitter Id: @MyBrownBaby

Approximate # of followers: 3,030

Online Involvements and associations: I've been a brand ambassador for Dove, Unilever and Parenting; I've also served as an ambassador to the Mom Bloggers Club.

Offline Involvements: Board member, The Greening Youth Foundation; committee head, local PTA; room mom, frequent journalist speaker at local schools and colleges.

What's the best way for companies to reach you as an influencer or as a mom? Companies can reach me as an influencer by acknowledging that moms of color deserve a say in the national parenting debate. It is important that we ALL be included, for two reasons: because we don't always parent the same way and do have some different ways of looking at particular situations, and because sometimes we fail to realize that we are way more THE SAME than we are different. So if a company invites moms of color and genuinely wants to hear our take on whatever message they're trying to get across, and genuinely LISTENS to our thoughts on the matter and uses that to tailor their message, then you've got a huge supporter in me and the MyBrownBaby brand. I feel the same way as a mother; companies that speak TO me rather than AT me get my utmost respect and loyalty.

What do you think is the biggest mistake companies make in trying to work with moms? I think when companies talk AT moms instead of TO us, we get turned off immediately. We are an opinionated lot and we're made up of a bunch of smart cookies, and the moment we sense that our emotional needs are not being fed (this, after all, is the very heart of social media—emotional connections) AND that you think we're stupid and will fall for the okey dokey? And that we are not worthy of respect, well then you've got yourself into a world of trouble with us. I think companies also fall into the trap of assuming we're a bunch of housewives sitting around wasting time on the internet and looking for creative outlets between diaper changes and dinner prep, when the truth of the matter is that we are business women, first and foremost. And if you don't treat us as such, we will call you out. Try to use us, and you will get burned—at least by the wise ones who value their businesses and their talent.

Are there companies who you feel are doing a great job connecting with moms? I love the job Parenting is doing in terms of putting an online voice to the emotional connections it makes online. I also adore sites like Momversation, DivineCaroline, and the Mom Bloggers Club for inviting moms to great conversation, and companies like Disney for really working hard to translate its brand to moms in meaningful ways. I think companies like General Mills, Kellogg's, Coca-Cola, Johnson & Johnson, Unilever, Dove and Toyota are catching on and, in no time, will make more meaningful connections.

How can companies best support your business or mission as a mom? Companies can best support the MyBrownBaby mission by opening up their doors and inviting moms of color into the conversation—and certainly by supporting us in every way that they can, by advertising on our sites (so that we can continue to provide solid content); by inviting us to participate in their campaigns (so that we can hear their messages and help them spread the word in a way that will truly speak to our audience); and by allowing us the space to be who we are—strong, beautiful, passionate women of color with a rich history and culture—within the context of their campaigns.

How do you feel companies can best connect with moms, particularly those who are influencers? By treating us with respect, having their stuff together, and knowing how to work social media. It really disgusts me when companies waste time, money and resources without first paying close attention to the most basic ways/tools needed to reach out to moms. If you're not on Twitter and Facebook, your page is static, you still require people to input practically their social security number, home address, cell phone number and first-born's full name to leave a comment, and you're not paying your influencers for their time and attention to detail, then you suck at your job and you should find another one. Those are just basic tenets of connecting with moms 101. Anyone doing more than those things is onto something.

Name: Beth Montgomery

Children: Three, ages 6, 3, and 1

Hometown: Fisher, Indiana

Company Name(s): In Good Cents, LLC

Short description of business: In Good Cents, LLC is a company that helps families save money on everyday items, so that they can worry less and spend more time together. It offers classes on cutting your budget, plus a website with daily grocery store deals with coupon match-ups, freebies alerts, hot coupons, samples, frugal recipes, and other great deals to help you save. My company started in 2009 when my friends were begging me to teach them how to save money like I did, picking up FREEbies and only spending $50 per week on groceries for a family of 5.

Websites or Blogs you own: In Good Cents http://ingoodcents.com

Approximate audience size: 50,000 page views per month

Websites or blogs you contribute to: Deal Seeking Mom, Coupon Dad, Money Saving Mom

Facebook Id: Beth Montgomery

Approximate # of followers: 2,450

Twitter Id: @ingoodcents

Approximate # of followers: 1,910

How many moms do you typically interact with during the week offline? 50-100

Offline Involvements: Northside Stay-at-Home Moms Group, volunteer, part-time Shepherd at Head of Infant-Toddler for Vacation Bible Camp, teach pro-bono Savings Classes at Shelters, Homes

What's the best way for companies to reach you as an influencer or as a mom? Email

What do you think is the biggest mistake companies make in trying to work with moms? I think the biggest mistake is form emails. Moms put their heart into their blogs, so they aren't interested in connecting with companies who don't know anything about them. "Dear Blogger" emails and other disconnected pitches are the quickest way to alienate mom bloggers. Also, seeing Mom bloggers as free advertising is taking advantage.

How do you feel you influence moms online? I have had some amazing emails from women struggling, who saved money and now feel all isn't lost, all because of me. It's overwhelming and so motivating. I also help connect other bloggers for big events, so that we can help each other spend less time online and more time with family.

How can companies best support your business or mission as a mom? Companies can support my business by offering me new ways to help my readers save money and also by helping me connect with other bloggers. They can support me as a mom and my mission as a mom, by proving opportunities for families to just be together and enjoy each other.

Final words: Mom bloggers are becoming the most powerful voice, influencing many purchases and opinions. Companies should connect with bloggers, since it can be a new, innovative way to reach their audience. But, more importantly, it will help them connect with their audience in a way that nothing else can.

Name: Sundae Montgomery

Children: Three, ages 13, 10 and 5 (all girls)

Hometown: Fruita, Colorado

Company Name(s): The Poppy Place

Short description of business: The Poppy Place is a website specializing in selling children's toys and gifts—from the hard-to-find, discontinued, and unique to the hottest and most popular!

The Poppy Place was started in 2007 with the intention of helping people make shopping easier. As a parent, I don't always have time to run all over town checking twenty different stores for the items my kids want for holidays. I love the ease of shopping online and having items delivered directly to my door. But I also love to receive personal attention. With incredibly large companies I often feel like I am "just a number." My goal is for my customers to always feel as if they will get friendly, personal attention from my company. If I don't know what is going on with your order then I will find out! If you need it fast then all you have to do is ask and I will move your order to top priority! If you want to know what my kids like or what toys we have tested lately—read my blog and find out! If you have a question while shopping then utilize our "click to chat" feature and ask!

I don't have an exit strategy for my business. I hope to keep growing and expanding, yet still provide the same quality service I love to receive. The Poppy Place started small in 2007 and has grown each year, with 2010 being our first year with our own independent website. I am really excited about the future with this business and I just want to keep going!

Websites or Blogs you own: The Poppy Place www.thepoppyplace.com

Facebook Id: The Poppy Place

What do you think is the biggest mistake companies make in trying to work with moms? The biggest mistake a company can make while trying to work with moms is telling us how busy THEY are. An example is a company I currently order from—every time I call I am told by my sales rep how busy she is, how hectic it is there, and how difficult it is for them to fill my order. As a busy mom of 3 running my own business I have a hard time feeling sympathetic! I just want to be treated like having my business is important to your company!

How do you feel you influence moms online? Moms are influenced online in so many ways. Facebook and blogs are huge. I learn so much from those two areas, get ideas, try new things, go new places ... all from things I have found out about from a friend on Facebook or reading a blog of someone I don't even know.

How can companies best support your business or mission as a mom? It is easy for companies to support my business—offer me great, friendly service and let me know you care whether I am happy with your company or not. The same goes for companies supporting my mission as a mom—I teach my daughters that we deserve to be treated with respect. We can always shop, eat, order from, watch movies, etc., somewhere else if we aren't happy.

What motivates you to tell other moms (good or bad) about a company, brand or product? I am usually motivated to tell other moms about a company, brand or product if I have a great experience or a terrible experience. Sometimes the experiences in between don't get talked about. One above and beyond, great experience can make a huge difference in whether something gets talked about. And bad experiences almost always get talked about. I am a firm believer in the fact that one bad experience can lose a customer, plus potentially more if they share their experience with others.

Name: Lisa Moore-Gee

Children: Three, ages 5, 3 ½, and 2

Hometown: Wenatchee, WA

Websites or Blogs you own: Frugal Family Fun http://www.frugalfamilyfunblog.com/, GeeSpot Reviews http://geespotreviews.blogspot.com/

Approximate audience size: 10,000 monthly loads

Twitter Id: @brianswifey05

Approximate # of followers: 1,800+

Online Involvements and associations: Mom Select, Giveaway Blogs, Eden Fantasys blogger, Eden Fantasy Ambassador, PTPA media blogger, CSN selected blogger

Are there companies who you feel are doing a great job connecting with moms? Companies that relate to families, such as Pampers, have great promotions and connections with moms. Also any company created by moms, like Piggy Paint or Boogie Wipes!

How do you feel you influence moms online? I share my thoughts, ideas and opinions with people who actually care what I have to say. I can reach a far larger audience and it is simple to do so.

Is there one moment when you realized you were impacting the life/lives of others? When my blog was picked up by some large companies and I was interviewed for a few e-magazines, I realized people look to me for advice and information. How powerful is that?

How do you feel companies can best connect with moms, particularly those who are influencers? By offering them the chance to try out new things and share their honest opinions with the company and the public. Moms are more likely to purchase something if a mom has tried it and shared their thoughts. This is a great way to connect.

Final words: NEVER underestimate the power of a mom.

Name: Marina Murphy

Children: Two, ages 3 and 1 (both girls)

Hometown: Atlanta, GA

Company Name(s): Blog "My Busy Children"

Short description of business: I have a bilingual blog: in English and Russian that I started in February 2010. In the English blog I write about kids' activities, how-to articles (for example: How To Raise Bilingual Children, How To Make Housework Easier, How To Buy Chemical-free Foods). I also write product reviews and host giveaways. In my Russian blog I write about raising kids in the U.S., about American food, and about American traditions.

Websites or Blogs you own: My Busy Children http://mybusychildren.com/; http://russian.mybusychildren.com

Approximate audience size: 1,000

Twitter Id: @mybusychildren

Approximate # of followers: 170

Online Involvements and associations: Mom Bloggers Club, http://www.momblog-gersclub.com/, Network or Russian Mom Bloggers, http://www.blogimam.com/

Offline Involvements: I organized a Mommy and Me group of Russian-speaking moms in North Atlanta. I also support a Russian language school in Atlanta: I help look for teachers; help spread the word among Russian parents about the school.

What's the best way for companies to reach you as an influencer or as a mom? Email: mybusychildren@gmail.com

Name: J.J. Newby, "JavaMom"

Children: Two, ages 4 and 6

Hometown: Chantilly, VA

Short description of business: Just a blog, not incorporated or an LLC, but I started Caffeine and a Prayer for a few reasons. First of all, I'm a writer but currently am primarily a stay-at-home mom, so I wanted a way to encourage myself to keep writing. Second, because I plan on returning to the workforce eventually and my most recent career (used to be a journalist) has been as a Marketing Communications professional for high tech companies, I began blogging as a way to keep my skills sharp and to prove that I could build an audience from scratch. And finally, I think there are a lot of negative people with a mouthpiece, and I like to put out positive, encouraging messages, especially for women.

Websites or Blogs you own: Caffeine and a Prayer, http://caffeineandaprayer.com

Approximate audience size: average 3,000 uniques a month

Websites or blogs you contribute to: Yahoo! Motherboard

Facebook Id: JJ Newby and Justine Newby

Twitter Id: @caffandaprayer

Approximate # of followers: 1,144

Online Involvements and associations: Clever Girls, Yahoo! Motherboard, Mom Select

How many moms do you typically interact with during the week offline? 20+

Offline Involvements: President of the Junior League of Northern Virginia, my church, my children's schools, Community Advisory Board member for the Katherine K. Hanley Family Shelter, Leadership Fairfax

What's the best way for companies to reach you as an influencer or as a mom? Email: javamom@caffeineandaprayer.com

Are there companies who you feel are doing a great job connecting with moms? PBS does a great job.

Is there one moment when you realized you were impacting the life/lives of others? Because a lot of people who read my blog are members of the Junior League and people who aren't typically blog readers, I realize I make an impact when someone says to me at a Junior League meeting, "I really liked that piece you blogged about ____." A more specific example is when I blogged about the fact I was going to have to have a hysterectomy due to a precancerous polyp that was discovered. I soon received a lot of emails from friends as well as strangers who told me either that they were concerned about a female health issue and asking me advice, or one friend who told me how brave she thought I was for putting it all out there, because when she went through a female health issue, she was too shy to tell anyone. I didn't expect such a strong reaction, and yet I wrote about it precisely because I felt like when I got the diagnosis, I couldn't find enough information about the process and recovery.

What motivates you to tell other moms (good or bad) about a company, brand or product? If a product is high quality, useful, and especially if it is also somehow socially responsible (recyclable or reduces waste, pesticide-free, etc.) then that catches my attention. If a company provides excellent customer service and knows how to communicate with its customers, that will often get great recognition—I often email the manager of people who give me great customer service. Conversely, if I have a really bad customer experience, you can be sure all my offline friends know for sure, and sometimes my online audience as well.

Final words: Moms are women with kids. We are influential in EVERY arena. We influence our kids, our husbands, our friends and our friends' husbands. In my blogging group of friends as well as offline, I have experts in practically every field. Blogging has allowed women to have even more influence than before. On my personal Facebook page, I have friends who are reporters, who are in television, who work in Silicon Valley, teachers, IT professionals, writers, musicians, politicos and so much more. Every discussion is an opportunity to influence.

Name: Janine Nickel

Children: Two, age 7 (twins)

Hometown: Washington, DC

Company Name(s): Buzz Cooperative & Idea-Ware

Short description of business: Buzz Cooperative assists PR and brand reps with blogger outreach programs. It was actually started by a friend of mine who brought me on as a partner, then had to give it up after taking a PR job (conflict of interest). I took it over July of 2009 and our mission has been to find creative ways to help small to mid-size brands and businesses connect with bloggers, while offering bloggers unique opportunities. Many smaller companies have never worked with bloggers and much of what we do is to explain the process, brainstorm a successful campaign, and connect them to bloggers who have expressed an interest in sampling or reviewing their product/service.

Website or Blogs you own: TwoferMom.com

Approximate audience size: 4-5,000 monthly unique visitors

Facebook Id: Janine Nickel

Approximate # of followers: 600

Twitter Id: @Twincident

Approximate # of followers: 5,000

Online Involvements and associations: Frigidaire Test Drive mom, Washington FAMILY Magazine highlighted bloggers, Lifetime Moms affiliate, Discovery Communications Toys for a Year, Next Day Blinds, Disney Social Media Mom

How many moms do you typically interact with during the week offline? 15-20

Offline Involvements: Brownies, PTA, Women's Club in my neighborhood, DC Moms group, MomzShare quarterly networking group, school volunteer, Brownie

What's the best way for companies to reach you as an influencer or as a mom? Email: scarytwins@yahoo.com

How is the best way to work with you and your company? Currently we work mostly on social media campaigns but we have partnered with other small firms to offer messaging, re-branding and website development in conjunction with an outreach program.

Are there companies who you feel are doing a great job connecting with moms? YES. Disney, Tiny Prints, Discovery Communications

How do you define influence among moms? Influence is not persuasion. Influence is based on honesty, trust, and personal relationships. I have a friend who is not on Twitter, Facebook, and does not have a blog. Yet she is a trusted resource. She always knows of a great place to eat, a fun place to go, and a cool new toy. She has maintained hundreds of friendships from childhood, through college, law school, and working. She is a true offline influencer.

Is there one moment when you realized you were impacting the life/lives of others? I was part of the first Frigidaire Test Drive mom campaign and I was using my Flip video camera to capture how much the washer can hold. It's cavernous! I received a message in Facebook from a stranger that said my video had really helped her decide to go with the Frigidaire set ... that's a $1000 decision someone made based on my video.

What motivates you to tell other moms (good or bad) about a company, brand or product? Again, I'm just naturally a "talker." I like to share things that are really working for me. I'm less focused on bringing down something that doesn't work, but I'll include that information when I'm talking to someone (or writing) if I think it's important.

Final words: Economically speaking, more moms are contributing to the family income either through gaining employment (inside or outside of the home) or finding creative ways to cut back on spending. Moms are educating themselves on products, reading reviews, and ALWAYS searching for online coupons. Thanks to sites like Retail Me Not and Groupon, we know a deal is out there. We just have to find it.

Name: Elizabeth Norton

Children: Two, ages 7 and 3

Hometown: Cape May, New Jersey

Company Name(s): Elizabeth Norton was Fitness Playhouse now T/A Party Planning Professor

Short description of business: For years I planned parties and weddings in beautiful Cape May. After a traumatic brain injury left me bed ridden, I began to learn how to take my creative ideas to the web for other parents to do the same. artyPlanningProfessor.com 2004—Create Moments that matter the most, came online after injury in January of 2009, (partyplanningprofessor.com); 2005—Blog created to help cope with being a foster mom (love is time).

Websites or Blogs you own: www.FosterCareReform.com/.org, www.LoveIsTime.com: My blog from 2005 that helped me heal as each child came and left. PartyPlanningProfessor.com over 6,000 uniques a month mainly coming from google. CapeMayMoms.com, a hyper-local site that is making a difference and connecting moms in the community.

Approximate audience size: over 6,000+

Websites or blogs you contribute to: CollectiveBias.com

Facebook Id: Eli Norton

Approximate # of followers: 900+

Twitter Id: @Elizabeth_N

Approximate # of followers: 4,000+

Online Involvements and associations: Speaker at the #140conference, Hershey Summer Celebrations leader, Tommy Nelson Mom, MomTV (let's read together), Genesis Today voting panel

How many moms do you typically interact with during the week offline? 100? between school moms and customers maybe more

What's the best way for companies to reach you as an influencer or as a mom? Email: Elizabeth@capemaymoms.com/ or Elizabeth@partyplanningprofessor.com

How do you feel you influence moms offline? Is it more than chatting in the carpool line? You have to walk the talk, talk the walk. People know me as Cape May Moms. If I start writing like I am awesome, then I have to be awesome, because otherwise someone will call me out. People ask me what makeup I am using and I better answer the latest product I reviewed, or someone will call me out ... it is a small town.

How can companies best support your business or mission as a mom? "JUST LISTEN." We are more than "just" stay-at-home moms. We are moms with minds, moms on a mission, and moms that can motivate others.

How do you feel companies can best connect with moms, particularly those who are influencers? "JUST LISTEN." If you listen to conversations, you can find leaders in the crowd. They may not be the loudest, they may not have the most tweets, but their statements are powerful and what they say is thought out.

Final words: If moms connect on one accord ... we can show the world what the power of being a mom really is and how with a click of a mouse we can find each other and make a difference.

Name: Trisha Novotny

Children: Five, ages 21, 19, 17, 11, and 9

Hometown: Gig Harbor, WA

Company Name(s): 24/7 MOMS

Short description of business: 24/7 MOMS hosts a weekly webcast and daily blog that has created an online community of moms count along the mom journey. 24/7 MOMS launched in 2007 to create a place for moms beyond the pre-school years—we started with a face-to-face conference, inviting moms to join us for speakers and workshops with a successful event. We moved forward to create an online experience of bringing a live webcast to the moms each week—we often explain ourselves as the Oprah, Rachel Ray and Martha Stewart show all wrapped into one just for MOMS. Our mission is to create the go-to place for moms and inspire them to keep it simple and make every moment count as they travel the mom journey.

Websites or Blogs you own: 247 Moms www.247moms.com

Approximate audience size: 6,000 Website readers, over 2,000 weekly viewers of the webcast, 4,900 Facebook friends, 27,000 Twitter followers, and 3,700 personal FB friends on Trisha Novotny FB

Websites or blogs you contribute to: www.scjohnson.com www.ideasthatspark.com,

Facebook Id: 247 Moms, Trisha Novotny

Twitter Id: @247moms and @millionmoms

Approximate # of followers: 27,000

Online Involvements and associations: Frigidaire Mom, Sears campaigns, Nestle campaigns, Operation Christmas Child blogger, Juicy Insider, Mom Congress for Parenting magazine, Baking with Betty, VTech Voices, SC Johnson Blogger

How many moms do you typically interact with during the week offline? 50 to 200

Offline Involvements: MOPS Speaker, MOMS Connect, Parent Council, VPO

What do you think is the biggest mistake companies make in trying to work with moms? Asking us to do things for which there is NO benefit to us or to our moms. Asking us to do more than they are willing to compensate for. Not having industry standards.

How do you feel you influence moms online? By sharing products, services and events that I trust, believe in and will benefit a mom along her mommy journey along with sharing my 21 years of MOM experience.

How can companies best support your business or mission as a mom? Be clear in what they are asking of me, offer opportunities that will be of benefit to our moms in their day-to-day mom journey.

What motivates you to tell other moms (good or bad) about a company, brand or product? When it works for me, simplifies my life, my kids love it.

Final words: Moms are online connecting, shopping, seeking deals and coupons, asking questions, looking for answers and resources. Moms influence each other in all areas; our voice is heard and makes a difference; we value the influence of other moms.

Name: Claudia Ochoa

Children: Five, ages 6, 4, 2, 1, and one deceased
Hometown: Las Vegas, NV

Company Name(s): For the Love Of 4

Short description of business: My blog is all about a day in the life of me with four sanity-sucking blessings.

Websites or Blogs you own: For The Love OF 4

Approximate audience size: Per Month I have 1,000 unique views.

Websites or blogs you contribute to: Seeds of Faith Women http://www.seedsoffaithwomen.com

Facebook Id: Claudia Ochoa

Twitter Id: @fortheloveof4

Approximate # of followers: 125

How many moms do you typically interact with during the week offline? 20+

Offline Involvements: church, playgroups, craft groups, soccer mom, softball team for me and a book club

What's the best way for companies to reach you as an influencer or as a mom? Email:fortheloveof4@gmail.com

What do you think is the biggest mistake companies make in trying to work with moms? The lack of interest in a mom's word of mouth. Most companies know how important we are and use it to their advantage!

How do you define influence among moms? By word of mouth and trust, I can use something and say it's great, but if a mom doesn't trust what I am saying then it doesn't make a difference. That is why I don't play the number game when it comes to followers because I want those who read my blog to actually care for what I have to say.

How do you feel you influence moms online? I stay honest and I am very picky about what I review or speak about in my blog. Because it is more of a personal blog yet at the same time a review blog, I only want things I will actually use in my home with my family. Other moms see this and can believe in what I have to say about a product.

How can companies best support your business or mission as a mom? By being a quality company and knowing that I am a quality mom. A company should be family/mom/kid friendly if wanting to work with me. A company could give more mom bloggers a chance to learn about what they have to offer. Money is not easy to come by, so if we are going to spend it we want to know it's worth it.

What motivates you to tell other moms (good or bad) about a company, brand or product? When my children or I love something, I want to share it with other moms and families. I feel quality fun-loving products should be in every home. Anything that will make a home more of a home for a family is an A+ in my book.

Name: Pamela Olsen

Children: Four, ages 5, 3 ½, 2 and one on the way

Hometown: Eugene, OR

Short description of business: I started my Mommy Blog in September of 2009 because I was looking for a way to connect with the outside world while still being a homemaker; in November I added my book blog to share my love of reading with other moms.

Websites or Blogs you own: The Busy Woman's Guide to Surviving Motherhood http://guidetosurvivingmotherhood.blogspot.com, Busy Moms Who Love to Read http://busymomswholovetoread.blogspot.com

Websites or blogs you contribute to: Busy Mommy Media http://busymommymedia.com Health Editor

Twitter Id: @loutnumberdmom

Approximate # of followers: 1,350

Online Involvements and associations: MomSpark, MyBlogSpark, MomSelect, MamaBuzz

How many moms do you typically interact with during the week offline? 30+

Offline Involvements: Monthly Book Club, Meadowlark Parent Organization, Relay For Life (American Cancer Society) planning committee

What's the best way for companies to reach you as an influencer or as a mom? Email: polsen11@comcast.net or loutnumberedmama@gmail.com

What do you think is the biggest mistake companies make in trying to work with moms? They tend to oversimplify things. Yes, moms want an easier way, but not because they can't understand the more difficult things; rather, because they are smart enough to know there is an easier way! They also tend to focus a "mom-targeted" product at only mom groups, when moms are members of all sorts of groups that have nothing to do with motherhood.

Are there companies who you feel are doing a great job connecting with moms? I think Kraft Foods, Lee Jeans and Curel Dermatologica Lotions are all doing wonderful work to make moms feel like their opinions matter.

How do you feel you influence moms online? With every post I write, I am trying to talk to at least one mom who might benefit from the topic. Whether it is a product review or just my thoughts and sharing of information, I hope to change just one woman's life—even if it is a small thing, it will make a big difference, because just knowing that someone else feels, or has felt the same things can make you feel stronger.

How can companies best support your business or mission as a mom? When companies are also community minded, it solidifies my actions. For example, when I request a donation for the American Cancer Society from a business, and they go above and beyond, they are showing the world that what one mom thought was a good idea really was.

What motivates you to tell other moms (good or bad) about a company, brand or product? When I am really impressed by a company I want to shout it from the roof tops; conversely I am one of those people that doesn't like the negative, so I will only speak negatively about a company if it comes up or I am directly asked. I am most impressed by companies that don't go for the gimmicks and flash but rather let their product or service speak for itself—sort of a "proof is in the pudding" philosophy.

How do you feel companies can best connect with moms, particularly those who are influencers? Being relatable is one of the best ways to connect with anyone. They have to think about what a mom needs in life—more time, more money and more patience. How can the company provide one or all of these things, is the question they need to ask themselves. If this means providing a product to a mom for trial, then go for it. If it means creating products that make life easier, make it happen.

Final words: As cliché as it may sound, the children are our future and the front line "molders" of those children are the mothers. Mothers are there to help a child to learn, grow and shape their views of the world. This means that the interaction between mothers is key to moving forward and helping society blossom with each generation.

Name: Marnie Omanoff

Children: One, age 6

Hometown: New York, NY

Short description of business: Marketing and Branding

Offline Involvements: Women's Leadership Exchange, Big City Moms, Best Buy WOLF Omega, PS 183 PTA/e-board, Kids In Distress Situations (KIDS)

What's the best way for companies to reach you as an influencer or as a mom? Email: omarien@nyc.rr.com, events

Are there companies who you feel are doing a great job connecting with moms? Diapers.com, Soap.com

Name: Candice Orpesa

Children: One daughter, age 15 months

Hometown: Atlanta, GA

Websites or Blogs you own: Stash Mama http://stashmama.blogspot.com

Approximate audience size: Over 1,200 Blog readers

Facebook Id: Stash Mama

Approximate # of followers: 500

Twitter Id: @stashMama

Approximate # of followers: 800

How many moms do you typically interact with during the week offline? Lots! I meet moms everywhere I go. It's like a universal thing that moms can just talk to one another because they have that one thing in common. I chat at church, playdates, and even places like the grocery store.

How do you define influence among moms? I'd say, there are tons and tons of kids'/babies' products and toys; some you have buyer's remorse and some it was the best most helpful purchase, it is our job to help out other moms and give them the hints, and help them to save money and spend well.

Is there one moment when you realized you were impacting the life/lives of others? After my blog's audience grew so large so quickly I started feeling like I have a voice, and I should do something with it. I feel like if there is something I think my readers absolutely must hear about whether it's a new band, awesome product, great event, fun thing to do, political view, etc., it will get safely delivered right to their inbox and that makes me smile.

What motivates you to tell other moms (good or bad) about a company, brand or product? Hmm, so an example would be me meeting pregnant women. I just HAVE to ask if they plan on cloth diapering. When they say no, because they always do, I simply must discuss the benefits, cost, how much easier it has gotten through the times, and why they should. I don't think my way is the only way, but I do want to share my experience to help them make an educated discussion.

Final words: Moms really do have their own network, every mom can understand certain things that only a mom would understand. Not only that, but a mom, whether a man thinks it or not, runs the household, buys the products, groceries, gifts, and talks with the other moms. We basically run the world.

Name: Kimberly Ortiz

Children: Three, ages 7, 5, and 2 (all boys)

Hometown: Olympia, WA

Short description of business: I started Pretty Pink Momma two years ago as a way of sharing the cool things that I found for moms and families when I was surfing the Internet. At the time, I was starting my own small online business and noticed that my competition all had blogs. I didn't know what a blog was but I knew that I needed to find out. I was waiting to get all my start-up money for my business so I started to learn blogging because there were no costs involved. Little did I know that I would get so into blogging that I would never get back to starting my business. My business became blogging. Currently my mission is to provide my readers of Pretty Pink Momma with as many product reviews and giveaways as possible. I am mainly a product review site but I love to infuse my knowledge and experience as a consumer, a mother and a woman that loves the newest products and innovations for women and families into each review. I have to have a way to relate to the product or I simply can't write about it. For now, there is no exit strategy. I love blogging and all the opportunities it has afforded my family and me.

Websites or Blogs you own: Pretty Pink Momma
http://www.prettypinkmomma.com/

Approximate audience size: 1,100 subscribers and 5,500 unique per month.

Twitter Id: @PrettyPinkMomma

Approximate # of followers: 1,800

Online Involvements and associations: My most recent and prominent association is being a blogger for Nutrisystem. It started as Nutrisystem Blogger 15 and now it has expanded into a new program called Nutrisystem Nation. I am also a Mommy Motivator for the launch of Community of Movement. I am also a brand ambassador for The View, Kleenex, Tropicana, Rice Krispies, Aquafresh and Mom Sends the Message.

What do you think is the biggest mistake companies make in trying to work with moms? I think that the biggest mistake is when companies assume that we care about their product. They need to sell it to us first before they expect us to try to promote it to our readers. I can't tell you how many media pitches I have deleted because they think I'm desperate to share info on my blog. They come off to me like I need them—really they need me. Those inquiries I generally don't reply to.

Are there companies who you feel are doing a great job connecting with moms? Yes there are many that understand that moms are the key. We not only shop for ourselves but each individual in our family. We are the reason our husbands wear the clothes they wear, eat the food they eat, most times drive the car they drive. We have a say and it's a big one.

How do you feel you influence moms online? I influence moms through my blog, Facebook and Twitter posts. By sharing content relevant to their lives on a regular basis, they know my experience with the ages of my children or the issues that I face personally, and because of that, my voice is trusted.

How do you feel you influence moms offline? Is it more than chatting in the carpool line? I think that moms everywhere—no matter how you meet them—like to share with other moms their experiences. Whether it's waiting at the bus stop or the doctor's office, if we find a common thread of communication, we love to give advice about products, services, people, and places—whatever fits the topic of conversation. We also ask other moms where they found that particular object or sitter or service. For me, I share the things I learn about with my friends, family, neighbors, my children's school, whoever will listen when I think that they would benefit from the knowledge I possess.

How can companies best support your business or mission as a mom? Give me something to boast about. If I think that it's an awesome solution to a typical mom or feminine problem I'm going to talk about it. I like the feeling that I get when someone tells me thanks for telling them about something that saved them time or money. Or even just their sanity!

What motivates you to tell other moms (good or bad) about a company, brand or product? It's nice to feel as if you are a part of something. When I became a SAHM I didn't realize how much I would miss those professional interactions that came with having a career. I felt like part of me was missing from the picture. I felt lonely and depressed. When I found blogging, it was the answer to my prayers. I felt whole again. And I could do it from home while watching my children. This is my main motivation. It's selfish but it's the truth. I like that I am useful and can serve a purpose to others beyond my family and my home.

How do you feel companies can best connect with moms, particularly those who are influencers? I think that it all comes down to research. If they do google searches that are relevant to their brand or product, then they can find bloggers, tweeters or Facebookers that are affected by the topic. That blogger in particular would have a reader base who already knows that they have a need for that brand or service. It's more than possible that the readers relate to the influencers because they have the same issues. Win over the group of moms that rate high in the search engines for those key words, and they can start the wave of word-of-mouth marketing. It's imperative that companies offer their product complimentary to the mom influencers because as with any product, a mom is going to be hard pressed to try something new just based on the word of the company if it involves out-of-pocket expense.

Name: Katie Owen

Children and ages: One, age 6 months

Hometown: Federal Way, WA

Short description of business: I started my blog as a way to reach out to other Moms like me, and to share the resources I had. Because saving money and giving back to my community is such a large part of who I am, I wanted a way of expressing that. The blog allows me a great place to speak my mind, interact with others like me, and learn about new resources to share.

Websites or Blogs you own: Saving for Change http://www.saving4change.blogspot.com

Websites or blogs you contribute to: Free Mania http://www.freemania.net

Facebook Id: Katie Owen

Online Involvements and associations: I am an affiliate of ErgoBaby Carriers, and actively participate with http://www.adoptivefamilies.com, and http://www.thebump.com.

Offline Involvements: I'm a foster Mommy, (well, a foster/adopt Mommy at the moment!) and I participate in biweekly support groups. One takes place in Auburn, WA, and the other in Federal Way, WA. We discuss topics like parenting, community resources, new products, feeding, healthcare, and anything and everything in between! I also attend my church on a weekly basis, and interact with parish mothers there. I currently am serving through AmeriCorps VISTA (Volunteers in Service to America) for the American Red Cross Mount Rainier Chapter. With them, I do volunteer coordination and help assist with disaster response. In my free time, I like to volunteer for a local homeless shelter.

What's the best way for companies to reach you as an influencer or as a mom? Electronically! Email: katie.lynn.owen1@gmail.com

What do you think is the biggest mistake companies make in trying to work with moms? They assume what needs and wants I have. If they simply asked, they might be surprised with my answer.

Are there companies who you feel are doing a great job connecting with moms? I really love ErgoBaby. That's why I'm an affiliate for them! I also love Gerber, BumGenius, BabiesRUs, and EvenFlo.

How do you feel you influence moms offline? Is it more than chatting in the carpool line? Definitely. I use my existing social networks to build new ones, and I'm constantly looking for ways of helping others. Because most of my life is centered on community, it only seems natural to share the resources I know. I appreciate companies that are transparent (like Gerber) who are an easier "sell" to other Moms. If you always know and feel a product is great, you've already sold the deal.

How can companies best support your business or mission as a mom? Be flexible, transparent, and easily accessible.

How do you feel companies can best connect with moms, particularly those who are influencers? Offering product samples or coupons is very effective, encouraging Moms to try the product before making an investment. Using available social media, like Facebook or Twitter, also helps to spread the word. A large part of the Mom-influence is getting information from a source you trust.

Final words: I remember a time where Moms didn't have a powerful voice in society. Being a homemaker or mother was something to hide, not flaunt for all to see! I am very proud to be a working mother, and I am excited for others out there who value family. I appreciate and support projects like this, because it's the most powerful way to drive change.

Name: Charlene Pacenti

Children: Two, ages 7 and 11

Hometown: Boca Raton, FL

Company Name(s): MomsMiami.com, owned by Miami Herald Media Company; BocaParent.com, owned by me, Charlene Pacenti

Short description of business: MomsMiami.com is an online community for moms in the Miami-Fort Lauderdale area, offering articles and guides with local information and resources on ALL stages of parenting. We also offer staff- and user-contributed blogs, videos, plus a calendar of kid-friendly events and forums on dozens of parenting topics.

BocaParent.com is a one-stop website with local information for things to do with the kids, advice from local experts, guides to local resources and more. I launched BocaParent.com on my own in January 2010, again to fill a need in the market. With the local newspaper closing in Boca Raton and the major dailies pulling back on coverage, there was a dearth of local information, as well as advertising opportunities. I want to fill that niche for Boca Raton families like mine.

Websites or Blogs you own: www.BocaParent.com

Approximate audience size: 1,750

Websites or blogs you contribute to: MomsMiami.com—audience 30,000

Facebook Id: MomsMiami.com and BocaParent

Twitter Id: @MomsMiami and @BocaParent

Approximate # of followers: 1,200 on MomsMiami and 200 on BocaParent

How many moms do you typically interact with during the week offline? About a dozen

What's the best way for companies to reach you as an influencer or as a mom? Email

How is the best way to work with you and your company? Joint promotions and banner advertising.

How do you define influence among moms? One word: credibility. You must give good, helpful, correct and timely information. You are a mom; you think like a mom. Ask the questions a mom would ask and give your followers the answers. That is the most valuable service you can provide. It's all about the content.

How do you feel you influence moms online? Through timely, credible, deep information. Tell them something they didn't know. Give them a tip that makes their lives easier, reduces their stress, lets them know they are not alone.

How do you feel you influence moms offline? Is it more than chatting in the carpool line? Chatting at school pickup and sports practices is part of it. But it's also through offline events. MomsMiami had a very successful workshop for moms looking to start their own businesses. Hundreds of moms came and they were still talking about it months later. We also have occasional Moms Night Out events where moms can meet offline. We have had morning coffees where they can bring the kids and we have an expert in to give a talk.

How can companies best support your business or mission as a mom? Advertise on our sites. Participate in our events.

Name: Colleen Padilla

Children: Two, ages 5 and 3

Hometown: Phoenixville, PA

Company Name(s): ClassyMommy.com

Short description of business: I Started ClassyMommy.com in May 2006 as a way to give me intellectual stimulation and potentially raise money to donate to charity when I decided not to return to work after finishing a 6-month maternity leave. Today, Classy Mommy is an indispensable website for moms featuring fabulous products that can be easily accessed in one of the largest catalogs of independent baby product reviews on the Web with over 1400 product reviews, fabulous giveaways for readers, and lively videos. Right now I don't have an exit strategy as I'd love to continue to grow my platform with speaking events, spokesperson opportunities, and TV segments with myself as Mom & Lifestyle expert, and write books on how moms can find a middle ground working from home thanks to social media. As for my new book—*The Digital Mom Handbook* and website/blog that goes along with it—I've found new passions. What started as a way to fill my spare time with intellectual stimulation and a goal of sharing my favorite shopping finds on ClassyMommy.com has turned into a mission to share the opportunity of the digital space with other moms since this has become my career. With an MBA from Cornell and years of FORTUNE 500 company experience under my belt, I truly feel I hit this magical middle ground when social media became a way for me to make a livelihood from home, while spending time with my children, and have a career on my own terms. I'm passionate now about sharing this "know how" with other moms and inspiring them to find a way to seek a better balance between their careers and their children that might give them more flexibility. I see moms who stay home frustrated and bored and wanting to find a way to work while those moms I know who are working are frustrated with their struggles to find balance and flexibility to put family first when they would at times prefer to do so.

Websites or Blogs you own: Classy Mommy http://classymommy.com/, DigitalHandbook.com http://digitalhandbook.com/, Gift Guide Girls http://www.giftguidegirls.com/

Approximate audience size: 80,000 Unique Monthly

Websites or blogs you contribute to: LifetimeMoms.com

Facebook Id: Classy Mommy and Colleen Costello Padilla

Twitter Id: @ClassyMommy

Approximate # of followers: 9,000

Online Involvements and associations: Brand Ambassador for Scrubbing Bubbles, TJ Maxx and Marshalls Back to School, Mattel Preschool Toys, Energizer Rechargeable, Hanes Comfort Crew, Frigidaire Test Drive Mom 2010, Frito Lay Fab 15, Healthy Choice, Johnson & Johnson's Real Mom Series, Carnival Cruise Lines, Healthy Child Healthy World Parent Ambassador, Lifetime Moms Channel Leader, Walmart Moms, Mom TV

Offline Involvements: YMCA member, Valley Forge Young Members, Member of the DAR (Daughters of the American Revolution), Philly Media Moms–this is a REAL LIFE group of blogging/social media people from the Philadelphia area, Valley Forge Mountain Swim & Tennis Club, upcoming speaker role at Reviewer's Retreat, upcoming speaker role at Reviewer's Retreat, spoke on the panel at Blissdom and Blog World Expo, spoke for NAWBO in Philadelphia Chapter on Social Media

What's the best way for companies to reach you as an influencer or as a mom? Email: colleen@classymommy.com

What do you think is the biggest mistake companies make in trying to work with moms? Besides everyday undervaluing moms' influence and expertise and not being willing to pay for that knowledge, the biggest mistake I see companies make is treating moms only as one dimensional "mommy" creatures and ignoring that moms are multidimensional with many other interests in addition to their children–from fashion to beauty to digital technology and a million other interests or areas of expertise.

Are there companies who you feel are doing a great job connecting with moms? Disney, Hanes, Land's End, Comcast, Apple

How do you feel companies can best connect with moms, particularly those who are influencers? By hosting local in-person events organized by influencers. This will enable them to engage closely and directly with the influencers (whether they be social media mavens or offline community mom mavens) to build a lasting relationship while also enabling companies to leverage the mom's influence in her own unique circle of real life friends–many of whom are also likely influencers. Plus, by engaging in an in-person real life event, moms can touch and feel a product and spend multiple hours engaging about the product–even if other activities happen during the party like lunch, games, dinner, drinks, or even the inclusion of kids–the brand will be TOP OF MIND as the host for the gathering and the key messages the companies hope to share will likely be spread.

Final words: I think moms have a huge influence on green products and sustainability. Those who are experts in this area are HUGE influencers as our society and moms in general continue to find ways to protect the environment for our children and protect our children and ourselves from what could "perhaps" be toxic products or foods that we casually come in contact with every day–as many of us do not know all the facts.

Name: Jendi Pagano

Children: Three, ages 8, 6, and 4

Hometown: Hershey, PA

Company Name(s): Scenes and Cinema

Short description of business: Media Assistants focusing on Video Creation and Marketing. It will be official in January 2011; a way to make an income from home doing something I love; support my family; outsourcing.

Websites or Blogs you own: http://simplevloggingtips.com; http://jendisjournal.com; http://scenesandcinema.com

Websites or blogs you contribute to: http://profitablemommyblogging.com; http://blissfullydomestic.com

Facebook Id: Jendis Journal and Simple Vlogging Tips

Twitter Id: @jendisjournal; @vloggingtips

Approximate # of followers: 3,500; 301

Online Involvements and associations: Dial Nutriskin Healthier You; Purex Insider

How many moms do you typically interact with during the week offline? 10-15

Offline Involvements: church and library

What's the best way for companies to reach you as an influencer or as a mom? jendivlogs@gmail.com

How do you feel you influence moms online? I do reviews and am not afraid to say the bad and good. I answer a lot of questions about cameras/video/hosting, etc.

How do you feel you influence moms offline? Is it more than chatting in the carpool line? I talk about products I like, and give them as gifts. I tell about deals and offer suggestions.

What motivates you to tell other moms (good or bad) about a company, brand or product? Whenever I think it is something that will benefit the other mom. If they have mentioned a problem or something they need I love to have suggestions.

How do you feel companies can best connect with moms, particularly those who are influencers? Twitter/Facebook is a great place to start. A forum or place where we can go and know that the company will see our questions/opinions is a wonderful option to have.

Final words: "For the hand that rocks the cradle is the hand that rules the world." ~William Ross Wallace

Name: Scarlet Paolicchi

Children: Three, ages 5, 3, and one on the way

Hometown: Born Center Sandwich, NH

Company Name(s): Moms Wear Your Tees Social Media Marketing

Short description of business: Provide marketing for companies, helping them spread their links and product buzz. I started my business in December 2009. My desire was to create a business to help supplement my husband's teacher salary and one that would allow me to work around my children's schedule. I just got the idea and went for it. It has been fun watching it develop!

Websites or Blogs you own: Young Living http://www.youngliving.org/scarlet and Moms Wear Your Tees http://momswearyourtees.blogspot.com

Approximate audience size: 11,000+ hits per month

Facebook Id: Moms Wear Your Tees

Approximate # of followers: 1,000+

Twitter Id: @MWYT

Approximate # of followers: 11,600+

Offline Involvements: I am president of MOMS Club Bellevue South and group owner of Bellevue Moms Yahoo Group

How is the best way to work with you and your company? 99% of my work is online. I create key word links for people's websites and this can only be done online. I also accept company t-shirts if they represent a company I believe in and I wear these to spread the word.

What do you think is the biggest mistake companies make in trying to work with moms? I think the biggest mistake is not working with moms! Some companies don't understand the value of the links and see the potential traffic that is to be gained by working with moms.

How do you feel you influence moms offline? Is it more than chatting in the carpool line? For me, influencing offline is just about being who you are talking about what interesst and affects you honestly. I would never try to sell anyone on any of the products I feature but I would be happy to let them know about something great I have tried that works for me. I also hope that others see me using cloth diapers, nursing my baby, and recycling and they notice it and think about trying it themselves.

Final words: I believe that every one of us, not just moms, influences every area of people's lives through our actions and words. It behooves us all to remember this in all of our actions!

Name: Ashley Paroli

Children: One, age 2

Hometown: New Orleans, LA

Company Name(s): "Closet of Free Samples" and "Scrappin A Moment"

Short description of business: Closet of Free Samples offers free samples from various companies, product reviews as well as giveaways. Closet of Free Samples was started in November 2008. I always loved free things in high school. When I discovered I could actually find free stuff just by doing internet searches I got excited. Then I just wanted to see how many freebies I was signing up for so I began a blog. Then I saw how other blogs were doing reviews and such and thought that was pretty neat. I began to fix up my blog a bit, promote it and build my readership. Once I had a decent amount of readers I began getting involved with other companies to host product reviews and giveaways which has helped a lot along the way of my site being where it is today. It's not only a hobby that I enjoy, but it also seems to help out others as well.

Scrappin A Moment offers handmade items such as scrapbooks, shadow boxes and things of that nature made by me. Scrappin A Moment is a new one. My friend and I both love making scrapbooks and handmade things similar to scrapbooking and cards and such. Basically, if we think of something to make and it comes out nicely, we're willing to share it and make it for you as well! We put a web site together last year. I love being able to share my crafts and projects while also being able to offer a service to others at affordable prices. Plus, we ship worldwide!

Websites or Blogs you own: Closet of Free Samples is http://www.closetsamples.com and Scrappin A Moment http://scrappinamoment.blogspot.com

Approximate audience size: 1,000

Facebook Id: Ashley Paroli, Closet of Free Samples

Twitter Id: @ashybaby87

Approximate # of followers: 1,730

Online Involvements and associations: Gather, Business2Blogger, Blogger Linkup, Mom Pancls, Logical Media

What's the best way for companies to reach you as an influencer or as a mom? Email: closetsamples@gmail.com or scrappinamoment@gmail.com.

How is the best way to work with you and your company? I offer advertising options, but my favorite is doing reviews of products. I'm mostly involved with social media at this point but am open to other suggestions! Help spreading the word about us is always a big help, also!

What do you think is the biggest mistake companies make in trying to work with moms? I think sometimes companies shoot us down a lot because they don't realize how important our work is. From what I've seen, they think we are too busy or can't give our best because of our involvement with our children.

How do you feel you influence moms online? I feel I influence moms by helping them find things for free or cheap, using coupons. I'm not an expert, but I think I'm a great start for those trying to live frugally. I also give honest opinions on the items I review. Knowing I'm a real person and a real mom, I believe it helps influence other moms that my opinion is honest and trustworthy coming from my point of view.

How can companies best support your business or mission as a mom? Simply spread the word about us! I have a whole new appreciation for businesses that do things to help support moms and online blogs/websites such as mine.

What motivates you to tell other moms (good or bad) about a company, brand or product? I guess it's mainly the quality of service I receive. I notice if my service was either REALLY good or REALLY bad. I want to spread the word about my experience, which in turn ends up getting me to talk about the product(s) I purchased.

How do you feel companies can best connect with moms, particularly those who are influencers? Honestly, for me, I like companies that reach out to me on their own. Not where I have to go to them. When they reach out to me it makes me feel important and of course, who doesn't like feeling important? I also like companies that have products really tested by moms, not just paying someone to say what they want them to say. I want to be able to trust the company and hear real opinions on them.

Final words: I honestly never realized how influential moms were until I started spending a lot of time online. I used to look at a mom just as a person who cares for a child. Now being a mom, and an influential mom online, I've realized how much more important and effective our opinions are to others. Others appear to have a greater respect for another mom's opinion, from what I've seen.

Name: Calley Pate

Children: 2, ages 7 years and 21 months

Hometown: Tampa, FL

Company Name(s): The Eco Chic blog and Eco Chic Parties

Short description of business: The Eco Chic blog is a blog for parents looking to make greener choices in their lives. I focus a lot on natural parenting and I am an avid cloth diaper advocate. Eco Chic Parties is a side project that features some of my favorite eco-friendly and cloth diaper companies as hosts for weekly Twitter parties. I also offer Social Media consulting for many of my clients. I began blogging in 2007 and branched out to offering Social Media consulting in early 2010. My original motivation was simply to write and learn the skills needed to become a successful blogger. As I continued my journey I became very passionate about natural parenting and cloth diapers. My mission is to continue to show families how they can make simple, small, easy steps to change their lifestyles to become more eco-friendly. My exit strategy? I'm not sure about that one yet; I'm just enjoying where I am at in the moment.

Websites or Blogs you own: The Eco Chic blog http://theecochic.com and Eco Chic Parties http://ecochicparties.theecochic.com

Approximate audience size: 200 to 2,000 people visit my blog each day

Websites or blogs you contribute to: I love Cloth Diapers – The SoftBums.com Blog http://loveclothdiapers.blogspot.com ,The Cloth Diaper Whisperer http://www.theclothdiaperwhisperer.com

Facebook Id: The Eco Chic and Eco Chic Parties

Twitter Id: @TheEcoChic and @EcoChicParties

Approximate # of followers: 4,262 and 2,750

How many moms do you typically interact with during the week offline? 200 to 600

Offline Involvements: Very active in the church community and with my son's Parent Teacher Association (PTA) community.

What do you think is the biggest mistake companies make in trying to work with moms? For me the biggest mistake I see is when a company sends me a proposal for a product or service that is clearly not an environmentally-friendly item. They need to do their homework and read their blogs—to find out what they are passionate about—before they approach them with a proposal. Moms are very educated and have a wealth of information available at their fingertips; if we don't know an answer we WILL go look for it.

How do you feel you influence moms online? To influence moms online, I like to offer them the most current and relevant content and information that I can. While I can't possibly share all of my knowledge with them (there just isn't enough time in the day), I make myself available to answer their questions. I can give them my opinions about a product or an idea but to influence them I must help change (or confirm) their opinions.

How do you feel you influence moms offline? Is it more than chatting in the carpool line? Again, the best way to influence anyone (a mom or otherwise) is to lead by example. The only way that will work is to surround yourself with people and become part of the community. By becoming part of a community you have the ability to influence more than just the moms that you chat with in the carpool line. Do life with others and they will begin to see what you are doing—and they will ask you questions about why you do things differently.

How can companies best support your business or mission as a mom? By giving us the tools and the resources we need to help make our communities better for everyone. We all want to have a healthy environment and healthy families.

What motivates you to tell other moms (good or bad) about a company, brand or product? It usually just comes up in conversation. Most of the time we are talking about our lives and our children and what challenges we are currently facing in our lives. If I have used a product that will make their lives easier, I usually tell them about it. Personal experience is very powerful.

Final words: Every mom has different values. We all want what's best for our families and we look at the products we purchase to help us with that. We have to be advocates for our children and teach them to make the best choices in their lives. The best way to influence a mom is to know that while not every mom will value what you have to offer, they may become influenced by other moms who do value what you have to offer.

Name: Desiree Peeples

Children: One, age 3

Hometown: Atlanta, GA

Company Name(s): Mommy Reporter Media, LLC

Short description of business: I do social media consulting for small businesses. I also do training and information classes, as well as report news and trends as it applies to women in social media. My company was formed late 2009 with the purpose of providing information and training to those interested in social media. I really had no idea what I wanted to do. All I knew is that I wanted to work in social media and that I wanted to share information. I love helping people discover the joy and power of connecting online. I love doing this so much that I would do it for free ... as a matter of fact, I was doing it for free until recently.

Websites or Blogs you own: MommyReporter.com http://www.mommyreporter.com/, The Better Mom Show http://bettermomshow.com/

Approximate audience size: 4,000 page views per month/6,000 unique

Websites or blogs you contribute to: SkyAngel.com, Autotrader.com, and Examiner.com

Facebook Id: Desiree Peeples and Mommy Reporter

Twitter Id: @mommyreporter

Approximate # of followers: 2,900

Online Involvements and associations: PBS Sprout Band of Bloggers, Soft Scrub Club Captain, Purex Insider, Team Mom, US Family Guide, Mom Central, Mommy PR, Global Influence, Mom Bloggers Club, Social Media Moms, Mom Select

How many moms do you typically interact with during the week offline? 20 to 50 via church and playgroups

Offline Involvements: Toastmasters, Atlanta Bloggers Club, National Association of Black Journalists, Volunteer for the Atlanta Children's Shelter

What's the best way for companies to reach you as an influencer or as a mom? Twitter @MommyReporter or via email at desiree@mommyreporter.com

How do you define influence among moms? I think influence is closely connected with being relatable. For instance, I would much rather take a recommendation from a single mom than I would from a mom who is married, because a single mom's life is much more like mine. In the same regard, I think a mom's status or lifestyle offline also determines her influence. I have seen some heavy hitters online who are virtually non-existent offline. I believe the ability to transfer authenticity and genuineness in various mediums is what truly determines a mom's influence.

How do you feel you influence moms offline? Is it more than chatting in the carpool line? I wish I had a dollar for every mom I discussed social media with. I've convinced three of my closest mom friends to start blogs and I'm known as the "online girl" at church and in social groups. I even advised former colleagues from my previous job in how to use social media to maximize their presence and how to connect with their audience. My former employer is in negotiations now to secure a contract for my consulting services.

How do you feel companies can best connect with moms, particularly those who are influencers? I think the best way is to support what moms are passionate about because in reality, no mom is excited about laundry detergent or batteries. If an influential mom is passionate about cancer research, then work with her on promoting that cause. I am super excited about sharing information and helping those who want to learn. Companies can help me do that by helping me to provide that information in an accessible way. If a brand does that, it will get noticed, and not because it bought ad space, but because it cares enough to add value to the lives of others and to be of service.

Final words: I think brands need to diversify their efforts. Just because a mom is a blogger doesn't mean she is necessarily a "mommy blogger." I have noticed that in many campaigns, companies tend to work with mom bloggers who are all very similar, instead of taking the time to try and find moms who are different, have different audiences or have different tastes. Moms have influence in other ways as well, not just via their blogs.

Name: Sarah Peppel

Children: Two, ages 13 and 12 (both girls)

Hometown: Phoenixville, PA

Employer: Valley Forge Christian College—part-time professor

Websites or Blogs you own: Genesis Moments http://www.genesismoments.com, DIYFrugal http://www.diyfrugal.com

Approximate audience size: Genesis Moments and DIYFrugal each average: 2,000-5,000/month depending on which I am giving more attention. (Weekly articles you see on DIYFrugal also appear in the local paper and on their website which increases the audience size to potentially 10,000 plus.)

Facebook Id: Sarah Oldham Peppel

Twitter Id: @GenMom, @DIYFrugal, @S_Peppel

Approximate # of followers: 7,500

Online Involvements and associations: Recently, a brand ambassador for Eggland's Best Eggs (Pink Dozen Blogger) and Wisk (BetaBlogger) and active as a Philly Social Media Mom. Participated in campaigns with The Motherhood, MomCentral,

MomSelect, Mom Central, JustCentsible consulting, Weber Shandwick (Hellmann's, Ragu), Rolemommy, and Disney and Paramount movie screenings.

How many moms do you typically interact with during the week offline? 20-30

Offline Involvements: Presbyterian church member, president of Women's Ministries in local presbytery and liaison to 11 churches, Republican Committee Woman, Cofounder of the annual Valley Forge Patriots TEA Party Rally, YMCA member, president of our neighborhood Home Owner's Association, active in our campground's women's association and planning for annual camp meeting, columnist in the local paper on Frugal Living.

What do you think is the biggest mistake companies make in trying to work with moms? Devaluing moms' time. They can't seem to set aside the company's agenda to see what really works for moms and incorporate that feedback so that both parties come away happy rather than one feeling taken advantage of—on either side.

Are there companies who you feel are doing a great job connecting with moms? The efforts of the PR firm, WeberShandwick, to work with moms and educate companies (and in turn work through the PR firms such as Mom Select) has been phenomenal. They have brought opportunities to mom bloggers from major companies like Hellman's and Ragu. Mom Select has also done a great job connecting mom bloggers to companies (for instance, Energizer and some of the toy companies to name a few).

How do you feel you influence moms online? I influence moms online through writing quality, fun content for both blogs and by participating in local events that highlight mom bloggers, and then posting them online so that others can see the opportunities available. I also use Facebook and Twitter and other forums to add input and insight to ongoing conversations. My DIYFrugal blog is a little more geared towards practical money-saving advice and resources, so some moms may find that site more helpful in the long run which is why I started it.

How do you feel you influence moms offline? Is it more than chatting in the carpool line? Offline, I am able to give moms spiritual guidance through an annual prayer retreat that I run for the women in the eleven churches of our presbytery. I also show moms that they can have a say through my volunteer efforts as president of our homeowner's association. I also encourage women to speak up for their country and ideals in my role as local committee woman for the Republican Party.

How can companies best support your business or mission as a mom? I love events that help the broader blogging community. If companies wish to engage someone locally, I am always willing to help for one-time events; or if I really like the product, I am still open to doing some reviews and giveaways, though my time is increasingly limited and my girls are getting older so toys are out of the question anymore.

Final words: Moms are making a statement. They are kicking butts and taking names; and now they are doing it online because it meets a core need in their lives to connect and use their education in a way that helps the family and if possible, allows them to stay home to do it. And, single moms are on the rise. They have to know what is going on in the world to survive.

Politically, moms are taking government by storm because they know how to multitask and strategize. Socially, they are the glue. Educationally, women are getting advanced degrees in every field. Opportunities are opening up everywhere and still women want to feel feminine, creative, loved, respected and appreciated for their efforts. Meet those needs and you go straight to the heart of those making radical changes in our society.

Name: Allyson Phillips

Children: Two, ages 7 and 2

Hometown: San Diego, CA

Company Name(s): Kiley Madison, Inc. (Tilty Cup); iPlayGroups.com

Short description of business: Kiley Madison Inc. is a company that brings new and innovative ideas to baby and toddler feeding. Kiley Madison Inc. was launched in 2004 when I designed a product, the Ki Kover, for my personal use and was motivated to produce it for others after constant requests from other parents about the product. We then sold and produced several thousands of the Ki Kovers and moved on to designing the Tilty Cup. The company has been rapidly expanding since then. Iplaygroups.com is the first online community dedicated to parents and their parenting support groups.

Websites or Blogs you own: Kiley Madison, Inc. (Tilty Cup) http://www.tiltycup.com/; iPlayGroups.com http://iplaygroups.com/

Approximate audience size: http://www.tiltycup.com/, 1,200/month; iPlayGroups.com, 9,000

Facebook Id: TILTY Cup and Allyson Phillips

Twitter Id: @tiltycup

Approximate # of followers: 1,000

Online Involvements and associations: Huggies® MomInspired™ Grant Winners, Mom of the Month for San Diego Parent Connection

Offline Involvements: Delta Gamma SDSU Alumni Group, Stroller Strides

What do you think is the biggest mistake companies make in trying to work with moms? I think the biggest mistake companies make when trying to work with moms is that they don't take into account all the things that a mom thinks about and deals with constantly throughout the day. For the most part her mind is never fully in one place but always thinking about what else has to be done and who needs what from her. It is very hard to ever have a mom's full and undivided attention. I also think that a lot of companies don't take into account how alone a lot of new moms feel and that they feel as if they are experiencing parenthood alone until they find that new group where they fit.

How do you feel you influence moms online? I feel I influence moms by providing useful information that I have learned about other companies, products, services, and health issues. Also, by helping them feel less alone in their parenting experiences, both good and bad.

How do you feel you influence moms offline? Is it more than chatting in the carpool line? I influence moms offline when they reach out to me for advice on parenting, diet, health, nursing, natural remedies, and relationships support on a daily basis, and they reach out because they know that I am there for them. I think it's amazing to be able to help these other amazing women through the trials of life and parenting and to have people value my opinion and actually follow through with my advice and then to hear they share it with other moms.

What motivates you to tell other moms (good or bad) about a company, brand or product? Simple: my experience whether it was good or bad makes me want to tell others about it. If I found a great new product or services, I will tell everyone and if I find an awful product or receive terrible service, I will tell everyone.

Name: Ana Picazo

Children: Three, ages 9, 6 and 6

Hometown: Palo Alto, CA

Short description of business: Stay-at-home parent, working part time as a features and deals editor for a preschool resource site, and as a freelance blogger/writer. I started blogging in April 2006 for the Silicon Valley Moms Blog, and then started my personal blog a few months later. In November 2007 I started my product review blog.

Websites or Blogs you own: Bonggamom Finds (product review blog) http://bonggafinds.blogspot.com/, Finding Bonggamom (personal blog) http://bonggamom.blogspot.com/

Approximate audience size: 8,000 unique visitors per month

Websites or blogs you contribute to: Silicon Valley Mamas (www.siliconvalley-mamas.com), Yahoo! Motherboard on shine.yahoo.com, Technocratic Women's Channel, Filipina Moms Blog (www.filipinamoms.blogspot.com)

Facebook Id: Bonggamom Finds

Twitter Id: @bonggafinds

Approximate # of followers: 4,500

Online Involvements and associations: I've been a Brand ambassador for various campaigns—Kellogs, Sprint, Yummie Tummie, Ubisoft, Energizer, Aquafina, Your-sphere, McDonalds, Sony, Ralph Lauren, etc. I'm a member of various marketing groups such as MomSelect, Clever Girls Collective, BlogHer Reviewers, MomImpact, Global Influence, Mom Bloggers Club, TwitterMoms, Team Moms/Childs Play, One2One Network, MyBlogSpark, and others.

Offline Involvements: PTA, class volunteering, local family shelters

What's the best way for companies to reach you as an influencer or as a mom? Email (bonggamom@yahoo.com) pitches work fine, but I also like being invited to events where I can interact with the product and with the people behind it.

How do you define influence among moms? When other moms listen to your opinion, when they go to your website for information on the latest products, or for sales/discounts/coupons, or for your opinion on whatever your blog deals with.

How do you feel you influence moms online? They come to my site for the giveaways, but they stay for the content!

Is there one moment when you realized you were impacting the life/lives of others? When I was asked to participate in blogging programs that would help people in my local communities (*i.e.*, providing Tag Readers to schools in underprivileged areas, gifting Zhu Zhu Pets to underprivileged kids).

How do you feel you influence moms offline? Is it more than chatting in the carpool line? My kids tell their friends about the cool new stuff we are testing (or they get to play with it when they're at our house for playdates) and they tell their moms about it, and maybe ask their moms to buy the toys as well.

How do you feel companies can best connect with moms, particularly those who are influencers? Make sure they are talking to the moms/influencers who are best suited to be advocates for their brand and their company (*i.e.*, don't pitch a videogame to a mom blogger who writes about natural/unplugged parenting!).

Final words: "Listen to your mother!"

Name: Sarah Pinnix

Children: Three, ages 10, 8, and 5 (all girls)

Hometown: Boone, NC

Company Name(s): Real Life Media, and High Country Mom Squad

Short description of business: Real Life Media publishes online content for women/moms as well as social media-savvy bloggers and webcasters. I run a family and faith blog at www.reallifeblog.net, and a local e-zine for Northwest NC moms at www.highcountrymomsquad.com. I also provide training for business people who want to use social media tools to change their marketing approach. I teach classes, and do consulting for businesses as well as employee social media training.

Location of business: I work at home. Or I occasionally work in my "mobile office," aka, in my minivan on my Droid.

Websites or Blogs you own: Sarah Pinnix www.sarahpinnix.net; Real Life Blog www.reallifeblog.net; High Country Mom Squad www.highcountrymomsquad.com; Talk of the Town Workshop www.talkofthetownworkshop.com

Facebook Id: Real Life Blog and HC Mom Squad

Twitter Id: @reallifesarah

Approximate # of followers: 6,980

Online Involvements and associations: BabyCenter's Momformation Blog Network, Operation Christmas Child Blogger Panel, Heart of Haiti Ambassadors

What's the best way for companies to reach you as an influencer or as a mom? Show me how your product or service will make my life easier, save me money, or cause me to have lots of fun with friends. If those criteria are met, you can count on me sharing it with everyone I know.

How is the best way to work with you and your company? I love to create original content with companies in the form of blog posts, online articles (on my site or yours), informal videos, or media interviews. I create short- and long-term campaigns for clients integrating multimedia, and advertising. Sponsoring my radio podcast or webcast on MomTV.com is a great way to reach a targeted audience of women aged 24-45.

What do you think is the biggest mistake companies make in trying to work with moms? I think sometimes they try to market to us using the old paradigm of interruption advertising, bait-and-switch, or fake deals. Moms these days are so much more marketing savvy. We know what we want in a good deal, and we want to be PART of the marketing conversation. And isn't it better when a company knows what we need first, and then provides it to us? Listen to moms first ... then market.

Are there companies who you feel are doing a great job connecting with moms? I think Zhu Zhu Pets has been ingenious in connecting with moms. Through their blog reviews, fun events around the country and the Random Acts of Zhu charity program, they've really gotten moms excited about supporting them! It's a great product, too.

Is there one moment when you realized you were impacting the life/lives of others? I participated in an Adoption campaign with Amy Lupold Bair and Global Influence Network. I wrote about the need for children in the system to have foster parents, and eventually be adopted. At a blogger conference later that year, a fellow mom told me that she had read that article. My post, as the final nudge among other influences she had experienced, caused her and her husband to begin the process of adoption. This, more than any other moment in my social media life, has shown me the power of moms online, and the community we have.

How do you feel companies can best connect with moms, particularly those who are influencers? Partner with us. This usually will involve a capital outlay of some sort, but today's mom influencers are talented writers, broadcasters, and content creators. They are professionally-minded women who work hard to build and interact with their community. Why reinvent the wheel when you can tap into great communities and content already out there? Also, most moms trust each other even more than they trust a company. You can leverage that for your brand.

Name: Kathryn Plasencia

Children: Five and a half, ages 8, 6, 5, 3 ½, 2, and baby due in March

Hometown: South-Central, PA

Company Name(s): Mommyhood by the Handful, HubPages

Short description of business: The blog is your standard mommy blog. My HubPages account is mostly essays on random topics, which I've used to earn a VERY minimal income. My number one job—that is, mommyhood—began in June 2002, when I first found out I was pregnant. I have since become all too familiar with abuse, miscarriage, raising children who suffer from trauma-based mental illness, single parenting, blending in a new daddy, and more. I also struggle with multiple chronic illnesses.

I began writing at age 4 and haven't put down my pencil yet. The blog/hub endeavor began in early 2009, as a time-killer while I was recovering from the very complicated delivery of baby number 5. My motivation: to help whomever possible by raising awareness of the issues I care and know about. There is a reason for every moment of suffering: if disclosing my pain can bring healing to another, my life has purpose.

Website or Blogs you own: Mommyhood by the Handful, http://mommyhoodbythe-handful.blogspot.com/; HubPages http://hubpages.com/profile/Kathryn+Plasencia

Facebook Id: Kathryn Plasencia

Twitter Id: @kpLibretto

Online Involvements and associations: Several survey panels such as NPDOR, MySurvey, Lightspeed, Mindfield, etc. Vocalpoint, Circle of Moms (on Facebook), What to Expect, Baby Center

Offline Involvements: Several therapy-type agencies, I sing occasionally on the worship team for our church's Spanish service; I do some work with Fruitbelt Farmworker Christian Ministries to help with mailings and fundraisers. I have taught and assisted children's classes at churches in the past.

Are there companies who you feel are doing a great job connecting with moms? Luvs was pretty much right on a few years ago. There are many professional blogs (think SITS) that do a good job of embracing moms of all kinds.

How do you feel you influence moms online? Through blogging and answering questions in various pregnancy and parenting forums, I am able to share my own experiences, love, and research findings with moms who may not be as experienced or may just need a shoulder to cry on.

Final words: I think that, generally speaking, being a mother is still looked down upon as a lesser goal. Society says we should focus first on education, then career, and then—if there's any time and/or money left—settle down and start a family. This must change! Our children really are our future, no matter how cliché it sounds. We must, as a nation, begin to focus more on LOVING our kids, on teaching them to live morally (regardless of religious affiliation or lack thereof), and on enjoying this period of life that lasts such a short time. Only then will education, economics, politics, and all that other "stuff" fall into place.

Name: Dianna Ranere

Children: Two, ages 12 and 7 (both boys)

Hometown: Baltimore, MD

Websites or Blogs you own: Free Sample Momma http://www.freesamplemomma.com, Free Sample Momma Blogs! http://www.freesamplemomma.com/blog and Free Coupon Momma http://www.freecouponmomma.com

Approximate audience size: 30,000 to 35,000 combined

Facebook Id: Free Sample Momma

Twitter Id: @freesamplemomma

Approximate # of followers: 5,530

Online Involvements and associations: Wisk betablogger, Tropicanna Juicy Insider, Aquafina FlavorSplash Mom, Your-Sphere Test-Dive Mom, Member of Mom Central, MyBlogSpark, One2One Network, BzzAgent, Business2Blogger, Giveaway Blogs, Bloggy Moms, Twitter Moms, CleverGirls Collective.

What's the best way for companies to reach you as an influencer or as a mom? Email: momma@freesamplemomma.com

How do you feel you influence moms offline? Is it more than chatting in the carpool line? I share the samples that I receive from my blog reviews with my fellow moms. This normally starts a dialogue about the brand and we often talk about how much we like or dislike a product.

What motivates you to tell other moms (good or bad) about a company, brand or product? I try not to post about bad experiences if they are minor, I don't feel it's a good way to develop a relationship with a brand. If the experience is a good one, I usually shout it from the virtual rooftop.

How do you feel companies can best connect with moms, particularly those who are influencers? The best way—make them feel connected to the company as more than just a mom with an opinion; maybe a mention here and there about a mom who is trying to make a difference or who has said something positive about their company.

Name: Jerri Ann Reason

Children: Two, ages 7 and 5

Hometown: Nauvoo, Alabama

Company Name(s): Four Reason's Media, The Blog Ambassador

Short description of business: Four Reason's Media is a culmination of all the work that my husband and I do comprehensively.

Websites or Blogs you own: Four Reason's Media www.fourreasonsmedia.com, The Blog Ambassador www.theblogambassador.com, Mom~E~Centric www.mome-centric.com, Education Uncensored www.educationuncensored.com, Don't Eat That www.doneteatthat.net www.donteatthat.com, Product Reviews by Me www.productreviewsbyme.com, Lebron Magnet www.lebron-magnet.info

Websites or blogs you contribute to: Virtual Field Trips www.virtualfieldtrips.info, Meet Me At The Corner www.meetmeattecorner.org, Vernon Croy www.vernon-croy.com, Hot Cappers www.hotcappers.com, Wager Run www.wagerrun.com, Live Strong www.livestrong.com, iParenting www.iparenting.com

Facebook Id: Jerri Ann Reason

Twitter Id: @The_Jerri_Ann

Approximate # of followers: 6,000

Online Involvements and associations: Mom Central, Twitter Moms, Mom Select, Global Influence, Mom Talk, YourSphere, The View, Collective Bias, Murphy USA , Mom Bloggers Club, Mom Spark, One to One Network, Pitch It To Me, MomFluential, SheBlogs, Clever Girls

How many moms do you typically interact with during the week offline? 25 to 35

Offline Involvements: PTO Admin for Newsletter, PTO Admin website, PTO Admin Notes Home, teaching parenting classes,

What's the best way for companies to reach you as an influencer or as a mom? jareason@gmail.com

Are there companies who you feel are doing a great job connecting with moms? Murphy USA is the number one company right now reaching out to mothers.

How do you define influence among moms? Influence is the ability to help others see various pieces of the issue by giving appropriate and specific information with just a bit of persuasion to attempt to sway one's opinion.

How do you feel you influence moms offline? Is it more than chatting in the carpool line? Offline I try to make sure that parents, both single parents and families, have the necessary skills to parent and the encouragement to work hard and pick themselves up when trouble arises. Through parenting classes, instructional classes on using the computer and the like, I hope they find their path to be a little easier each day because of me.

Final words: The first time I heard the words "Blogging is the New Black" was in 2003. I'm absolutely certain that I may have started hyperventilating at the thought. I had been doing a blog post for many years prior to that but emailing it to everyone I knew. My heart sank and I headed straight for a free platform service. I had no idea at that time that the idea of a weblog would grow to include complicated methods of SEO.

Name: Jennifer Rees

Hometown: Grand Rapids, Michigan

Websites or Blogs you own: http://www.thebigbinder.com

Approximate audience size: total daily reach is currently approximately 1000, my blog is locally focused

Websites or blogs you contribute to: Michigan Mom/Mom TV

Facebook Id: Bigbinder

Twitter Id: @bigbinderblog

Approximate # of followers: 490

Online Involvements and associations: MomSelect, Collective Bias

How many moms do you typically interact with during the week offline? I am at my kids' school, tae kwan do classes, church (both Sunday mass/children's worship classes and Wednesday night CCD)—I would have to say hundreds.

Offline Involvements: Great Start Parent Coalition, First Steps Collaborative (Initiatives developing and early childhood system in Grand Rapids), Media Sponsor for Children's Marathon, Great Start Parent Coalition active member and volunteer, Grand River Clean Up, Kids Food Basket Committee Member (working towards ending childhood hunger in Grand Rapids)

What do you think is the biggest mistake companies make in trying to work with moms? Thinking that a blogger is a blogger is a blogger. They need to read the posts and weed out the ones that are just cut and paste jobs of the press release. No moms are reached—their subscriber numbers might be huge but that is a very different number than what their actual influence is. Influence means getting someone to act. It takes a trusted, skilled writer to get someone to act. Companies need to do the hard work of sorting those people from the pack. Hard—but so very worth it.

How do you feel you influence moms online? I have a simple strategy: 1) inform, 2) encourage, and 3) lead by example, and document (pictures, video) it.

Is there one moment when you realized you were impacting the life/lives of others? Yes. I decided to raise money for a hunger walk using only social media—not email to my family or friends. I wanted to measure my influence and see if I could call people to action. I exceeded my monetary goal, and got notes from donators that they were supporting me in this because I helped make them a better mom, or made their kids' childhood better, or got them involved in the community by making them unafraid of attending cultural events. It was amazing.

Final words: Kids need to be involved in their communities. They need to attend events that are not "sanitized" for their protection. They need to learn how to eat at fancy restaurants, not just Chuck E Cheese. They need to learn how to interact with people who have different ideas and different faces and maintain their foundation while learning from people different from them. They need to not be intimidated by art, music, and theater. They need to go with their parents to vote and understand that they do have a voice, and rather than making a bunch of noise about things needing to change—to work for it. They need to meet their legislators, and see their parents volunteer. They need to be raised to be good citizens.

Name: Cinella J. Reyes

Children: Two, ages 6 and 19 months (both girls)

City and home state: Donna, Texas

Short description of business: Mommy, wife, blogger, writer and independent contractor/mystery shopper

Websites or Blogs you own: The Mommy Blog, http://cjrthemommyblog.blogspot.com

Approximate audience size: 100

Websites or blogs you contribute to: Living Smart Girl, Hidalgo Metro

Facebook Id: CinellaJReyes

Twitter Id: @vetsmom_rgv

Approximate # of followers: 324

Online Involvements and associations: Own a group on CafeMom.com, brand ambassador for Kraft, Mom Bloggers Club reviewer, Mom's Meet

How many moms do you typically interact with during the week offline? I interact with as many moms as I can. I love to spread the word about being green and using cloth diapers.

Offline Involvements: CafeMom playgroup, Mom's Meet, Owner/Moderator of my local Freecycle group

How do you define influence among moms? I define influence or see it as trust in that company and that moms share their passion, story or experience with other moms. Whether it's good or bad you will have a personal influence because you know the other mom goes through the same exact situations you do on a daily basis.

How do you feel you influence moms offline? Is it more than chatting in the carpool line? I believe I influence moms offline by acting and being a hands-on demonstrator of what I believe in. In return they see that I practice what I preach.

What motivates you to tell other moms (good or bad) about a company, brand or product? What motivates me is how the company, brand or product has a passion for what they do. I can see that passion and that's what motivates me to tell other moms about their products. Even if it's something bad I will still tell other moms about it.

How do you feel companies can best connect with moms, particularly those who are influencers? Get more involved with how moms are communicating today. Get our attention and add your own personal touch on how you connect with us. Whether it's on Facebook or Twitter, let us know that you hear our questions and/or concerns.

Name: Connie Roberts aka ConnieFoggles

Children: Two, ages 24 and 12 (both girls)

Hometown: Spring Hill, FL

Short description of business: BrainFoggles.com is a blog that provides product reviews on family-friendly items in the author's own voice, provides bloggers with helpful tips, and parents with advice and information. I began my blog, BrainFoggles.com, in April of 2007 as a means to cope with a new medical diagnosis I received in 2000 (I had an earlier blog on Yahoo 360). I also wanted to create a space for others with chronic illnesses to learn that it was possible to live your life to the fullest, to attempt new things, and to earn some money as well. Now my blog has morphed into a product review blog, where I share my personal experiences with items, services and websites. I also write about nonprofits, travel, parenting and information about blogging. Writing about educational and social issues, as well as travel adventures, will be more of my focus in 2011.

Websites or Blogs you own: BrainFoggles.com, ConniesView.com and MyChronicLife.com

Approximate audience size: 3,600 to 16,000

Facebook Id: Connie Melucci Roberts

Twitter Id: @ConnieFoggles

Approximate # of followers: 1,390

Online Involvements and associations: Brand Ambassador for Hershey's Summer Celebrations, Crayola Pop Art Pixies, Random Acts of Zhu, Random Acts of Wellness (Walgreens), Hebrew National (Better Than a Picnic in Tampa), Yoursphere Test Mom Driver, Aqufina Test Drive Mom, City of Hope Ambassador, Scrubbing Bubbles Circle of Influencers, member of the AT&T Power Mom's panel and The Online Mom team.

How many moms do you typically interact with during the week offline? Dozens

Offline Involvements: PTSA, Title 1 (both at my daughter's school), and the Democratic Party in my county. I volunteer for my daughter's current school and her previous elementary school, take calls from people who are newly diagnosed with two of the specific medical conditions that I have (Myasthenia Gravis and Sjogren's Syndrome), help raise money and awareness for specific local nonprofits and just answer the call where I'm needed.

What's the best way for companies to reach you as an influencer or as a mom? Email, conniefoggles@gmail.com, or on Twitter and Facebook.

What do you think is the biggest mistake companies make in trying to work with moms? Not valuing us for our worth, by expecting work for free, for a product that doesn't cost much; and by just looking at numbers and not taking into consideration what our social reach is online and offline.

How do you define influence among moms? Influence among moms is defined as how we connect and trust opinions about anything from soap detergent to the best preschools. When moms get together online or offline, we talk and listen, and then form opinions based on the trustworthiness of the person or group.

How do you feel you influence moms online? I'm honest on my blog and all areas of social media. I share the positives and negatives of products and the ups and downs of my life. I do my best to answer questions from my commenters, tweets or Facebook messages. My readers know me and can trust me.

Is there one moment when you realized you were impacting the life/lives of others? Oh yes! When an online friend told me she ordered a product just because of my review. I was thrilled! Some of my posts about health issues get comments or emails from people that have the same diagnosis or need information about it.

How can companies best support your business or mission as a mom? First, please recognize that I am a business. I work hard maintaining three blogs. Next, reach out to me personally, perhaps read a few of my blog posts or my "about" page to get to know a bit about me, especially my name. Don't expect me to post press releases, or to review a product that you won't supply me with. If you want me to write something for you, pay me for it. I have a fee schedule that I can send to you. If you want my advice, pay me for that, too. If you need me to help you out and we've worked before, be upfront about it. Treat me like you would another company and be genuine.

Final words: Mothers are influential in all areas of society. We are the backbone of schools where we volunteer and we help our children at home with school work. In politics, more mothers are being voted in to serve locally, statewide and federally. Mothers are also volunteering for candidates, political parties, and action groups. We use our life experiences to help make decisions. Mothers are working outside the home, shaping businesses' and companies' corporate policies. Mothers are active in social issues that affect us, our children, our families, our loved ones. We don't sit idly by when an injustice occurs. We take action and gather others to fight. One mother is strong alone, but as a group we can change things that others believe to be set in concrete.

Name: Felicia Rogers

Children: Three, ages 12, 9, 6

Hometown: Caryville, TN

Job title: Novelist

Short description of business: I'm a homeschooling mom of three kids. Last year I started writing "clean" romance novels at home. My first was published in December 2010 with Solstice Publishing. Also, I have a novella with Solstice Publishing. I won their Celebrate the Season contest for Christmas stories. I started writing last year because my cousin suggested a joint novel. In the end, I finished on my own.

Websites or Blogs you own: Felicia's Finds www.feliciasfinds.blogspot.com and Felicia Rogers www.feliciarogersauthor.webs.com

Websites or blogs you contribute to: www.graceelliot.webs.com and www.vernaclay.webs.com

Facebook Id: Felicia Rogers

Online Involvements and associations: Mom Select, Vocalpoint, All You Ambassador, Dove Ambassador

Offline Involvements: Church, homeschool group, Girl Scouts

What do you think is the biggest mistake companies make in trying to work with moms? They make things too complicated. We don't have as much time to just delve into the product. As a homeschooling mom of three children, I'm constantly looking for the simplest and easiest way to get anything done. I also need to save money while getting it done. Show me something simple and show me a deal and I'm hooked.

How do you feel you influence moms offline? Is it more than chatting in the carpool line? I'm constantly telling people I meet in the store and in other places about great deals that I've found online or in the store. Or about places that you can go for free.

How do you feel companies can best connect with moms, particularly those who are influencers? Free samples, is the biggest thing. Or if it is a business that charges, do a free day. One free day may bring in 1,000 people that run out and tell others about your business. Each sample you give could tell 1,000 people about that product.

Final words: There have always been moms influencing the world. Look at June Cleaver. She was the ultimate mom. Everyone knows about her. Everyone remembers watching her on TV: taking care of her kids, cooking for her husband and staying at home. Now in today's society we have a different perspective on moms. Now moms work, take care of the cooking, the housework, and the kids. Or if they're lucky, their spouse shares in the responsibility. Being a "mom" is not just being a "mom." We have so many hats to wear in today's world that time is our number one enemy. We have to be careful not to forget that even though our home and hearth is not the only hat we have on like it was for June Cleaver, those things are still important. We do influence those around us. Our children look to us for who they are going to be and who they should be.

Name: Renee J. Ross

Children: One, age 3

Hometown: Atlanta, GA

Websites or Blogs you own: Cutie Booty Cakes http://cutiebootycakes.blogspot.com/

Approximate audience size: 10,000 monthly

Websites or blogs you contribute to: BlogHer.com, Moms of Hue, Snackpicks.com, Walmart YouTube channel

Facebook Id: Renee Ross

Twitter Id: @reneejross

Approximate # of followers: 10,000

Online Involvements and associations: Snackpicks.com, Walmart Mom, EA SPORTS Active, Yummie Tummie, Children's Hospital of Atlanta, Mom 2 Mom blogger, American Cancer Society Blogger Advisory Council,

Offline Involvements: Mocha Moms, Preschool, Atlanta Food Bank, raised over $5000 for the Leukemia & Lymphoma Society with Team in Training and ran a 1/2 marathon, donation of diapers and school supplies to Atlanta Children's Shelter

What's the best way for companies to reach you as an influencer or as a mom? Email: cutiebootycakes@gmail.com

How do you feel you influence moms online? I think the largest influence I've had on moms is in regard to healthy living. By documenting my personal journey to a healthy weight and meeting the goal of running a half-marathon, I've inspired others to do the same. I've done it as the mother of a young son and if I can do it, anyone can do it.

Is there one moment when you realized you were impacting the life/lives of others? When several people on Twitter decided to run the Disney Princess Half-Marathon after hearing that I was going to run it.

How do you feel you influence moms offline? Is it more than chatting in the carpool line? Most times it is all about conversation. Talking to other moms about things I like and have had positive experiences with, influences moms offline.

Name: Jamie Roth

Children: Two, ages 5 and 3

Hometown: Pearl, Mississippi

Company Name(s): Intuitive Encounters, Empowered Birthing Doula Services and September Dawn Publishing Company

Short description of business: Intuitive Encounters is a service in which I guide people on how to live empowered, inspired and joyful lives through one-on-one Intuitive Counseling sessions. I have been using my Intuitive gifts for over a decade to help people around the world find their true inner spirit, as well as passions. We also discuss how to move past any emotional or mental blocks they have that are preventing them from living at their highest level of well-being. An Intuitive counseling session helps people make the body/mind/spirit connection, allowing them to move forward towards all the joy, abundance and fulfillment that is rightfully theirs. I also do energy healing work called Reiki. It is a traditional Japanese hands-on healing technique. Reiki is a massage for the soul. It leaves a person relaxed, centered and in a balanced state of mind/body/spirit.

I have been doing my Intuitive and energy healing work for over a decade. However, when I became a mom, I put the Intuitive hat away in order to focus on my children. I thought I was done with it, except for continuing to use the guidance for my own personal life. Then in April of 2008, a local man, who was a massage client of mine, went missing. I became a part of the search process, offering Intuitive guidance. That situation brought my Intuitive work back to the forefront of my life, along with parenting. Soon after, I put up my website; a year later I started my radio show and things have just exploded from then on. It became clear to me as my business really developed, that I deal with a lot of mothers who are reaching out because they have lost themselves somewhere in parenting. And they are getting "stuck" and don't know how to get unstuck. That is where I come in. My mission is to help mothers, or anyone get in touch with their true spirit. Who they really are without the stigma, the boxes placed around them by society, family or even religion. I help people become strong within themselves and find their own inner voice/inner guidance; thus they begin to move forward through life with more ease, more satisfaction and completely empowered. It is a complete joy to me to do my work!

Websites or Blogs you own: www.IntuitiveEncounters.com, www.LivingInspiredTour.com , www.IntuitiveEncounters.com/forum/, www.TheGeneralManagerOfTheUniverse.com

Approximate audience size: 5,000 per month

Facebook Id: Jamie Roth or Intuitive Encounters Group

Approximate # of followers: 1,000

Twitter Id: @IntuitiveJamie

Approximate # of followers: 1,000

Online Involvements and associations: I host an international radio show, called Intuitive Encounters, on Mondays, www.ContactTalkRadio.com. I have a listenership of 30,000+. I also have a live Web TV show on MomTV.com called

Intuitive Encounters. www.Mothering.com community—I I have an "Ask an Intuitive" pay per question subforum. CTR HotSpot—spiritual forum. Ravelry—online Crochet and Knit community

How many moms do you typically interact with during the week offline? 10-20

Offline Involvements: La Leche League, Mississippi friends of Midwives, International Cesarean Awareness network of Jackson MS, MOPS (Moms of preschoolers). I support Project Night Night non-profit, which is based in Oakland, California. This is a program that gathers a book, blanket and stuffed animal in a Night Night bag to give to homeless children staying in shelters. I have been fortunate enough to put together 70 Night Night bags to give to children staying in homeless shelters in Mississippi.

What's the best way for companies to reach you as an influencer or as a mom? Email: intuitiveencounters@gmail.com

How do you feel you influence moms offline? Is it more than chatting in the carpool line? I have learned about myself that I am a leader, adviser, empowerment coach, healer and a voice. And I do all of these things in everything I am a part of. Whether that is just as your friend, or as part of a local group or with my clients. I empower people to make educated, intentional choices in their own lives. I do this particularly with pregnancy and birth work as a doula. I support women in having an educated pregnancy and natural labor. I support women in breastfeeding. Actually, I support moms in general: being who they are and having confidence and pride in all of their choices.

How can companies best support your business or mission as a mom? Help me network my business and I'll help you network yours. I love barter and trade and working together. I love to make connections with all kinds of other companies, mom-based and more, and supporting one another through all of our social networking sites. Sharing blog buttons and reviews and interviews and such. Power in numbers!

What motivates you to tell other moms (good or bad) about a company, brand or product? When a product or service is provided and works exactly as advertised and the company has great customer service.

How do you feel companies can best connect with moms, particularly those who are influencers? Get to know these women. Understand who they are, what their preferences are, where they are coming from in life and most definitely appeal to their emotional needs. Women are emotional creatures and need to be emotionally fulfilled in all that they do.

Name: Kim Rowley

Children: Four ages 19, 16 (twins), and 12

Hometown: Pierce, NE

Company Name(s): Key Internet Marketing, Inc., www.kimarketing.com

Short description of business: What originally began with a hobby of a "coupon code site" has grown into a multitude of growing websites and niche blogs. My expertise in performance-based marketing has been carried over to consult merchants, businesses and publishers on affiliate management options as well. My coupon code site—ShoppingBookmarks.com—was actually started as a hobby as I love to save money. I was sharing my finds with friends and family who in turn were sharing with their family and friends. When I discovered that I could make money by teaching others to save money, I knew I had it made!

Location of business: I built my dream home around my home office proving that a single mom can build a new house without a man!

Websites or Blogs you own: www.KIMarketing.com; www.ShoppingBookmarks.com; www.ShoeaholicsAnonymous.com; www.StealTheStyle.com; www.WorkInMyPajamas.com;www.Preemietwins.com; www.HouseForKim.com; www.EnterOnlineSweeps.com

Approximate audience size: Millions

Websites or blogs you contribute to: www.MoneyMindedMoms.com; www.Examiner.com

Facebook Id: kimarketing, shoppingbookmarks, shoeaholics, stealthestyle

Twitter Id: @kimarketing, @shoppingkim, @shoeaholics, @stealthestyle, @preemietwins

Approximate # of followers: 20,000

Online Involvements and associations: Adjunct Professor for the University of San Francisco/ USanFranOnline.com, teaching about online affiliate marketing; "The View" television show Ambassador; writer for Suze Orman's MoneyMinded-Moms.com website; Affiliate Summit/ AffiliateSummit.com Advisory Board; panelist on TheSpew.fm podcasts.

How many moms do you typically interact with during the week offline? 100

Offline Involvements: In my spare time, I volunteer for several civic organizations, including being a past president and current Board member of my local Kiwanis club, serve on the Board of Directors of my local school's Booster Club, and I also share my marketing expertise as a SCORE counselor for small business start-ups.

What's the best way for companies to reach you as an influencer or as a mom? Using the contact forms on my respective websites.

How is the best way to work with you and your company? I'm willing to try anything once! But I usually write blog posts which are in turn automatically cranked out to all my corresponding social media avenues.

How do you feel you influence moms online? My blogs are my exact sentiments on how I feel about everything, from my family to my favorite foods, so my readers feel as if they know me personally, thus value my opinion on products and services.

How do you feel you influence moms offline? Is it more than chatting in the carpool line? I have lunch every Thursday with my Kiwanis club, whom I always update on my favorite blog posts or product reviews (they especially like it when I share free goodies)!

Name: Ku'ulei Sako

Children: One, age 15 months

Hometown: Atlanta, GA

Company Name(s): Ku'ulei Sako Photography

Short description of business: Lifestyle and event photography

Websites or Blogs you own: Every Mom Has Her Day http://everymomhasherday.com/

Facebook Id: Every Mom Has Her Day

Twitter Id: @momhasherday

Approximate # of followers: 900

What's the best way for companies to reach you as an influencer or as a mom? Learn a little about me by finding out what I care about, what's important to me and what my interests are.

What do you think is the biggest mistake companies make in trying to work with moms? The biggest mistake companies make in trying to work with moms is approaching them with services or products that are not relevant to the mom's or her kid's interests.

How do you feel you influence moms online? I talk about my experiences as a mom, a wife and as an individual. I share my opinions and experiences with products, services, recipes, parenting and more, so I am able to relate to other moms on many different levels from the nursery to the kitchen to the play ground and beyond.

How do you feel you influence moms offline? Is it more than chatting in the carpool line? I'm a part of a play group, where I host and attend play dates, so I have the opportunity to talk to moms regularly, and we share our experiences when our children get sick, meet milestones and more. I always share information if it could help another mom in some way, whether it is a home remedy or a recommendation on a sippy cup or a dinner recipe.

How do you feel companies can best connect with moms, particularly those who are influencers? By providing a service, a product that can help her in some way, whether it's to save time, save money or save energy, while keeping her kid safe and happy.

Name: Jennifer Salazar Hutcheson

Children: One, age 2

Hometown: Suburban Atlanta, GA

Company Name(s): Ash Breeze Media, LLC. http://ashbreezemedia.com

Short description of business: Public relations, social media, and marketing consulting. My company was just recently launched in January 2011 after the realization that the consulting work that I had been doing for more than 6-plus years was already an established business, so it was just a matter of making it official. I have always had a passion for working in communications, public relations, marketing and social media so it made the transition from the corporate world to becoming an entrepreneur much smoother. I was strongly motivated by an incredible person who helped me to see that I could take my "side hustle" and make it a full-time gig ... Kimberly Seals-Allers of http://MochaManual.com. She was truly an inspiration to me. And the overall mission for my company is to not only provide the client with amazing work but to teach/educate them on what it is that I have done so that they can walk away with much more. As the proverb goes, "Give a man a fish and you feed him for a day. Teach a man to fish and you feed him for a lifetime." In regard to an exit strategy, I had to give it much thought. I didn't want to admit to myself that this might possibly not work out so I didn't want to even put the "bad ju ju" or negative energy out into the universe. But the reality of being a mother and wife made me realize that I needed to. However, I firmly believe that an exit strategy will be something that should continuously be developing as your company grows. Someone who started a company alone and then took on a partner or hired employees will need to revamp their strategy to keep up with the changes. Right now my exit strategy is quite simple. If the financial aspect of it doesn't equal the time I'm putting into it and continues to not do so then I will re-evaluate and take the next steps. I am fortunate because at this time my household does not depend on my income, but rather my husband's.

Websites or Blogs you own: Mami 2 Mommy http://mami2mommy.com and Blog Talk Radio Show http://blogtalkradio.com/chicaschatting–Chicas Chatting with co-host Joscelyn Ramos of Mami of Multiples http://mamiofmultiples.com

Approximate audience size: 1,500 per month

Websites or blogs you contribute to: http://momtourage.com, http://beinglatino.wordpress.com, http://care2.com, http://clicklatina.com

Facebook Id: www.mami@mommy.com, Chicas Chatting

Twitter Id: @Mami2Mommy/@ChicasChatting

Approximate # of followers: 5,930

Online Involvements and associations: Brand Ambassador for Pampers Latino, Swagg Mobile, and Macy's Heart of Haiti, Super Bowl Gospel Celebration, Discovery Familia, Logitech, Zhu Zhu Pets, Allconnect, and many more. Also a part of Hispanicize(http://www.hispanicprconference.com/), Conference Advisory Board Member, Community Manager for Being Latino (http://twitter.com/beinglatino), Social Media Atlanta (http://socialmediaclub.org/chapter/atlanta/blog/social-media-club-atlanta-re-launches), Social Media Club, Promotions Director, Atlanta Chapter (http://socialmediaclub.org/chapter/atlanta) and Social Media Strategist for TEDxPeachtree (http://tedxpeachtree.com).

Offline Involvements: Social Media Atlanta, Social Media Club, local Meetup.com groups, and do various community services through my church.

What do you think is the biggest mistake companies make in trying to work with moms? The biggest mistake that I see companies making now is assuming that they are doing the mom a favor by just approaching them and not being willing to compensate the mom for her time. We are now at a pivotal point with blogger compensation and I think it is extremely important to continue the dialogue. Because I have had the opportunity to work on both sides I know that there is still much to be discussed. And keep in mind that "compensation" may mean something different to each mom being approached; so again, make sure to do your homework to see what makes that mom tick.

Are there companies who you feel are doing a great job connecting with moms? Newell Rubbermaid (Graco), General Mills (Que Rica Vida) and Discovery (Discovery Familia). They all understand the true value of today's mom, know exactly how to speak to us in a very organic way, and support us 100%!

How do you feel you influence moms online? I hope I am influencing moms online in a positive way. Providing them with the support as a parent, the guidance of a friend, and the advice and tools of a business owner. For all the moms who have inspired me, this is my way of honoring them by passing along the knowledge I've gained from them and helping other moms reach their goals.

Is there one moment when you realized you were impacting the life/lives of others? There have been a few times and it was incredibly humbling. In October 2010 I was asked to speak at the Blogalicious conference on the Social Media Moms panel. At the end of the panel I was approached by a fairly new blogger who seemed so overwhelmed but excited about everything she just took in. She thanked me over and over again and said that she knew that the information she received during the panel was going to help her take her blog to the next level, which in turn would allow her to work from home and be with her son. It was the passion in her voice that made me cry because that was me just a year ago.

How do you feel you influence moms offline? Is it more than chatting in the carpool line? I have always shared offline with other moms but I feel that with my online presence I share more often and with more moms offline than ever before. My blog and the other social media platforms provided me with a stronger voice and I wanted to share all that I've learned with other moms. You can't get me to stop sharing now!

How do you feel companies can best connect with moms, particularly those who are influencers? If a company wants to connect with moms they must be respectful of these moms and fully understand that we come from all walks of life and have many sides to us. The perception of us being "just moms" should be long over. I wear my mom badge very proudly. My son and family will always be my top priority and joy in my life; however, there is more to me. So when reaching out to us please don't start off your pitch with "Dear Mom Blogger." Take the time to at least learn our names and remember that it doesn't define us, we define it.

Final words: I would be remiss not to mention the increasing influence of the Latina mami blogger. We are seeing a tremendous increase in outreach in the overall Latino social media community so I hope that this proves that companies/brands need to not only continue, but to increase their initiatives in this area. Even though we are *Una Comunidad* (one community) of moms, we are still *Many Voices* that are still looking to be heard!

Name: Lisa N. Samples

Children: Two, ages 17 and 6 (both boys)

Hometown: Atlanta, GA

Company Name(s): The Product Review Place

Short description of business: A company that offers bloggers the opportunity to learn about doing reviews.

Websites or Blogs you own: The Product Review Place Company, http://theproductreviewplace.com; The Product Review Place Community, http://productreviewplace.ning.com; Life with Lisa (personal blog), http://lifewithlisa.com; The Brand Ambassador (brand focused blog), http://thebrandambassador.com

Approximate audience size: 75,000 page views each site monthly

Facebook Id: Lisa N Samples (personal), Life with Lisa (fan page)

Twitter Id: @lisasamples

Approximate # of followers: 11,670

Online Involvements and associations: Ralph Lauren Ambassador, Frigidaire Ambassador, Hickory Farms Brand Ambassador, and others

How many moms do you typically interact with during the week offline? 50

Offline Involvements: PTA, Room Mom, Atlanta Food Bank, RIF (reading is fundamental)

What's the best way for companies to reach you as an influencer or as a mom? Email: lisa.samples@gmail.com

What do you think is the biggest mistake companies make in trying to work with moms? I think the biggest mistake companies make when trying to work with moms is not researching. Many times companies send out a blanket pitch and neglect the opportunity to form a relationship. Any mom that is going to promote a company will do a much better job if she feels she is valued and that the company took the time to get to know her.

Are there companies who you feel are doing a great job connecting with moms? I've worked with a lot of great companies such as Barber Foods (did a Twitter campaign for them), PUR, P&G, Nestle and more.

Name: LaTasha Sams

On my blogs I go by Daisy@The Deal Fanatic and Lala@LenzLove. This simply happened because my daughter loved the character that was on The Deal Fanatic and named her Daisy. Lala is short for LaTasha.

Children: Two (twins)

Hometown: Las Vegas, NV

Company Names: The Deal Fanatic.com, LenzLove Photography

Short description of business: LenzLove—I have recently jump-started my Natural light photography business and love the freedom it has brought to me and the level of personal growth it gives me daily. DealFanatic—I've successfully operated The DealFanatic.com for two years now. It was launched in winter of 2009. It was created out of a need to save. My husband and I went from two incomes, two people, to an astonishing four people, one income in a matter of three months. My grandmother has always told me, "Great things can happen when there is a need." I had no idea she was speaking of me. My mission is to assist in being able to live a rich life on a frugal budget. The DealFanatic.com has no exit strategy. This is not a momentary thing. It is my way of life. If I were to make millions, there is still no way I would go directly to the store without a coupon for groceries. It's just not smart. My photography is justified because I'm able to save so much in other areas of my life. LenzLove officially launched winter of 2009. My motivation for starting my Photography blog is because my need to connect and save had been taken care of through my Deal blog. However, my need to create and feel had still not been met. I've loved photography and art all of my life. I live it and breathe it every day. My official website will be launched in the winter of 2011 and I can't wait. It's been a long process. My mission is and has always been to capture life as it happens and share it with the world. I am a natural light photographer that loves creating art as I watch it play out in front of me. Again, there is no exit strategy. Even if I were not paid to photograph others, art will always be a part of me in one shape or form. My blogs are me! Exiting from them would be like leaving me.

Websites or Blogs you own: TheDealFanatic.com, LenzLove.com

Approximate audience size: 1,040

Facebook Id: LenzLove, DealFanatic

Twitter Id: @LenzLove, @DealFanatic

Approximate # of followers: 1,500

Online Involvements and associations: SFSmarties for Smart and Final, Green Moms Meet, Fresh and Easy Ambassador @ The Deal Fanatic.

How many moms do you typically interact with during the week offline? 26 to 30

What do you think is the biggest mistake companies make in trying to work with moms? Assuming we should be grateful they are even considering us. Many times I've been approached and the product was simply not a good fit. I've had companies reply with much sarcasm because I wasn't grateful. I will not promote a product I do not believe in. This goes back to trust. If my readers cannot trust me, there will be no relationship.

Are there companies who you feel are doing a great job connecting with moms? I do feel there are a few. I can only speak of the ones that I have worked with but those few are: Fresh and Easy, RC Willey, Ross, Smart and Final.

How do you feel you influence moms online? My connections with other moms online are ones that are truly unique. When you are online you seek out others that are like you. So before we even begin our relationship we know that there is a connection. Being that I am a mother of multiples (set of twins), also an African American mom blogger, photographer, and in a biracial marriage, I tend to stick out. I also do not hide all of my attributes. I knew that there were many others like me but could not find them. I influence my readers that I have similarities with and I love that we've connected.

How can company's best support your business or mission as a mom? Companies can best support my business as a mom owner by allowing me to test the product out. I have very specific niches: deals and photography; very different but yet very specific. Allowing me to try the product will not only give me insight to share with my readers but also personal touch that I believe we all appreciate. In my photography profession, one of my biggest connections is other photographers. We all want to know what the next best product is so that we can buy it, use it and share it with our clients.

How do you feel companies can best connect with moms, particularly those who are influencers? Becoming a mom opened the doors to lots of great gatherings that I had never heard of before. It would be great if companies could connect through their current known and trusted sources such as Maria Bailey's Companies and maybe even a connected trusted Twitter place for quick and immediate connections that are needed. Whatever the venue, it needs to be one that is a trusted source. I have had many companies contact me but without references, it's difficult to trust them. I solely go by reference.

Final words: Being able to tap into a mom, and the level of motherhood she is in, is valuable. We learn more about being a mother with each stage our child is in. I would love to see a program that was designed for mothers in stages. By that I mean different age groups. We can have more of an influence if we can speak in our current life and it's noted that way.

Name: Lorraine Sanabria Robertson

Children: Two, ages 9 and 7

Hometown: Atlanta, GA

Company Name(s): 30 Miles Media, Inc.; and I co-own The BlogRollers Media

Short description of business: 30 Miles Media, Inc. houses my writing ventures. I published a book, do freelance magazine writing and blog regularly. The BlogRollers is a social media marketing company. I launched 30 Miles Media to house my writing career. Writing off and online is my passion. While I do both, I really enjoy the interaction of social media and online writing. I've recently started my blog, Run Wifey Run, where I talk about marriage, motherhood and my marathon running. My mission is to grow that blog in hopes of motivating others while taking care of myself.

Websites or Blogs you own: Run Wifey Run www.RunWifeyRun.blogspot.com; Ask Wifey www.AskWifey.com; The Blog Rollers www.TheBlogRollers.com

Facebook Id: Lorraine Sanabria Robertson; Run Wifey Run

Twitter Id: @AskWifey

Approximate # of followers: 3,800

Online Involvements and associations: Heart of Haiti; Path to Peace; Allconnect; Social Media Moms; Purex Insider

What do you think is the biggest mistake companies make in trying to work with moms? When companies treat moms as if they are not business savvy; because many of us are!

Are there companies who you feel are doing a great job connecting with moms? Sure. I've had wonderful experiences with Walt Disney World and recently spent time at Coca Cola. They are just coming into the social media world but are doing an awesome job.

Is there one moment when you realized you were impacting the life/lives of others? I've really seen it since I started running. The tweets, Facebook notes and blog comments that I received while training for my marathon and after I ran it were awesome: really supportive and people actually told me that I make them want to run. That's such an incredible thing.

How can companies best support your business or mission as a mom? I like to arrange social media and in-person events so sponsorships are key. Also, providing seminars and education activities/conferences are beneficial.

What motivates you to tell other moms (good or bad) about a company, brand or product? If I like it, feel it's beneficial and authentic, then I will happily spread the word. On the flipside, I won't talk negative about a company unless they do something really bad—I'd rather just not deal with them.

How do you feel companies can best connect with moms, particularly those who are influencers? I think by being authentic and respectful. Realize it's a two-way street and the relationship should be a win-win for everyone involved.

Final words: Moms rule and run this world. Our influence and impact is immeasurable. It's so priceless ... we don't get paid!

Name: Amy Schuler

Children: Four, ages 8, 6, and 3 ½-year-old twin boys

Hometown: Fairfax, VA

Websites or blogs you contribute to: http://shalomnovayouthedu.blogspot.com/

Facebook Id: Amy Schuler

Online Involvements and associations: BzzAgent, House Party, MomSelect, Growing Jewish Family Listserv, BigTent, VocalPoint, VIP Beauty Access

Offline Involvements: PTO at kids' school (very involved in children's private school), Moms group, Jewish Study Class, Growing Jewish Families Committee Chair (JCC of Northern VA), Shalom Baby Volunteer (past 7 yrs), ran a Mommy & Me program for the past three years (at kids' school, volunteer)

What's the best way for companies to reach you as an influencer or as a mom? To advertise in such a way that we can relate to and connect with, *i.e.*, Kaiser

Permanente has some great new radio advertisements with their "Thrive" Campaign about kids and being a parent: "How kids drive us crazy, but there's nothing that makes us happier."

What do you think is the biggest mistake companies make in trying to work with moms? Making assumptions that they know what we want and need. The best way to truly know is to have the parent test a product and evaluate its effectiveness. There are companies that provide this opportunity, such as P&G (VocalPoint) and MomSelect.

How do you feel you influence moms online? I use social media such as Facebook, Yahoogroup Listserv, and email to post recommendations and I frequently get requests for referrals. This is how I know I've been successful.

How can companies best support your business or mission as a mom? Continuing to produce items which lets us achieve more. Cost is not the limiting issue; value and time are.

How do you feel companies can best connect with moms, particularly those who are influencers? I feel that companies such as MomSelect, VocalPoint, House Party, BzzAgent, and similar companies, which give moms the opportunity to receive free products to test and review, are using one of the best ways to connect. However, there are also companies like Trader Joe's that connect with moms, not through strategic advertising, but through stocking shelves with value and kid-friendly items.

Name: Debbie Schuster

Children: Four, ages 20, 17, 8, and 4

Hometown: Kenosha, Wisconsin

Short description of business: I launched Frugal Diva Frenzy in March of 2009; it is my way of helping other parents and others with their budgets and to help them save more. It combines two of my passions: blogging and helping others. The motivation behind Frugal Diva Frenzy was to have an outlet that was just mine.

Since I have two sons that are special needs, I cannot work outside the home, as they need constant care; so it's a great way for me to have me time, while helping others at the same time. It gives me an outlet for those not-so-easy days and always puts a smile on my face. I enjoy helping other moms, dads and others who follow my blog. I find it just amazing when I see from how far away they are and following. I have followers in Russia, China, and other countries as well. I love hearing their opinions and sharing their thoughts on the topic of being frugal. It's a learning experience for me as well as for them.

Websites or Blogs you own: Frugal Diva Frenzy (Freebies, Deals and coupons blog)

Approximate audience size: 5,100 views a month

Websites or blogs you contribute to: Frugal Diva Frenzy, and other blogs by doing guest blog posts

Facebook Id: Frugal Diva Frenzy

Twitter Id: @frugaldivafrenz

Approximate # of followers: 350

Online Involvements and associations: Mom central, Mom Select, Fritos fan club

Offline Involvements: Cub Scouts, miracle league baseball, we donate to the local food pantries with our freebies and other stock-up deals that I post on my blog to help out those who need them.

What's the best way for companies to reach you as an influencer or as a mom? The best way to reach me is usually by email: frugaldivafrenzy@gmail.com.

How do you feel you influence moms online? I do influence them with my blog by helping them to save money, learn to make freezer meals to cut kitchen time and save money at the same time; help them to get freebies and deals to help their budget and give them tips on saving as well.

However, I would say that I do a lot of other things online to also influence moms as well. I support many moms who have children with brain tumors, cancer and other very life-threatening diseases. I'm there when they need to laugh, cry, scream, or just vent. Being a mom of two special needs children, I know how hard it can be on those not-so-good days. There are times I will get a call at 3 a.m. from one of the moms having a rough day and their child just finally fell asleep and they need to talk. That is our time to listen, to give advice if needed, or to just say you're doing a great job, it's going to be a better day tomorrow.

I am that mom who has very large voice, no matter if it's on my blog and I'm helping parents or others with saving for their family if I'm helping another mom cope with the day that she has had or if I'm just letting them vent. I love everything that I do and I wouldn't change a thing other than maybe making life a little easier on my sons and being able to give my daughters more "Us" time.

How do you feel you influence moms offline? Is it more than chatting in the carpool line? I would love to go back to it just being chatting and carpooling at times. However, my influencing now pertains more to health problems, couponing, how to save money, where to buy that GREAT dress for a great price for Homecoming, and so much more. It's helping moms shop at the grocery store and teaching them about saving for their family. It's going to the hospital to provide some moral support, and giving hugs to show it's going to be okay, because they are not alone. Being a mom, well for me, is being a Jack-of-all-Trades and learning about medical advantages and disadvantages as we go.

What motivates you to tell other moms (good or bad) about a company, brand or product? I feel that my opinions are honest, about companies, products or brands that I review for my blog. I give everything I do 100% of me. So my opinion of a company, product or brand does go a long way with my readers. I do get products from companies to test and tell my readers about. I do tell them if there are positives or negatives to the product, company or brand. I tell them about my experience with a company, and I am always 100% honest. I feel I owe it to myself, my readers and the company, product or brand to be completely honest. I can be picky about things at times because of the way I need things to work for my family. However, I do note in my reviews that my needs may not be the same as theneeds of others.

How do you feel companies can best connect with moms, particularly those who are influencers? I feel that companies can best connect with moms on many levels. One of the best ways would be getting the moms' feedback on their products; having the products reviewed on blogs and other media pulls a lot of weight with moms. Also, have excellent customer service; it will get you everywhere with a mom! We don't have all day to sit on hold waiting, if there is a problem with the product or if it was missing a part that should have come with it. Don't give us the run-around because I have to say that as moms, we are going to be spreading that word like lightening.

Name: Lori Seaborg

Children: Four, ages 15, 13, 10, and 7

Hometown: Fairhope, AL

Websites or Blogs you own: FreelyEducate.com http://FreelyEducate.com and Just Pure Lovely http://JustPureLovely.com

Approximate audience size: 15,000+ unique visitors each month, 55,000+ page views across each month

Websites or blogs you contribute to: Contributed to Suite101.com and Homeschool-Blogger.com and PreciousMoms.com

Facebook Id: Freely Educate

Twitter Id: @justpurelovely and @freelyeducate

Approximate # of followers: 2,000

Online Involvements and associations: PreciousMoms.com

How many moms do you typically interact with during the week offline? 200+ in our homeschooling groups

What's the best way for companies to reach you as an influencer or as a mom? Email: loriseaborg@gmail.com

How is the best way to work with you and your company? I offer many sponsorship methods for a company to be featured on my blogs or in my social media feed.

What do you think is the biggest mistake companies make in trying to work with moms? Companies think we work for free. Too many moms *do* work for free, but we should be paid to promote company's products. We have a *niche* audience, we have influence. A blog post should be worth at least what a magazine or newspaper ad with about the same "circulation" would be worth.

Are there companies who you feel are doing a great job connecting with moms? I'm not having much luck here, so can't think of any company that is doing well. Usually, I am approached only by those wanting to access my sites for free.

How do you feel you influence moms online? When I recommend a product, my readers usually buy it, so I am very careful about which products or companies I recommend.

How can companies best support your business or mission as a mom? By supporting FreelyEducate.com through sponsored posts, they help me keep it up and going. For Just Pure Lovely, I simply want to see more children go outdoors, more moms unafraid of taking photos and more people with hope.

What motivates you to tell other moms (good or bad) about a company, brand or product? I only speak badly about it if the product should have a warning on it or is a dangerous one. I speak well about a product only if I truly do use it and enjoy it. Useful products at inexpensive pricing are appealing to me.

How do you feel companies can best connect with moms, particularly those who are influencers? Contact moms directly by finding those of us who have a large following, or those of us who are leaders. Through the leaders, you can find many moms who are willing to learn more about your product. And by working with the influencer in this way, you are building a relationship with her.

Name: Denise Seegobin

Children: Three, ages 11, 5 and 2

Hometown: Brooklyn, New York

Employer: Lehman College

Short description of business: I work for a math program that offers professional development for teachers in public school. My company's history is providing leadership and professional development for teachers and schools. The company has been around for more than 20 years.

Facebook Id: DSeegobin

Twitter Id: @Nico2317

Approximate # of followers: 299

Online Involvements and associations: Modern Mom, Mom Central, FWA

How many moms do you typically interact with during the week offline? 40

Offline Involvements: I am part of mom parenting groups and book clubs. I participate in a lot of volunteer association that help with educational issues.

What's the best way for companies to reach you as an influencer or as a mom? I think the best ways for companies to reach us is through websites that allow us to sign up and be ambassadors for the programs. Also through a social network site, that allows us to follow the brand and give comments and feedback.

How do you define influence among moms? What I think defines influence is the ability to reach us. Are you taking us into consideration when you do your advertisement, are you asking us what we would like to see you do better?

How do you feel you influence moms online? I influence moms online by talking about products that I find work well, on products that companies talk truthfully about, if they allow me to sample the product before I buy it. I think a great thing also is providing surveys for us to do follow-up on products.

What motivates you to tell other moms (good or bad) about a company, brand or product? My motivation is to be someone who can help other moms make better decisions and I feel that if I try something and have a good or bad experience, then me sharing it does my part in educating others about things.

Name: Jo-Lynne Shane

Children: Three, ages 11, 8, and 5

Hometown: Philadelphia, PA

Short description of business: I have several businesses under one umbrella. I started my personal blog in spring of 2006. It was just a whim. I thought it might be fun and never expected to stick with it. I discovered I loved writing, and then I discovered the mom blogging community and I was hooked. Then companies discovered me, and it became a vocation. I started a beauty/fashion blog in January of 2008. My mission was to create a beauty/fashion blog with real women behind it. We have 8 writers and Chic Critique and everyone brings her own voice to the site. I began my blog design business in March of 2008. There was a market for it; most blog designers were swamped and hard to reach. I taught myself how to use Adobe Illustrator and with the help of a mentor, I started designing for Blogger. I've expanded now and I also design blogs for Wordpress. I started my hyper local blog, Eat Local Philly, in the fall of 2010 with a mission to promote our local food economy. So far, it's off to a great start.

Websites or Blogs you own: www.musingsofahousewife.com, www.chic-critique.com, www.eatlocalphilly.com, www.dcrdesign.com

Approximate audience size: That's hard to say. I have almost 2,000 subscribers to my personal blog, almost 4000 followers on Twitter as well as fan pages on Facebook for all 3 blogs.

Websites or blogs you contribute to: Blogging Your Way, Plan To Eat, Therapon

Twitter Id: @JoLynneMusings, @ChicCritique, @EatLocalPhilly

Approximate # of followers: 4000

Online Involvements and associations: Therapon brand ambassador, Wisk Beta Blogger, Frigidaire Mom

How many moms do you typically interact with during the week offline? 50-100

What's the best way for companies to reach you as an influencer or as a mom? Email: dcrmom@gmail.com

What do you think is the biggest mistake companies make in trying to work with moms? Mass marketing, irrelevant press releases. Moms are looking for the personal touch, something relatable.

Is there one moment when you realized you were impacting the life/lives of others? I think it was the first time I posted about shopping for an item and someone said they went out and bought it on my recommendation. I started taking everything I write more seriously after that.

How do you feel companies can best connect with moms, particularly those who are influencers? Get involved in our conversations. Connect with us on our blogs, on Twitter, at conferences. Get to know us, and then, AND ONLY THEN, pitch us with ideas on working together. Ask us for our input, respect our ideas. Make sure the relationship is mutually beneficial. Don't ask us to work for free when you're getting paid a fair wage. That's insulting.

Final words: Moms are incredibly influential, and companies who are not harnessing the power of social media are missing out on great opportunities. But companies who are doing it incorrectly are digging their own graves. As with most things, watch and learn, dip your toe into the pool and tread carefully. Be personal and relatable, and don't take our time and talents for granted. There are many opportunities to work together in ways that are mutually beneficial. It's just a matter of figuring out who is right for you and what's the best way to promote your product or service in a way that is relatable and relevant.

Name: Debi Silber, MS, RD, WHC, The Mojo Coach®

Children: Four ages 15, 13, 10 and 8

Hometown: Dix Hills, New York

Company Name(s): Lifestyle Fitness, Inc.

Short description of business: Lifestyle Fitness, Inc. through www.TheMojoCoach.com is dedicated to inspiring and empowering people to become their personal and professional best by helping them create their ultimate body, mind, image and lifestyle. The company is also dedicated to helping companies boost productivity, morale, health, wellness and their bottom line while reducing health care costs from chronic illness, absenteeism and turnover as a result of poor health and morale.

I started in 1991 as a Dietitian/Trainer with new direction (as a Whole Health Coach-health expert trained to teach how your lifestyle creates health/wellness or illness/disease) in 2008. New direction occurred due to my own health decline—illnesses, symptoms, conditions, disease. My life came to an abrupt stop as I had to give up my entire practice, could barely move, stay awake, raise my kids, etc. I was in constant, chronic pain, very sick, depressed, etc. During surgery, I had a feeling there was a link between my lifestyle and my health because as a dietitian/trainer, I was eating well and exercising so there was something obviously wrong. Toxic relationships, chronic stress, emotional upheaval was the catalyst for my deteriorating mental, physical, emotional health. I slowly changed everything and as I did, everything slowly healed. I got my mojo back, started working with clients again and they got their mojo back. They branded me "The Mojo Coach" and I've been on a mission to inspire and empower women to become their personal and professional best ever since. Books, products, programs have been designed to help women when I'm unable to coach one-on-one or speak in groups or at events.

Websites or Blogs you own: The Mojo Coach www.TheMojoCoach.com and The Mojo Coach blog www.TheMojoCoach.com/blog

Approximate audience size: 10,000+

Websites or blogs you contribute to: Women on Their Way-Wyndham Worldwide, GirlGetStrong.com, 5MinutesForMom.com, BookieBoo.com, HealthyMoms.net, SoulSalonInternational.com, MomeoCommunity.com, SelfGrowth.com, ExtraordinaryResultsCoachingCommunity.com, TooMuchOnHerPlate.com, Fabulously40.com, NurseTogether.com, BestLifeDesign.com, MenuPlanningCentral.com, TheFitAdvocate.com, FitBusinessWoman.com, MeTime.com, Examiner.com, Wellness.com/Workplace, myvillagegreen.com, The National Institutes of Health (NIH), MSN.com, SheKnows.com, North Valley Magazine, SparkPeople, Bringham and Women's Hospital, Today's Dietitian, St. John Health System, Examiner.com, All Educational Software, Pregnancy Today, Health Online Plus, Integration Health, Kroger, Medi-Care First, Meridian Health, MomToBe-Depot, Helping Moms at Home, The Holistic Option, Health Mart, Nurse Zone, Well Sphere, Main Street Mom, Exceptional People Magazine, Mom Central, Go Workout Mom, DivaToolBox.com, HealthyStyleNY.com, MyVillageGreen.com, CorporateWellnessMagazine.com

Facebook Id: Debi Silber

Twitter Id: @themojocoach

Approximate # of followers: 5,900

How many moms do you typically interact with during the week offline? Depends on the week. Private clients (one-on-one), speaking events, networking events, etc.

Are there companies who you feel are doing a great job connecting with moms? I just attended the Working Mother Media WorkLife Congress which celebrated the best 100 companies for working moms. They all had great programs which gave moms more flexibility, maternity leave, fitness facilities, health care, onsite daycare, nursing rooms and other programs which gives moms greater work/life balance

How do you feel you influence moms online? I share weight loss, fitness and lifestyle information that gives moms the opportunity to gather information and make informed decisions about what will work for them. Having worked with many moms and being a mom of four myself, moms trust my material because they see that I practice what I preach!

How do you feel you influence moms offline? Is it more than chatting in the carpool line? It's thrilling to influence moms to make changes that will help them create a better body, mind, image and lifestyle. Sometimes it can be something as simple as complimenting someone who rarely receives one and you know she's a little bit happier and who knows what else that will inspire? Other times it's a conversation with a friend and our conversation leads to pursuing a new idea, talent or direction. Other times it's through my coaching where the work is deeply personal and a mom is making big breakthroughs to create the life she wants most. Finally it's through speaking where I can see the "a-ha" moment in a mom's eyes as I talk about something she never even realized was holding her back.

How do you feel companies can best connect with moms, particularly those who are influencers? Companies need to connect with moms in the way that works best for the moms. If moms get most of their information online or through word of mouth, companies should use those channels first. Companies can also connect best with moms by speaking with moms to find out what their needs are, how they want to be promoted to, what would best serve them, etc. Unfortunately, many companies want to serve moms but aren't consulting the very market they want to reach.

Final words: Moms have a huge influence in today's world. They're the ones buying most of the household products/services, promoting brands they use, etc. They're also a powerful presence in the workforce. If companies are willing to work around the demands of a mom (allowing flexibility within the work schedule, etc.) they'll retain a highly productive and successful employee. Moms are already used to doing so much, but need the ability to work around a schedule that personally works best for them. If companies recognize that and are willing to be flexible in their approach, they'll attract and retain incredible talent.

Name: K. Melissa Smallwood

Children: Three, ages 17, 14, and 13

Hometown: Falling Waters, WV

Company Name(s): Young Lives of Eastern Panhandle

Short description of business: Young Lives is a nonprofit organization that provides mentoring, life skills training and other services to teen moms and their children. I became involved with Young Lives after hearing a presentation in October of 2009. In April of 2010 I became the assistant area director. I was a teen mom myself, becoming pregnant with my son at 16. I found support to obtain my GED, enroll in college and more through a program similar to Young Lives, so the mission immediately appealed to me. I am privileged to spend my days working alongside the current director, effecting change in the lives of young girls with nowhere else to turn.

Websites or Blogs you own: Multi-Tasking Mama http://www.multitaskingmama.com and Eastern Panhandle Moms http://www.easternpanhandlemoms.com

Approximate audience size: 400 RSS subscribers, newsletter subscribers 1,200+

Websites or blogs you contribute to: http://www.themobsociety.com

Facebook Id: Melissa Nicholson Smallwood

Twitter Id: @multitaskingme

Approximate # of followers: 6,700

How many moms do you typically interact with during the week offline? I frequently speak about teen pregnancy and parenting to MOPS groups, MOMS clubs, etc., at least weekly. I also have a group of about 10 friends who meet weekly for a coffee club to discuss parenting adolescents, etc. I am active in the local school system and my local church so I also encounter 10-30 moms a day that way as well.

What's the best way for companies to reach you as an influencer or as a mom? It is important to me that companies are authentic, that they reach out to me (both as an influencer and especially as a mom) through cause marketing and giving back to the community, both on and offline.

What do you think is the biggest mistake companies make in trying to work with moms? Companies undervalue the impact that moms can have on both their online and offline sphere of influence. Campaigns that offer me a way to reach out to both communities are appealing versus generic press releases in my inbox.

How do you feel you influence moms online? I hope I offer inspiration and authenticity to other moms who may be struggling with similar issues such as parenting teens, living with chronic illness and finding a way to live a fulfilling life that has purpose. I also give my unabashed opinion on products I like (or don't), issues I feel strongly about and charities that strike a chord in my heart. Usually I find that my opinions and posts resonate with other women through the feedback (emails, tweets, comments, etc.) that I receive.

How can companies best support your business or mission as a mom? Companies can help raise awareness of important issues, like teen pregnancy, poverty and more. At times, companies seem hesitant to jump into assisting with a particular cause because of the stigma attached to some issues. While I understand that, the companies I respect and support are those that take a stand for something and are willing to put their resources where their mouth is.

What motivates you to tell other moms (good or bad) about a company, brand or product? Providing information is my primary motivation for writing about a product or campaign. On my local blog, I will write about a bad experience (or good) with a product or establishment to save my readers the time and energy of having to find out themselves and to listen to feedback from those who have had a similar or totally different experience. Oftentimes the company will respond as well, and I truly appreciate that interaction.

How do you feel companies can best connect with moms, particularly those who are influencers? By getting to know the woman behind the blog. Since I blog about parenting teens, many marketers assume I am not interested in issues affecting small children. But I work with moms of small children every day. Taking the time to get to know the influencer is key and developing a mutually beneficial relationship is well worth the companies' time.

Final words: Moms have more influence in today's media driven society than at any other time in history. We have individual and collective voices with the tools (internet and social media) for those voices to be heard. We can affect change in so many realms, if we just give ourselves the permission to stand up and speak up for the issues that we are passionate about.

Name: Deirdre Smith

Children: One, age 2

Hometown Simpsonville, South Carolina

Short description of business: I started my blog in 2009. My mission is to share with other toddler moms what I am learning.

Websites or Blogs you own: JDaniel4's Mom http://www.jdaniel4smom.com/

Approximate audience size: 1,700 subscribers

Websites or blogs you contribute to: I am a Mom Loop Community Leader.

Facebook Id: Daniel Foursmom

Twitter Id: @jdaniel4smom

Approximate # of followers: 1,320

Online Involvements and associations: I am a member of TwitterMoms, WeTeach, and several other mom groups. I am not on any special panels.

How many moms do you typically interact with during the week offline? 30

Offline Involvements: Weekly playgroup, story time at the library, and Mentor Moms group at church. I am a member of Alpha Delta Kappa (a teaching soriority).

What's the best way for companies to reach you as an influencer or as a mom? Email: jdaniel4smom@aol.com is the best way to reach me directly.

What do you think is the biggest mistake companies make in trying to work with moms? I don't think they remember that moms don't have tons of free time.

How do you define influence among moms? Respected moms whose opinions can lead others to buy and try new products.

How do you feel you influence moms online? I think by writing fair and honest reviews, moms that read my blog have come to trust my opinion.

How do you feel you influence moms offline? Is it more than chatting in the carpool line? During playgroup while the children are playing, I share what I have going on with the blog.

What motivates you to tell other moms (good or bad) about a company, brand or product? I just like to share.

Final words: I think moms influence every area of the world. They are raising future leaders as well as wonderful children. They care about everything that will affect their child.

Name: Courtney Solstad

Children: Three, ages 5, 3, and 2 (all girls)

Hometown: McKinney, TX

Company Name(s): MyDFWMommy

Short description of business: This blog was started in July 2009. It was created to give the DFW area moms a place to find HOT local deals and coupons!

Website or Blogs you own: MyDFWMommy.com

Approximate audience size: 10,000+ per day

Websites or blogs you contribute to: MyDFWMommy.com, MyCityMommy.com

Facebook Id: Personal: Courtney Solstad, Professional: MyDFWMommy

Twitter Id: @MyDFWMommy

Approximate # of followers: 3,000

Online Involvements and associations: MyCityMommy Network Blogger, TeamMom, Wisk Mom Blogger, MomBloggersClub, MomSelect Member, Mom Central Member, MomDot Member, Social Spark Member, Totsy Mom Blogger, and Collective Bia's Member

What's the best way for companies to reach you as an influencer or as a mom? I think the best way is to email me at mydfwmommy@gmail.com.

What do you think is the biggest mistake companies make in trying to work with moms? They offer time-consuming promos and don't consider that the typical mom doesn't have that kind of time on her hands.

How do you define influence among moms? If moms are excited about something and talking about it often, the brand has a strong influence!

Is there one moment when you realized you were impacting the life/lives of others? Yes, when my college-aged babysitter wanted to learn how to coupon and used my site.

How do you feel you influence moms offline? Is it more than chatting in the carpool line? Yes, I love to show and tell at my MOPS group or in the line waiting at the grocery store.

How can companies best support your business or mission as a mom? I would love for companies to send me deals and/or products to try and talk about.

What motivates you to tell other moms (good or bad) about a company, brand or product? If I have an out-of-the-box experience with a product I am more apt to tell others about it ... good or bad. For example, I expect that diapers will work, so I want to talk about them if they leak a lot, or if they go beyond expectations and hold in the smell.

Final words: Companies have to make things personal for moms. If it's not personal, moms will overlook it. A personal experience goes a LONG way. I love to talk to ACTUAL people when I call 1-800 #'s ... not press this, now that ... etc.

Name: Melanie Somnitz

Children: Two, ages 5 and 2

Hometown: Columbus, OH

Short description of business: I started my blog because I was so amazed at all the moms out there that had lives similar to mine. I found myself talking to other moms all the time and wanted to share what I have learned about mothering, balancing work and life, raising special needs kids in my unique family.

Websitse or Blogs you own: www.sunshinepraises.com

Approximate audience size: 250+

Facebook Id: Sunshine Praises

Twitter Id: @SunshinePraises

Approximate # of followers: 250+

How many moms do you typically interact with during the week offline? 20 to 30

Offline Involvements: I am the recent past President of the Ohio Chapter of the Registry of Intepreters for the deaf. I am also involved in our church. I have served on the State board of the Ohio Chapter of the Registry of Interpreters for the Deaf for the past nine years. This organization is made up of over 90% women and almost all of them are moms.

Is there one moment when you realized you were impacting the life/lives of others? Yes, when other moms starting coming to me for advice about cloth diapers and breastfeeding allergy-sensitive babies; when I started having my email passed to strangers for my "list" of safe foods to eat while breastfeeding.

How can companies best support your business or mission as a mom? Be proactive. Find out what moms really need to make their lives easier. The more time I have with my family, the happier a mom I am. If it eats up too much of my time, I am not interested. However, fast does not mean cheap. Companies need to understand that quality matters.

What motivates you to tell other moms (good or bad) about a company, brand or product? The thrill of sharing something that they might not already know about; I love helping my mommy friends' lives become easier, healthier and more productive.

Final words: Moms that have a cause really appeal to me. I love blogs or moms that believe in something and walk it out, when companies partner with moms that have kids/families in need or are working to better the world for someone else, that always gets my attention.

Name: Laura "Lou" Spencer

Children: One, age 10

Hometown: Orlando, FL

Company Name(s): Professional experience in publishing (Addison Wesley/Pearson) wellness (YMCA) and owned a family business with my mother for 10 years (beauty salon)

Twitter Id: @LauraSpencerOne

Approximate # of followers: 2,000

How many moms do you typically interact with during the week offline? Up to 100

Offline Involvements: Sustainer member of the Junior League, Board member of my community's HOA, member of the finance and marketing committees of daughter's school

How is the best way to work with you and your company? On a personal level, no mass emails or recorded phone calls.

What do you think is the biggest mistake companies make in trying to work with moms? Thinking that we are all the same. I am a New Englander, who skis, loves the Red Sox; I am conservative AND liberal; I am cheap, but will spend money on what's important to my family. I also think marketers COMPLETELY miss the mark when dealing with African American moms by labeling us "urban" and assuming our life circumstances.

Are there companies who you feel are doing a great job connecting with moms? Johnson and Johnson, Dove, Justice for Girls, MAC cosmetics, DSW, Franklin Covey

How do you feel you influence moms online? I don't attempt to, but because of my job I have a more visible blogosphere presence.

How do you feel you influence moms offline? Is it more than chatting in the carpool line? I usually am the mom who takes charge. I am the committee leader, the organizer, the planner.

How can companies best support your business or mission as a mom? By creating products that I can use to make my life easier and exciting.

How do you feel companies can best connect with moms, particularly those who are influencers? Meet them where you find them. Everyone is not online.

Final words: I believe that if women truly banded together we could achieve amazing things. Politically, socially, and emotionally we tend to be divisive. We should be each other's "sisters."

Name: Steph, Be Positive Mom

Children: Two, ages 4 and 10 months

Hometown: (Northern Bay Area) California

Company Name(s): Be Positive Mom

Short description of business: Be Positive Mom (http://www.bepositivemom.blogspot.com) is a compilation of my personally written content based on my own experiences of being a working mom, of family life, motherhood and parenting. The purpose of Be Positive Mom is to provide working moms or moms who are just overworked with some positive tips, insights and perspective on how to manage the day-to-day grind and still have some fun. It can't all be work and no play! My site includes The Working Mom Interviews, a monthly newsletter that features a new topic and working mom each month, along with tips and resources. http://bepositivemom.blogspot.com/p/working-mom-interviews.html

Be Positive Mom launched June 2010. The motivation for my blog, my purpose came out of my own personal tragedy in 2007.

See "What's The Story Behind Be Positive Mom?" http://bepositivemom.blogspot.com/2010/10/whats-story-behind-be-positive-mom.html

Mission: To empower every working mom with a positive perspective and some imagination to help manage the juggle between family and the world of work—grab hold of that balancing act and pull out some "me time" from the day-to-day grind.

Websites or Blogs you own: Be Positive Mom www.bepositivemom.com

Approximate audience size: About 500 including all outlets (Twitter, Facebook, etc.) plus my reach on the mom blog sites listed below.

Websites or blogs you contribute to: Mom Bloggers Club http://www.mombloggersclub.com/, Bloggy Moms http://www.bloggymoms.com, MommyMo http://mommymo.com, BlogFrog http://theblogfrog.com/, Work It Mom http://www.workitmom.com/, Work Wife Mom... Life! http://www.workwifemom-life.com (Working Mommy Wednesday Posts)

Facebook Id: Be Positive Mom

Twitter Id: @bepositivemom

Approximate # of followers: 300

What's the best way for companies to reach you as an influencer or as a mom? Email: bepositivemom@gmail.com

How do you define influence among moms? Moms connect for different reasons. Influence is achieved if fellow moms like or want to hear what you have to say. Even with social media, it's about building your relationship (your brand) with the group of moms you interact with. It's that connection to others that can establish you as an influencer even if it's with a small group of moms.

Is there one moment when you realized you were impacting the life/lives of others? When I first launched the blog, I received very positive feedback and people commented on how important it is to be positive in a world that is filled with such negativity. Just recently, I realized how I influence others when I encountered negative feedback about having my babies in daycare and working 40+ hours a week. An anonymous commenter really shook my blog purpose and mission to the core with comments that were really demeaning and judgmental about choices my husband and I made for "our" family. Rather than responding emotionally and attacking the commenter because I knew it would spark debate, I wrote specifically about the choices we make as parents and how we can support our differences rather than condemn them. See my post at http://bepositivemom.blogspot.com/2010/10/choices-we-make.html.

How can companies best support your business or mission as a mom? Try to better understand how truly frazzled moms are even if they seem to have it all together. For me, I prefer to promote products with a purpose (*i.e.*, positive, healthy, promote green living, etc.).

What motivates you to tell other moms (good or bad) about a company, brand or product? The best tips come from other moms. Regardless if free products are involved or not, I genuinely love telling other moms about a good product experience. On my site, I stay away from negative product promotion but if a product is unsafe or recalled, I help get the word out. Twitter is great for that.

How do you feel companies can best connect with moms, particularly those who are influencers? Surveys, product trial group. Freebies are always looked at positively but should require some follow-up on the part of the mom who is reviewing. Coupons are great (but tough to use when they are cumbersome; for example, with Babies R Us, you have to purchase three to get one, or they have many stipulations to get a percentage off). Sometimes it's harder to use them than not use them at all.

Final words: I believe that moms in high-powered, visible positions are influencing on a daily basis. My hope is that they use their power and influence wisely, make meaningful decisions and that they value the opportunity this country affords us.

Name: Amanda (Mandee) Suchland

Children: Five, ages 10, 7, 5, 2 and 3 months (all boys)

Hometown: Ohio

Short description of business: I started my blog in July of 2009. In the beginning, I blogged about the funny things my boys did and about our day-to-day outings. Over time I my blog has grown to not only writings about my boys, but also reviews of products that we have tried, some great, some not so great, and giveaways for my readers.

Blog: Raising My 5 Sons http://raisingmy5sons.com

Approximate Audience Size: Over 1,500 fans

Facebook Id: http://www.facebook.com/RaisingMy5Sons

Approximate Number of Facebook Fans: 2,000

Twitter Id: @RaisingMy5Sons

Approximate Number of Twitter Followers: 1,200

Online Involvement and Association: Mom Bloggers Club Reviewer, My BlogSpark Member, Mom Select Member, Popsicle Mom

How do you feel you influence Moms online? I feel that I am an experienced mother. I have a voice that likes to be heard and I like to give advice. I feel that I have helped other moms determine products that will be right, or not so right for their families. I have also given advice that may have helped some mothers with breastfeeding, raising children and so forth.

What motivates you to tell other Moms about a company? I really love to help others out. I love having my opinion be heard, and if we purchase a product and really don't like it, I like to let other moms know so that they don't waste their money on it, especially if it is a big dollar product. I also love to tell Moms about the great products on the market! If I love a product, why not share my thoughts with others so that they can experience that, too?

How can companies best connect with Moms? I think they need to listen to what Mothers have to say and take that into consideration. Moms really do have a very loud voice in the market. Why not use that to their advantage?

Name: Dr. Daisy Sutherland

Children: Five, ages 19, 17, 14, 10 and 7

Hometown: Tampa, Florida

Company Name(s): CEO & Founder of Dr. Mommy Online

Short description of business: As a doctor, published author and speaker—our company's main goal is to encourage, motivate and inspire for your health, wealth and sanity ... this is accomplished by written books, webinars, writing services as well as individual/group mentoring programs.

Dr. Mommy was created in 2007 and continues to this day to encourage, motivate and inspire women.

As a mom, a doctor, published author and entrepreneur, I am able to help many, but the main mission is Going Retro, where I incorporate what worked in the past into today. By Going Retro, I can help empower you to be the best person you can be. Health is very important and living a healthy lifestyle is something I preach and encourage others to achieve.

My mission is to Help YOU... Going Retro in your health, wealth and sanity. Yes, sanity! I completely understand the role of a parent and more importantly one that is also an entrepreneur. It is one of joy, wonder and sometimes one that can drive us a bit crazy. Those are all wonderful qualities and emotions that make us all unique, and I can help you balance them all.

Website or Blogs you own: http://drmommyonline.com , http://drmommy-healthtips.com , http://retroparenting.com , http://drmommywrites.com

Approximate audience size: website visits of over 50,000 per month

Facebook Id: Dr Mommy, Dr Mommy Online, and Retro Parenting

Approximate # of followers: over 2,000

Twitter Id: @drmommy

Approximate # of followers: over 13,500

Online Involvements and associations: (Brand ambassadors, Mom Panels, etc.) Involved with Collective Bias, P&G as well as Mom Select

How many moms do you typically interact with during the week offline? With an active chiropractic office as well as activities through homeschooling and church, my interaction with moms is non-stop.

Offline Involvements: Church groups, home school groups, Praxis Haiti, Metropolitan Ministries

What's the best way for companies to reach you as an influencer or as a mom? The best way to reach me is through my website: http://drmommyonline.com/contact.

How do you define influence among moms? The influence is huge! Moms will gladly speak highly of a product they truly like and will yell it from the rooftops, but the same will also apply if they dislike a product or company. Moms usually run the households, do the shopping, and develop the menus as well as make many more decisions, so it is wise to work with moms in a cohesive relationship that would benefit all the parties involved.

Is there one moment when you realized you were impacting the life/lives of others? I've always wanted to serve others, which is the main reason I became a doctor. It wasn't until women of all ages were seeking my advise on not only the rearing of their children, but maintaining a healthy relationship with their spouses, as well as building a successful business, that I realized I was impacting others. I truly love what I do.

How do you feel you influence moms offline? Is it more than chatting in the carpool line? Moms are so much more tech savvy and many feel they must be in order to keep up with their tech savvy children. It is much more accessible to influence moms online and many are more willing to learn than those that are merely chatting in a carpool line. The changes that can be made to impact the many lives via online communities are truly amazing.

What motivates you to tell other moms (good or bad) about a company, brand or product? As humans, but more importantly as women, we naturally enjoy sharing both good and bad news. We will gladly share information on a product that has worked for us, or perhaps the great customer service we may have received. We will just as quickly share if we received bad service or received a faulty product. It's part of the social network that connects us as women to support each other.

How do you feel companies can best connect with moms, particularly those who are influencers? It is important for companies to do their homework as well as connect with companies that connect with moms online. There are many of us that are important influencers in different departments and allowing us to share our expertise and work together with larger companies will not only benefit the company but the community as a whole. It is easy to connect with such influencers today, thanks to the Internet and the social networks available such as Twitter and Facebook.

Name: Nina Sutton

Children: Two, ages 4 ½ and 3

Home state: Hermosa Beach, CA

Short description of business: TV host, Beauty and Mommy Lifestyle Expert. I write and speak about easy and affordable beauty and lifestyle tips for moms to feel good about themselves, and am a TV Host and a Beauty Expert and Mommy Lifestyle Expert. I just wrapped the show Pretty.Smart, which was shown at www.walmart.com/PrettySmart (the show ran from April 2010 to October 16, 2010). I do not have a company per se, I am my own brand. It started when I wrote my first book, *The Chic Mom's Guide to Feeling Fabulous* in 2008. I wrote my book after the birth of my first son. I was inspired by my Mommy and Me class and everyone discussing how they looked and felt, etc. Since I had been in the beauty and fashion industry, I felt like I had some quick tips to offer to help everyone feel pretty, and ultimately happier with themselves, so they could be the best moms. Those conversations sparked the book and it seems so obvious, but moms do need to be reminded and nudged to take care of themselves. My goal with my books, my blogs and TV segments is to create an ultimate brand personality that will make moms feel "Everyday Fabulous." A brand personality can then grow into multiple revenue platforms (from books to websites to TV shows and products) and I can feel good doing it since I know I am helping moms in America and beyond.

Websites or Blogs you own: Author, *The Chic Mom's Guide to Feeling Fabulous*, blog, TheChicMomsGuide.com, and website: www.NinaSutton.com. I am also the lead Beauty Expert for SheKnows.com, ranked third largest website for women.

Websites or blogs you contribute to: SheKnows.com (1.6 million users), BestEverYou.com (50,000 members)

Twitter Id: @NinaSutton

Approximate # of followers: 230

How many moms do you typically interact with during the week offline? With school activities (church, birthdays, soccer, etc.), at least 100-plus a week. Not to mention my love of mommy and me happy hour.

What do you think is the biggest mistake companies make in trying to work with moms? I think they need to understand that moms are TIME restricted—but we do still want to be involved. Anything lengthy or too complicated will not take priority.

Are there companies who you feel are doing a great job connecting with moms? I think Nestle and Johnson and Johnson are doing well on the CPG end. For beauty, Proctor and Gamble and Unilever are doing a good job of targeting moms as well, with mom-focused advertising and communication.

How do you feel you influence moms online? I feel that I influence moms by giving them easy tips on beauty, style, health and well-being. I am giving them PERMISSION to take care of themselves, because we all need reminding! I show them how to do it quickly and inexpensively and that is why they like my tips; I am not asking them to buy a $250 cream, but giving them simple, everyday tips.

How do you feel you influence moms offline? Is it more than chatting in the carpool line? Yes, I always give moms samples of beauty products—even if I squeeze a little into a small jar for them from my bottle. My mom friends ALWAYS email me or call me with questions or advice and I love giving it. If I love a product or service, I will proactively tell everyone about it—moms and non-moms!

How can companies best support your business or mission as a mom? I think the best way a company could support my mission as a mom would be to integrate their product with my message. I did that recently as the host of Pretty.Smart. I wrote most of the copy and all of the tips were mine. I would integrate the products as I saw fit.

What motivates you to tell other moms (good or bad) about a company, brand or product? If it is good—if I love the product I talk about it all day long! If I see results from a product, I want others to try it, too. If I have a bad experience, I hate to say this ... I talk about that, too—but only offline if I am asked, and I tell the truth.

How do you feel companies can best connect with moms, particularly those who are influencers? Email/social media, in-person events, samples—and some to give to other moms as well—similar to the Mommy Parties, where you send the products.

Final words: I believe that moms are the most important influence in society. We are raising the next generation of citizens. Moms do 80+% of the household purchases, moms feed their families, moms help with homework, moms take care of the family budget—the duties are endless. Companies and even government needs to understand moms' busy lives and provide products and services that make life easier and more streamlined—without being expensive.

Name: MJ Tam

Children: Three, ages 11, 8, and 4

Hometown: Chicago, IL

Company Name(s): City Connect Media, Inc./Chicagonista

Short description of business: It is a city online magazine designed for active city families. I have a profound love for my city and the way my family lives a robust and exciting life in Chicago. The word "Chicagonista" (in my mind) embodies someone who is actively in the know of what's going on around her. It was a perfect fit since I also came from the fashion industry background. It was about me being a mom and living a moving and shaking kind of lifestyle, but this time with my kids in tow.

Websites or Blogs you own: SugarMyBowl.com http://www.sugarmybowl.com/, Chicagonista http://chicagonista.com/, Chicagonista Live http://chicagonistalive.com/,Young Chicagonista http://youngchicagonista.com/, Next Gen Chicagonista http://nextgenchicagonista.com/, NY Metropolista http://nymetropolista.com/, The Chicago Moms http://thechicagomoms.com/

Approximate audience size: 5,000 Online Newsletter Subscribers

Websites or blogs you contribute to: DigiFams.com, Yahoo! Motherboard, and Technorati

Twitter Id: @mjtam

Approximate # of followers: 5,000+

Offline Community Service: I've taught and continue to teach "Embracing the True Nature of our Children in Today's Digital Age" to parents in my community. I am about to start a session with kids as well.

What's the best way for companies to reach you as an influencer or as a mom? I am very active in social media; any channel will do. If it fits what I do in life, then I am more than likely interested.

What do you think is the biggest mistake companies make in trying to work with moms? When companies forget to factor in the kids and family that mom has and instead just zero in on her followers.

Are there companies who you feel are doing a great job connecting with moms? Yes, I think Kraft has done a wonderful job.

Is there one moment when you realized you were impacting the life/lives of others? Yes, a first-time mom came out to meet me in an event one time and told me that she lost a lot of her outgoing self until she found Chicagonista. It made me feel really good!

How can companies best support your business or mission as a mom? Quick and instant information is always something I want: like QR-coded products in this cell phone age is such a great idea.

What motivates you to tell other moms (good or bad) about a company, brand or product? Good experience with a company motivates me. Good relationships motivate me. Bad companies and products, I don't bother giving a single space in my digital world. I realize how powerful I can be online, so there is no need to be ruining someone else's business because I had a bad experience. But then again, if it is completely unforgivable, then maybe I would say something. It hasn't happened yet.

How do you feel companies can best connect with moms, particularly those who are influencers? Build better relationships. Don't drop the ball when you get what you want like a blog post or a tweet. Keep carrying on the conversation with us.

Final words: With social networking around, I see every mom online equally influential. Whether you have 10 or 100,000 followers, the voices that will resonate will multiply endlessly. Each person's followers are taken into the equation when imagining the kind of current that can result from one wave of statement.

Name: Sheena Tatum

Children: One, age 3

Hometown: Chicago, IL

Short description of business: I'm an overall entrepreneur. I specialize in Web & Graphic Design, Freelance Writing/Blogging, and Social Media Strategy.

Websites or Blogs you own: Sophistishe http://sophistishe.com and Sheena Tatum http://sheenatatum.com

Approximate audience size: Sophistishe: 3,300 RSS subscribers

Websites or blogs you contribute to: http://strollerdepot.com/conectar

Facebook Id: Sophistishe

Twitter Id: @SheenaTatum

Approximate # of followers: 6,500

Online Involvements and associations: Ralph Lauren Mombassador, Walmart Moms, Panasonic LIHD Family

What do you think is the biggest mistake companies make in trying to work with moms? Expecting their blogs to be information powerhouses. And expecting them to have no lives outside of their online world. Content must be a good fit. Be upfront with any deadlines and compensate fairly. Also believing that bloated stats = great influence. Anyone can publish a post to thousands of readers, but what about the blogger with the smaller audience ... who may even be an expert, who is willing to publish a more creative post than the popular blogger, vlog it, and regularly mention your brand because she genuinely likes it? Don't miss out on potential advocates because you're set on numbers.

Are there companies who you feel are doing a great job connecting with moms? Guidecraft, Wilton, CSN Stores, Olive Kids, KidStuffPR, Litzky PR

Is there one moment when you realized you were impacting the life/lives of others? There are times when I feel no one is reading my blog, like what I write really doesn't matter. Then I get an email or message inquiring about a product, photography, natural hair, or eczema remedies. I've had moms tell me that they purchased a product or took a certain action because of me. That really lifts my spirits and motivates me to maintain my online presence.

How can companies best support your business or mission as a mom? Understand that we are moms and our families come first. It takes time away from our families and other obligations when we work with them. We deserve to be compensated fairly, based on the amount of work involved in a partnership. As bloggers, many of us don't operate like other publications. Some of us (especially personal bloggers) don't have editorial calendars and we don't post information just for the heck of it. The content we publish must be in tune with our lifestyles and blog focus. I personally don't do much spokesmom video work because I am uncomfortable doing so. I'm an introvert, so companies that give me the freedom to execute a campaign how I see fit receive cool points from me.

What motivates you to tell other moms (good or bad) about a company, brand or product? Well, their product/brand has to meet or even exceed my expectations whether by functionality, affordability, or how they present themselves publically (including events). Brands who are overall kind hearted win me over.

Name: Maggie Taylor

Children: Four

Hometown: Carlisle, PA

Company Name(s): OMG! It's Maggie Photography

Short description of business: I run a photography studio from home. I started it this year with my daughter. It's a mommy daughter photography studio.

Website or Blogs you own: OMG! It's Maggie Photography www.omgitsmaggie.com / The Busy Baby Mama www.thebusybabymama.com

Approximate audience size: 1,000+

Facebook Id: Maggie Oohmygod Taylor

Approximate # of followers: 2,700

Twitter Id: @0MGitsMaggie

Approximate # of followers: 5,000+

How many moms do you typically interact with during the week offline? Over 50, I'm in a ton of moms' groups

Offline Involvements: 5 moms and the PTO/PTA, I help part time at a homeless shelter/rehab

Is there one moment when you realized you were impacting the life/lives of others? Last year when I helped a family get sponsored for Christmas gifts, which I did simply by talking about it on Facebook.

Final words: Moms make up most of this country's biggest sales. With that in mind, companies should work on their marketing to be a lot more family friendly.

Name: Sarah Elizabeth Teres

Children: Three, ages 3, 7, 9

Hometown: Andover MA

Short description of business: Motherwords is a company dedicated to presenting an irreverent, humorous, and "reality based view" of motherhood. Motherwords was born in May of 2007, with the official launch of subscription and newsstand issues in January 2008. I developed Motherwords after having been the editor-in-chief for a regional periodical for mothers that was published by a mother's outreach and support network called "The Mother Connection." Motherwords developed the voice of reality in motherhood as a backlash to the judgmental, unrealistic and sometimes offensive expectations of motherhood pushed by traditional parenting magazines and general media. Motherwords began as a regional print magazine, with plans to become a national magazine and publishing house for women's literature, fiction and non-fiction, as well as a production company for mom-oriented television and educational programming; additionally, to include a nonprofit arm to provide community outreach and support for mothers, and classes on writing and artistic expression of their motherhood experiences. Currently in transition from a print format to an online format, Motherwords is continuing to develop the long-term goals of a media conglomerate incorporating the publishing house, production company, and nonprofit community outreach and support for women with children everywhere. The hope for Motherwords is to keep growing and developing until all goals are met, and to become a permanent brand and fixture synonymous with outreach, support, and humor for mothers; like the voice of Erma Bombeck on steroids.

Websites or Blogs you own: Motherwords www.motherwords.com

Approximate audience size: 940

Facebook Id: Sarah Teres (motherwords) and Motherwords

Twitter Id: @motherwords

Approximate # of followers: 134

What do you think is the biggest mistake companies make in trying to work with moms? Making assumptions that all moms have brains the size of a pea, and have no clue about how to make purchasing decisions; having a condescending attitude, an offensive or obnoxious pitch that often plays to the idea of a "June Cleaver" type of mother, instead of the modern, connected, savvy, and smart mothers of the 21st Century.

How do you define influence among moms? Impacting their lives, creating a network of support, discussing decisions—whether purchasing, or otherwise—in such a way as to build a voice that is trusted for accuracy and real understanding of their needs.

How do you feel you influence moms online? By presenting reality that can often be isolating, maddening, depressing, and ego-depleting in an irreverent and humorous way. When you make mothers feel connected, supported, and can make them smile—and hopefully laugh out loud—about the community of motherhood and their experiences, they tend to follow you and trust your words.

Final words: The last figures I saw in relation to the buying power of mothers, it seemed that mothers are responsible for nearly 70% of all purchasing decisions. Mothers spend billions of dollars every year. This means that mothers are extremely powerful economically. Mothers dictate the success of whether or not products and brands succeed in the marketplace. The failed "Motrin" campaign from 2008 was a great example of how mothers via Twitter, Facebook, blogs, and vocally had an entire Motrin campaign scrapped within 24 hours. That is true economic influence. Likewise, politically, mothers are a powerful force who can change the course of an election, and can often guarantee the success or failure of a particular candidate. Bill Clinton was probably the first presidential candidate to acknowledge the power of women, particularly "soccer moms," a term coined during his election. It is clear that mothers create incredible networks with one another. That was always the case in any community; however, now with the development of social media, computers, Internet, and all the technological advancements in the past 25 years, mothers have the ability to reach across miles into a global community that carries with it the incredible power of millions of mothers instantaneously. As a result of the strong connectivity between mothers, a variety of political ideas, causes, and needs become platforms that mothers support, or oppose in force. The political influence of mothers has become more than strength in numbers. Mothers have become more involved with the causes that are significant to their families, children, and the environment. Any candidate that does not take the strength of women/mothers seriously does so at their own peril.

Name: Wendy Tibbetts

Children: Two, ages 19 and 4

Hometown: Lombard, IL

Websites or blogs you contribute to: Cafemom, Twitter, Facebook

Online Involvements and associations: I have a group on Cafemom called Freebies & More! This is a great informational and support site for moms anywhere in the world. My group is a great resource for freebies and great deals that I find out on the Internet and through emails I receive directly in one location. My group has been in the top 250 most popular groups on Cafemom for the last 11 months and still going strong. And I will tell you there are thousands and thousands of groups on Cafemom. I am one of the most frugal and savvy moms I know and I'm all about paying it forward to help other moms like me. I also belong to many other mom panels and reputable survey sites (sorry, too many to list here—but I would be happy to tell you those sites if you contact me). I value these panels and sites and they value my opinions as a mom and shopper in today's world. I take pride in providing my honest feedback and ideas to these companies to help shape and change our world. Here is the website for Cafemom: Cafemom.com. It's very easy to join.

Offline Involvements: I belong to a great group called the Independent Order of Foresters. They have many functions and involvements in the community and world. They also have excellent financial services and products that you won't find anywhere else. I have belonged to the IOF for over 38 yrs. Here is a link to their website if you would like to find out more about them and what they offer: http://www.foresters.com/.

What's the best way for companies to reach you as an influencer or as a mom? Either by direct mail or email: wwrezzes@yahoo.com.

What do you think is the biggest mistake companies make in trying to work with moms? I think some companies ask for too much of our time in one sitting sometimes. If they want our valuable feedback or to get our attention about something they are trying to promote or sell, they need to be direct and to the point; give us a clear meaning of what they are providing or provide us with short surveys that are straight to the point with enough information for us to go on so that we can give them our honest feedback within a reasonable amount of time without taking away from our families. In addition, most companies give you some type of compensation for your valuable time and some do not (which is okay), but incentives add a little more to getting more feedback. As the saying goes, "you catch more flies with honey."

Are there companies who you feel are doing a great job connecting with moms? Cafemom, Fisher Price, Leap Frog, Parents Insights Program, Know It All's, and many more

How do you define influence among moms? Making a product or offering a service like we have not seen or heard before. Companies getting creative and wanting mom's honest and valuable feedback so they can market their product should it be a success in the early stages.

Is there one moment when you realized you were impacting the life/lives of others? Yes! After I joined Cafemom and started my own group within Cafemom, I received many emails and messages from moms who are so grateful they found my group. Sometimes you can hardly ever find anything for free anymore, or even just finding that great deal is the highlight of someone's day. Then they tell their friends about it, and so on and so on. Some moms have been hit so hard by this economic downfall we have been experiencing that they look forward to checking out my group daily just to see what great freebies and deals I have to share with them. I had one mom reply to me who was having such a struggle in her life that she didn't even have money to buy pull-ups for her child. Through my group, just those free pull-ups showing up in the mail brought tears to her eyes and she was thankful. You would not think something that small would impact someone, but it did and she let me know about it as other moms have as well. It makes me feel so good inside to know I am impacting people even in the smallest or biggest way. That's why I'm all about paying it forward!

How do you feel you influence moms offline? Is it more than chatting in the carpool line? I talk with many moms both after school, while I'm in the stores, at functions or anywhere else I happen to be. I am a very sociable, knowledgeable and resourceful mom. Many moms look to me for advice on parenting, where to bargain shop and so much more. It always feels so good inside to help any mom with anything I can help her with.

What motivates you to tell other moms (good or bad) about a company, brand or product? If I have had a great experience I surely would want other moms to know about the company and their product or services so that others could utilize them as well. There's nothing like finding a reputable company and knowing someone who has personally used them or their products to make someone want to trust that person and use them, also. It's all about networking! And of course vice versa when I have had a bad experience. If it's bad, I certainly am going to let that company know about it. And then it's up to them to change or improve their service or product.

Final words: I think companies do have to consider the economic mess our world is in. All countries around the world are being impacted in every way and form. Companies need to find solutions to problems we are currently having including any potential problems that may lie down the road, and then put their ideas out there. They need to find cost effective means of marketing and selling their product in today's and the future's world. And keeping that in mind, their products should be "smart" so that other moms will see them as a resourceful company. Mom influencers are very sociable people in today's world, and if a company can impress us with their products and services, we are a key to help spreading the word about their company to help them be successful.

Name: Romina Tibytt

Children: Three, ages 8, 5, and 2

Hometown: Teaneck, NJ

Website and blog: Mamá XXI www.MamaXXI.com

Approximate audience size: 20,000 visitors per month

Facebook Id: Mama XXI and Romina Tibytt

Twitter Id: @MamaXXI

Twitter Followers: 710

How do you define influence among moms? The influence of moms to other women always existed and always will, with or without blogs. Women always turn to mothers for advice, but now with the Internet, this amazing tool, this influence grows at levels that I beleive we never imagined before. Moms and women can share the adventures and misadventures of every day with a lot of other women who are the same, maybe living similar experiences, and can discuss a lot of topics and issues, and maybe never meetup in person. In my case, as a latina mommy, I've got a lot to say and share, from my perspective and about experiences with women in my virtual community.

Final words: Again, as a latina mommy blogger, I believe the power of blogs is amazing, and I never imagined the helpful tool that this could be; but now I am so happy helping others, latinas mommys and women like me, to live better lives in this beautiful country. Reading a blog is like talking with a person, so in today's world the influence is extended to every aspect of life.

Name: Karrie Truman

Children: Four, ages 11 (twins), 6, and 4

Hometown: Pasco, WA

Company Name(s): Happy Money Saver

Short description of business: HappyMoneySaver.com is a modern blog, sharing freebies and great deals to inspire you to save money, reduce your grocery bill by using coupons, and live happily on less. My dream was to be a stay-at-home mother of my four kids. However, even with my hard-working wonderful accountant husband, having four children on one income often left us struggling financially to make ends meet. We were living payday to payday, found ourselves in debt and felt like we would never get out of that cycle. I lived as thriftily as I could, trying to make money a little here or there by offering daycare or working part time, but I can remember praying a lot for help. One day a friend of mine told me she was a couponer and scored tons of items for FREE! I was intrigued. She taught me some basic couponing strategies and I tried them out at the stores. To say the least, I was hooked. The savings were just so amazing. I didn't even realize that it was possible to get things for FREE or cheap! After about six months of slowly learning and couponing as much as I could, I started to notice my monthly budget for food and toiletries had been cut in half! Plus I had food bursting from my pantry shelves and was able to have a nice food storage built up for a rainy day. I am able to give freely now to others in need with my excess as well. With the money I saved I was able to become a full-time stay-at-home mommy. I realize that couponing and living a thrifty life was the answer to my prayer and continues to be a great blessing the Lord has given to me.

Why did I start my blog? I was passionate about couponing and saving money, and you know what they say ... do something you are passionate about! So I decided to start a blog to post the deals I was doing, to share them with my many family members and friends. I fell in love with blogging about the deals, and I found that sharing and helping others brings a lot of joy and happiness to me. My blog has just taken off with thanks to the many wonderful readers who spread the word. My goal is to help families and individuals save money, give back and realize that they *can* make a great difference in their families and communities.

Websites or Blogs you own: Happy Money Saver http://happymoneysaver.com/

Approximate audience size: 17,000 + unique each month!

Facebook Id: HappyMoneySaver

Twitter Id: @HappyMoneySaver

Approximate # of followers: 250

How many moms do you typically interact with during the week offline? With church and school moms I would say I interact with more than 15-20 other moms during the week.

Offline Involvements: I offer once a month a FREE, with three food item donation, coupon class to people. Then I donate the huge bins of food plus toiletries to the local shelter or food bank.

What's the best way for companies to reach you as an influencer or as a mom? Email: happymoneysaver@gmail.com

How is the best way to work with you and your company? I love hosting giveaways, offering reviews of items and being sponsored by companies for blogging conferences. I love promoting companies via Facebook, and posting on my blog.

Are there companies who you feel are doing a great job connecting with moms? Groupon is a fun place where moms can go to save money and have fun.

How do you feel you influence moms online? By sharing great deals that inspire moms and dads to save money, reduce their grocery bills by using coupons and live happily on less. I have received a lot of emails from moms sharing how my website has helped them save enough money to stay home with their children. Family is so very important and the time we spend with them is priceless.

Final words: Moms are the first teachers a child will know in this world. It's important that they provide a good example and show lots of love so that children will grow healthy and strong. I think every mom should try to become as well rounded as possible so that they can pass on important lessons to their children.

Name: Emily VanVeelen

Children: Three, ages 4, 2.5 and 1

Hometown: Augusta, GA

Websites or Blogs you own: Fun with the VanVeelens http://vanveelenfun.blogspot.com/

Approximate audience size: 500

Facebook Id: Emily VanVeelen

Twitter Id: @emvanveelen

Online Involvements and associations: Momselect, Vocalpoint, One2One Network, BlogFrog, My BlogSpark

How many moms do you typically interact with during the week offline? 100+

Offline Involvements: Church, MOMS Club, Meetup group

What do you think is the biggest mistake companies make in trying to work with moms? Forgetting how busy life can get!! As a mom, we tend to forget about ourselves. I think companies should focus more on how their product or service can make life easier for moms.

How do you define influence among moms? I go to my friends for parenting advice, recipes, house cleaning tips, marriage tips, car buying advice. I think we as moms rely on each other's advice very much. I can do research on the web. But if one of my friends comes to me asking about Webkinz, for example, I can tell them how much my kids enjoy them and it will more than likely influence their decision to buy. Like I said before, I really think giving moms an opportunity to try things hands-on is a great marketing tool. If I really love something I tell everyone I know about it.

How do you feel you influence moms online? On the blog I do product reviews. I let my friends and family know if I have a new review or post via Facebook or phone. They check it out and I have had a lot of friends then ask about the product. Facebook has been an awesome tool for me. My friends and I are always sharing tips and telling one another about new products.

What motivates you to tell other moms (good or bad) about a company, brand or product? If a product I have tried is no good, I want to make sure my friends don't waste their time or money on it. If it is a great product, I feel the need to share. Because if it makes my life easier I can't keep that to myself.

How do you feel companies can best connect with moms, particularly those who are influencers? Give us more "try and tells" with a giveaway to readers. If I really enjoy the product I will push it! But more than likely if I get a coupon for one dollar off or something, I am not going to waste my money on trying it because I might not like it. I have really enjoyed the Mommy Parties. Even if some of my friends couldn't make it, if 10 moms did, I have reached those 10 moms and every person they have gone home to tell.

Name: Lori Vaughn

Children: Two, ages 19 and 9

Hometown: Keller, TX

Company Name(s): Southern Girl Bakery www.etsy.com/shop/twosoutherngirls

Short description of business: Bakery, mainly featuring Decorated Sugar Cookies. I also have started a new line called Cuppy Cakes which are my signature cupcakes squished into a container with topping and frosting; I saw a need for these when I was constantly getting requests to ship cupcakes. All of our products are available on ETSY under www.etsy.com/shop/twosoutherngirls. I started Two Southern Girls in July 2009 as a cooking website because I was sad that there are so many women who don't know how to cook. I decided to build my own site so I went online and learned CSS and HTML from W3schools. Once I got my feet wet I decided to expand my site into first a section on crafts and tutorials and then my Southern Living Section. After about six months when things were starting to pick up I added in my review and giveaway portions which I just love doing; I get to share some great products and give them away to my loyal readers. After a year and a half my website now consists of Southern Living; Reviews, Giveaways, Articles from Southern Living; My Life; Southern Recipes; Recipe Tutorials; Crafts; crafts Tutorials and ETSY Finds; Southern Girl Bakery; Link to my ETSY Shop. Southern Girl Bakery has always been in the picture, but I only decided to take it to ETSY 2 months ago. In the past my bakery items consisted mainly of cakes and cupcakes locally and I started thinking about what I could make that ship well: cookies. I got a few cookie cutters and watched a video on how to frost them and I was off. The funny part is that I can't draw to save my life, but when I use frosting I become an artist. I started with a few different items on ETSY and found that it's hard when people have never tasted your cookies. That's when I found my new avenue, sampler boxes; each month I participate in four different samplers which gets my product to the masses as a form of advertising. I think that I have found my new love in Sugar Cookies.

Websites or Blogs you own: Two Southern Girls www.twosoutherngirls.com; it's all about Southern Living Texas Style. I feature product reviews, giveaways and a daily section from Southern Living. I also have a recipe section with tutorials on cooking, which is why I started my website. I was sad that so many women and men today don't know how to cook, then I found out it was because no one ever showed them. So I give step-by-step instructions with pictures that everyone can understand. I was super excited when my own mom started getting my recipes; I am truly honored by this. I also have a craft section which features my daily finds on ETSY and other blogs with some great products and then I post a weekly craft tutorial with step-by-step instructions with pictures. Oh and the book reviews; I love to read, so I post as many reviews as I can. The last section is all about me, the rule is that if you interact with me it's fair game and anything can be posted, it's really just what happened in my life that day.

Approximate audience size: 63,000+ Page Views

Websites or blogs you contribute to: Crazy Coupon Mommy; I have a weekly craft post that I write for her which is a tutorial or party themed.

Twitter Id: @twosoutherngirl

Online Involvements and associations: Brand Ambassadors; Pear Tree Greetings, Milano Cookies, Gorton's Seafood, Frito Lay, Carmex Social Groups; Bloggy Moms, DFW Bloggers, Double Duty Divas, Mom TV, Southern Mamas

How many moms do you typically interact with during the week offline? About 20

Offline Involvements: All of my involvement is online, I used to be the President of The Social Committee with our HOA which hosted all of our community functions and parties, but since starting my own business some things had do go and this was one of them. My main involvement is online. It's funny how many "bloggy friends" that I have and talk to every day, but who I've never met.

What do you think is the biggest mistake companies make in trying to work with moms? They believe that we are just a bunch of women sitting around talking about who was on Dancing with the Stars last night when really we are the people who influence others. Think about all of those women without sites who are on Facebook and Twitter, they see your reviews and giveaways and it makes them go to the product site and see something that maybe they would not have seen before. Mom bloggers are the advertising of the present and future.

Are there companies who you feel are doing a great job connecting with moms? I work with several PR Firms that I just love; this is one place that moms' influence has caught on. Some of the other major brands are Frito Lay, Gorton's, and Tropicana. I also work with sites like Product Review Place, Pitch It to Me, Tomoson, She Blogs, Moms Select, and Business2Blogger that connect you to businesses that are mom friendly.

How do you feel you influence moms online? I do a lot of Link Love, especially in my Craft Section. I show ETSY Sites with very unique items and I am always getting feedback that people have gone to this site and bought from them. I also influence moms with my product reviews, which show you before you buy whether it's worth the money or not.

How do you feel you influence moms offline? Is it more than chatting in the carpool line? The main place that I influence offline is at the grocery store. I find myself giving advice on products and chatting to people in line, whereas before my website I would have never done this. The best part is when they take my advice and add the item to their cart.

What motivates you to tell other moms (good or bad) about a company, brand or product? The impact that it has on me. Recently I had a very bad experience at the grocery store which prompted a write-up on my site; this is actually very rare, but there are too many times to count the good products that I encounter every day. My favorite thing is to review TV shows, I tell a little bit about the background and why I love them. This is not a sponsored review, just my own.

How do you feel companies can best connect with moms, particularly those who are influencers? Reaching out to them on the different sites such as Product Review Place, Tomoson and Pitch It To me to bring more mom bloggers into their advertising campaign.

Name: Déa Viola

Children: Five, ages 23, 21, 9, 4, 22 months

Hometown: NJ, Essex County

Company Name(s): The Baby Flamingo Co., LLC5.

The Baby Flamingo Co. specializes in unique gift ideas for parents and their baby's basic needs. Starting date May 2006. I was motivated to launch my company when I realized how many creative ideas were out there, and that these ideas were not things that people necessarily needed to have but things that people wanted to have, either to give it as a gift or for personal use. The Baby Flamingo Co.'s mission is to create products that are unique gifts and products that help parents with their baby's basic needs. Also, we offer products that are a part of "an experience" as opposed to just a product/commodity only; *i.e.*, The Mama Taco Towel™, for instance. This is more than just a towel, it allows the caregiver and baby to bond before, during and after the bath; because it's hands-free, worry-free, and so soft, and the whole idea of the baby being The Mama Taco Towel's most wonderful filling, moms are given an extra reason to feel that the bath is a wonderful experience as opposed to a messy and slippery one. And for someone who is giving the towel as a gift, it makes them feel special for having brought something other than a bib or a blanket, a gift that no one else will likely bring to the baby shower.

Websites or Blogs you own: www.thebabyflamingoco.com

Websites or blogs you contribute to: Product-n-Press, ShopSight, BabyShowerGifts.net

Facebook Id: The Baby Flamingo Co.

Twitter Id: @thebabyflamingo

How many moms do you typically interact with during the week offline? 20 to 25

Offline Involvements: I volunteer as a music teacher for preschool children in my community for a Kindergarten Preparation Program. I am a part of a National Registry for Bone Marrow. I honestly hope to be given the honor to give back the gifts I have already been given.

Are there companies who you feel are doing a great job connecting with moms? I do hear of companies out there that are providing childcare facilities, and ways for moms to connect with other moms as a way of making moms' working experience less stressful. Also, in my own experience, Kimberly Clark/Huggies with the Huggies® MomInspired™ Grant Program, provides moms like myself the seed money to encourage us to continue to pursue our companies; these grants allow moms to work from home while parenting, thus encouraging moms to still pursue a career even though they are not sitting in an office.

How do you define influence among moms? Relatedness. Moms are nurturers by nature and they love to connect and relate to one another. They listen, they feel each other's pain and cheer for each other's triumph, particularly when it comes to sharing stories about their children. When they "relate" they can understand it, then they can "endorse" it.

How can companies best support your business or mission as a mom? By creating venues of advertising that are more than just feature to my product. People tend to relate to other people and then look at their companies. They may like a company, or a product, but they will love a person and then everything they are about. Perhaps my business account bank can feature me in an article as a "person in the community" in their monthly newsletter, in which they could share about me as person, business owner, mom, and client. I think it would be a good way to create a good business relationship and influence others to do the same. Personally, I would feel extremely validated and supported this way.

What motivates you to tell other moms (good or bad) about a company, brand or product? My customer service experience. That can make or break the deal for me. I've cancelled orders, no matter how much I've wanted a product, because of bad customer service; and I have purchased things I did not need just because I was encouraged by the customer service experience.

How do you feel companies can best connect with moms, particularly those who are influencers? Encourage them to tell their stories. Have newsletters that encourage moms to speak up. Everyone has something to share.

Final words: To me it all goes to the "personal input" and really how we relate to others. So moms should be heard because they are naturally looking for the well-being of others. They are powerful in the way they relate to everyone around them and because most of their decisions come from the necessity of making it work.

Name: Marcie Wahrer

Children: Three, ages 6, 4, and 2

Hometown: Las Vegas, NV

Short description of business: Obviously MARvelous started as a personal blog about myself and my family after much pushing from friends and family. I had been entering giveaways on other blogs for some time, but never thought of hosting my own product review/giveaway blog. When one opportunity fell into my lap, I accepted, and everything seemed to snowball from there! "If you build it, they will come."

Websites or Blogs you own: Obviously MARvelous, www.obviously-MARvelous.com

Approximate audience size: 1,200-1,300

Facebook Id: Obviously MARvelous

Twitter Id: @Mdub70deuce

Approximate # of followers: 790

Offline Involvements: I am an active member of the PTA in my daughter's elementary school, and I help in her school as time allows.

What do you think is the biggest mistake companies make in trying to work with moms? I think sometimes companies automatically assume we're in mom mode ALL the time. I think I speak for most of us when I say that we are still women, individuals, with goals that are not totally focused on just our children.

Are there companies who you feel are doing a great job connecting with moms? Go Gaga, Joovi, Youcast, Zehn Naturals, Funky Fleece, and Newhall Coffee.

Is there one moment when you realized you were impacting the life/lives of others? I recently hosted a giveaway of a baby carrier, and when I contacted the winner (who's won on my site before) she informed me that she was newly pregnant after a stillbirth and was so excited to have won a baby carrier, since she's been too nervous to buy anything herself.

How can companies best support your business or mission as a mom? I feel companies can best support my mission and my blog by understanding that it's a mutual agreement. I am not here for free products; however, I love to review, so by allowing me to do so you will get your name out there that much more. A review product is always cheaper than TV advertising and usually cheaper than Internet ads as well! This is a hobby for me, one I enjoy, and have fun doing.

Final words: I feel that mothers trust other mothers. New mothers trust mothers who have a bit more experience. It's amazing what word of mouth can truly do.

Name: Tamara Walker

Children: Two, ages 18 and 16

Hometown: Edmond, Oklahoma

Company Name(s): MomRN

Short description of business: MomRN.com and the Ask MomRN Show provide practical advice for raising a happy, healthy family. MomRN and her expert guests offer information and advice mixed with a healthy dose of encouragement and support for today's families.

MomRN was created in 2000 and the website launched in March 2001. MomRN was initially started as a ministry to offer support, encouragement, information and advice for parents using my combined knowledge and expertise as a mom, nurse, and professional child care provider. That mission has remained a constant even though the company has undergone several changes over the last decade. MomRN was started when my children were very young and has, until recently, been a part-time outlet for me to help others as I raise my kids. Now that my kids are older teenagers, I am working to expand MomRN's outreach through our website, talk show, videos, social networks, and through partnering with brands and other bloggers.

Websites or Blogs you own: MomRN.com (http://www.MomRN.com) and Ask MomRN Show (on BlogTalkRadio.com) at http://www.blogtalkradio.com/MomRN

Approximate audience size: Current average of nearly 3,100 listeners per month, and approximately 1,000 visitors per month to MomRN.com (newly redesigned and re-launched, so we are rebuilding our traffic right now to the site).

Websites or blogs you contribute to: PediatricSafety.net, and I have written guest posts for several other sites.

Facebook Id: Ask Mom RN Show and Mom RN

Twitter Id: @MomRN

Approximate # of followers: 6,640 followers

Online Involvements and associations: Prilosec OTC Official Internet Talk Show Host, Chevy Girl on the Go blogger, Earth Footwear Mom-Certified Exer-Walk shoe tester (wrote reviews and was featured in ad campaign in several national magazines), Chef Requested sponsored blogger, Tavern Direct blogger, Disney Social Media Moms member, MomSelect member, Global Influence member, Mom Spark Media member, judge for Moms Choice Awards, Brandfluential member, Mom Central member, Collective Bias member, CleverGirls Collective 1000 member and more. I have also been a Twitter party panelist for several brands and organizations.

What's the best way for companies to reach you as an influencer or as a mom? Send an email to MomRN@MomRN.com.

How is the best way to work with you and your company? MomRN is open to working with other companies, brands, and bloggers in multiple ways. I am very active on social media and have experience writing reviews, blogging and vlogging for companies, along with radio and TV interview experience. I'd love to partner with a family-friendly brand or a health-oriented brand to be their spokesperson for satellite media tours, promotional events, and ad campaigns.

What do you think is the biggest mistake companies make in trying to work with moms? The biggest mistake I see companies make is sending out an email or pitch with a generic greeting, such as, "Hi Blogger" or "Dear Blogger" instead of a personalized greeting, and/or sending a pitch that does not fit with the blogger's (or mom's) interests or site. Companies will be more successful in working with moms and especially with bloggers by taking the time to research who they are pitching to before the initial contact email or phone call. "Blind pitches" are a waste of time for both parties. As for reaching moms who are not bloggers, companies who talk down to moms are making a huge mistake. No mom wants to be made to feel like she is doing a bad job if she doesn't buy your product or use your services.

Is there one moment when you realized you were impacting the life/lives of others? It has been an honor to hear from many people about the impact MomRN and the Ask MomRN Show has had on their lives, but one that really stands out has to be hearing that my show helped save a struggling marriage.

How do you feel you influence moms offline? Is it more than chatting in the carpool line? I influence moms offline through my friendships, child safety classes, community service, and through my involvement in church and several organizations.

How can companies best support your business or mission as a mom? Companies can best support my business by advertising on my site, hiring me for blogger campaigns or as a brand ambassador or spokesperson, and by providing content that is useful for my audience. They can support my mission as a mom by providing products, services, and information that make my job as a parent easier.

Final words: There is no denying the powerful influence moms have upon all of these areas and more. I believe moms are more influential right now than at any time in the past. Moms make 80% of the purchasing decisions for their households and are the key decision makers for the health choices of their families. Moms are, in general, great at banding together to create positive change and to support good causes to make our world better for our children.

Name: Terri Walsh

Children: Three, ages 7, 4 and one on the way

Hometown: Richmond Va

Company Name(s): Stay at home mom

Websites or Blogs you own: Mom's Point of View http://mompointofview.blogspot.com and our personal website http://chrisandterri.com

Approximate audience size: 46 followers on Mom's Point of View

Websites or blogs you contribute to: N/A

Facebook Id: Moms Point of View

Twitter Id: @momspointofview

Offline Involvements: I have a girls' night out each month with women from my church.

What do you think is the biggest mistake companies make in trying to work with moms? I think companies are not all aware that each mom is different. They don't all do the same thing. Just because we are all moms doesn't mean we raise our kids the same. Some work and some stay at home, some do cloth diapers while others use disposables. There are so many different things out there that each mom does.

Are there companies who you feel are doing a great job connecting with moms? So far the best companies I have found for moms are Maria Bailey and Business to Blogger.

How can companies best support your business or mission as a mom? To get to know me as an individual person. I am not like every other mom out there.

What motivates you to tell other moms (good or bad) about a company, brand or product? My children are my biggest motivators. If I know there is a product out there that will help or hurt my children I am one of the first people to say so.

Final words: Educationally I have influenced a lot of moms to take the leap and start homeschooling with me. Some were not able to do it this year but a lot are considering it for next year. A lot of moms are scared that their kids will be antisocial but that is so not true. There is so much out there. So many groups in people's areas and so many other connections for mom to start. I know I couldn't be happier about my decision to homeschool so I love sharing that with my friends.

Name: Barb Webb

Children: Three, ages 8, 10, and 21

Hometown: Salt Lick, KY

Short Description of business: I began writing early in my career, settling into curriculum writing for the business sector. I entered the mainstream writing market in 2003, beginning with mom blogging, magazine articles and short stories. In 2005, McGraw Hill published my first non-fiction book, *The Mom's Guide to Earning and Saving Thousands on the Internet*. From 2005 forward I have continued to write magazine articles, short stories, and to develop my mom blogs. My motivation for writing has always been two-fold: a) my love of the craft and, b) to empower others to learn, grow, and succeed.

Websites or Blogs you own: Rural Mom www.ruralmom.com, MOMdotCOM.net www.momdotcom.net, BarbWebb.com www.BarbWebb.com, Country Bookshelf www.countrybookshelf.blogspot.com

Approximate audience size: 36,500 monthly

Websites or blogs you contribute to: Gather.com, AssociatedContent.com (feature craft write,), CreativeMindandHands.com (paper crafts editor), TwitterMoms.com, FTRHW.com, and a number of parent-friendly forums.

Facebook ID: Barb Webb or Rural Mom

Approximate # of Followers: 2,400

Twitter ID: @ruralmoms

Approximate # of Followers: 1,620

Online Involvements and associations: Nutrisystem Blogger, Clever Girls Collective member, Wisk Beta Blogger, TwitterMoms member, MomBloggers member, MySpark member, SheBlogs Network member, and maintain various other members in parenting and/or blogging communities throughout the web.

How many moms do you typically interact with during the week offline: 100 to 150+

Offline involvements: Student at MSU, substitute teacher at Menifee County School system, Menifee County Library Board Chairperson, Menifee County Sports and Recreation (coach), Wildlife Improvement Project volunteer, volunteer work with local charities, member of Romance Writers of America.

What's the best way for companies to reach me as an influencer or as a mom? Via email or mail. Send me a note or a product/service worth paying attention to that I feel compelled to share with others and it's a win.

What do you think is the biggest mistake companies make in trying to work with moms? The biggest mistake companies make in trying to work with moms is not taking the time to research their client to address needs and personalities. Often "moms" are lumped into one big category, the obvious—women with child(ren). But, there are many facets to consider, including location, profession, culture, and so forth. Every product/service is not always a good fit with every group of moms.

Nutrisystem has done a wonderful job connecting with mom bloggers and therefore, mom blogger followers. Very simply, they treat their mom clients as they would family and they work with us to understand the diverse needs of each mom.

How do you define influence among moms? I feel that I influence moms online by providing quality information that moms need, accurate product information and reviews, and by interacting with and offering support to my fellow moms. My mission is to empower, not to preach or to sell.

How can companies best support your business or mission as a mom? Companies can best support my mission by providing quality information and resources. Also, I'm a stickler for hands-on. If I'm going to support something, I have to have firsthand knowledge of the initiative or product. My pet peeve is being sent press releases from a company for a new product with an expectation that I will share it with my readers—when the company has no idea who my readesr are and I have no comfort level that the company offers an effective product.

Final words: I feel companies can best connect with mom influencers by building individual relationships and seeking to understand the audience the mom influencer connects with. For example, my audience comprises primarily rural and suburban moms. Sending me information on businesses located only in urban areas is not the best fit. Also, my blogs are not overtly promotional, they are conversational. Sending me a press release filled with promo information is not applicable and I'll rarely be able to use the information.

Name: April Welch

Children: Two, ages 16 and 12 (both boys)

Hometown: Leavenworth, WA

Company Name(s): The Mental Clutter Coach

Short description of business: I began as an Organizing Expert several years ago after asking myself that famous question: "What do I want to be when I grow up?" I knew I loved teaching skills and many friends and family commented on my innate ability to conquer chaos without batting an eye. Over the years I became the most educated and accredited organizer in WA State, working with clients ranging from students to families to elderly to hoarding. After speaking at the Mom 2.0 Summit 2010 in Houston on "Mental Clutter in a wired world," I realized I wanted to be a larger part of the social media industry. Throughout 2010 I worked to "re-brand" and essentially mold my old organizing business into a new (fully online) clutter coaching social media business. My next big project is what I'm calling "an experiment in social media." Using my experience as an organizer (seeing the big overwhelming picture and breaking it down into manageable pieces) I have launched the BE project: the Beyond Engagement project. The goal of the BE project is to collect as many bloggers into one database as possible, get to know their voices and connect them with up and coming campaigns via blogging tours, geo-tagging, guest contributions and quarterly columns; going Beyond the Engagement of just Facebook, Twitter, YouTube, and giving them a farther reach with their influence. This is the closest I've come to my mission statement. As for an exit plan, I don't have one. I believe social media is a fluid industry and I intend to continue riding the wave of change for a very long time.

Approximate audience size: 1,400 a month

Websites or blogs you contribute to: VolunteerSpot.com, MomItForward.com, BurbMom.net

Facebook Id: The Mental Clutter Coach

Twitter Id: @mental_clutter, @April_in_WA, @mental_clutter2

Approximate # of followers: 1,720

How many moms do you typically interact with during the week offline? 50-100

Offline Involvements: Blogger Outreach, Geo-Tagging Campaigns, Brainstorming and Goal Sessions, Curating Editorial Calendars, school volunteer

What's the best way for companies to reach you as an influencer or as a mom? Email if they want to understand my consulting programs, Twitter if they just want to chat and get to know me, Facebook if we run in the same circles, and the submission page on TMCC if they want to be considered for a video or picture campaign that can help others with their clutter or social media dilemmas. First and foremost though, they need to ask themselves if they are really advocating for an improved lifestyle. Those who listen to me and my team are looking for truthful, honest connections and I deliver on that daily.

What do you think is the biggest mistake companies make in trying to work with moms? By-passing the "getting to know you" stage: the moms you really want representing you will feel offended if you haven't taken the time to read them or even care what type of audience they attract. I'm a mom of a tween and a teen, I'm not exactly in the loop anymore on diapers and strollers. Hit me with ways to engage with the hormone-infested child claiming he's mine, then we've got something to discuss.

How do you define influence among moms? Those who stay connected to their support systems, have innovative ideas, are "listed" on Twitter, make people laugh and are able to inspire movement with their passions. Look for the folks who carry average scores among the PeerIndex, Klout and their own blog comments as a "report card" style assessment.

How do you feel you influence moms offline? Is it more than chatting in the carpool line? Absolutely! I've been told by clients that they "have my voice in their head." When they are about to purchase something, they ask themselves the questions we've discussed and determine whether they will bring the item home. Or when I receive an email that working through the clutter has been difficult but listening to my radio show on their iPod has helped them understand the baby steps necessary to move forward. But the single most influential "offline" action, is attending conferences, chatting it up during the networking time and then staying connected after the experience. This is where the village aspect of raising children nurtures us as women.

How can companies best support your business or mission as a mom? Easy: listen. If a company thinks I'm doing something in line with their goals, it should reach out and ask for my input, then listen to the answers. Compensate me for the consulting through both monetary means as wells as enacting the change we discussed.

Final words: I think there is plenty of room for everyone. I also think that anyone invested in this social media industry needs to understand not only are we changing with advances of technology but also as generations. The first group of "moms" are now facing tween/tweenhood, aging parents and possibly becoming a grandparent. All the while we still have "new moms" starting blogs every day. You couldn't grab a more diverse group if you tried. There is no formula, just finding where the positive outcomes are and backtracking to what worked, hopefully finding the intangible that worked and continuing forward with each new innovation.

Name: Stephanie Wetzel

Children: Three, ages 13, 11, and 8

Hometown: Atlanta, GA

Company Name(s): Story Gurus

Short description of business: Social media and blog management and consulting, personal humor blog. Started 2/09. Launched to fill a need for John C Maxwell (author and speaker) to enter the online realm. Created and designed his blog, started his Twitter and Facebook accounts. Mission: Grow and maintain a valid audience and community online, for purposes of connection and marketing.

Websites or Blogs you own: John Maxwell on Leadership http://johnmaxwellon-leadership.com and Red Clay Diaries http://redclaydiaries.com

Approximate audience size: John Maxwell: 11,000 feed subscribers, average 50,000 views/month. Red Clay Diaries: 130 feed subscribers, average 1,500 views/month.

Facebook Id: Stephanie Wetzel

Twitter Id: @redclaydiaries

Approximate # of followers: 5,500

What's the best way for companies to reach you as an influencer or as a mom? Email: redclaydiaries@gmail.com

What do you think is the biggest mistake companies make in trying to work with moms? Generic pitch, especially when they tell me that my blog is educational or profound (since it's a humor blog). Or a straight press release, no cover letter, no indication of what kind of offer they're making or what they're asking of me.

Are there companies who you feel are doing a great job connecting with moms? Disney seems to do well.

How do you feel you influence moms online? By talking about what I've tried out and what I like. Helping them find cool stuff online (*e.g.*, JibJab, Think Geek).

How can companies best support your business or mission as a mom? Impress me. If you or your product impress me, I'll write about you.

What motivates you to tell other moms (good or bad) about a company, brand or product? Extremes. Really bad or really good experience. "Cool" factor for me, personally.

How do you feel companies can best connect with moms, particularly those who are influencers? Let us try your product if you think it's something we'll like. Using focus groups, consulting, as well as brand ambassador gigs.

Name: Molly Wey

Children: One, age 2 ½

Hometown: Gainesville, VA

Short description of business: I started my blog in January 2009 after realizing how lonely being a stay-at-home mom could be. It was simply to vent and connect with other people in the same situation. Now some of my closest friends are ones met through blogging.

Websites or Blogs you own: Stilettos and Diapers www.stilettosanddiapers.com

Approximate audience size: 620

Twitter Id: @stilettodiapers

Approximate # of followers: 450

What do you think is the biggest mistake companies make in trying to work with moms? Probably thinking that we are only interested in "mom" things.

Are there companies who you feel are doing a great job connecting with moms? Disney is fantastic.

How do you feel you influence moms online? I love fashion and I try to show moms that you don't have to look frumpy to be comfy and a mom.

How can companies best support your business or mission as a mom? I think there are a lot of companies that do a great job via advertising: moms test groups, and giveaway items. I would like to see companies use larger groups of moms, though.

What motivates you to tell other moms (good or bad) about a company, brand or product? If I love it, I'll talk about it! I try to be very careful about talking about bad experiences until there has been adequate time for things to be made right.

How do you feel companies can best connect with moms, particularly those who are influencers? I have found that Twitter is my favorite place to connect with companies. Most mom influencers are on Twitter on a regular basis.

Name: Meg Wilson

Children: Two, ages 6 and 4

Hometown: Anderson, SC

Websites or Blogs you own: Muses of Megret http://www.musesofmegret.com; Muse Reviews http://www.musesofmegret.com/reviews, plus two private blogs to document children's homeschooling

Approximate audience size: 4,200 unique visitors monthly

Websites or blogs you contribute to: Heart of the Matter Online (www.heartofthematteronline.com)

Facebook Id: Megret7; MuseReviews

Twitter Id: @mgt777; @MuseReviews

Approximate # of followers: 370

Online Involvements and associations: Mom Select, BlogHer, Global Influence, MyBlogSpark, BookSneeze, Soft Scrub Captain, BSM Media, Skin MD Natural, CSN Stores Preferred Blogger

Offline Involvements: Local church involvement/attendance, homeschool association, church writing team volunteer

What's the best way for companies to reach you as an influencer or as a mom? Email: musesofmegret@gmail.com

Are there companies who you feel are doing a great job connecting with moms? Learning Curve, VTech, and Eleven Collection.

Is there one moment when you realized you were impacting the life/lives of others? When I gave away a car seat once to a family with a fifth child on the way, they weren't sure how they would afford another car seat for their family car, and the contest win was an answered prayer. I love it when random drawings end up being big blessings!

How do you feel you influence moms offline? Is it more than chatting in the carpool line? Yes, I have biweekly girl hang outs here at my house with like-minded moms. We talk about baby and kid products, clothes, toys. I show them some of the current items I'm reviewing in person. I also am asked often what I'm wearing and where'd I get it, where'd I buy my child's clothes or shoes, etc., by total strangers I come across day to day.

How do you feel companies can best connect with moms, particularly those who are influencers? More personal interaction–prompt reply to emails sent and questions asked–willingness to agree to giveaways when possible (to boost visibility and participation from readers).

Final words: As a stay-at-home, homeschooling mom, I do sometimes feel as if my voice doesn't matter as much–but when it comes to products for my family, my home, my children, who knows best? I do. I'm here 99.9% of the time. I'm the most qualified expert on the subject. Being treated as such would empower and uplift moms–make us more willing and excited to tell about products and services. When it comes to how I raise my children and run my home, I am more than just a number ... or a targeted, prospective blogger to bring in company revenue.

Name: Robyn Wright

Children: One, age 16

Hometown: St. Louis, MO

Short description of business: I've had various websites and work-at-home jobs over the years. For my blog, I just started it as a hobby in June of 2008 and it just sort of grew legs and took off. My only motivation was to share a bit of myself with friends and family and anyone else that wanted to listen. My goal now is to continue to do the same while also generating an income allowing me to continue to be at home as needed.

Website or Blogs you own: Robyn's Online World www.RobynsOnlineWorld.com

Twitter Id: @RobynsWorld

Approximate # of followers: 7,500

What's the best way for companies to reach you as an influencer or as a mom? As a person. I'm that above all; yes I'm a mom (and wife, geek, foodie, etc.) and I happen to have influence in those areas in social media, but above all I'm a real live person.

What do you think is the biggest mistake companies make in trying to work with moms? They seem to throw a very wide net out and try to find "Mom Bloggers" to work with and while they will find them that way, they really should be focusing in a bit more. Look for a few bloggers in different categories that all tie into the target you are trying to reach. Also, take the time to read about the moms you are trying to work with before pitching to them.

Are there companies who you feel are doing a great job connecting with moms? Definitely! Kellogg's has really been fabulous I think and has many different events happening at once to help spread the brand out. I think Microsoft is really working on reaching the mom audience as well and realizes that moms are tech savvy these days, too, and we rely on technology daily in our lives.

What motivates you to tell other moms (good or bad) about a company, brand or product? Honestly, I've got an opinion on just about everything and I like to talk. It really is as simple as that. Social media gives me multiple channels to talk and share those opinions and there always seems to be someone who is interested no matter what the topic.

Name: Dana Zeliff

Children: Two, ages 6 and 3 (both girls)

Hometown: Chesapeake, VA

Company Name(s): The Coupon Challenge

Short description of business: The Coupon Challenge provides coupons, freebies, store matchups, deal scenarios, giveaways, recipes, free/cheap events and much more! January 2010, I was always emailing out deals to friends and family. I felt like I was bombarding their inboxes with deals (which I was). I started the site as a place for them to view deals at their leisure, but it has become so much more.

Websites or Blogs you own: http://www.thecouponchallenge.com/

Approximate audience size: 6,000 unique visitors per month

Websites or blogs you contribute to: Money Saving Mom, Madame Deals, BeCentsAble's Grocery Gathering and more

Facebook Id: The Coupon Challenge

Approximate # of followers: 1,044

Twitter Id: @couponchallenge

Approximate # of followers: 1,275

Online Involvements and associations: Mom Select, Mom Bloggers Club, My Blog Spark

How many moms do you typically interact with during the week offline? 15+

Offline Involvements: PTA

What's the best way for companies to reach you as an influencer or as a mom? Email: thecouponchallenge@gmail.com

Are there companies who you feel are doing a great job connecting with moms? I've worked with a lot of amazing companies. Kidorable, EasyLunchBoxes, Gorton's Seafood & Gourmet Gift baskets to name a few.

How do you define influence among moms? Moms have always used the advice and opinions of other moms. We share parental strategies and products on everyday tasks such as diapers and baby food to nursery school and first reader books. The Internet has provided more opportunities for moms to reach out from their immediate surroundings and connect with moms all over the world.

How do you feel you influence moms offline? Is it more than chatting in the carpool line? I talk with my close friends regularly and with moms in my children's classes. I also chat with readers I meet at my local stores.

How can companies best support your business or mission as a mom? Remembering that our blogs are our business, but our first priorities are to our family.

What motivates you to tell other moms (good or bad) about a company, brand or product? I like to share companies and products that I believe will be either helping them save money or time.

SECTION 4
Moms Worth Mentioning

In this section I feel like an award winner on stage trying to thank everyone involved. For months the team at BSM Media has gathered names, interviewed moms and collected data on mothers we classify as Power Moms. The information contained in this directory was gathered from interviews, media kits, websites, bios and other public sources. We did our best to assemble the most accurate information for you, but we also encourage you to visit their sites, blogs or other media outlets for updates. The key thing is that these mothers meet our criteria to be called a Power Mom. You'll find community and business leaders, popular bloggers and podcasters. They vary in age, race and political thinking but all are engaged in impacting, influencing and engaging other mothers.

Alexandra Allred

Mother of 3, Texas

Website/Company: Author, (www.alexandrapoweallred.com)

Description: AlexandraPoweAllred.com is the official online home of author and screenwriter, Alexandra Allred. In addition to being an author, Alexandra enjoys sports and has won a gold medal at the US Olympic Nationals for bobsledding and competed on a Women's Professional Football team. Media may reach Alexandra on her site.

Affiliations: Mature Living, Muscle & Fitness Hers, Columbus Parenting Magazine, Sports Illustrated, Reading for the Blind & Dyslexic, Pregnancy.org

Awards: iParenting.com's Mom of the Month, qCircuit.com's Author of the Month

Offline: Alexandra has written 13 books including *Passion Rules! Inspiring Women in Business, Entering the Mother Zone: Balancing Self, Health and Family* and *Atta Girl! A Celebration of Women in Sports.*

Amilya Antonetti

Mother of 1, Pheonix, Arizona

Website/Company: Founder and Author, Amilya Antonetti, (www.amilya.com)

Description: Amilya's blog offers articles and advice on being a successful mother and businesswoman as well as green living, where all articles are based on a monthly theme. Amilya works with marketers and media on several opportunities including speaking engagements and interviews; more information about these opportunities can be found on her site.

Offline: Amilya is the author of *Why David Hated Tuesdays: One Courageous Mother's Guide to Keeping Your Family Toxin and Allergy Free* and *The Recipe: A Fable for Leaders and Teams*

Twitter: @amilya

Heather Armstrong

Mother of 2, Salt Lake City, UT

Website/Company: Founder, Dooce (www.dooce.com)

Description: For more information on these opportunities, please visit the site.

Offline: Author, *It Sucked and Then I Cried* and *Things I Learned About my Dad in Therapy*

Twitter: @dooce

Joanne Bamberger

Washington, DC

Website/Company: Founder, Pundit Mom (www.punditmom.com)

Description: Pundit Mom is the go-to source for all that is politics and motherhood, featuring articles on women in politics, presidential campaigns, feminism, equal pay, the economy, and changing the world. Pundit Mom works with media and marketers on a variety of opportunities including speaking engagements and interviews. For more information on these opportunities, please visit the site.

Awards: BlogHer's 2010 Voices of the Year Finalist, Blogtrepreneur Top 50 Mommy Blogs, Type-A Parent Top 20 Women Political Bloggers, Babble's 2010 Top (and Most Controversial!) Twitter Moms, BlogHer's 2010 Must-Read Political Blogs by Women, Babble's 2010 Top 50 Mom Blogs

Offline: Author, *Mothers of Intention: How Women & Social Media are Revolutionizing Politics in America*

Twitter: @punditmom

Lisa Belkin

Mother of 2, New York

Website/Company: Author, Motherlode (www.parenting.blogs.nytimes.com)

Description: In Motherlode, Lisa Belkin tackles homework, friends, sex, baby sitters, eating habits, work-family balance and so much more: subjects culled from the news, from her own experience as a parent, from the latest books and studies and reader input.

Offline: Author, *Life's Work: Confessions of an Unbalanced Mom*

Twitter: @lisabelkin

Lorin Beller Blake

Mother of 1, San Diego, California

Website/Company: Founder, Big Fish Nation (www.bigfishnation.com)

Description: Lorin and her team create programs that educate Women Business Owners to set obtainable goals and how to be successful. She offers practical hands-on ideas with a fresh perspective that leaves her audience inspired. Lorin has written her first book, *From Entrepreneur to Big Fish: 7 Principles to Wild Success* and is a contributing author in the book, *Roadmap to Success*. She's shared her powerful perspective for organizations such as the National Association of Women Business Owners, Canada's Women in Business National Expo, Sales and

Marketing Executives, Young Entrepreneurs Organization, eWomenNetwork as well as large Chambers and Associations. Lorin also co-hosts the Kathryn Zox Radio show on Voice America.

Awards: Women Supporting Women Award, Mentor of the Year

Twitter: @LorinB and @BigFishNation

Carla Birnberg

Mother of 1, Austin, Texas

Website/Company: Founder, Miz Fit Online (www.mizfitonline.com)

Description: Miz Fit Online offers musings on health and fitness from personal trainer, body building competitor and mom, Carla Birnberg. Featuring articles and tips, product reviews and giveaways, Miz Fit Online serves as a one-stop shop for moms looking to get fit. Carla offers several opportunities for partnership, from advertising to product reviews. More information on these opportunities is available on her site.

Affiliations: Yahoo Mother Board, Mom Talk Radio, Life...Supplemented™, Sears Fit Club

Awards: Austin Fit Magazine Fittest Mom

Offline: Author, *The Whole Megillah: Mitzvahs, Matzo Balls & Everything in Between*

Twitter: @mizfitonline

Gabrielle Blair

Mother of 6, Washington, DC

Website/Company: Founder, Design Mom (www.designmom.com), Co-Founder, Kirtsy (www.kirtsy.com)

Description: Design Mom merges motherhood with design, featuring articles and eye candy on artful living, written by graphic designer and mother, Gabrielle Blair. Kirtsy is described as that friend who always finds the best stuff, only better. The site features a collective of articles throughout the blogosphere on topics such as arts and entertainment, family and parenting, fashion and style, food and home, and more. Various partnership opportunities are available and are viewable through their respective sites.

Affiliations: Dwell Partner Network, Café Mom, Family Style

Awards: Time Magazine Top 50 Websites of 2010

Twitter: @designmom, @kirtsy

Beth Blecherman

Mother of 3, California

Website/Company: Founder, TechMamas (http://www.TechMamas.com/main/), Cool Mom Tech (http://www.coolmomtech.com/)

Description: Beth's personal blog, TechMamas, discusses technology, social media, and her obsession with consumer electronics. She has been covered in Wall Street Journal, Laptop Magazine, MSNBC, Parents.com, BBC, PBS, Forbes.com, Advertising Age and has written articles for Real Simple and Scholastastic.com. Beth is a host of MommytoMommy.tv, a new show online for moms. She is teaming up with the top female tech bloggers to launch vlog: Gadgetspin.com. Beth is also on the Board of Advisors for MommyTech summit at the Consumer Electronics Show.

Awards: Nielson Power Mom 50 influencers, Parents Magazine Power Mom, Forbes 100 Best Websites for Women, and @ForbesWoman Best Branded Women on Twitter

Twitter: @TechMama

Alice Bradley

Mother of 1, Brooklyn, New York

Website/Company: Founder, Finslippy (www.finslippy.com)

Description: Finslippy is the personal site of writer Alice Bradley, featuring a blog of her works including articles on motherhood.

Affiliations: Contributor, Berkeley Fiction Review, Fence Magazine, Redbook, Nerve, Wellesley Magazine, Good Housekeeping, Parents, the Onion, the Sun, and PBS.org

Twitter: @finslippy

Fiona Bryan

Mother of 3, Denver, Colorado

Website/Company: Founder, Bantering Blonde, (http://banteringblonde.com/), MomActive (http://momactive.com/)

Description: MomActive is a Multi Media outreach that includes a weekly Blog Talk Radio program, MomTV live stream video program, and the MomActive.com community and blog. Fiona started her blog, Bantering Blonde in 2008, and then launched MomActive in 2009. Mom Active is geared towards motivating and empowering women to be positive role models for their families. MomActive inspired her to create Active Mom Media, Inc. a company that focuses on connecting brands with the "active mom" community.

Affiliations: Fiona is involved with MomTV, Social Mom, Heart of Haiti Ambassador, Social Media panelist for CNN and Earth Footwear.

Awards: 2009 Top 50 Tweeple on PRSarahEvans.com

Twitter: @banteringblonde

Angela Burgin Logan

Mother of 1, Buffalo, New York

Website/Company: Founder, Ladies Live and Learn (www.ladiesliveandlearn.com)

Description: Ladies Live and Learn is the online home of Angela Burgin Logan, where she communicates and connects with moms on living happy and healthy lives, drawing from her own experience and from a community of moms to educate, support, and entertain. A large focus on the site is on public awareness of the pregnancy disorders preeclampsia and peripartum cardiomyopathy, which Angela has experienced herself with the birth of her child. Ladies Live and Learn offers partnerships with brands and media including advertising and sponsorships, which are viewable on the site.

Affiliations: Lifetime Moms

Twitter: @angelablogan

Kristen Chase

Mother of 4, Atlanta, Georgia

Website/Company: Founder, Motherhood Uncensored (www.motherhooduncensored.typepad.com)

Description: Motherhood Uncensored features the adventures of motherhood including the sometimes funny and often challenging parts. Kristen welcomes opportunities to work with brands and media. For more information on these opportunities, please visit the site.

Affiliations: Contributor, Cool Mom Tech, The Stir, Cool Mom Picks and The Shredheads

Offline: Naptime Nookie with the Mominatrix radio show

Twitter: @thatkristen

Mallika Chopra

Mother of 2, Santa Monica, California

Website/Company: Founder, Intent (www.intent.com), MyPotential.com (www.BabyPromises.com)

Description: Mallika is the founder and CEO of Intent.com. She launched Intent in hopes to connect with others by sharing and listening to their stories. Intent.com lets women create profiles and posts their goals/intents for the day, week, month, and year. She launched mypotential.com with her father, Deepak Chopra in earlier 2000. Mallika is also the president of Chopra Media LLC and is on the board of directors of Virgin Comics. She has also written two books, *100 Promises to My Baby*, and *100 Questions from Her Child*. Mallika is a spokesperson for UNICEF, raising awareness for orphans who have been affected by HIV and AIDS.

Twitter: @mallikachopra

Kathryn Cloward

Mother of 1, San Diego, California

Website/Company: President and Owner, Guardian Foods, Natural Kidz, Kandon Unlimited and Owner and Author, Kathryn the Grape Company (www.kathryncloward.com)

Description: KatherynCloward.com serves as the online home of Kathryn Cloward, author, entrepreneur and mom, with more than five resolutions for everything from healthy foods and organic products to public speaking and publishing. Media may reach Kathryn through her site.

Offline: Kathryn has written a children's book series titled *Kathryn the Grape*.

Twitter: @kathryncloward

Janice Croze

Mother of 2, Vancouver, Canada

Website/Company: Co-founder, 5 Minutes for Mom (www.5minutesformom.com)

Description: 5 Minutes for Mom is an essential, go-to site for moms that entertains and informs, while promoting the online mom community, created by twin sisters, Janice and Susan Croze. The Croze sisters offer several opportunities to partner with brands and media. For more information on these opportunities, please visit the site.

Twitter: @5minutesformom

Susan Croze

Mother of 2, Vancouver, Canada

Website/Company: Co-founder, 5 Minutes for Mom (www.5minutesformom.com)

Description: 5 Minutes for Mom is an essential, go-to site for moms that entertains and informs, while promoting the online mom community, created by twin sisters, Janice and Susan Croze. The Croze sisters offer several opportunities to partner with brands and media. For more information on these opportunities, please visit the site.

Twitter: @5minutesformom

Hollie Danklefsen

Mother of 2, Idaho Falls, ID

Website/Company: Co-founder, Real Moms Real Views (www.realmomsrealviews.com)

Description: Real Moms Real Views features articles and tips, product reviews and giveaways for real moms. Real Moms Real Views works with brands and media on a number of opportunities. For more information on these opportunities, please visit the site.

Affiliations: Wisk Mom, Kolcraft Mom, Infantino Test Drive Mom

Twitter: @agiveawaydaily

Lisa Douglas

Mother of 6, Fort Polk, Louisiana

Website/Company: Founder, Crazy Adventures in Parenting, (www.crazyadventuresinparenting.com)

Description: Crazy Adventures in Parenting features the adventures of an Army wife of six, featuring product reviews and tips on parenting, travel and more. Lisa is happy to work with media and marketers on promotional opportunities including advertising, product reviews, and sponsorships. More information regarding these opportunities is available on the site.

Affiliations: Nintendo, Constructive Playthings Moms, Unilever, Truvía

Twitter: @crazyadventures

Stephanie Elie

Mother of 2, California

Website/Company: Founder, Bizzie Mommy (www.bizziemommy.com)

Description: Bizzie Mommy is an online resource for busy moms on topics such as motherhood, working from home, technology, and photography. Bizzie Mommie works with media and brands on everything from advertising to product reviews. More information regarding these opportunities is available on the respective sites.

Affiliations: Lifetime Moms

Awards: Nielsen Top 50 Power Moms (2009 & 2010), Forbes Top 100 Websites for Women,

Twitter: @bizziemommy

Carol Evans

Mother of 2, Chappaqua, New York

Website/Company: Founder, Bonnier Corporation: Working Mother Media (www.workingmothermediainc.com)

Description: A dedicated champion of culture change, Working Mother Media, a subsidiary of Bonnier Corp., is the largest multimedia company in the country focused on diversity and the advancement of women. Encompassing *Working Mother* magazine, Diversity Best Practices, the National Association of Female Executives (NAFE), the Working Mother 100 Best Companies for Working Mothers, Best Companies for Multicultural Women, NAFE Top Companies for Executive Women, Working Mother & Flex-Time Lawyers Best Law Firms for Women, Balance Seekers, Best Green Companies for America's Children and Best Practices in Corporate Communications, Working Mother Media also includes a dynamic conference and events division.

Twitter Id: @CarolEvansWM

Awards: Highest Leaf Award from the Women's Venture Fund, the Work-Life Legacy Award from the Families and Work Institute, YWCA Women Achiever's Hall of Fame award, Admiral Grace Hopper Women's Diversity Champion Award from the U.S. Navy, 21 Most Intriguing People by *MIN* magazine in 2003.

Anna Fader

Mother of 2, New York, New York

Website/Company: Founder, Mommy Poppins (www.mommypoppins.com)

Description: Mommy Poppins is the New York Mom's one-stop shop for parenting news, free weekend events, art and nature activities, kid-friendly itineraries, day trips and giveaways. The site also includes an in-depth guide for navigating New York's preschools, summer camps, classes, birthday parties and more. Anna offers advertising on her site in addition to other marketing opportunities. Complete advertising and media information can be found on her website.

Twitter: @mommypoppins

Lori Falcon

Mother of 2, Texas

Website/Company: Founder, A Cowboy's Wife (www.acowboyswife.com), E-living Media and My Wooden Spoon (www.elivingmedia.com)

Description: Lori is the Owner and Founder of three blogs. My Wooden Spoon is where she shares family recipes and her passion for food & kitchenware. A Cowboy's Wife is where she chronicles her reflections in words and photos of cowboy life and shares her personal thoughts and feelings on just about anything. eLiving Media is a lifestyle featuring articles about technology and the latest in hot topics such as sports and the auto industry. Lori works with media and marketers on a number of opportunities. For more information on these opportunities, please visit the site.

Affiliations: WalMart Mom, Velveeta Kitchenista, Wilton Ambassador

Twitter: @acowboyswife

Beth Feldman

Mother of 2, Westchester, New York

Website/Company: Founder, Role Mommy (www.rolemommy.com)

Description: Role Mommy was created on the premise that helping your children realize their dreams doesn't mean you have to give up on your own. Featuring blog articles on mommyhood, product reviews, a book club, radio show, events, and even a business directory, Role Mommy is an online community where moms become role mommies. Role Mommy welcomes the opportunity to work with marketers and brands on everything from advertising to event sponsorships. More information regarding these opportunities is available on the site.

Affiliations: Lifetime Moms, MTVN Tribes

Twitter: @rolemommy

Nicole Feliciano

Mother of 2, New York, New York

Website/Company: Founder, Mom Trends (www.momtrends.com) and Mom Trends NYC (www.momtrendsnyc.com)

Description: Mom Trends is the one-stop shop for fashionable moms, featuring trends and tips for living a fashionable and fabulous life. Mom Trends partners with brands and media on various opportunities including advertising and product reviews, as well as speaking engagements. For more information on these and other opportunities, please visit the site.

Affiliations: Momtastic Expert Contributor, Lifetime Mom Affiliate

Twitter: @momtrends

Justice Fergie

Mother of 3, Seattle, Washington

Website/Company: Co-Founder, Blogalicious Weekend (www.blogaliciousweekend.com), Mama Law (www.mamalaw.com), and Founder, Food"e"(www.justfergie.com)

Description: Blogalicious Weekend serves as the web space for the

Blogalicious Weekend conferences, which place women bloggers face-to-face with their peers, marketers and brands. Mama Law is an award winning blog run by three lawyers, who just happen to be moms. Best known as a lifestyle parenting blog, Mama Law focuses mainly on the topics of work-life balance, homemaking and pop culture. Justice Fergie offers various online and offline marketing opportunities which are viewable on their respective sites.

Affiliations: Mom Bloggers Club, BitMoms, member of Yahoo Mother-Board, Work It Mom

Offline: Blogalicious Weekend

Twitter: @justicefergie, @mamalawgrp, @beblogalicious

Alyssa Francis

Mother of 4, Texas

Website/Company: Founder, Keeping the Kingdom First (www.kingdomfirstmom.com)

Description: Kingdom First Mom aims to balance the journey of motherhood while offering new and creative ways to reduce spending in order to increase giving, featuring topics such as faith, family, and frugality. Kingdom First Mom offers a variety of opportunities to work with brands and media. For more information on these opportunities, please visit her site.

Affiliations: Lifetime Moms

Twitter: @kingdomfirstmom

Leslie Gail

Mother of 2, Denver, Colorado

Website/Company: Founder, New Life Focus (www.newlifefocus.com)

Description: New Life Focus is the online home of Leslie Gail, professional life coach, who offers practical advice on topics from finding your purpose, improving relationships, and simply having more fun in life. Leslie offers a variety of partnerships including advertising and sponsorship opportunities. For more information on these opportunities, please visit her site.

Affiliations: MomTV

Offline: Author of *Life Simplified: A weekly guide to creating a life you love!*

Twitter: @gr8lifecoach

Jessica Gottlieb

Mother of 2, Los Angeles, California

Website/Company: Founder, (www.jessicagottlieb.com)

Description: JessicaGottlieb.com serves as the personal blog and website of Jessica, featuring tips on social media and technology. Jessica works with advertisers and media on a number of opportunities. For more information on these opportunities, please visit the site.

Affiliations: Contributor, Momovation

Awards: Nielson's 2008 & 2009 Power Mom, Babble's Top 50 Mom Bloggers, Forbes 14 Women to Follow on Twitter, Hive Awards Honorable Mention

Twitter: @jessicagottlieb

Trisha Haas

Fort Collins, Colorado

Website/Company: Founder, Mom Dot (www.momdot.com)

Description: Mom Dot features personal life stories from Trisha, including crafting ideas, Amazon finds, coupon codes and fashion. Mom Dot works with advertisers and media in a number of ways. For more information on these opportunities, please visit the site.

Twitter: @momdot

Julie Hammerstein

Mother of 2, Denver, Colorado

Website/Company: Founder (www.juliehammerstein.com) (www.fatisnotafourletterword.com)

Description: JulieHammerstein.com serves as the online home of Julie Hammerstein, certified nutritionist, speaker and author, where she offers advice on nutrition, creating a healthy mindset and raising healthy children, as well as yummy recipes any mother (and child) is sure to love! Julie partners with brands and media on opportunities including advertising and speaking engagements. For more information on these opportunities, please visit her site.

Affiliations: MomTV

Offline: Author, *Fat is Not a Four-Letter Word*

Catherine Hickem

Mother of 2, Delray Beach, Florida

Website/Company: Founder, Intentional Moms (http://www.intentionalmotherhood.com/)

Description: Catherine started Intentional Moms in 2005, to serve as the national resource for information, support and insights on motherhood. She encourages moms to be proactive in their relationships in all seasons of mothering. Catherine has contributed to NewBaby.com and PreciousMoments.com, she is also known as the "Monday Morning Mom Coach" in several radio markets. Catherine wrote her book, *Raising Your Children With No Regrets – 7 Principles of an Intentional Mother*, in 2007 and is currently working on a book that addresses parenting adult children. She has appeared on Lifetime's show Balancing Act and is currently featured on Fox 10 News.

Twitter: @CatherineHickem

Nirasha (Niri) Jaganath

Mother of 1, Boston, Massachusetts

Website/Company: Founder, Mommy Niri (www.mommyniri.com)

Description: Mommy Niri features content ranging from, philanthropic blogger, Niri's personal opinions on parenting and education, to product reviews, contests and sage social media advice. Niri blogs about her various charitable projects, including Rwanda Path2Peace, building playgrounds with Kabloom, and the End Child Hunger campaign. You can find more information on brand marketing through Mommy Niri on her site.

Affiliations: Office Max Moms, Serves on Sprout's team of experts, Heart of Haiti Ambassador

Sugar Jones

Mother of 4, San Diego, California

Website/Company: Founder, Sugar In the Raw (www.sugarjonesblog.com)

Description: Sugar in the Raw serves as the personal website of Sugar Jones, social media consultant, writer, traveler and mom of four, where she blogs about her life, riddled with tips and news covering a wide range of topics including lifestyle, travel, family, learning, food and religion. Sugar offers various marketing opportunities to brands large and small. More information on these opportunities is available on her site.

Affiliations: Lifetime Mom Affiliate

Twitter: @sugarjones

Twitter: @mommyniri

Isabel Kallman

Mother of 1, New York, New York

Website/Company: Founder, Alpha Moms (www.alphamoms.com)

Description: Alpha Moms serves as the go-to resource for new and current moms, featuring advice on pregnancy, parenting and family fun. Alpha Moms works with marketers to reach their vast networks of mothers in a variety of ways. More information on these opportunities is available on the site.

Twitter: @alphamom

Amy Keroes

Mother of 2, Mill Valley, California

Website/Company: Founder, Mommy Tracked (www.mommytracked.com)

Description: Mommy Tracked features regular columns by experts on motherhood–moms! Other content includes free downloads for the modern mommy toolbox, interviews of working moms, an online book group featuring book recommendations, and the site even offers product reviews, deals and discounts. Mommy Tracked offers a large variety of marketing opportunities for brands. More information is available on the site regarding these opportunities.

Twitter: @mommytracked

Christine Koh

Mother of 2, Boston, Massachusetts

Website/Company: Founder, Boston Mamas (www.bostonmamas.com)

BostonMamas is a one-stop source for cool ideas and resources for families in Boston and beyond. Marketers and media can work with Christine in a number of ways from paid advertising to traditional product pitches. Complete media kits and advertising guidelines are available on her site.

Affiliations: March of Dimes Mom, The Mom Bloggers Club, Columnist of Minimalist Mama for Shoestring Magazine, Parent Ambassador for Healthy Child Healthy World, Founding Mother of Be Out There by the National Wildlife Federation.

Awards: 2009 Nielsen's Power Moms 50 List, Babble.com's 50 best Mommy Bloggers

Twitter: @bostonmamas

Erika Lehmann

Mother of 1, Louisiana

Website/Company: Founder, Chic Shopper Chick (www.chicshopperchick.com)

Description: Chic Shopper Chick is the go-to source for women to find tips on fashion, beauty, travel, technology, kids gear, and more. Featuring articles from blogger Erika Lehmann, a self-professed shopping, beauty, and fashion addict. Chic Shopper Chick works with brands and media on everything from advertising and giveaways to conference and event sponsorships. More information about these opportunities can be found on the site.

Affiliations: Wal-Mart Moms, Frito Lay's Fabulous 15, Wishpot Mom Expert

Twitter: @erikalehmann

Lindsay Maines

Mother of 3, District of Columbia

Website/Company: Founder, Rock and Roll Mama (www.rockandrollmama.com)

Description: Rock and Roll Mama was created as a way to "to explore the different ways music shapes the past, present and future of mamas far and wide." Featuring articles, reviews, and giveaways on topics such as diy, motherhood and, you guessed it, rock and roll. Rock and Roll Mama welcomes partnerships with brands and media. More information regarding these opportunities can be found on the site.

Affiliations: Lifetime Moms

Twitter: @rockandrollmama

Jennifer McCullar

Mother of 3, Tracy, California

Website/Company: Founder, Cal Delta Mommies (www.caldeltamommies.com) and The Mommies Network (www.themommiesnetwork.blogspot.com)

Description: The Mommies Network is a 501c(3) non-profit organization dedicated to helping moms find support and friendship in their local community. As part of The Mommies Network, CalDeltaMommies.com is a free community for moms in San Joaquin and Stanislaus Counties, California. Jennifer works with brands and media on a number of opportunities. For more information on these opportunities, please visit the site.

Twitter: @greenidmama

Emily McKhann

Mother of 2, Larchmont, New York

Website/Company: Co-Founder, The Motherhood (www.themotherhood.com), The Motherhood Creative (www.themotherhoodcreative.com)

Description: The Motherhood is a website dedicated to mothers helping mothers make life a little better every day. Centered around Circles, on-going conversations by members, and Talks, scheduled live conversations featuring expert hosts, The Motherhood is a one-stop social network by moms and for moms. Through her site, The Motherhood Creative, The Motherhood offers a wide range of opportunities to work with brand both online and off. For more information on these opportunities, please visit the site.

Awards: 2008 WebAward for Family Standard of Excellence, Parents Magazine Top Power Moms on the Web

Offline: Co-Author, *Living With the End in Mind*

Twitter: @emilymckhann, @themotherhood

Dawn Meehan

Mother of 6, Chicago, Illinois

Website/Company: Founder, Because I Said So (www.mom2my6pack.com), Because I Said So Reviews (www.dawnmeehan.blogspot.com)

Description: Mom 3 My 6 Pack is the home of author Dawn Meehan, where she blogs about her often humorous adventures as a single mom with six kids. Dawn also offers product reviews on her review site, Because I Said So Reviews. Dawn offers to brands several marketing solutions, including advertising and product reviews. More information on these opportunities is available on her respective sites.

Awards: 2008 Best Parenting Blog by Blogger's Choice, Babble's Top 35 Mom Bloggers

Offline: Dawn is the author of *Because I Said So: And other Tales from a Less-than-Perfect Parent* and *You'll Lose the Baby Weight: And Other Lies about Pregnancy and Childbirth*

Twitter: @mom2my6pack

Jennifer Mercurio

Mother of 2, Orlando, Florida

Website/Company: Founder, Double Duty Mommy (www.doubledutymommy.com)

Description: Double Duty Mommy features the life and times of mother Jennifer featuring useful articles, giveaways and reviews. Jennifer welcomes the opportunity to work with brands and media on a number of opportunities. For more information on these opportunities, please visit the site.

Affiliations: Business 2 Blogger, Bloggy Moms, Purex Insider

Twitter: @mommaJWoww19

Cooper Munroe

Mother of 4, Pittsburgh, Pennsylvania

Website/Company: Co-Founder, The Motherhood (www.themotherhood.com), The Motherhood Creative (www.themotherhoodcreative.com)

Description: The Motherhood is a website dedicated to mothers helping mothers make life a little better every day. Centered around Circles, on-going conversations by members, and Talks, scheduled live conversations featuring expert hosts, The Motherhood is a one-stop social network by moms and for moms. Through her site, The Motherhood Creative, The Motherhood offers a wide range of opportunities to work with brand both online and off. For more information on these opportunities, please visit the site.

Awards: 2008 WebAward for Family Standard of Excellence, Parents Magazine Top Power Moms on the Web

Twitter: @coopermunroe, @themotherhood

Clarissa Nassar

Mother of 3, New York

Website/Company: Founder, The Posh Parent & Company (www.theposhpreneur.com)

Description: After the birth of her second child in 2006, her company The Posh Parent began to take shape. Being a stay at home mom gave Clarissa the ability to grow into something bigger; she began gaining attention as her handmade blankets were being gifted to celebrities such as Jessica Alba, Tori Spelling, Nicole Richie and Gwen Stefanie to name a few. Shortly after, she began to blog about her journey. Her blog consists of fashion and beauty, social media, reviews and give-aways, entertaining and traveling tips, and much more! Clarissa has worked with Medela as a Breastfeeding Maven, Glamour Magazine Glambassador for the Upstate New York area, Miss April in the upcoming Hot Bloggers Calendar for 2011, Walmart Mom's, Sam's Club Bloggers, Soft Scrub Team Captain, Purex Insider and MomTV's The Glam Life with The POSHpreneur.

Twitter Id: @thePOSHpreneur, @momtvclarissa, @glamlifemama

Shaina Olmanson

Mother of 4, Minnesota

Website/Company: Founder, Food for my Family (www.foodformyfamily.com)

Description: Food for my Family is a website featuring for foodie moms trying to help their family to eat right and enjoy food while still saving money and time. Shaina works with brands and media on a number of opportunities. For more information on these opportunities, please visit the site.

Affiliations: Lifetime Moms

Twitter: @foodformyfamily

Kim Orlando

Mother of 3, Connecticut

Website/Company: Founder, Traveling Mom (www.travelingmom.com)

Description: Traveling Mom is the go-to source for stories and tips for the modern traveling mom, featuring content from and for every type of mom, including moms with small kids, big kids, and even grandparents. Traveling Mom works with brands and media on customized promotional concepts to harness the power of their network of traveling moms. More information is available on the site regarding these opportunities.

Affiliations: Lifetime Digital

Awards: Top 4 Traveling Site by Sherman Travel

Twitter: @travelingmoms

Amy Platt

Mother of 2, Long Island, New York

Website/Company: Founder, Long Island Parent Source (www.liparentsource.com)

Description: Long Island Parent Source is an online guide that centralizes resources for families on Long Island, featuring a directory of local resources, playgroups, an events calendar, activities and parent tips for pregnancy through the teen years. Amy is happy to work with media and marketers on a number of partnership opportunities. For more information on these opportunities, please visit the site.

Twitter: @liparentsource

Katja Presnal

Mother of 3, New York, New York

Website/Company: Founder, Skimbaco Lifestyle (www.skimbaco-lifestyle.com), Skimbaco Home (www.skimbacohome.com), Skimbaco Travel (www.skimbacotravel.com) and launching soon is Skimbaco Food (www.skimbacofood.com)

Description: Skimbaco means living life to its fullest, and Skimbaco Lifestyle, Home, Travel and Food offer up great advice on doing just that. With featured content on each separate site with tips, product reviews, photos, recipes and more. Skimbaco offers various opportunities for partnership including advertising and product reviews. For more information on these opportunities, please visit the respective sites.

Affiliations: Lifetime Digital

Twitter: @skimbaco, @katjapresnal

Jaime Prideaux

Mother of 2, Kansas

Website/Company: Founder, Coupons and Freebies Mom (www.couponsandfreebiesmom.com)

Description: Coupons and Freebies Mom is the one-stop shop for moms looking for great deals, freebies and coupons, featuring money saving tips for even the most frugal moms. Jaime has numerous opportunities available to work with brands and media. For more information on these opportunities, please visit the site.

Twitter: @couponsfreebie

Janet Ridgeway

Mother of 2, Pace, Florida

Website/Company: Founder, Frugal and Focused (www.frugalandfocused.com)

Description: Frugal and Focused is the online destination for moms interested in saving money and living frugally, including articles, tips, and resources covering a wide range of topics, quick and cheap recipes and menu plans, to coupons and giveaways. Opportunities for partnership with brands and media are viewable on the site.

Twitter: @frugalfocused1

Kimberly Seals Allers

Mother of 2, New York

Website/Company: Founder, The Mocha Manual (www.mochamanual.com)

Description: The Mocha Manual serves is a fast growing online lifestyle publication for today's African American moms and moms-to-be, covering topics such as pregnancy, baby's first year, toddler years, single moms, mompreneurs, and more. The Mocha Manual partners with media and marketers on a number of opportunities, which are viewable on the site.

Affiliations: Lifetime Moms, Lifetime Digital

Offline: Creator and Author of The Mocha Manual™ series of books including: *The Mocha Manual to a Fabulous Pregnancy*, *The Mocha Manual* *to Turning Your Passion into Profit*, *The Mocha Manual to Military Life—A Savvy Guide for Wives, Girlfriends & Female Service Members* (written with Pamela McBride)

Twitter: @mochamanual

Joyce Shulman

Mother of 2, New York

Website/Company: Co-founder, Macaroni Kid (www.national.macaronikid.com)

Description: Macaroni Kid is dedicated to delivering the scoop on all the family-friendly events and activities happening in various communities each week. A weekly newsletter is sent out giving readers events, shows and family hot spots. The newsletter is emailed to thousands of moms and dads each Thursday and then posted onto the website.

Twitter: @macaronikidhq

Sharon Silver

Mother of 2, Arizona

Website/Company: Founder, Proactive Parenting (www.proactiveparenting.net/home)

Description: With an education in Parenting and Early Childhood Development, four certifications as a Parent Educator, as a facilitator for The Cline/Fay Institute and Redirecting Children's Behavior, and with practical experience as the mother of two young adults, Sharon has the knowledge to teach parents how to respond, and not react. The methods used at Pro*active* Parenting™ are responsive, firm yet empowering, and instinctual, allowing parent and child to remain connected, no matter what issue they're facing. Sharon is currently the host of Stop Reacting – Start Responding on MomTV.com. Through Pro*active* Parenting, Sharon does telephone and online seminars for corporations and working parents and does live seminars. Sharon has also been on the Oprah Winfrey Show talking about "Hitting, Spanking, Smacking: Should it happen to your child?"

Twitter: @Sharon_Silver

Shelby Skrhak

Mother of 1, Plano, Texas

Website/Company: Founder, Fat Head Dog (www.fatheaddog.com)

Description: Fat Head Dog offers valuable tips and articles to any mother looking to save a buck, from freebies and product reviews to coupons and giveaways. Brands and media may work with Fat Head Dog on a variety of opportunities viewable on the site.

Affiliations: Mom Select, Mom Central, Psst...Network, TJX Insider, Member of the CVS Pharmacy Advisory Panel, BlogHer, One2One Network

Twitter: @fatheadtweet

Jennifer Houck Spink

Mother of 2, Raleigh, North Carolina

Website/Company: Founder, One Mom's World (www.onemomsworld.com)

Description: One Mom's World features regular tips and reviews on everything from life as a mom to travel destinations, recipes and technology. Jennifer is happy to work with brands on advertising, giveaways and product reviews. More information on these opportunities is available on her site.

Affiliations: Pillsbury My Crescent Wow

Twitter: @onemomsworld

Twitter: @jhammerstein

Lisa Stone

Mother of 3, San Francisco, California

Website/Company: Co-founder of BlogHer (www.blogher.com)

Description: BlogHer is the leading participatory news, entertainment and information network for women online. Lisa blogs on her personal blog, Surfette, and also blogs on BlogHer, often on politics and media. Lisa has launched successful online networks and interactive programming for many national brands, including Hearst and Rodale magazines, E! Television/Online, HBO's Sex and the City, Bloomberg, Glam Media, Knight Ridder and Law.com. She has written for The New York Times, the Los Angeles Times, CNN, The Oakland Tribune, Publisher's Weekly and Frommer's, among other publications.

Awards: First internet journalist awarded a Nieman Fellowship by Harvard University.

Twitter: @lisastone

Aparna Vashisht-Rota

Mother of 2, San Diego, California

Website/Company: Founder, Parentella (www.parentella.com)

Description: Parentella is an online social network for parents and teachers. Their goal is to allow better communication about kids' education by enabling free-flowing conversations between parents and teachers. Parentella has various advertising opportunities available to brands. For more information about these opportunities, please visit the site.

Twitter: @parentella, @ApsatParentella

Christine Young

Mother of 7, Sacramento, California

Website/Company: Founder, From Dates to Diapers (www.fromdatestodiapers.com)

Description: On From Dates to Diapers, Christine Young blogs about life as a young mom with seven kids, shares parenting advice, and writes her thoughts and opinions about family-friendly products. Christine welcomes partnerships with marketers and media from advertising to product reviews. More information about these opportunities is available on her site.

Affiliations: Backyard Discovery Ambassador, WalMart Moms

Awards: Nielsen's Top 50 Power Moms

Twitter: @youngmommy

Section 5
Celebrity Moms

Reese Witherspoon, Sarah Palin, Tori Spelling and Felicity Huffman. These are just a few of the women who not only grab the headlines but also have children. Is it enough to be famous and a mother to be a Power Mom to the average Middle American, Main Street mother? While we didn't have the opportunity to ask these women ourselves about the ways they feel they influence other moms, we did feel it was important to include some of the most visible Celebrity Moms in our directory of Power Moms. Notice I didn't say most *popular* moms. This is because some of the most media-saturated mothers don't earn the Power Mom title even though we often see photos or videos of them toting a toddler on their hip or pushing a stroller down a busy New York City street.

So why aren't they in our directory? There are many reasons for this. The first begins with the word "real." Authenticity and attainability are important components of how Millennial and Generation X moms define reality. Social media has a great deal to do with this: moms want to stay in touch with what's real to their families and their world, and tend to focus on issues that relate to their piece of Americana. She may see Madonna and admire her fit arms but they don't seem real to her because in her mind, she knows that Madonna has something she herself will likely never have: several nannies and a personal trainer. However, when she sees Michelle Obama's arms, albeit not nearly as cut as Madonna's, it seems real because she sees images of Mrs. Obama gardening and caring for her children. A typical mom can identify with those homey kinds of realities and simply bypass the thought that Mrs. Obama probably has several housekeepers and a personal trainer, too. It's all a *perception* of what's real.

Look at Sarah Palin. You may love or hate her political views but I bet if you are a mother of a physically-challenged child, you can relate to her parenting tasks.

The fact is, the more a celebrity or well-known mom is pictured doing everyday mom tasks, the more she is seen as a peer. In January of 2008, before Hillary Clinton announced her candidacy for president, I got a call from a high-ranking Democrat. He wanted my advice. "If a mother ran for president," he asked, "what would she have to do to earn the votes of U.S. mothers?"

My response in retrospect was pretty gutsy but it went something like this. "Well, if it's Hillary, I would tell you something very different from what I'd say about another female candidate." What did I mean by this answer? My advice to him was if it's Hillary, make sure she gets photographed shopping with Chelsea at Old Navy or Gap. In order for Hillary to be seen as a mom, she needed to connect with moms by demonstrating that they had something in common beyond political issues.

Interestingly, Hillary Clinton's strategic team brought in Chelsea to campaign in Iowa with her mother...and she won, having just lost New Hampshire the week before. I'm not saying that I had anything to do with Hillary's Iowa victory but I *am* trying to illustrate the impact that a Celebrity Mom has on the opinions of Main Street moms and how it's directly related to how much the latter group identifies her with her role as a mother. It is true that some Celebrity Moms purposely keep their motherhood in the background and that's fine. It's their prerogative to do so but the less the public sees them in a role of mom, the less they are an influencer in the world of moms.

Let's take a closer look at some Celebrity Moms.

Felicity Huffman

Actress, author, entrepreneur and Power Mom, Felicity Huffman was born on December 9, 1962. She has two children with her husband, actor William H. Macy: Sophia Grace, born in 2000, and Georgia Grace, born in 2002. Six months after her first daughter was born, she created the Head's Up Comfort Pillow for rocking your baby to sleep comfortably. It's won a Good Housekeeping Excellence Award and is now sold at Bed Bath & Beyond stores. Felicity's role on *Desperate Housewives* reinforces her authenticity in the eyes of moms, who can relate to her not only as the mother of five on television but as a mom of two day in and day out. She is a definite Mom Influencer.

Brooke Burke

Television personality, model, dancer and entrepreneur, Brooke Burke was on born September 8, 1971. Her children, Neriah Fisher, born in 2000, and Sierra Sky Fisher, born in

2002, were fathered by her then-husband Garth Fisher. Heaven Rain Charvet, born in 2007, and Shaya Braven Burke, born in 2008, are fathered by her fiancé David Charvet. In 2007 Brooke began Baboosh Baby, which offers Tauts belly wraps and l'huile de Baboosh organic stretch mark prevention oil, among other items for pregnant women. Brooke is also co-CEO of ModernMom.com, founded in 2003, which features practical advice for moms and now the author of, "Naked Mom." Although ModernMom.com is popular among mothers, in a recent survey Brooke was rated only a moderate influencer. Most moms do not link her identity to that of a mom but to one of her many other roles.

Teri Hatcher

Actress Teri Hatcher was born on December 8, 1964. Her daughter, Emerson Rose Tenney, was born on November 10, 1997. Her husband from 1994 to 2003 was Jon Tenney. Teri began her acting career as Lois Lane in *Lois & Clark: The New Adventures of Superman* which ran from 1993 to 1997. Since then, she has starred in numerous television series and films, including her most successful role in *Desperate Housewives.* In May 2010, Teri created her blog, "Get Hatched: A Chick's Guide To Life," where she offers up advice for women on style, love, health and nesting, among other popular topics. Teri is viewed as a hip, involved mom but Main Street mothers cannot truly relate to her life as a mom. Her numerous online videos, magazine articles that highlight her in the kitchen with her daughter and her on-air role as a mother all contribute to her authenticity as a mother but she lacks Power Mom influence.

Kelly Ripa

Actress, television personality and spokesperson, Kelly was born on October 2, 1970. She's married to Mark Consuelos and they have three children: Michael Joseph, born in 1997, Lola Grace, born in 2001, and Joaquin Antonio, born in 2003. Kelly received her first big role when she was cast as Hayley Vaughn on the soap opera *All My Children*, and has since appeared in a variety of roles in both television and film. Aside from her role in daytime TV, Kelly is best known for being herself, as co-host of *Live with Regis and Kelly*. Kelly was voted Favorite Celebrity Mom in 2008 by *USA Today* readers, and has since served as spokesperson for Electrolux; together they run regular campaigns on their joint website, Kelly Confidential, to raise money for various causes including the Ovarian Cancer Research Fund. She is popular among Mom Bloggers, many of whom have done online interviews with her for Electrolux or attended events with her in New York City. Although many moms envy her petite, fit physique, they still love and respect her as a real Power Mom.

Angelina Jolie

Actress and humanitarian, Angelina Jolie was born June 4, 1975. She has six children with her husband since 2008, Brad Pitt: Maddox Chivan, born in 2001 and adopted in 2002, Zahara Marley, born and adopted in 2005, Shiloh Nouvel, born in 2006, Pax Thien, born in 2003 and adopted in 2007, and twins Knox Léon and Vivienne Marcheline, born in 2008. Angelina is no stranger to show business, having been born into a family of actors, but it wasn't until her role as Cornelia Wallace in the 1997 biographical TV film *George Wallace* that she was recognized for her ability with her first Golden Globe award. Angelina has won several awards for her work since. In 2009, Angelina was named World's Most Powerful Celebrity by Forbes magazine. In addition to her busy acting career, in 2001 Angelina joined forces with the UN Refugee Agency and is hugely involved with its humanitarian efforts. Angelina receives mixed reviews from moms when it comes to influence. Although many admire her parenting efforts, her lifestyle and product selections seem somewhat unattainable to the average mother. They may like the shoes little Shiloh is wearing and may even research them online, but they won't necessarily purchase them.

Tori Spelling

Actress, television personality, author, fashion and jewelry designer and entrepreneur, Tori Spelling was born on May 16, 1973. Her husband is Dean McDermott; their children are Liam Aaron, born in 2007, and Stella Doreen, born in 2008. Growing up with a powerful TV producer father, there was no shortage of roles for Tori as a budding actress; however, she is most recognized for her role as Donna Martin on *Beverly Hills, 90210.* Tori went on to appear in several independent films and made-for-TV movies. Her most recent projects are in reality television. Aside from her current reality TV show, *Tori and Dean: Home Sweet Hollywood*, Tori has written three books about life and motherhood including *sTori Telling, Mommywood* and *Uncharted TerriTori*, as well as a newly released children's book, *Presenting...Tallulah.* In addition to her active acting and writing career, Tori added designer to the list with her jewelry line at HSN and a children's fashion line named Little Maven. Tori has done a good job establishing respect among Main Street moms. She's believable in her role as mother and many moms look to her for advice, product suggestions and entertainment.

Jennifer Lopez

Actress, dancer, singer, television producer and host, fashion designer, entrepreneur and Power Mom, Jennifer Lopez was born on July 24, 1969. Her children, twins Emme Maribel and Maximilian David, born in 2008, are fathered by her husband since 2004, Marc Anthony. After winning several awards for both her music and film projects, Jennifer has proven to critics that she is indeed a triple threat. In addition to her busy music and film career, she's also a successful entrepreneur with several ventures including her fashion and fragrance lines JLO and Glow, a Cuban restaurant called Madre's and a film and television company, Nuyorican Productions. Most moms respect JLo as a mother although they might not totally relate to her lifestyle.

Celine Dion

Singer, songwriter and entrepreneur, Celine Dion was born on March 30, 1968. She and her husband Rene Angelil have three children: Rene-Charles, born in 2001, and twins Eddy and Nelson, born in 2010. Celine made a name for herself beginning in the 1990s with her powerful vocal range in the release of her first English-language album, *Unison*, placing her among the likes of Whitney Houston and Mariah Carey and making her one of the most successful pop artists of all time. In 2003, Celine entered into a deal with Coty, Inc. to release Celine Dion Parfums, her line of fragrances, which have since grossed more than $850 million. The recent birth of her twins was welcomed by Main Street moms.

Elisabeth Hasselbeck

Television personality, host and author, Elisabeth Hasselbeck was born on May 28, 1977. She is married to Tim Hasselbeck; their children are Grace Elisabeth, born in 2005, Taylor, born in 2007, and Isaiah, born in 2009. Elisabeth began her career in television with her appearance on *Survivor: The Australian Outback* in 2001 and is now a co-host on the popular daytime talk show *The View*, where she is best known for her controversial commentary. More recently, Elisabeth is also the newest contributor on the television news show *Good Morning America*. As a Mom Influencer, Elisabeth can be polarizing. She would serve well as a Power Mom in a conservative segment of mothers but has suffered many negative comments in the more liberal mom blogosphere and on Twitter.

Jada Pinkett Smith

Actress, producer, director, author and Power Mom, Jada Pinkett Smith was born on September 18, 1971. She and husband Will Smith have two children, Jaden Christopher Syre, born in 1998, and Willow Camille Reign, born in 2000. In 2004, Jada published her first children's book, *Girls Hold Up This World*, whose cover features both herself and daughter Willow. This Hollywood power couple also founded the Will and Jada Smith Family Foundation, a charitable organization focusing on inner-city youth and family support. Jada is one cool mom and receives praise among most mothers in the blogosphere. We would call her a Power Mom for sure!

Jennifer Hudson

Singer, actress and spokesperson, Jennifer Hudson was born on September 12, 1981. She has a son, David Daniel, born in 2009, with her fiancé David Ortunga. After her acting debut in 2006's *Dreamgirls*, Jennifer's performance earned her 29 awards, including a Golden Globe award, Screen Actors Guild award and an Academy Award. In addition to her prestigious acting career, her 2008 self-titled album, *Jennifer Hudson*, debuted at #2 on the Billboard 200. In 2010, Jennifer made headlines with her tremendous weight loss after the birth of her son and began serving as spokesperson for Weight Watchers. What mom can't relate to the struggle of eliminating baby weight after a pregnancy? Jennifer has won the hearts of moms by being real and allowing us to applaud her successes and share in her losses.

Sarah Palin

American politician, author, speaker, political commentator and television personality, Sarah Palin was born on February 11, 1964. She and husband Todd have five children: Track, born in 1989, Bristol Sheeran Marie, born in 1990, Willow, born in 1994, Piper, born in 2001, and Trig Paxson Van, born in 2008. Sarah is best known as the ninth governor of Alaska and for her running in the 2008 presidential campaign as Republican vice-president hopeful alongside John McCain. Since resigning as governor in 2009, Sarah has kept herself busy with the release of her autobiography, *Going Rogue: An American Life*, in 2009, providing political commentary to the Fox News channel and more recently hosting her own show, beginning 2010, called *Sarah Palin's Alaska*. Hate her or love her, you can't ignore the influence she has over people in general and you don't often see her without a child in her arms or close by. It's difficult to forget she's a mom and if you share her political views, you'd agree that she's a Power Mom.

Jennifer Garner

Actress and Power Mom, Jennifer Garner was born on April 17, 1972. She's married to Ben Affleck and they have two daughters, Violet Anne, born in 2005, and Seraphina, born in 2009. Jennifer first gained recognition as an actress on the television show *Alias*, which has since led to roles in many box-office hits such as *Pearl Harbor*, *Catch Me If You Can*, *Daredevil*, *Juno* and *Valentine's Day*. Gen X and Millennial moms love Jennifer. She's real and thanks to People magazine, most moms know she shares in the everyday tasks of motherhood. There's nothing that makes a Power Mom an influencer like seeing her in the grocery store in jeans.

Victoria Beckham

English singer-songwriter, dancer, model, actress and fashion designer, Victoria Beckham was born on April 17, 1974. She's married to David Beckham; their children are Brooklyn Joseph, born in 1999, Romeo James, born in 2002, and Cruz David, born in 2005. Victoria is expecting a girl in 2011. Victoria began her rise to fame in the late 1990s as Posh Spice in the pop group Spice Girls. Since her days in the music industry, Victoria's career in the spotlight continued on British and American television; however, it is her status as international style icon which makes her most recognizable. She's a Celebrity Mom who is often pictured casually dressed (albeit in four-inch stilettos) and with her children. Beckham influences fashion choices, although most mothers will find a way to wear it on a Target budget.

Gwyneth Paltrow

Actress and singer, Gwyneth Paltrow was born on September 27, 1972. She and husband Chris Martin have two children: Apple Blythe Alison, born in 2004, and Moses Bruce Anthony, born in 2006. Gwyneth leapt onto the movie screen in 1991, but it was her performance in *Shakespeare in Love* in 1998 that won her numerous awards, and has since launched her into stardom with both leading and supporting roles in blockbuster hits such as *The Talented Mr. Ripley*, *Bounce* and *Iron Man*. In 2008, she started Gwyneth "Goop," an online lifestyle newsletter focusing on one action per week: make, go, get, do, be or see. She's a hip mom and one who wins praise from most Main Street moms.

Kimora Lee Simmons

Actress, model and television personality, Kimora Lee Simmons was born on May 4, 1975. With then-husband Russell Simmons she has two daughters, Ming Lee, born in 2000, and Aoki Lee, born in 2002. She and current boyfriend Djimon Hounsou have a son, Kenzo Lee, born in 2009. Kimora has made a name for herself in the fashion industry, beginning with her modeling career when in 1988, she was awarded an exclusive modeling contract with Chanel and worked with famed Chanel designer Karl Lagerfeld. Her mark on fashion continued in 2007, when she was promoted to president and creative director of Phat Fashions, the former clothing company of ex-husband Russell Simmons. In 2007, Kimora allowed a glimpse into her world with the premiere of *Kimora: Life in the Fab Lane*, a reality TV show chronicling her daily life. Call her the fashion queen of Power Mom. Kimora's designs for children are very popular, and she keeps producing clothing lines that win the hearts of her target market. Many mothers also admire her mompreneur spirit.

Jenny McCarthy

Actress, model, comedian, author and activist, Jenny McCarthy was born on November 1, 1972. She and then-husband John Mallory Asher have a son, Evan Joseph, born in May 2002. After beginning her acting career as the sexy, goofy host of MTV's *Singled Out* from 1995 to 1997, Jenny moved on with roles in both film and TV. Since announcing the diagnosis of her son's autism in 2007, Jenny became an autism activist and served as spokesperson for Talking About Curing Autism from 2007 to 2008. Jenny has written several books on pregnancy and motherhood, including *Belly Laughs: The Naked Truth about Pregnancy and Childbirth; Baby Laughs: The Naked Truth about the First Year of Mommyhood;* and *Life Laughs: The Naked Truth about Motherhood, Marriage, and Moving On.* In addition, she has written three books about children and autism. Jenny has definitely solidified her role as a mom. Her books inform and impact moms on a regular basis.

Reese Witherspoon

Actress and producer, Reese Witherspoon was born on March 22, 1976. With then-husband Ryan Phillippe she has two children: Ava Elizabeth, born in 1999, and Deacon Reese, born in 2003. Reese began her acting career in 1990, when she was cast in a leading role for *The Man in the Moon*. Since then, she's starred in several blockbuster hits, earning accolades for many of them. In 2000, Reese founded Type A Films, her film production company, and has produced films such as *Legally Blonde 2: Red, White and Blonde*, *Penelope* and *Four Christmases*. She is also actively involved in children's and women's advocacy organizations such as Save the Children and the Children's Defense Fund. Reece's role as a mother gets lost in the fine print of her latest relationships. We know she's a good mom who is involved with her children but she's not the first mom who comes to mind as an influencer.

Gwen Stefani

Singer and fashion designer, Gwen Stefani was born on October 3, 1969. She's married to Gavin Rossdale and they have two children, Kingston James McGregor, born in 2006, and Zuma Nesta Rock, born in 2008. Gwen began her rise to stardom with her alternative band, No Doubt, after signing to Interscope Records in 1991. The band released several successful albums; however, in 2004 Gwen took a break from the band to launch her solo career in pop music. Her first two albums earned high accolades and subsequently increased fan following. In addition to music, Gwen developed the clothing line L.A.M.B. in 2003, and has since expanded to include the Harijuku Lovers line in 2005. There is little doubt that Gwen has embraced her role as mother. She's often photographed with her sons, and moms appreciate the step back from work she made after her pregnancies. If there's a way to become a stay-at-home mom as a celebrity, she's done it.

Brooke Shields

Actress, model and author, Brooke Shields was born on May 31, 1965. She is the mother of two girls. When she was just under a year old, Brooke appeared as a child model for Ivory soap; it was the beginning of a very successful career as both a model and actress. At the age of 14 she became the youngest fashion model to appear on the cover of Vogue. Most notably, Brooke is known for her role in the movies *Blue Lagoon* in 1980 and *Endless Love* in 1981. In 2005, Brooke appeared on the *Oprah Winfrey Show* to speak out about her experience with postpartum depression. She has written two books on the subject of postpartum depression, in addition to two children's books. Brooke also serves as the spokesperson for Tupperware's SMART Girls campaign, whose goal is to teach young girls to nurture their mental and physical well-being. Mothers relate to Brooke as a fellow mom thanks largely to Tom Cruise, who, with his famously insensitive remarks, helped publicize her post-partum depression. Never doubt the power of moms who team up to support a new mother. Most Boomers grew up with Brooke and it's fun to share motherhood with her. Brooke is definitely a Power Mom.

Kate Gosselin

TV personality and author, Kate Gosselin was born on March 28, 1975. She was married to Jon Gosselin with whom she had twins Cara Nicole and Madelyn Kate, born in 2000, and sextuplets Hannah, Aaden, Joel, Alexis, Leah and Collin, born in 2004. Kate is best known for her reality television show, *Jon & Kate Plus 8,* which follows Kate and then-husband Jon on their journey through parenthood with eight kids. After her divorce and the end of her show in 2009, Kate competed on the reality series *Dancing With the Stars* and has since begun her own show, *Kate Plus 8.* In addition to her reality TV stardom, Kate has written three nonfiction books: *Multiple Blessings, Eight Little Faces* and *I Just Want You to Know.* Kate is currently working on her next book, a cookbook titled *Love Is in the Mix,* due to release in 2011. Is Kate a Mom Influencer? The jury is still out on this one. She's got a large fan base who are rooting for her to succeed now that she is a single mother; however, there are many who believe she needs to take a step back and raise her children.

Natalie Morales

Television anchor and national correspondent, Natalie Morales was born on June 6, 1972. She and her husband Joe Rhodes have two children: Joseph Stockton, born in 2004, and Luke Hudson, born in 2008. Natalie is best known for her current role as national correspondent on NBC's *Today Show.* Prior to becoming a *Today Show* correspondent, Natalie began her on-air career at News 12, the Bronx, as the first morning anchor. In addition to her journalistic career, Natalie appears on NBC's *The Marriage Ref* and also hosted the 2010 Miss USA and Miss Universe pageants. Natalie has done a good job staying relatable to moms. She is often seen gracing the cover of smaller parenting publications such as *Mom* magazine. For companies looking for a mother who comes across as authentic, she's a great selection.

Julie Chen

Television personality, news anchor and producer, Julie Chen was born on January 6, 1970. She's married to Leslie Moonves; their son Charlie was born in 2009. Julie serves as the moderator of the CBS talk show *The Talk*, featuring a panel of five other moms. Since 2000, Julie has also served as the host of *Big Brother*, a reality TV show on CBS. Prior to launching her career as an on-air personality, Julie worked at *CBS Morning News* where she answered phones and copied faxes, a far cry from her future days in the spotlight. As a mom older than most first-time mothers, Julie has stayed hip and connected with Millennials by hosting shows like *Big Brother*. She's the perfect example of how a peer group isn't dictated by your generational cohort but by having children of similar ages. She might be a Boomer but her peer group is definitely Millennial and younger Generation X moms.

Cynthia McFadden

News anchor and correspondent, Cynthia McFadden was born on May 27, 1956. She and then-husband James Hodge have a son, Spencer Graham, born in 1998. Before becoming a famed news anchor and correspondent on *ABC News* and co-anchor of *Nightline* and *Primetime*, Cynthia began her on-air career in 1991 as an anchor and producer on the Courtroom Television Network. Since she began working on the show as an anchor, *Nightline* has seen a resurgence in its ratings and prominence. Cynthia is also a contributor for wowOwow.com, a website geared toward women and covering topics such as pop culture and politics. Cynthia can often be seen at mom events in NYC and recently keynoted the Executive Moms luncheon. She embraces her motherhood, and is not afraid to talk about her child and the challenges she faces being a mom juggling a career and family. Her words and actions definitely influence mothers.

Sandra Bullock

Actress Sandra Bullock was born on July 26, 1964. Her son, Louis Bardo, was adopted in January 2010, just one week after his birth. Sandra first made a name for herself in the mid-1990s with her performance in *Speed* and *While You Were Sleeping*. She then reappeared as a leading lady in the 2000s with several hit movies such as *Miss Congeniality*, *Divine Secrets of the Ya-Ya Sisterhood* and *Crash*. In 2009 Sandra received her highest accolades yet, winning an Academy Award, a Golden Globe Award and a Screen Actors Guild Award for her performance in *The Blind Side*. Sandra has won the hearts of most moms, but whether she is considered an influencer or not depends on how much she is in the public eye at any given time.

Section 6
Global Moms

As the song goes, "It's a small world after all." Thanks to social media, it keeps getting smaller. For moms, their influence has gone global, which is why I wanted to include a selection of Global Mom Influencers. As I've traveled around the world studying mothers, I've discovered moms who are engaging and influencing others in their region of the world. Everywhere there are peer leaders who seize the opportunity to share information with mothers in their community or online.

I've learned that the greatest difference with Power Moms is the way the Word of Mom travels. In some parts of the world, blogging is just taking off. The most accurate way to describe social media and moms outside the United States is that it's like going back in time. The same debates that moms in the U.S. have with each other about the transparency of product reviews is going on all over the world. In fact, there are some areas where Mom Blogging has yet to catch on as a trend. In those regions where it's still in the infant stage, product reviews are almost nonexistent. In the United Kingdom, where mothers have started forming blog networks, there are still few Mom Bloggers who will review products provided by a company. It was only a few years ago that most female bloggers in the UK posted anonymously to their blogs. The debate about whether to review or not to review is present elsewhere as well. In Italy, there is a strong debate about receiving products from brands and even more debate about monetizing a blog.

Moms around the globe are fascinated by the growth of Mom Blogging in the U.S. and look to American mothers for guidance. During my travels, I've met so many social media Mom Influencers seeking information about what American moms are doing online that I launched GlobalMomBloggers.com to create a platform for these moms to share ideas, know-how and stories.

The use of Twitter by moms outside the United States is very limited. They're not using it for Twitter parties, product mentions or promotional codes. In fact, BSM Media held the first ever transatlantic Twitter party in the summer of 2010 for ZhuZhu Pets. We invited moms around the world to attend and although we were successful in attracting hundreds of moms to join us, we did need to spend a significant amount of time bringing European moms up to speed on Twitter party basics.

Moms elsewhere are using Facebook in greater numbers than Twitter and the blogosphere. My theory about the slow adoption of blogging in some areas can be traced back to the key motivators of mothers that I discussed in section one. American moms adopted blogging to help combat the isolation of motherhood. It was a means to socialize with like-minded women and share the journey through parenthood. However, while moms were blogging, Facebook entered the social media landscape. Mothers in

Europe and other developed regions entered directly into the world of Facebook. For these mothers, there wasn't the need to write posts and upload photos. They can achieve the same objectives of memory archiving and socializing on their wall with Facebook friends. Thus rather than adopting blogging, many moms in other areas of the world are Facebooking with peers.

It's not surprising that the influence of moms is happening offline as well. Culture plays a major role in how and where moms pass along ideas and suggestions to each other. You can be assured that travel advice is being traded on the side of an Argentinian *futbol* field just as recipes are being swapped on the side of a U.S. soccer field. Moms are talking and spreading ideas everywhere from the plains of Africa to the Alps of Austria.

Global Power Moms

Veronica Faole

Australia

Website/Company: Founder, Sleepless Nights (www.somedaywewillsleep.com), cofounder, Aussie Mummy Bloggers (www.aussiemummybloggers.com)

Twitter Id: @sleeplessnights, @ausmumbloggers

Brenda

Australia

Website/Company: Founder, Mummy Time (www.mummy-time.com), cofounder, Aussie Mummy Bloggers (www.aussiemummybloggers.com)

Twitter Id: @mummytime, @ausmumbloggers

Catherine

Australia

Website/Company: Founder, Adventures with Kids (www.adventureskids.blogspot.com)

Twitter Id: @adventureskids

Jo White

Australia

Website/Company: Founder, Media Mum (www.mediamum.net)

Twitter Id: @mediamum

Rachel

Australia

Website/Company: Founder, A Juggling Mum (www.ajugglingmum.com)

Twitter Id: @ajugglingmum

Karen Andrews

Australia

Website/Company: Founder, Miscellaneous Mum (www.miscmum.com)

Corrie

Australia

Website/Company: Founder, Retro Mummy (www.retromummy.blogspot.com)

Twitter Id: @retromummy

Jodie Ansted

Australia

Website/Company: Founder, Mummy Mayhem (www.mummy-mayhem.blogspot.com)

Twitter Id: @jodieansted

Catherine Bolt

Australia

Website/Company: Founder, An Ordinary Life (www.catherinebolt.com)

Mandi Gussenberger

Australia

Website/Company: Founder, Babyology (www.babyology.com.au)

Twitter Id: @babyology

Chantelle Ellem

Australia

Website/Company: Founder, Fat Mum Slim (www.fatmumslim.blogspot.com)

Twitter Id: @fatmumslim

Felicity Moore

Australia

Website/Company: Founder, Moore For Mums (www.mooreformums.com.au)

Twitter Id: @felicitymoore

Catherine Oehlman

Australia

Website/Company: Founder, Squiggle Mum (www.squigglemum.com)

Twitter Id: @squigglemum

Janaina Medeiros

Brazil

Website/Company: Owner, Baby Boo Emporium (www.babyboo.com.br)

Twitter Id: @babybooemporium

Alyssa Kingsbury

Canada

Website/Company: www.amotherhoodexperience.wordpress.com

Twitter Id: @AMotherhoodBlog

Tammi

Canada

Website/Company: Founder, My Organized Chaos (www.myorganizedchaos.net)

Twitter Id: @mychaos

Christine Louise Hohlbaum

Germany

Website/Company: www.powerofslow.wordpress.com, www.thedailybrainstorm.com, www.wowOwow.com, http://www.psychologytoday.com/blog/the-power-slow

Twitter Id: @powerofslow

Aparna

India

Website/Company: Founder, Adventures In Mommyland (www.advaithandyukta.blogspot.com)

Deepa

India

Website/Company: Founder, Devis with Babies (www.deviswithbabies.blogspot.com)

Jolanda Restano

Italy

Website/Company: Founder, www.filastrocche.it, www.blogmamma.it, www.mammacheblog.com, www.mammacheclub.com, www.mammamamma.com

Twitter Id: @filastrocche

Kori

Japan

Website/Company: Founder, Smile Smile (www.momkori.blogspot.com)

Sarah

Japan

Website/Company: Founder, Mommy In Japan (www.mommyinjapan.blogspot.com)

Mande

Japan

Website/Company: Founder, Working Mom In Japan (www.workingmominjapan.blogspot.com)

Twitter Id: @mandejlife

'Little Mama'

Malaysia

Website/Company: Mom Bloggers Planet (www.mumbloggersplanet.com)

Twitter Id: @mombloggers

Hanz

Malaysia

Website/Company: Founder, Triple Colour Life (www.triplecolourlife.com)

Habibah Ismail

Malaysia

Website/Company: Founder, Habibah & Anas (www.blog.beba-anas.com)

Twitter Id: @beba_anas

Sarah Rasmussen

New Zealand

Website/Company: www.buy4babydirect.com, www.buy4babydirect.co.nz, www.buy4babydirect.com.au, www.buy4babydirect.co.uk

Twitter Id: @buy4babydirect

Angela Noelle

New Zealand

Website/Company: Founder, Mormon Mommy Blogs (www.mormonmommyblogs.com)

Twitter Id: @mmbcommunity

Michelle

Poland

Website/Company: Founder, Warsaw Mommy (www.warsawmommy.com)

Twitter Id: @warsawmommy

Clare Taylor

Russia

Website/Company: Founder, The Potty Diaries (www.potty-diaries.blogspot.com)

Twitter Id: @thepottydiaries

Jane Linley-Thomas

South Africa

Website/Company: Founder, Moms Matter (www.momsmatter.co.za)

Twitter Id: @AMotherhoodBlog

Michele Bates

United Kingdom

Website/Company: http://www.ukmums.tv

Producer of Practical Pre-School Awards

Twitter Id: @UKMumstv

Susanna Scott

United Kingdom

Website/Company: Founder, A Modern Mother (www.amodernmother.com) and British Mummy Bloggers (www.britishmummybloggers.ning.com)

Twitter Id: @amodernmother

Jo Beaufoix

United Kingdom

Website/Company: Founder (www.jobeaufoix.com)

Twitter Id: @jobeaufoix

Becky

United Kingdom (Ireland)

Website/Company: Founder, English Mum (www.englishmum.com)

Twitter Id: @englishmum

Emily Carlisle

United Kingdom

Website/Company: Founder, More Than Just a Mother (www.morethanjustamother.com)

Twitter Id: @mtjam

Becky Goddard-Hill

United Kingdom

Website/Company: Founder, Baby Budgeting (www.babybudgeting.co.uk)

Twitter Id: @babybudgeting

Tara Cain

United Kingdom

Website/Company: Founder, Sticky Fingers (www.stickyfingers1.blogspot.com)

Twitter Id: @tara_cain

Laura Chora

United Kingdom

Website/Company: Founder, Are We Nearly There Yet Mummy? (www.arewenearlythereyetmommy.com)

Twitter: @lauraawntym

Erica Douglas

United Kingdom

Website/Company: Founder, Little Mummy (www.littlemummy.com)

Twitter Id: @erica

Henrietta Pretty

United Kingdom

Website/Company: Founder, Marketing To Milk (www.marketingtomilk.wordpress.com)

Twitter Id: @marketingtomilk

Emma

United Kingdom

Website/Company: Founder, Mummy Musings (www.mummymusings.com)

Twitter Id: @b4kersgirl

Natalie Lue

United Kingdom

Website/Company: Founder, Bambino Goodies (www.bambinogoodies.co.uk)

Twitter Id: @bambinogoodies

Jo Rheam

United Kingdom

Website/Company: Founder, Mummo (www.mummo.co.uk), *Mummo* magazine (www.mummomag.co.uk)

Twitter Id: @mummojo

Deborah

United Kingdom

Website/Company: Founder, Metropolitan Mum (www.metropolitanmum.co.uk)

Twitter Id: @metropolitanmum

Jennifer James

United Kingdom

Website/Company: Founder, Mum Bloggers Club (www.mumbloggersclub.ning.com)

Twitter Id: @mumbloggersclub

Kiran Singh

United Kingdom

Website/Company: Founder, Vivacious Mums (www.vivaciousmums.com), Vivacious Business Mums (www.kiransingh.net/vivaciousbusinessmums), *Vivacious Mums* online magazine (www.content.yudu.com/library/alppp2/vivaciousmum/resources.index.htm)

Twitter Id: @vivaciousmum, @kiransingh

SECTION 7
Influential Dads

At every presentation I've delivered over the past decade, I can be sure I'm going to hear "What about dads?" It's not that I haven't been interested in the interface between marketing and men who have children. In fact, in 2008, I toyed with the idea of writing a book provisionally titled *Marketing to the New American Family.* I'd noticed a shift in how parents were sharing responsibility in the home. Additionally, I had watched the growth of gay couples becoming parents, so I knew that dads were taking on a new, and might I say, improved role. I turned my attention instead to the topic of moms and technology, but stay tuned for more from me on this subject in the future. Times have definitely changed and there is a growing pool of Dad Influencers made prominent through social media. Some brands that previously had exclusively Mom Panels and mom advisory boards have been taking a second look at their approach to marketing. Social media dads are becoming so popular that it is absolutely necessary to include Dad Influencers in this book.

In the list, you'll meet some of the dads I've watched for many years as they've worked relentlessly to get their voices heard—men like Tim Sullivan, who launched "PTO Today" before blogging was a verb, and Gregory Keers who launched FamilyMan.com before Twitter even existed. I'm so pleased that brands are starting to bring these men (and others in parenting roles) into the mix of Parenting Marketing. Does this mean that it's time to abandon Mom Marketing for Parenting Marketing? I wouldn't go that far just yet. However, the men I've listed here are bringing greater attention to the role of fathers.

As a marketer, I caution you to use the same protocol used in finding Mom Bloggers who match your company's value and mission. Additionally, it's important to recognize that the motivators I described in previous sections do not drive Dad Bloggers. Few would tell you that they blog as a way to socialize with other dads or to eliminate social isolation in their life. Many are motivated to have the voice of dads heard and to elevate the position of fatherhood by sharing their more involved role in raising their children.

There are many very talented men out there writing roll-on-the-ground funny stories of fatherhood and parenting advice and many attract as many moms to their content as dads. It's important to get to know the dad who is behind the site and in particular read his views on advertising, product reviews and sponsorships. Some are uninterested in the commercialization of their blogs while others are quite innovative about their approach to working with brands. Some, like the guys at DadLabs, have found their place in front of the webcam, producing digital content that entertains and informs and often carries a sponsor's message as well.

Dad's day has finally come and I'm proud to introduce you to these remarkable Dad Influencers.

Mitchell Chaitin

Father of 1, New York, NY

Website/Company: Founder, Gay NYC Dad (www.gaynycdad.com)

Twitter Id: @gaynycdad

Facebook: Mitch_GayNYCDad

Mitch prides himself on being part of the mom blogger community as well. He's a great example of a dad blogger that integrates into the mom blogger space. I asked Mitch to answer a few questions in his own words below.

Short description of business: The blog was started so I can share the story of my family, a gay couple with a child adopted at birth. It is about a parent's life, with fun blog stuff that is starting to include my son as my assistant, until he starts a kid's blog next year! The blog is almost 1 year old.

Approximate audience size: 3600/month

Approximate # of followers: 1700

What do you think is the biggest mistake companies make in trying to work with moms? Slow lag time in responding to us and asking for our help without offering anything in return (not monetary).

Are there companies who you feel are doing a great job connecting with moms? I have worked with over a dozen companies and I find all of them very respectful and wanting to work with me and my fellow bloggers. The ones that don't answer emails are the ones I have no use for.

How do you define influence among moms? I am part of a group of NYC bloggers, we meet at events and we share information. We all reach several thousand people across the USA and that is how we spread our opinions and influence.

How can companies best support your business or mission as a mom? I would love if they advertised and supported me financially. I also enjoy keeping the products that I review for myself and my family for future use.

How do you feel companies can best connect with moms, particularly those who are influencers? Reach out to bloggers, the mom blog community is growing daily and reaching more and more people. More blog events would help.

Final Word: Firstly, the recognition that I am a mom blogger for all intensive purposes; the phrase now includes some stay-at-home dads. Not all stay-at-home dads do the functions that I do. I do most of the mom functions in the family since I am not working, *i.e., take care of the kid and the house, etc*. There are mostly moms in the school playground after school that I talk with and influence, and they, me. I think as a group we control a lot of the purse strings and with more information can guide our spouses to better purchases when they need something. I believe that the more of us that share our information about our loves and care giving advice, and product info, the quicker and better our decisions can be—I know that is one of my goals. And I am having a great time doing this!

Adam Cohen

Father of 1, New York, New York

Website/Company: Founder, Dada Rocks (www.dadarocks.com)

Description: DaDa Rocks provides a great mix of real-life stories of fatherhood with cool product reviews, especially tech items, and give-aways. Adam offers advertising on his site as well as other marketing or review opportunities. More information can be found on his site.

Twitter: @dadarocks

Facebook: DaDa Rocks!

How do you think the influence among dads is changing today? Dad's role has been evolving for the last several generations. It follows a similar curve much like that of women rights—the more equal we are, the more the role of Dad is equal to that of the role of mom.

There is a generation, let's say two/three generations ago, where Dad was just the provider—few and far between truly engaged in the family direction much beyond the fiscal concerns. Today's generation of dads want to be involved, they want work life balance, they want to be on the little league fields but now struggle with the images of being that good man and fully providing for their family. It is a very interesting paradigm shift unfolding today.

Do you influence moms as much as you influence dads? When I first started DaDa Rocks the stats I pulled showed a majority of visitors were moms, 70% actually. It took a much longer time to find a dad-based audience. Now I'm at 60% dad-based audience. Part of that I attribute to my writing style and the other part I attribute to the way men socially connect. Men aren't as likely to befriend total strangers or strike up conversations while in check out lines as women. I think it took a long time and a lot of work to prove myself and my site to other dads. In terms of influence, that's a whole different story. I think men typically look for the blunt answer to questions, such as I need a birthday gift for my wife. Guys don't want reviews of dozens and dozens of items, they want one list featuring 10 items that clearly describes the item and the price.

Please briefly describe how companies may be able to work with you. Since I've started, companies have approached me to reach that male audience or that parenting audience—so much so that I removed my address from my contact page just after a few weeks of receiving dozens of unwanted packages. I carefully sort my options and which brands/products I want to post/endorse. At this current juncture I'm now looking for base level or site-based sponsorship that will allow me to travel to more social media conferences, as I'm not keen on the idea of strict advertising-based site and I want to control who I'm partnering with much more closely than others. Lately I've built such a following that I'm being asked to consult with companies on building their brands or on their outreach to the Dad market or the parenting market.

Greg Allen

Father of 1, New York, New York and Washington, D.C.

Website/Company: Founder, Daddy Types (www.daddytypes.com)

Description: DaddyTypes is a blog geared toward new dads, offering a dad-friendly perspective in the baby-making and -raising world. Greg started DaddyTypes in 2004 and was one of the first dad bloggers to begin filling the then-absent gap in the market. DaddyTypes doesn't typically do product reviews or giveaways, but does offer advertising opportunities. More information can be found on the site.

Twitter: @daddytypes

Jason Avant

Father of 2, Carlsbad, California

Website/Company: Founder & Managing Editor, Dad Centric (www.dadcentric.com)

Description: DadCentric, founded by Jason Avant, is a group of ten smart, edgy, and talented writer-dads, whose common goal is to overthrow the outdated notions of Fatherhood. Here you'll find stories, essays, reviews, and interviews—written by and for modern fathers. Marketing and PR information is available on the site.

Affiliations: Contributor to Manofthehouse.com

Twitter: @PetCobra

Jeremy Biser

Father of 3, Washington, D.C.

Website/Company: Founder, Discovering Dad (www.discoveringdad.net)

Description: Discovering Dad is a site about learning what it means to be a good dad. Its main objective is to build connections between dads, encourage fathers to get involved in their kids' lives, and to help fathers establish their own voice in society as something more than the "second" parent. Jeremy offers advertising on his site as well as other marketing opportunities. More information about these opportunities can be found on the site.

Twitter: @jnbammer

Shawn Burns

Father of 2, Mountain View, California

Website/Company: Founder, Backpacking Dad (www.backpackingdad.com)

Description: Backpacking Dad is Shawn Burns' witty take on his journey as a husband, father of 2 young children, and Philosophy student. His posts are down-to-earth and relatable, making Backpacking Dad entertaining and enlightening for dads of all types. You can contact Shawn on his site for marketing and advertising information.

Twitter: @BackpackingDad

Frederick Goodall

Father of 3, Houston, Texas

Website/Company: Founder, Mocha Dad (www.mochadad.com)

Description: Mocha Dad began in 2008 to chronicle Frederick's life as a father and to counter the negative stereotypes regarding black fatherhood. He now uses his blog not only to capture his experiences as a father, but also to help motivate other fathers to be more actively engaged and involved with their children. Mocha Dad offers various marketing opportunities, including product reviews and advertising. Complete marketing and advertising information can be found on the site.

Affiliations: Co-founded MakingItLastForever.com with his wife

Twitter: @mochadad

Joey Donovan Guido

Father of 2, Madison, Wisconsin

Website/Company: Founder, Daddy Brain (www.daddybrain.wordpress.com)

Description: Daddy Brain is a place for modern-day dads to talk about what's on their minds, in their hearts and what they struggle with as parents and men. No matter if you're a working dad, stay-at-home dad, or something in between—this blog is a place for dads to be heard. To learn more about Daddy Brain and for media information, contact Joey Guido via email.

Affiliations: Started the Daddy Brain Dads' Group, Founder of The Daddy Brain Workshop

Twitter: @daddybrain11

Jared Hoylman

Father of 1, Columbus, Ohio

Website/Company: Founder, Dad Thing (www.dadthing.com)

Description: Dad Thing is a PR-friendly blog where Jared Hoylman shares his stories and experiences of fatherhood, from his son's first steps to his last time riding in a rear facing car seat. Contact Jared for more information on advertising and product reviews.

Twitter: @dadthing

Gregory Keer

Father of 3, Los Angeles, California

Website/Company: Publisher, Family Man Online (www.familymanonline.com)

Description: FamilyManOnline, the fastest growing resource for the modern father, is home to Gregory Keer's online fatherhood magazine, featuring articles on parenting, discussion boards, reviews, and more. In addition, Gregory's Family Man column also appears in publications across the country, including L.A. Parent, Bay Area Parent, and Boston Parents' Paper. Marketers can contact Gregory via email, provided on his site.

Affiliations: Contributor for Parenting Magazine, the Parents' Choice Foundation, USA Today, and the New York Times, as well as DrLaura.com, ParentingBookmark.com, Parenthood.com, and CanadianParents.com

Twitter: @FamilyManOnline

Joe Kelly

Father of 2, Saint Paul, Minnesota

Website/Company: Founder, The Dad Man (www.thedadman.com), Dads and Daughters (www.dadsanddaughters.blogspot.com), Co-Founder, New Moon Girls magazine (www.newmoongirls.com)

Description: The Dad Man is a place to learn how men can be better fathers, and how everyone can activate fathers to help enrich and strengthen our families, communities, organizations, workplaces, and schools. Joe Kelly, founder of The Dad Man, is a father, best-selling author, blogger, speaker and primary media source on fathering. To learn more about Joe Kelly or to contact him for media information, go to TheDadMan.com.

Affiliations: Contributor to Mothering.com, Featured author on GreatDads.com.

Offline: Joe Kelly is the author of seven books including *Dads and Daughters: How to Inspire, Understand and Support Your Daughter, The Dads and Daughters Togetherness Guide: 54 Fun Activities to Help Build a Great Relationship* and *The Pocket Idiot's Guide to Being a New Dad.*

Awards: iParenting.com Father of the Year, Women's Sports Foundation Father of the Year

Elliott Kim

Father of 2, Oak Ridge, Tennessee

Website/Company: Founder, 21st Century Dad (www.21stcenturydad.com)

Description: 21st Century Dad provides Elliott Kim's insights not only into fatherhood as the dad of a little girl, but step-fatherhood as well to his wife's teenage son. For more information on advertising and media, contact Elliot Kim.

Twitter: @21stcenturydad

Troy Lanier, Clay Nichols and Brad Powell

Fathers of 2, 3, 3; respectively, Austin, Texas

Website/Company: Co-Founders, Dad Labs (www.dadlabs.com)

Description: DadLabs is a one-stop shop providing resources to expecting, new, and veteran fathers that will launch them into a more active and creative role in their children's lives. Their mission is to strengthen families and benefit children by empowering today's fathers. With blog posts, videos including live weekly shows, and an online forum—they cover it all at DadLabs. Complete advertising and media information can be found on the website.

Awards: 27th Annual Bronze Telly Award for their DVD *DueDads: The Man's Survival Guide to Pregnancy*

Affiliations: Weekly show on MomTV.com

Offline: Co-authors of *DadLabs: A Guide to Fatherhood: Pregnancy and Year One*. The company has also released its first DVD, *DueDads: The Man's Survival Guide to Pregnancy.*

Twitter: @DadLabs

C. Lewis

Father of 2, Michigan

Website/Company: Founder, Dad of Divas (www.dadofdivas.com), The Great Minivan Trade Up (www.minivantradeup.blogspot.com)

Description: As a father of 2 girls, Dad of Divas works every day to regain control of his kingdom. His site is dedicated to chronicling the experiences and challenges in being a father, as well as providing some food for thought to other dads. There are many opportunities for marketers and media to work with Dad of Divas, including paid advertising, sponsorships, and product reviews. Complete advertising and media information can be found on his site.

Twitter: @dadofdivas

Jim Lin

Father of 2, Los Angeles, California

Website/Company: Founder, Busy Dad Blog (www.busydadblog.com)

Description: The Busy Dad Blog documents author Jim Lin's adventures in parenting as a busy working father. His site features stories, pictures, videos, and even comic strips of some of his best real-life parenting adventures. To reach Jim regarding any marketing and media inquiries, his contact information can be found on his site.

Affiliations: Blissdom '11

Twitter: @BusyDadBlog

David Mott

Father of 2, San Francisco, California

Website/Company: Founder, Dad's House (www.dadshouseblog.com)

Description: Dad's House is a single dad's blog offering stories, tips and opinions on single parenting, two-home families, cooking, cocktails, self-awareness and dating as a single parent. David Mott is considered to be a leading voice in the Single Parent blogosphere and has appeared as a guest on ABC News, CBS radio, and has been interviewed for CNN.com. Advertising and media information can be found on his website.

Affiliations: Contributor to Manofthehouse.com, Contributed to the Silicon Valley's Mom Blog, Founded the Facebook group Single Parents Connection

Twitter: @dadshouseblog

PJ Mullen

Father of 2, Charlotte, North Carolina

Website/Company: Founder, Real Men Drive Minivans (www.realmendriveminivans.com)

Description: Real Men Drive Minivans is the humorous and insightful chronicles of PJ Mullen's adventures in fatherhood. Here he talks about life as a stay-at-home dad, husband, amateur chef, and anything else that crosses his mind. For marketing information, you can contact PJ on his site.

Affiliations: Contributor for Manofthehouse.com, DigitalDads.com, and RoadToThin.com; Launched Spread Your Warmth campaign for The Sweatshirt Blanket Blog (www.sweatshirtblanket.com) and Get in the Game campaign for The Adirondack Fleece Blog (www.adirondackfleece.com)

Twitter: @pjmullen

Buck Rogers

Father of 1, Memphis, Tennessee

Website/Company: Founder, BuckDaddy (www.buckdaddyblog.com)

Description: Buck Rogers talks about life from his point of view as a father, husband, and guy on his site BuckDaddy. Buck is considered one of the original daddy bloggers as well as a marketer and Internet media enthusiast. Information regarding reviews, sponsorships, and other marketing opportunities can be found on his site.

Affiliations: Founded RulesForMyDaughter.com, Contributing writer for Dad-O-Matic.com and Blogalogues.com

Twitter: @buckdaddy

Jim Silver

Father of 3, New York, New York

Website/Company: Editor-in-Chief, Time To Play Magazine (www.timetoplaymag.com)

Description: Jim Silver is recognized as one of the preeminent experts in the toy, licensing, and family entertainment industries. He is currently editor-in-chief of Time to Play Magazine, a playful destination website which provides adults with information, entertainment, and services on what's fun for children and their families. Twice a year Silver and his TimetoPlayMag.com team host industry-wide press events in NYC to unveil the season's must-have toys and children's products hitting store shelves. For media inquiries, you can contact Jim Silver on twitter or through the site.

Affiliations: Weekly host of #TimetoPlayLive, a virtual game show on twitter; weekly co-host of *Time to Play with Jim & Chris* on MomTV.com, the number one viewed toy and family entertainment show on the web

Offline: Editor-in-Chief of trade publications *Royaltie$: The Journal of the Licensing Industry* and *Toys & Family Entertainment*

Twitter: @jimsilver

Jeremy Adam Smith

Father of 1, Palo Alto, California

Website/Company: Founder, Daddy Dialectic (www.daddy-dialectic.blogspot.com)

Description: Jeremy Adam Smith started Daddy Dialectic as a journal of his experience as a stay-at-home dad. Today Daddy Dialectic has become a group blog by and about dads who take care of kids. With around 11 contributing writers, there is something for every twenty-first-century father on this site. While Daddy Dialectic doesn't typically offer opportunities for marketers, Jeremy Adam Smith can be contacted with any questions or media inquiries.

Affiliations: Editor of Shareable.net

Offline: Author of *The Daddy Shift*, Co-editor of *The Compassionate Instinct* and *Are We Born Racist?*, Contributing Editor of *Greater Good* magazine

Twitter: @jeremyadamsmith

Tim Sullivan

Father of 4, Attleboro, Massachusetts

Website/Company: Founder, PTO Today (www.ptotoday.com), Schools Fight Hunger (www.schoolsfighthunger.org)

Description: Founded in 1999 by Tim Sullivan, PTO Today quickly established itself at the center of the school parent group world (PTOs and PTAs) as both a valuable resource and a trusted voice for the entire parent group market. PTO Today is the only company dedicated exclusively to providing a full suite of products, programs and services to the entire K-8 school parent group market. Since the founding of PTO Today, Tim has been a featured columnist in every issue of the flagship magazine, has been the host of the ptotoday.com online community and has penned the "Tim's Tip" email feature every week for nearly a decade. PTO Today offers a broad range of marketing opportunities. Complete advertising and marketing information can be found on the site.

Twitter: @TimPTO

David Wright

Father of 1, Florida

Website/Company: Founder, Blogger Dad (www.bloggerdad.com), Project 30 Days (www.projcct30days.com)

Description: BloggerDad puts a humorous spin on topics ranging from musings on parenthood, blogging, and life to parenting wisdom and thoughts on writing. David's latest website is Project30Days.com, where he will document his attempts to change 12 things about his life, 30 days at a time. For advertising and marketing information, contact David Wright.

Affiliations: Contributor to Manofthehouse.com

Twitter: @bloggerdad

Acknowledgements

My books are never written alone. You can always be assured that behind each one is a team of folks who help edit, research, cook dinner and put up with an overly focused writer. This book is no different. I have to thank the group that brought this book to life either directly or indirectly.

Thank you to the team at BSM Media. I am the most fortunate business owner in the world. Not only because I love my work, but because I am blessed with the amazing support of my talented associates. Thank you to Laura Motsett, Amy Sobel, Valika Shivcharran, Mary Donnellan, Melanie Yerman, ElizaBeth Fincannon Wilson, Shauna Lewis, Megan Crosby, Carey Piascik and Kim Mishler. These ladies worked feverishly to help me assemble the data, lists and interviews that are such a big part of this book. It was hectic but we got it done! Thanks, gals.

Moms are busy people, and they're *really* busy people during the holidays. Knowing this, I still asked moms to share their precious time with me so I could complete this book. Thank you, thank you and thank you to all the moms who endured my questions, emails and constant reminders that I had a deadline looming. I greatly appreciate the time you took away from your family, your business and your own me-time.

To the friends who support me at work and at home and make being away from home feel a little more comfortable: Audrey Ring, Bridget Brennan, Carter Auburn, Larry Earnheart, Leanne Jakubowski, Laura Spencer and Amy Lupold Bair. I am blessed to have you in my life.

To my dad, Bill Telli, and my siblings and all their children: thank you for inspiring me to be my best.

My clients make my work so interesting and so much fun. I work with the best brands in the world and feel privileged that you trust your business to me. In the business world we all have leaders we admire and continually learn from when we interact with them. Mine are Craig Derzen of the Walt Disney Company; Michael Mendenhall, former CMO of HP; and my dear friend Maxine Clark of Build-A-Bear Workshop. Thank you for the example you set for me and others who admire your work.

And finally, to my family. To my children Madison, Owen, Keenan and Morgan: you make being a mom the best job in the world. I am fortunate to have the best children in the world to go along with the job. And finally to my husband Tim: thank you for always being there.

FOOTNOTES

[1] Young & Rubicam, "The Intelligence Factory," *The Single Female Consumer* (Young & Rubicam, July 2000), www.yr.com.

[2] Center for Women's Business Research, *Women-Owned Business in the United States, 2002: A Fact Sheet* (Washington, D.C.: Center for Women's Business Research, 2002), www.nfwbo.org.

[3] Ibid

[4] Connie Glaser, "The Women's Market Rules," *Competitive Edge* (May/June 2001).

[5] US Bureau of Labor Statistics, *Working in the Twenty-first Century* (Washington, D.C., 2000).

[6] James Bennet, "Soccer Mom 2000," *New York Times* (April 9, 2002).

[7] US Department of Agriculture, *Expenditures on Children by Families*, Washington, D.C.: GPO, June 2001.

[8] Ibid

[9] Bureau of the Census, Population Projections of the United States by Age, Sex, Race and Hispanic Origin: 1995 to 2050, Washington, D.C.: GPO, 1996 Business Research, Women-Owned Business in the United States, 2002: A Fact Sheet.

[10] Center for Women's Business Research, *Women-Owned Business in the United States, 2002: A Fact Sheet* (Washington, D.C.: Center for Women's Business Research, 2002), www.nfwbo.org.

[11] Ibid

[12] Connie Glaser, "The Women's Market Rules," *Competitive Edge* (May/June 2001).

[13] Faith Popcorn, *EVEolution: Understand Women: Eight Essential Truths That Work in Your Business and Life*, (Dimensions, 2001).

[14] US Bureau of the Census, *Population Projections of the United States by Age, Sex, and Race*: 1995 to 2050 (Washington, D.C.: GPO, 2000), www.census.gov.

[15] US Bureau of the Census, *Population Projections of the United States by Age, Sex, and Race*: 1995 to 2050 (Washington, D.C.: GPO, 2000), www.census.gov.

[16] Ibid

[17] *2004 Direct Selling Growth and Outlook Survey Fact Sheet,* http://www.dsa.org (accessed September 14, 2004).

[18] US Bureau of the Census, *Population Projections of the United States by Age, Sex, and Race*: 1995 to 2050 (Washington, D.C.: GPO, 2000), www.census.gov.

[19] Zell Center for Risk Research Conference Series, *The Risk of Misreading Generation Y: The Need for New Marketing Strategies,* January 25, 2002, www.kellogg.nwu.edu/research/risk/archive.htm (accessed September 14, 2005).

[20] Zell Center for Risk Research Conference Center.

[21] Ellen Newborne and Kathleen Kerwin, "Generation Y," Business Week Online, February 19, 1999, http://www.businessweek.com/1999/99.htm (accessed May 12, 2004).

[22] Ibid

INDEX

A

Acuna, Amanda, 80
advisory boards, 72–78
Aigner Clark, Julie, 45
Akemann, Lorraine, 80–81
Alamilla, Jen, 81–82
Alferink, Beth, 83
Allred, Alexandra, 278
alpha moms, 40
Antonetti, Amilya, 278
Armstrong Heather, 278
Arndt, Betsy, 84–85
Axtell, Bridget, 85–86

B

baby boomers. *See* boomers
Baby Einstein, 45
Bair, Amy Lupold, 54, 86–87
Baker, Mimi, 88
Bamberger, Joanne, 14, 279
Barry, Halle, 44
Bastien, Suzanne, 89
Baxter, Amy, 89–91
Be Positive Mom, 249
behavior matrix, 54, 55
Belden, Heather, 91–92
Belkin, Lisa, 279
Beller Blake, Lorin, 279–280
Bellgardt, Amy, 92
Bender, Rachael, 11
Benuck, Kathy, 92
Berg, Tisha, 93–94
Berry, Emily, 94–95
Berry, Jill, 95–96
Besecker, Suz, 96–97
Best Buy, 3
beta moms, 40–41
Birnberg, Carla, 41, 280
Blair, Gabrielle, 57, 280
Blecherman, Beth, 281
bloggers, 3–4, 17, 56, 62–64, 71
boomers, 19–20
Boone, Clair, 97–98
Bradley, Alice, 281
Brady, Nicole, 98–99
Breidenbach, Angela, 99–101
Brett Elspas, Janis, 101–102
Broom, Candice, 102–103
Bryan, Fiona, 281–282
Buccieri, Cindy, 103–104
Bullock, Jennifer, 105
Burgin Logan, Angela, 282
Byrd, Amy, 106

C

Cain, Kris, 106–107
Calhoun, Jennifer, 57–58
Campbell, Tricia Chinn, 112
Carpenter, Sheri, 107–108
Carter, Felicia, 108–109
Celebrity Moms
    Beckham, Victoria, 44, 308–309
    Bullock, Sandra, 315
    Burke, Brooke, 301–302
    Chen, Julie, 314
    Dion, Celine, 305–306
    Garner, Jennifer, 44, 308
    Gosselin, Kate, 313
    Hasselbeck, Elisabeth, 306
    Hatcher, Teri, 302
    Hudson, Jennifer, 307
    Huffman, Felicity, 301
    Jolie, Angelina, 44, 303–304
    Lopez, Jennifer, 305
    McCarthy, Jenny, 310–311
    McFadden, Cynthia, 314–315
    Morales, Natalie, 313–314
    Palin, Sarah, 307–308
    Paltrow, Gwyneth, 309
    Ripa, Kelly, 44, 303
    Shields, Brooke, 312
    Simmons, Kimora Lee, 309–310
    Smith, Jada Pinkett, 306–307
    Spelling, Tori, 304–305
    Stefani, Gwen, 311–312
    Witherspoon, Reese, 311
Charlene Chronicles, 113
Chase, Geri, 109–111
Chase, Kristen, 282
Cherry, Jennifer, 60
child enrichment, 33–35
Chopra, Mallika, 282–283
Clawson Fletcher, Danielle, 114
Cloward, Kathryn, 283
Colton, Amy, 114–115
core values, 29–37
Cote, Randa, 115–116
Coulsey, Sarah, 116–117

coupon moms, 43
Cowan, Laura K., 117–118
Crane, Anne, 118–119
Cross, Lucinda, 119–120
Croze, Janice, 283
Croze, Susan, 283–284
Cunningham, Lori, 121–122
Cupido, Onica, 123

D

D'Addario, Jeannine, 123–124
Danklefsen, Hollie, 284
DeCarlo, Dori, 124–126
Deckard, Andrea, 43
Denay, Jessica, 126–127
Denton, Melissa, 127–128
DiSilvio, Niki, 128–129
Disney In-Home Celebrations, 66–67
Disney World Moms Panel, 77–78
divorce, 22
Douglas, Lisa, 284
drmommyonline.com, 6, 54, 251–252
Druxman, Lisa, 45, 59–60, 129–131

E

eco moms, 42–43
Edwards, Elizabeth, 14
Edwards, Melanie, 131–132
Elie, Stephanie, 284
engagement, consumption vs., 17
Engberg, Erika, 132
entrepreneurs, 45
Erickson, Melissa, 133–134
Etheridge, Yakini, 134–135
Evans, Carol, 285

F

Fader, Anna, 285
Falcon, Lori, 285–286
family enrichment, 33–35
Feldman, Beth, 286
Feliciano, Nicole, 286
Fergie, Justice, 286–287
Filip, Amy, 136
Filleman, Tonya, 136–137
finding Power Moms, 58–61
fitness moms, 41–42
Francis, Alyssa, 287
Franklin, Laura (Lolli), 138
Frawley, Sandra, 138–139
Frederick, Alaina, 139–140
Freelove, Emily, 140–141

G

Gahrmann, Natalie, 141–142
Gail, Leslie, 287
Gawlik, Cara, 142
Generation X moms, 21–26, 44
Generation Y moms, 26–29
Glascoe Crowder, Christie, 143–145
Global Moms
- Australia, 319–321
- Brazil, 321
- Canada, 322
- Germany, 322
- India, 322
- Italy, 322
- Japan, 323
- Malaysia, 323
- New Zealand, 324
- Poland, 324
- Russia, 324
- South Africa, 324
- United Kingdom, 324–327
- United Kingdom (Ireland), 325

Go Mom!, 6, 145–146
Gold, Molly, 6, 145–146
Good-Enough Mother: The Perfectly Imperfect Book of Parenting (Sylver), 40
Gorkow, Stacie, 146–147
Gorman Newman, Robin, 147–148
Gottlieb, Jessica, 287–288
Grant, Linda, 148–149
Green, Natalie, 149–150
GreenAndCleanMom (blog), 42
GreenMomReviews.com, 42
Gregg, Melissa, 150
Grenon, Kim, 151–152
Griffith, Apryl, 152
Grisham, Kimberly, 152–153
groups, belonging to, 24, 28
Guadagna, Maricris, 153–154
Gully, Lisa, 42
Gumbiner, Liz, 57

H

Haas, Trisha, 62, 288
Hall, Renee, 154–155
Hammerstein, Julie, 288
Hamrick, Rachel, 155–156

health and safety, 30–31
Heilman, Leanne, 156–157
Heinold, Dawn, 157–159
Herrmann, Paula, 159–160
Hess, Brenda, 160–162
Hess, Stephanie, 162
Hickem, Catherine, 288–289
Hilbrich Davis, Amy, 162–165
Hipwell, Deana, 165–166
Hoage, Natalie, 166–167
Hochreiter, Lauren, 167–169
Hoffer Weckstein, Stacey, 169–170
Huggies MomInspired program, 45
Hughes, Linda, 170–171
hybrid moms, 41

I

individuality, quest for, 23
influencers. *See* Power Moms
Influential Dads
  Allen, Greg, 333
  Biser, Jeremy, 333–334
  Burns, Shawn, 334
  Chaitin, Mitchell, 331–332
  Cohen, Adam, 332–333
  Goodall, Frederick, 334
  Guido, Joey Donovan, 334–335
  Hoylman, Jared, 335
  Keer, Gregory, 335
  Kelly, Joe, 335–336
  Kim, Elliott, 336
  Lanier, Troy, 336
  Lewis, C., 337
  Lin, Jim, 337
  Mott, David, 337
  Mullen, PJ, 338
  Nichols, Clay, 336
  Powell, Brad, 336
  Rogers, Buck, 338
  Silver, Jim, 338–339
  Smith, Jeremy Adam, 339
  Sullivan, Tim, 339
  Wright, David, 340
in-home parties, 69–71

J

Jaganath, Nirasha (Niri), 289
Jennings, Milissa, 171–172
Jones, Sugar, 289
Jordan, Bryana, 172–174

K

Kallman, Isabel, 289–290
Kellogg, Cecily, 174
Keroes, Amy, 290
King Steimer, Shelley, 171–172
Kirby, Alicia, 174–175
Kirkland-Andrews, Sherrelle, 175
Knutson, Angie, 176
Koh, Christine, 290
Kopulos, Maura, 176–177
Kotecki Vest, Erin, 14
Kratka, Trish, 177
Kripalani, Karen, 178–179

L

Lamb, Tiffany, 179–180
latchkey kids, 21
Lavelle, Susan, 41
learning, visual aspect of, 25
Lehmann, Erika, 290–291
Lettre, Dina, 180–181
Levey, Rebecca, 181–183
locating Power Moms, 58–61
Lopez, Heather, 183–185
Lord, Jazerai, 185–186
Loubet, Kelly, 186–187
Lowe, Misty, 187–188

M

Maines, Lindsay, 291
Manongdo-Joya, Sarah, 188–189
Marchese, Julie, 54
Marketing to Moms: Getting Your Share of the Trillion-Dollar Market (Bailey), 2, 17
marriage, 22
matrix, behavior, 54, 55
Mattke, Lynette, 189–190
mavens, 52–54. *See also* Power Moms
McCullar, Jennifer, 291
McDonald's Mom Panel, 74–77
McGraw, Michele, 190–191
McKhann, Emily, 291–292
Meehan, Dawn, 292
Mercurio, Jennifer, 292
Merritt, Tiffany, 191–192
Millennial moms, 26–29
Millner, Denene, 193–194
mining Power Moms, 58–61
mixers, 68
mojo moms, 39–40

Mom 3.0: Marketing with Mothers by Leveraging New Media and Technology (Bailey), 3, 17
Mom Market
  boomer moms in, 19–20
  busy moms and, 16–18
  core values in, 29–37
  Generation X moms, 21–26, 44
  Generation Y moms, 26–29
  generations, defined, 18–19
  overview, 11–13
  spending by, 11–15
  subsegments of, 37–45
mom matrix, 54, 55
Mommy parties, 69–71
mompreneurs, 45
Montgomery, Beth, 194–195
Montgomery, Sundae, 195–196
Moore-Gee, Lisa, 197
motivators, 23, 36–37
moxie moms, 41–42
Munroe, Cooper, 293
Murphy, Marina, 197–198

N

Nassar, Clarissa, 293
Nelson, Melanie, 57
Nestlé Nesquik, 66
Newby, J. J. (JavaMom), 198–199
Nickel, Janine, 199–200
Norton, Elizabeth, 200–201
Novotny, Trisha, 201–202

O

Ochoa, Claudia, 202–203
Olmanson, Shaina, 293–294
Olsen, Pamela, 203–204
Omanoff, Marnie, 204–205
Online Media Tours, 71
Orlando, Kim, 294
Orpesa, Candice, 205
Ortiz, Kimberly, 205–207
Owen, Katie, 207–208

P

Pacenti, Charlene, 208–209
Padilla, Colleen, 209–211
Pagano, Jendi, 211
panels, 72–78
Pantley, Elizabeth, 57
Paolicchi, Scarlet, 212
Paroli, Ashley, 212–214
Pate, Calley, 214–215
Peeples, Desiree, 215–216
peer groups, values and, 38
Peppel, Sarah, 216–218
Phillips, Allyson, 218–219
Picazo, Ana, 219–220
Pinnix, Sarah, 220–221
Plasencia, Kathryn, 221–222
Platt, Amy, 294
Power Moms, 3–4, 17, 56, 62–64, 71
  activity programs for, 67
  bloggers, 3–4, 17, 56, 62–64, 71
  building relationships with, 61
  business goals and, 4–5
  characteristics of, 55–58
  defined, 4
  directory overview, 6
  finding, 4, 58–61
  marketing with, 61–67
  mavens and, 52–54
  overview, 3–5
  power of, 6–7, 47–52
  word of mouth marketing, 47–51, 55, 66–67
Presnal, Katja, 294–295
price, value vs., 32–33
Prideaux, Jaime, 295
product kits, 71

R

Ranere, Dianna, 222–223
Reason, Jerri Ann, 223–224
Rees, Jennifer, 224–225
Reyes, Cinella J., 225
Richie, Nicole, 44
Ridgeway, Janet, 295
Roberts, Connie (ConnieFoggles), 226–227
Rogers, Felicia, 227–228
Ross, Renee J., 228–229
Ross, Shellie, 54
Roth, Jamie, 229–230
Rowley, Kim, 230–231

S

safety, health and, 30–31
Sako, Ku'ulei, 231–232
Salazar Hutcheson, Jennifer, 232–234
Samples, Lisa N., 234–235

Sams, LaTasha, 235–236
Sanabria Robertson, Lorraine, 236–237
saving time, 31–32
Schuler, Amy, 237–238
Schuster, Debbie, 238–239
Seaborg, Lori, 240
Seals Allers, Kimberly, 295–296
Seegobin, Denise, 241
self-confidence, 27
Shane, Jo-Lynne, 57, 241–242
Shulman, Joyce, 296
Silber, Debi (Mojo Coach), 39, 42, 242–244
Silver, Sharon, 296
simplicity, 35–36
single mothers, 22
Skrhak, Shelby, 296–297
Smallwood, K. Melissa, 244–245
Smith, Deirdre, 246
soccer moms, 19
Solstad, Courtney, 246–247
Somnitz, Melanie, 247–248
Spencer, Laura (Lou), 248–249
spending habits, 11–15
Spink, Jennifer Houck, 297
Stone, Lisa, 297
Stroller Strides, 45, 59–60
Suchland, Amanda (Mandee), 250–251
Sutherland, Daisy, 6, 54, 251–252
Sutton, Nina, 253–254

T

Tam, MJ, 254–255
Tatum, Sheena, 255–256
Taylor, Maggie, 256–257
technology, 27–28
Teres, Sarah Elizabeth, 257–258
Tibbetts, Wendy, 258–260
Tibytt, Romina, 260
Tiemann, Amy, 39
time, saving, 31–32
Trillion-Dollar Moms: Marketing to a New Generation of Mothers (Bailey), 2, 3, 17, 18, 19
Truman, Karrie, 260–261

U

Ultimate Mom (Bailey), 2

V

value, 32–33
values, core, 29–37
VanVeelen, Emily, 262
Vashisht-Rota, Aparna, 297–298
Vaughn, Lori, 262–264
Viola, Déa, 264–265

W

Wahrer, Marcie, 266
Walker, Tamara, 266–268
Walsh, Terri, 268–269
Webb, Barb, 269–270
Welch, April, 270–271
Wetzel, Stephanie, 272
Wey, Molly, 272–273
Williams, Dave, 3
Wilson, Meg, 273–274
Women's Home-Based Business Book of Answers, The (Bailey), 2
Word of Mom, 25, 50–51
word of mouth marketing, 47–51, 55, 66–67
Wright, Robyn, 274–275

Y

Young, Christine, 298
yummy mummies, 44
Yummy Mummy (Williams), 44

Z

Zeliff, Dana, 275
ZhuZhu Pets, 65